Edward Robinson

A harmony of the four gospels in English:

According to the common version

Edward Robinson

A harmony of the four gospels in English:
According to the common version

ISBN/EAN: 9783337714406

Printed in Europe, USA, Canada, Australia, Japan

Cover: Foto ©ninafisch / pixelio.de

More available books at **www.hansebooks.com**

A

HARMONY

OF THE

FOUR GOSPELS IN ENGLISH.

ACCORDING TO THE COMMON VERSION.

NEWLY ARRANGED, WITH EXPLANATORY NOTES.

BY

EDWARD ROBINSON, D. D. LL. D.

Professor of Bibl. Literature in the Union Theol. Seminary, New-York.
Author of Biblical Researches in Palestine, etc, etc.

TWELFTH EDITION.

BOSTON:
PUBLISHED BY CROCKER & BREWSTER
LONDON: WILEY & PUTNAM
1867.

PREFACE.

The Harmony of the Four Gospels in Greek, published in 1845, having been favourably received, I have been requested by many persons whose advice I could not disregard, to prepare a similar Harmony of the Gospels according to the common English Version. This I have attempted to do in the present work.

In the Gospels we have four different narratives of the life and actions of our Lord, by as many different and independent historians. The narrative of John, except during the week of the Saviour's passion, contains very little that is found in either of the other writers. That of Luke, although in its first part and at the close it has much in common with Matthew and Mark, comprises nevertheless in its middle portions a large amount of matter peculiar to Luke alone. Matthew and Mark have in general more resemblance to each other; though Matthew, being more full, presents much that is not found in Mark or Luke; while Mark, though briefer, has some things not contained in any of the rest. The Evangelists were led, under the guidance of the Spirit, to write each with a specific object in view, and for different communities or classes of readers; much as in the case of the authors of the Epistles. Hence, while the narratives all necessarily exhibit a certain degree of likeness, they nevertheless bear also each for itself the stamp of independence.

The four writers vary likewise in their chronological character. On the one hand, it appears, that Mark and John, who have little in common, follow with few exceptions the regular and true order of the events and transactions recorded by them; as may be more fully seen at the close of the Introduction to the Notes. On the other hand, Matthew and Luke manifestly have sometimes not so much had regard to chronological order, as they have been guided by the principle of association; so that in them, transactions having certain relations to each other are not seldom grouped together, though they may have happened at different times and in various places.

Some other diversities in the character and manner of the Evangelists, are pointed out in the Introduction to the Notes.

In view of the preceding considerations, it follows, that in order to obtain a full and consecutive account of all the facts of our Lord's life and ministry, the four Gospel-narratives must be so brought together, as to present as nearly as possible the true chronological order; and, where the same transaction is described by more than one writer, the different accounts must be placed side by side, so as to fill out and supply each other. Such an arrangement affords the only full and perfect survey of all the testimony relating to any and every portion of our Lord's history. In this way alone can be brought out and distinctly presented the mutual connection and dependency of the various parts, and the gradual development and completion of the great plan of redemption, so far as it was manifested in the life and ministry, the death and resurrection, of our Lord Jesus Christ. Yet without such a survey, our knowledge on all these great topics can only be fragmentary and partial.

To afford just the aid here proposed, is the object of a Harmony of the Gospels ; and by this consideration I have been governed in preparing such a work both in Greek and in English. Other uses and advantages, as also the particular objects aimed at in the present volume, are specified near the close of the Introduction to the Notes.

In all the preceding particulars, a Harmony in English is not less useful and important than one in Greek. It is mainly in respect to the verbal parallelisms of the sacred writers, that a comparison in the original language is of greater weight. These of course often disappear in a translation.

In a work of this kind, no great amount of novelty can be expected, on subjects which have more or less occupied the ablest minds of the Church during many centuries. Yet even here, knowledge has not been stationary. In a course of years, and especially within the last half century, there has been great progress in the observation and discovery of new facts and circumstances bearing upon both the social and physical history of the Hebrews and other ancient nations. These all serve to enlarge the circle of Biblical knowledge ; and they often shed light on topics which before were dark or doubtful. The accumulated facts and results of this progress, it is the duty of the Harmonist to apply to the elucidation of the narratives of the four Evangelists. This I have attempted to do in the present, as well as in my former work ; and have endeavoured every where faithfully to judge and write, according to the impressions left upon my mind by a personal inspection of most of the scenes of the Gospel history.

The Sections, and the general arrangement of the Text in this volume, are the same as in the Greek Harmony. The notation of place is every where given ; and may be regarded as a not unimportant feature of the work.

The Notes are for the most part those appended to the Greek Harmony, with such curtailments, additions, and changes, as seemed advisable in order to adapt them to the reader acquainted only with the English tongue. In using the Notes, I would particularly request the reader to search out all the scriptural references; inasmuch as very often they alone contain the evidence on which particular statements rest.

In the Text, I have inserted in two places (Matth. 6, 1. John 5, 2) the marginal reading of the English Version, for the reasons assigned in the Notes, and in accordance with all critical authority at the present day. In a few instances, a merely expletive word, added by the translators in *Italic*, has been silently dropped.

My hope is, that this little work may be found useful to those who love and seek the truth, in their closets, in families, in Sabbath Schools and Bible Classes. If it shall thus aid in extending the knowledge and influence of God's Holy Word, the object of my labours and prayers will be accomplished.

EDWARD ROBINSON.

Union Theological Seminary, }
New-York, July, 1846. }

Note.—The only point in the order of time, in which this work differs from the Greek Harmony, is in respect to our Lord's arrival at Bethany "six days before the passover," and the chronology of the passion week. In this I was formerly misled *one day*, by relying too implicitly upon the authority of the learned Lightfoot.

CONTENTS

AND

SYNOPSIS OF THE HARMONY.

PART III.

OUR LORD'S FIRST PASSOVER, AND THE SUBSEQUENT TRANSACTIONS
UNTIL THE SECOND.

TIME: *One year.*

PART IV.

OUR LORD'S SECOND PASSOVER, AND THE SUBSEQUENT TRANSACTIONS
UNTIL THE THIRD.

TIME: *One year.*

PART V.

PART VI.

**THE FESTIVAL OF TABERNACLES, AND THE SUBSEQUENT TRANS-
ACTIONS UNTIL OUR LORD'S ARRIVAL AT BETHANY SIX
DAYS BEFORE THE FOURTH PASSOVER.**

TIME: *Six months less six days.*

PART VII.

OUR LORD'S PUBLIC ENTRY INTO JERUSALEM, AND THE SUBSEQUENT
TRANSACTIONS BEFORE THE FOURTH PASSOVER.

TIME : *Four days.*

PART VIII.

THE FOURTH PASSOVER; OUR LORD'S PASSION; AND THE ACCOMPANYING EVENTS UNTIL THE END OF THE JEWISH SABBATH.

TIME: *Two days.*

PART IX.

OUR LORD'S RESURRECTION, HIS SUBSEQUENT APPEARANCES, AND
HIS ASCENSION.

TIME: *Forty days.*

CONTENTS OF THE NOTES.

PART VII.

PART VIII.

PART IX.

TABLE

FOR FINDING ANY PASSAGE IN THE HARMONY.

MATTHEW.

Chap.	Verse.	Sect.	Page.	Chap.	Verse.	Sect.	Page.	Chap.	Verse.	Sect.	Page.
i.	1-17	13	8, 9	xiii.	1-23	54	47-50	xxii.	41-46	121	117
	18-25	6	4		24-53	55	50-52	xxiii.	1-12	122	117, 118
ii.	1-12	10	6		54-58	61	59		13-39	123	118, 119
	13-23	11	6, 7	xiv.	1, 2	63	62	xxiv.	1-14	127	121, 122
iii.	1-12	14	10, 11		3, 5	24	18		15-42	128	123-125
	13-17	15	12		6-12	63	62		43-51	129	125
iv.	1-11	16	12, 13		13-21	64	63, 64	xxv.	1-30	129	125, 126
	12	24	18		22-36	65	65, 66		31-46	130	126, 127
	13-16	28	21	xv.	1-20	67	68, 69	xxvi.	1-16	131	127, 128
	17	26	20		21-28	68	70 .		17-19	132	129
	18-22	29	21, 22		29-38	69	70, 71		20	133	130
	23-25	32	24		39	70	71		21-25	135	131, 132
v.	1-48	41	32-34	xvi.	1-4	70	71, 72		26-29	137	133, 134
vi.	1-34	41	34, 35		4-12	71	72		30	142	138
vii.	1-29	41	35-37		13-20	73	73		31-35	136	132, 133
viii.	1	41	37		21-28	74	73, 74		36-46	142	138, 139
	2-4	33	24	xvii.	1-13	75	74-76		47-56	143	140, 141
	5-13	42	37, 38		14-21	76	76, 77		57, 58	144	141, 142
	14-17	31	23		22, 23	77	77		59-68	145	143, 144
	18-27	56	52, 53		24-27	78	78		69-75	144	142, 143
	28-34	57	53, 54	xviii.	1-35	79	78-80	xxvii.	1, 2	146	144, 145
ix.	1	57	55	xix.	1, 2	94	93		3-10	151	149
	2-8	34	25, 26		3-12	104	99, 100		11-14	146	145
	9	35	26		13-15	105	100		15-26	148	146, 147
	10-17	58	55, 56		16-30	106	101, 102		26-30	149	147, 148
	18-26	59	56-58	xx.	1-16	106	102, 103		31-34	152	149, 150
	27-34	60	58, 59		17-19	107	103		35-38	153	150, 151
	35-38	62	59		20-28	108	104		39-44	154	151
x.	1	62	59		29-34	109	104, 105		45-50	155	152
	2-4	40	31	xxi.	1-11	112	107-109		51-56	156	153
	5-42	62	60, 61		12, 13	113	109, 110		57-61	157	154
xi.	1	62	61		14-17	112	109		62-66	158	155
	2-19	44	38, 39		18-19	113	109	xxviii.	1	160	156
	20-30	45	40		20-22	114	110		2-4	159	156
xii.	1-8	37	29		23-32	115	111, 112		5-7	161	157
	9-14	38	30		33-46	116	112, 113		8-10	162	157, 158
	15-21	39	30, 31	xxii.	1-14	117	113, 114		11-15	165	159
	22-37	48	41, 42		15-22	118	114, 115		16	169	161
	38-45	49	42, 43		23-33	119	115, 116		16-20	170	162, 163
	46-50	50	44		34-40	120	116				

MARK.

Chap.	Verse.	Sect.	Page.	Chap.	Verse.	Sect.	Page.	Chap.	Verse.	Sect.	Page.
i.	1–8	14	10, 11	vii.	24–30	68	70	xii.	41–44	124	119
	9–11	15	12		31–37	69	70	xiii.	1–13	127	121, 122
	12, 13	16	12	viii.	1–9	69	71		14–37	128	123–125
	14	24	18		10–12	70	71	xiv.	1–11	131	127, 128
	14, 15	26	20		13–21	71	72		12–16	132	129
	16–20	29	21, 22		22–26	72	72		17	133	130
	21–28	30	22, 23		27–30	73	73		18–21	135	131, 132
	29–34	31	23		31–38	74	73, 74		22–25	137	133, 134
	35–39	32	23, 24	ix.	1	74	74		26	142	139
	40–45	33	24, 25		2–13	75	74–76		27–31	136	132, 133
ii.	1–12	34	25, 26		14–29	76	76, 77		32–42	142	138, 139
	13, 14	35	26		30–32	77	77		43–52	143	140, 141
	15–22	58	55, 56		33	78	78		53, 54	144	141, 142
	23–28	37	29		33–50	79	78, 79		55–65	145	143, 144
iii.	1–6	38	30	x.	1	94	93		66–72	144	142, 143
	7–12	39	30, 31		2–12	104	99, 100	xv.	1–5	146	144, 145
	13–19	40	31		13–16	105	100		6–15	148	146, 147
	19–30	48	41, 42		17–31	106	101, 102		15–19	149	147, 148
	31–35	50	44		32–34	107	103		20–23	152	149, 150
iv.	1–25	54	47–50		35–45	108	104		24–28	153	150, 151
	26–34	55	50, 51		46–52	109	104, 105		29–32	154	151
	35–41	56	52, 53	xi.	1–11	112	107–109		33–37	155	152
v.	1–21	57	53–55		12–19	113	109, 110		38–41	156	153
	22–43	59	56–58		20–26	114	110		42–47	157	154
vi.	1–6	61	59		27–33	115	111	xvi.	1	159	156
	6–13	62	59–61	xii.	1–12	116	112, 113		2–4	160	156, 157
	14–16	63	62		13–17	118	114, 115		5–7	161	157
	17–20	24	18		18–27	119	115, 116		8	162	157
	21–29	63	62		28–34	120	116, 117		9–11	164	158, 159
	30–44	64	63, 64		35–37	121	117		12–13	166	159, 160
	45–56	65	65, 66		38, 39	122	117		14–18	167	160, 161
vii.	1–23	67	68, 69		40	123	118		19, 20	172	163

LUKE.

Chap.	Verse.	Sect.	Page.	Chap.	Verse.	Sect.	Page.	Chap.	Verse.	Sect.	Page.
i.	1–4	1	1	iv.	14, 15	26	20	vi.	32–36	41	34
	5–25	2	1, 2		16–31	28	20, 21		37–49	41	35, 36
	26–38	3	2		31–37	30	22, 23	vii.	1–10	42	37, 38
	39–56	4	3		38–41	31	23		11–17	43	38
	57–80	5	3, 4		42–44	32	23, 24		18–35	44	38, 39
ii.	1–7	7	4	v.	1–11	29	21, 22		36–50	46	40, 41
	8–20	8	5		12–16	33	24, 25	viii.	1–3	47	41
	21–38	9	5, 6		17–26	34	25, 26		4–18	54	47–50
	39, 40	11	7		27, 28	35	26		19–21	50	44
	41–52	12	7		29–39	58	55, 56		22–25	56	52, 53
iii.	1–18	14	10, 11	vi.	1–5	37	29		26–40	57	53–55
	19, 20	24	18		6–11	38	30		41–56	59	56–58
	21–23	15	12		12–19	40	31, 32	ix.	1–6	62	59–61
	23–38	13	8, 9		20–26	41	32		7–9	63	62
iv.	1–13	16	12, 13		27–30	41	33, 34		10–17	64	63, 64
	14	24	18		31	41	36		18–21	73	73

LUKE CONTINUED.

Chap.	Verse.	Sect.	Page.	Chap.	Verse.	Sect.	Page.	Chap	Verse.	Sect.	Page.
ix.	22-27	74	73, 74	xvii.	1-10	101	98	xxii.	21-23	135	131, 132
	28-36	75	74, 75		11-19	82	81, 82		24-30	133	130
	37-43	76	76, 77		20-37	102	98, 99		31-38	136	133
	43-45	77	77	xviii.	1-14	103	99		39-46	142	138, 139
	46-50	79	78, 79		15-17	105	100		47-53	143	140, 141
	51-56	81	81		18-30	106	101, 102		54-62	144	141-143
	57-62	56	52		31-34	107	103		63-71	145	143, 144
x.	1-16	80	80		35-43	109	104, 105	xxiii.	1-5	146	144, 145
	17-24	89	88	xix.	1	109	105		6-12	147	146
	25-37	86	86, 87		2-28	110	105, 106		13-25	148	146, 147
	38-42	87	87		29-44	112	107-109		26-33	152	149, 150
xi.	1-13	88	87, 88		45-48	113	109, 110		33-34	153	150
	14, 15	48	41	xx.	1-8	115	111		35-37	154	151
	16	49	42		9-19	116	112, 113		38	153	151
	17-23	48	41, 42		20-26	118	114, 115		39-43	154	151, 152
	24-28	49	43		27-40	119	115, 116		44-46	155	152
	29-36	49	42, 43		41-44	121	117		45	156	153
	37-54	51	44, 45		45, 46	122	117		47-49	156	153
xii.	1-59	52	45-47		47	123	118		50-56	157	154, 155
xiii.	1-9	53	47	xxi.	1-4	124	119	xxiv.	1-3	160	156, 157
	10-21	94	93		5-19	127	121, 122		4-8	161	157
	22-35	95	93, 94		20-36	128	123-125		9-11	162	158
xiv.	1-24	96	94, 95		37, 38	113	110		12	163	158
	25-35	97	95	xxii.	1-6	131	127, 128		13-35	166	159, 160
xv.	1-32	98	95, 96		7-13	132	129		36-49	167	160, 161
xvi.	1-13	99	96, 97		14-18	133	130		50-53	172	163
	14-31	100	97		19, 20	137	133, 134				

JOHN.

Chap.	Verse.	Sect.	Page.	Chap.	Verse.	Sect.	Page.	Chap.	Verse.	Sect.	Page.
i.	1-18	17	13, 14	ix.	1-41	90	88, 89	xviii.	13-18	144	141, 142
	19-34	18	14	x.	1-21	90	89, 90		19-24	145	143
	35-52	19	14, 15		22-42	91	90, 91		25-27	144	142, 143
ii.	1-12	20	15	xi.	1-46	92	91, 92		28-38	146	144, 145
	13-25	21	16		47-54	93	92		39, 40	148	146, 147
iii.	1-21	22	16, 17		55-57	111	106	xix.	1-3	149	147, 148
	22-36	23	17, 18	xii.	1	111	106		4-16	150	148
iv.	1-3	24	18		2-8	131	127, 128		16, 17	152	149, 150
	4-42	25	18-20		9-11	111	106		18-24	153	150, 151
	43-45	26	20		12-19	112	107, 108		25-27	154	152
	46-54	27	20		20-36	125	120		28-30	155	152
v.	1-47	36	27, 28		37-50	126	120, 121		31-42	157	153, 154
vi.	1-14	64	63, 64	xiii.	1-20	134	130, 131	xx.	1, 2	160	156, 157
	15-21	65	65		21-35	135	131, 132		3-10	163	158
	22-71	66	66, 67		36-38	136	132, 133		11-18	164	158, 159
vii	1	66	67	xiv.	1-31	138	134, 135		19-23	167	160, 161
	2-10	81	81	xv.	1-27	139	135, 136		24-29	168	161
	11-53	83	83	xvi.	1-33	140	136, 137		30, 31	173	164
viii	1	83	84	xvii.	1-26	141	137, 138	xxi.	1-24	169	161, 162
	2-11	84	84, 85	xviii.	1	142	138		25	173	164
	12-59	85	85, 86		2-12	143	140, 141				

ACTS.　　　1 CORINTHIANS.

Chap.	Verse.	Sect.	Page.	Chap.	Verse.	Sect.	Page.	Chap.	Verse.	Sect.	Page.
i.	3–8	171	163	xi.	23–25	137	133, 134	xv.	6	170	162
	9–12	172	163	xv.	5	166	159		7	171	163
	18, 19	151	149		5	167	160				

NOTE.

In the Text, the Dash [—] is used to mark a break or transposition in the order of the verses; and, also, to denote a break or division in single verses.

In the Notes, the work of Josephus on the Jewish Wars is quoted by the initials of its Latin title, viz. B. J. for *de Bello Judaico*.

PART I.

EVENTS CONNECTED WITH THE BIRTH AND CHILDHOOD OF OUR LORD.

Time: About thirteen and a half years.

§ 1. *Preface to Luke's Gospel.*

LUKE I. 1—4.

1 FORASMUCH as many have taken in hand to set forth in order a dec-
2 laration of those things which are most surely believed among us, ' even
as they delivered them unto us, which from the beginning were eye-wit-
3 nesses, and ministers of the word ; ' it seemed good to me also, having had
perfect understanding of all things from the very first, to write unto thee
4 in order, most excellent Theophilus, ' that thou mightest know the certainty of those things wherein thou hast been instructed.

§ 2. *An Angel appears to Zacharias.* — JERUSALEM.

LUKE I. 5—25.

5 There was in the days of Herod the king of Judea, a certain priest
named Zacharias, of the course of Abia : and his wife was of the daughters
6 of Aaron, and her name was Elisabeth. And they were both righteous before God, walking in all the commandments and ordinances of the Lord
7 blameless. And they had no child, because that Elisabeth was barren ;
8 and they both were well stricken in years. And it came to pass, that,
while he executed the priest's office before God in the order of his course,
9 ' according to the custom of the priest's office, his lot was to burn incense
10 when he went into the temple of the Lord. And the whole multitude of
11 the people were praying without, at the time of incense. And there appeared unto him an angel of the Lord, standing on the right side of the
12 altar of incense. And when Zacharias saw *him*, he was troubled, and fear
13 fell upon him. But the angel said unto him, Fear not, Zacharias : for thy

1

LUKE I.

prayer is heard ; and thy wife Elisabeth shall bear thee a son, and thou
14 shalt call his name John. And thou shalt have joy and gladness, and
15 many shall rejoice at his birth. For he shall be great in the sight of the
Lord, and shall drink neither wine nor strong drink ; and he shall be filled
16 with the Holy Ghost, even from his mother's womb. And many of the
17 children of Israel shall he turn to the Lord their God. And he shall go
before him in the spirit and power of Elias, to turn the hearts of the fathers
to the children, and the disobedient to the wisdom of the just ; to make
18 ready a people prepared for the Lord.[a] And Zacharias said unto the angel,
Whereby shall I know this ? for I am an old man, and my wife well strick-
19 en in years. And the angel answering, said unto him, I am Gabriel, that
stand in the presence of God ; and am sent to speak unto thee, and to
20 shew thee these glad tidings. And behold thou shalt be dumb, and not
able to speak, until the day that these things shall be performed, because
thou believest not my words, which shall be fulfilled in their season.
21 And the people waited for Zacharias, and marvelled that he tarried so
22 long in the temple. And when he came out, he could not speak unto
them : and they perceived that he had seen a vision in the temple ; for he
23 beckoned unto them, and remained speechless. And it came to pass, that
as soon as the days of his ministration were accomplished, he departed to
his own house.
24 And after those days his wife Elisabeth conceived, and hid herself five
25 months, saying, Thus hath the Lord dealt with me in the days wherein he
looked on *me*, to take away my reproach among men.

§ 3. *An Angel appears to Mary.* — NAZARETH.

LUKE I. 26—38.

26 And in the sixth month the angel Gabriel was sent from God unto a city
27 of Galilee, named Nazareth,[1] to a virgin espoused to a man whose name
was Joseph, of the house of David ; and the virgin's name *was* Mary.
28 And the angel came in unto her, and said, Hail, *thou* highly favoured, the
29 Lord *is* with thee : blessed *art* thou among women. And when she saw
him, she was troubled at his saying, and cast in her mind what manner of
30 salutation this should be. And the angel said unto her, Fear not, Mary :
31 for thou hast found favour with God. And behold, thou shalt conceive in
32 thy womb, and bring forth a son, and shalt call his name JESUS. He
shall be great, and shall be called the Son of the Highest ; and the Lord
33 God shall give unto him the throne of his father David. And he shall reign
over the house of Jacob for ever ; and of his kingdom there shall be no end.[b]
34 Then said Mary unto the angel, How shall this be, seeing I know not a
35 man ? And the angel answered and said unto her, The Holy Ghost shall
come upon thee, and the power of the Highest shall overshadow thee :
therefore also that holy thing which shall be born of thee, shall be called
36 the Son of God. And behold, thy cousin Elisabeth, she hath also conceived a son in her old age ; and this is the sixth month with her who was
37 38 called barren :[1] for with God nothing shall be impossible. And Mary
said, Behold the handmaid of the Lord, be it unto me according to thy
word. And the angel departed from her.

---

a 17. Comp. Mal. 4, 5. 6.　　　　　b 33. Comp. Mic. 4, 7.

§ 4. *Mary visits Elisabeth.* — JUTTAH.

LUKE I. 39—56.

[39] And Mary arose in those days, and went into the hill-country with haste, [40] into a city of Juda,' and entered into the house of Zacharias, and saluted [41] Elisabeth. And it came to pass, that when Elisabeth heard the salutation of Mary, the babe leaped in her womb : and Elisabeth was filled with the [42] Holy Ghost. And she spake out with a loud voice and said, Blessed *art* [43] thou among women, and blessed *is* the fruit of thy womb. And whence *is* [44] this to me, that the mother of my Lord should come to me ? For lo, as soon as the voice of thy salutation sounded in mine ears, the babe leaped in [45] my womb for joy. And blessed *is* she that believed : for there shall be a performance of those things which were told her from the Lord.
[46] [47] And Mary said, My soul doth magnify the Lord,' and my spirit hath [48] rejoiced in God my Saviour. For he hath regarded the low estate of his handmaiden : for behold, from henceforth all generations shall call me [49] blessed. For he that is mighty hath done to me great things ; and holy *is* [50] his name. And his mercy *is* on them that fear him, from generation to [51] generation. He hath shewed strength with his arm ; he hath scattered the [52] proud in the imagination of their hearts. He hath put down the mighty [53] from *their* seats, and exalted them of low degree. He hath filled the hun- [54] gry with good things, and the rich he hath sent empty away. He hath [55] holpen his servant Israel, in remembrance of *his* mercy ;' as he spake to our fathers; to Abraham, and to his seed, for ever.[a]
[56] And Mary abode with her about three months, and returned to her own house.

§ 5. *Birth of John the Baptist.* — JUTTAH.

LUKE I. 57—80.

[57] Now Elisabeth's full time came that she should be delivered ; and she [58] brought forth a son. And her neighbours and her cousins heard how the Lord had shewed great mercy upon her ; and they rejoiced with her. [59] And it came to pass, that on the eighth day they came to circumcise the [60] child ; and they called him Zacharias, after the name of his father. And [61] his mother answered and said, Not *so ;* but he shall be called John. And they said unto her, There is none of thy kindred that is called by this [62] name. And they made signs to his father, how he would have him called. [63] And he asked for a writing-table, and wrote, saying, His name is John. [64] And they marvelled all. ' And his mouth was opened immediately, and his [65] tongue *loosed,* and he spake, and praised God. And fear came on all that dwelt round about them : and all these sayings were noised abroad [66] throughout all the hill-country of Judea. And all they that heard *them,* laid *them* up in their hearts, saying, What manner of child shall this be ! And the hand of the Lord was with him.
[67] And his father Zacharias was filled with the Holy Ghost, and prophesied, [68] saying, Blessed be the Lord God of Israel ; for he hath visited and redeem- [69] ed his people,' and hath raised up an horn of salvation for us, in the house [70] of his servant David :' as he spake by the mouth of his holy prophets, which

---

LUKE I.

[71] have been since the world began : ' that we should be saved from our ene-
[72] mies, and from the hand of all that hate us ; ' to perform the mercy *prom-*
[73] *ised* to our fathers, and to remember his holy covenant ; ' the oath which
[74] he sware to our father Abraham,[a] ' that he would grant unto us, that we
being delivered out of the hand of our enemies, might serve him without
[75] fear, ' in holiness and righteousness before him all the days of our life.
[76] And thou, child, shalt be called the prophet of the Highest, for thou shalt
[77] go before the face of the Lord to prepare his ways ; ' to give knowledge of
[78] salvation unto his people, by the remission of their sins, ' through the tender
mercy of our God ; whereby the day-spring from on high hath visited us,
[79] ' to give light to them that sit in darkness and the shadow of death, to
guide our feet into the way of peace.
[80] And the child grew, and waxed strong in spirit, and was in the deserts
till the day of his shewing unto Israel.

§ 6. *An angel appears to Joseph.* — NAZARETH.

MATTH. I. 18—25.

[18] Now the birth of Jesus Christ was on this wise : When as his mother
Mary was espoused to Joseph, before they came together, she was found
[19] with child of the Holy Ghost. Then Joseph her husband, being a just *man*,
and not willing to make her a public example, was minded to put her away
[20] privily. But while he thought on these things, behold, the angel of the
Lord appeared unto him in a dream, saying, Joseph, thou son of David,
fear not to take unto thee Mary thy wife : for that which is conceived in
[21] her is of the Holy Ghost. And she shall bring forth a son, and thou shalt
[22] call his name JESUS : for he shall save his people from their sins. Now
all this was done, that it might be fulfilled which was spoken of the Lord
[23] by the prophet, saying,[b] Behold, a virgin shall be with child, and shall bring
forth a son, and they shall call his name Emmanuel, which being interpreted
is, God with us. -
[24] Then Joseph, being raised from sleep, did as the angel of the Lord
[25] had bidden him, and took unto him his wife : ' and knew her not till she
had brought forth her first-born son : and he called his name JESUS.

§ 7. *The birth of Jesus.* — BETHLEHEM.

LUKE II. 1—7.

[1] And it came to pass in those days, that there went out a decree from
[2] Cesar Augustus, that all the world should be taxed. (This taxing was
[3] first made when Cyrenius was governor of Syria.) And all went to be
[4] taxed, every one into his own city. And Joseph also went up from
Galilee, out of the city of Nazareth, into Judea, unto the city of David
which is called Bethlehem, (because he was of the house and lineage of
[5] David,) ' to be taxed with Mary his espoused wife, being great with child.
[6] And so it was, that while they were there, the days were accomplished
[7] that she should be delivered. And she brought forth her first-born son,
and wrapped him in swaddling-clothes, and laid him in a manger ; because
there was no room for them in the inn.

---

a **73.** Gen 22, 16 sq.　　　　　b **22.** Is. 7, 14.

§ 8. *An Angel appears to the Shepherds.*—NEAR BETHLEHEM.

LUKE II. 8—20.

8 And there were in the same country shepherds abiding in the field, keeping
9 watch over their flock by night.   And lo, the angel of the Lord came upon
them, and the glory of the Lord shone round about them ; and they were
10 sore afraid.   And the angel said unto them, Fear not: for behold, I bring
11 you good tidings of great joy, which shall be to all people.   For unto you
is born this day, in the city of David, a Saviour, which is Christ the Lord.
12 And this *shall be* a sign unto you ; Ye shall find the babe wrapped in swad-
13 dling-clothes, lying in a manger.   And suddenly there was with the angel
14 a multitude of the heavenly host praising God, and saying, Glory to God
in the highest, and on earth peace, good will toward men.
15   And it came to pass, as the angels were gone away from them into
heaven, the shepherds said one to another, Let us now go even unto Bethlehem, and see this thing which is come to pass, which the Lord hath made
16 known unto us.   And they came with haste, and found Mary and Joseph,
17 and the babe lying in a manger.   And when they had seen *it*, they made
18 known abroad the saying which was told them concerning this child.   And
all they that heard, wondered at those things which were told them by the
19 shepherds.   But Mary kept all these things, and pondered *them* in her
20 heart.   And the shepherds returned, glorifying and praising God for all the
things that they had heard and seen, as it was told unto them.

§ 9. *The circumcision of Jesus, and his presentation in the Temple.*—BETHLE-
HEM, JERUSALEM.

LUKE II. 21—38.

21   And when eight days were accomplished for the circumcising of the child,ᵃ
his name was called JESUS, which was so named of the angel before he
22 was conceived in the womb.   And when the days of her purification according to the law of Moses were accomplished, they brought him to Jeru-
23 salem, to present *him* to the Lord ; ' (as it is written in the law of the Lord,ᵇ
24 Every male that openeth the womb shall be called holy to the Lord ;) ' and
to offer a sacrifice according to that which is said in the law of the Lord,ᶜ
A pair of turtle-doves, or two young pigeons.
25   And behold, there was a man in Jerusalem, whose name *was* Simeon ;
and the same man *was* just and devout, waiting for the consolation of Israel :
26 and the Holy Ghost was upon him.   And it was revealed unto him by the
Holy Ghost, that he should not see death, before he had seen the Lord's
27 Christ.   And he came by the Spirit into the temple ; and when the parents
28 brought in the child Jesus, to do for him after the custom of the law, ' then
29 took he him up in his arms, and blessed God, and said,' Lord, now lettest
30 thou thy servant depart in peace, according to thy word: ' for mine eyes
31 have seen thy salvation, ' which thou hast prepared before the face of all
32 people ; ' a light to lighten the Gentiles, and the glory of thy people Israel.
33   And Joseph and his mother marvelled at those things which were spoken
34 of him.   And Simeon blessed them, and said unto Mary his mother, Be-

ᵃ 21. Gen. 17, 12.   Lev. 12, 3.   ᵇ 23. Ex. 13, 2.   Comp. Num. 8, 16. 17
ᶜ 24. Lev. 12, 6. 8.
1*

LUKE II.

hold this *child* is set for the fall and rising again of many in Israel; and
15 for a sign which shall be spoken against;*' (yea, a sword shall pierce
through thy own soul also;) that the thoughts of many hearts may be
revealed.

36 And there was one Anna, a prophetess, the daughter of Phanuel, of the
tribe of Aser: she was of a great age, and had lived with an husband seven
37 years from her virginity;' and she *was* a widow of about fourscore and four
years, which departed not from the temple, but served *God* with fastings
38 and prayers night and day. And she coming in that instant, gave thanks
likewise unto the Lord, and spake of him to all them that looked for redemption in Jerusalem.

§ 10. *The Magi.*—JERUSALEM, BETHLEHEM.

MATTH. II. 1—12.

1 Now when Jesus was born in Bethlehem of Judea in the days of Herod
2 the king, behold, there came wise men from the east to Jerusalem,' saying,
Where is he that is born King of the Jews? for we have seen his star in
3 the east, and are come to worship him. When Herod the king had heard
4 *these things,* he was troubled, and all Jerusalem with him. And when he
had gathered all the chief priests and scribes of the people together, he de-
5 manded of them where Christ should be born. And they said unto him,
6 In Bethlehem of Judea: for thus it is written by the prophet,[b] ' And thou
Bethlehem, *in* the land of Juda, art not the least among the princes of Juda:
for out of thee shall come a Governor, that shall rule my people Israel.
7 Then Herod, when he had privily called the wise men, inquired of them dili-
8 gently what time the star appeared. And he sent them to Bethlehem, and
said, Go, and search diligently for the young child; and when ye have
found *him,* bring me word again, that I may come and worship him also.
9 When they had heard the king, they departed; and lo, the star, which they
saw in the east, went before them, till it came and stood over where the
10 young child was. When they saw the star, they rejoiced with exceeding
11 great joy. And when they were come into the house, they saw the young
child with Mary his mother, and fell down, and worshipped him: and when
they had opened their treasures, they presented unto him gifts; gold, and
12 frankincense, and myrrh. And being warned of God in a dream, that they
should not return to Herod, they departed into their own country another
way.

§ 11. *The flight into Egypt. Herod's cruelty. The return.*—BETHLEHEM, NAZARETH.

MATTH. II. 13—23.

13 And when they were departed, behold, the angel of the Lord appeareth to
Joseph in a dream, saying, Arise, and take the young child and his mother,
and flee into Egypt, and be thou there until I bring thee word: for Herod
14 will seek the young child to destroy him. When he arose, he took the young
15 child and his mother by night, and departed into Egypt: ' and was there
until the death of Herod: that it might be fulfilled which was spoken of
the Lord by the prophet, saying,' Out of Egypt have I called my Son.

---

* **34.** Comp. Is. 8, 14.   b **5, 6.** Mic. 5, 2.   c **15.** Hos. 11, 1

MATTH. II.

16 Then Herod, when he saw that he was mocked of the wise men, was exceeding wroth, and sent forth, and slew all the children that were in Bethlehem, and in all the coasts thereof, from two years old and under, according to the time which he had diligently inquired of the wise men.
17 Then was fulfilled that which was spoken by Jeremy the prophet, saying,[a]
18 In Rama was there a voice heard, lamentation, and weeping, and great mourning, Rachel weeping *for* her children, and would not be comforted, because they are not.
19 But when Herod was dead, behold, an angel of the Lord appeareth in a
20 dream to Joseph in Egypt,¹ saying, Arise, and take the young child and his mother, and go into the land of Israel : for they are dead which sought the
21 young child's life. And he arose, and took the young child and his mother,
22 and came into the land of Israel. But when he heard that Archelaus did reign in Judea in the room of his father
Herod, he was afraid to go thither : notwithstanding, being warned of God in a dream, he turned aside
23 into the parts of Galilee :¹ and he came and dwelt in a city called Nazareth : that it might be fulfilled which was spoken by the prophets, He shall be called a Nazarene.[b]

LUKE II. 39, 40.

39 And when they had performed all things according to the law of the Lord, they returned into Galilee, to
40 their own city Nazareth. And the child grew, and waxed strong in spirit, filled with wisdom ; and the grace of God was upon him.

§ 12. *At twelve years of age Jesus goes to the Passover.*—JERUSALEM.

LUKE II. 41—52.

41 Now his parents went to Jerusalem every year at the feast of the passover.
42 And when he was twelve years old, they went up to Jerusalem after the
43 custom of the feast. And when they had fulfilled the days, as they returned, the child Jesus tarried behind in Jerusalem ; and Joseph and his mother
44 knew not *of it.* But they, supposing him to have been in the company, went a day's journey ; and they sought him among *their* kinsfolk and ac-
45 quaintance. And when they found him not, they turned back again to
46 Jerusalem, seeking him. And it came to pass, that after three days they found him in the temple, sitting in the midst of the doctors, both hearing
47 them, and asking them questions. . And all that heard him were astonished
48 at his understanding and answers. And when they saw him, they were amazed : and his mother said unto him, Son, why hast thou thus dealt with
49 us ? behold, thy father and I have sought thee sorrowing. And he said unto them, How is it that ye sought me ? wist ye not that I must be about
50 my Father's business ? And they understood not the saying which he spake
51 unto them. And he went down with them, and came to Nazareth, and was subject unto them : but his mother kept all these sayings in her heart.
52 And Jesus increased in wisdom and stature, and in favour with God and man.

a 17. Jer. 31, 15.   Comp. Jer. 40, 1.
b 23. Heb. Is. 11, 1.   Comp. Is. 53, 2.   Zech. 6, 12.   Rev. 5, 5.

MATTH. I. 1—17.

1 The book of the generation of Jesus Christ, the son of David, the son of Abraham.

2 Abraham begat Isaac; and Isaac begat Jacob; and Jacob begat Judas 3 and his brethren; ' and Judas begat Phares and Zara of Thamar; and Phares begat Esrom; and Esrom 4 begat Aram; ' and Aram begat Aminadab; and Aminadab begat Naasson; and Naasson begat Sal- 5 mon; ' and Salmon begat Booz of Rachab; and Booz begat Obed of 6 Ruth; and Obed beget Jesse; ' and Jesse begat David the king; and David the king begat Solomon of her *that had been the wife* of 7 Urias; ' and Solomon begat Robo- am; and Roboam begat Abia; and 8 Abia begat Asa; ' and Asa begat Josaphat; and Josaphat begat Jo- 9 ram; and Joram begat Ozias; ' and Ozias begat Joatham; and Joatham begat Achaz; and Achaz begat 10 Ezekias; ' and Ezekias begat Manas- ses; and Manasses begat Amon; 11 and Amon begat Josias; ' and Josias begat Jechonias and his brethren, about the time they were carried 12 away to Babylon. And after they were brought to Babylon, Jechonias begat Salathiel; and Salathiel begat 13 Zorobabel; ' and Zorobabel begat Abiud; and Abiud begat Eliakim, 14 and Eliakim begat Azor; ' and Azor begat Sadoc; and Sadoc begat Achim; and Achim begat Eliud; 15 ' and Eliud begat Eleazar; and Eleazar begat Matthan; and Mat- 16 than begat Jacob; ' and Jacob begat

LUKE III. 23—38, inverted.

39 The son of God, *the son* of Adam, *the son* of Seth, *the son* of Enos, 37 ' *the son* of Cainan, *the son* of Maleleel, *the son* of Jared, *the son* 36 of Enoch, *the son* of Mathusala, ' *the son* of Lamech, *the son* of Noe, *the son* of Sem, *the son* of Arphaxad, 35 *the son* of Cainan, ' *the son* of Sala, *the son* of Heber, *the son* of Phalec, *the son* of Ragau, *the son* of Saruch, 34 ' *the son* of Nachor, *the son* of Thara, *the son* of Abraham, *the son* 33 of Isaac, *the son* of Jacob, ' *the son* of Juda, *the son* of Phares, *the son* of Esrom, *the son* of Aram, *the son* 32 of Aminadab, ' *the son* of Naasson, *the son* of Salmon, *the son* of Booz, 31 *the son* of Obed, *the son* of Jesse, ' *the son* of David, *the son* of Nathan, *the son* of Mattatha, *the son* of 30 Menan, *the son* of Melea, ' *the son* of Eliakim, *the son* of Jonan, *the son* of Joseph, *the son* of Juda, *the son* of 29 Simeon, ' *the son* of Levi, *the son* of Matthat, *the son* of Jorim, *the son* 28 of Eliezer, *the son* of Jose, ' *the son* of Er, *the son* of Elmodam, *the son* of Cosam, *the son* of Addi, *the son* 27 of Melchi, ' *the son* of Neri, *the son* of Salathiel, *the son* of Zorobabel, *the son* of Rhesa, *the son* of Joanna, 26 ' *the son* of Juda, *the son* of Joseph, *the son* of Semei, *the son* of Matta- 25 thias, *the son* of Maath, ' *the son* of Nagge, *the son* of Esli, *the son* of Naum, *the son* of Amos, *the son* of 24 Mattathias, ' *the son* of Joseph, *the son* of Janna, *the son* of Melchi, *the*

MATTH. I.	LUKE III.

Joseph, the husband of Mary, of whom was born Jesus, who is called Christ.

17 So all the generations from Abraham to David *are* fourteen generations; and from David until the carrying away into Babylon *are* fourteen generations; and from the carrying away into Babylon unto Christ *are* fourteen generations.

son of Levi, *the son* of Matthat, **23** ' *the son* of Heli, the son of Joseph,— And Jesus himself ... being (as was supposed)—

PART II

ANNOUNCEMENT AND INTRODUCTION OF OUR LORD'S PUBLIC
MINISTRY.

TIME: *About one year.*

§ 14. *The Ministry of John the Baptist.* — THE DESERT. THE JORDAN.

LUKE III. 1—18.

[1] NOW in the fifteenth year of the reign of Tiberius Cesar, Pontius Pilate
being governor of Judea, and Herod being tetrarch of Galilee, and his
brother Philip tetrarch of Iturea and of the region of Trachonitis, and Lysanias
[2] the tetrarch of Abilene,[1] Annas and Caiaphas being the high priests, the word
of God came unto John
the son of Zacharias in
[3] the wilderness. And he
came into all the coun-
try about Jordan,
preaching the baptism
of repentance, for the
[4] remission of sins; [1] as
it is written in the
book of the words of
Esaias the prophet,
saying,[b] The voice of
one crying in the wil-
derness, Prepare ye the
way of the Lord, make
his paths straight.
[5] Every valley shall be
filled, and every moun-
tain and hill shall be
brought low; and the
crooked shall be made
straight, and the rough ways made smooth;
[6] [1] and all flesh shall see the salvation of God.

MATTH. III. 1—12.

[1] In those days came
John the Baptist,
preaching in the wil-
[2] derness of Judea,[1] and
saying, Repent ye: for
the kingdom of hea-
[3] ven is at hand. For
this is he that was
spoken of by the pro-
phet Esaias, saying,[b]
The voice of one cry-
ing in the wilderness,
Prepare ye the way of
the Lord, make his
paths straight.

MARK I. 1—8.

[1] The beginning of
the gospel of Jesus
Christ the Son of God.
[4] —John did baptize in
the wilderness, and
preach the baptism of
repentance, for the re-
[2] mission of sins.—As it
is written in the proph-
ets,[a] Behold, I send
my messenger before
thy face, which shall
prepare thy way be-
[3] fore thee: The voice of
one crying in the wild-
erness,[b] Prepare ye the
way of the Lord, make
his paths straight.—

---

[a] 2 Mal 3, 1. Is. 40, 3   [b] 3 etc. Is. 40, 3 sq.

MATTH. III.

4 And the same John had his raiment of camel's hair, and a leathern girdle about his loins ; and his meat **2** was locusts and wild honey. Then went out to him Jerusalem, and all Judea, and all the region round **5** about Jordan, ' and were baptized of him in Jordan, confessing their sins.

7 But when he saw many of the Pharisees and Sadducees come to his baptism, he said unto them, O generation of vipers, who hath warned you to flee from the wrath to come ? **8** bring forth therefore fruits meet for **9** repentance : ' and think not to say within yourselves, We have Abraham to *our* father : for I say unto you, that God is able of these stones to raise up children unto Abraham. **10** And now also the axe is laid unto the root of the trees : therefore every tree which bringeth not forth good fruit is hewn down, and cast into the fire. •

MARK I.

6 And John was clothed with camel's hair, and with a girdle of skin about his loins ; and he did eat locusts and **5** wild honey.—And there went out unto him all the land of Judea, and they of Jerusalem, and were all baptized of him in the river of Jordan, confessing their sins.—

LUKE III.

7 Then said he to the multitude that came forth to be baptized of him, O generation of vipers, who hath warned you to flee from the **8** wrath to come ? Bring forth therefore fruits worthy of repentance, and begin not to say within yourselves, We have Abraham to *our* father : for I say unto you, that God is able of these stones to raise up children unto Abraham. **9** And now also the axe is laid unto the root of the trees : every tree therefore which bringeth not forth good fruit, is hewn down, and cast **10** into the fire. And the people asked

11 him, saying, What shall we do then ? He answereth and saith unto them, He that hath two coats, let him impart to him that hath none ; and he that hath meat, let him do **12** likewise. Then came also publicans to be baptized, and **13** said unto him, Master, what shall we do ? And he said unto them, Exact no more than that which is appointed **14** you. And the soldiers likewise demanded of him, saying, And what shall we do ? And he said unto them, Do violence to no man, neither accuse *any* falsely ; and be con**15** tent with your wages. And as the people were in expectation, and all men mused in their hearts of John, whether **16** he were the Christ, or not ; John answered, saying

MATTH. III.

11 I indeed baptize you with water unto repentance ; but he that cometh after ~me is mightier than I, whose shoes I am not worthy to bear ; he shall bap.tize you with the Holy Ghost, and *with* fire : **12** ' whose fan *is* in his hand, and he will thoroughly purge his floor, and gather his wheat into the garner ; but he will burn up the chaff with unquenchable fire.

MARK I.

7 And preached, saying, There cometh one mightier than I after me, the latchet of whose shoes I am not worthy to stoop down and un**8** loose. I indeed have baptized you with water : but he shall baptize you with the Holy Ghost.

unto *them* all, I indeed baptize you with water ; but one mightier than I cometh, the latchet of whose shoes I am not worthy to unloose : he shall baptize you with **17** the Holy Ghost, and with fire : ' whose fan *is* in his hand, and he will thoroughly purge his floor, and will gather the wheat into his garner ; but the chaff he will burn with fire unquenchable. **18** And many other things in his exhortation preached he unto the people.

§ 15. *The Baptism of Jesus.* — THE JORDAN.

MATTH. III. 13—17.	MARK I. 9—11.	LUKE III. 21—23.
13 Then cometh Jesus from Galilee to Jordan unto John to be bap- 14 tized of him. But John forbade him, saying, I have need to be bap- tized of thee, and com- 15 est thou to me? And *it to be so* now : for thus ness. Then he suf- 16 fered him. And Jesus, when he was baptized, went up straightway out of the water: and lo, the heavens were opened unto him, and he saw the Spirit of God descending like a dove, and lighting upon 17 him : ' and lo, a voice from heaven, saying, This is my beloved Son, in whom I am well pleased.	9 And it came to pass in those days, that Jesus came from Naz- areth of Galilee, and was baptized of John in Jordan.	21 Now when all the people were baptized, it came to pass, that Jesus also being bap- tized,

Jesus answering said unto him, Suffer it becometh us to fulfil all righteous-

| | . 10 And straightway com- ing up out of the water, he saw the heavens opened, and the Spirit like a dove descend- 11 ing upon him. And there came a voice from heaven, *saying,* Thou art my beloved Son, in whom I am well pleased. | and praying, the heaven was opened, 22 ' and the Holy Ghost descended in a bodily shape like a dove upon him, and a voice came from heaven which said, Thou art my be- loved Son ; in thee I am well pleased. 23 And Jesus himself began to be about thirty years of age.— |

§ 16. *The Temptation.* — DESERT OF JUDEA.

MATTH. IV. 1—11.	MARK I. 12, 13.	LUKE IV. 1—13.
1 Then was Jesus led up of the Spirit into the wilderness to be tempted of the devil. 2 And when he had fast- ed forty days and forty nights, he was after- wards an hungered. 3 And when the tempter came to him, he said, If thou be the Son of God, command that these stones be 4 made bread. But he answered and said, It is written,ᵃ Man shall not live by bread alone, but by every word that proceedeth out of the	12 And immediately the Spirit driveth him into the wilderness. 13 And he was there in the wilderness forty days tempted of Sa- tan ; and was with the wild beasts ; and the angels ministered unto him.	1 And Jesus being full of the Holy Ghost, re- turned from Jordan, and was led by the Spirit into the wilder- 2 ness, ' being forty days tempted of the devil. And in those days he did eat nothing: and when they were ended, 3 he afterward hungered. And the devil said unto him, If thou be the Son of God, command this stone 4 that it be made bread. And Jesus answered him, saying, It is written,ᵃ that man shall not live by bread

---

ᵃ 4. Deut. 8, 3.

MATT. IV.	LUKE IV.
5 mouth of God. Then the devil taketh him up into the holy city, and setteth him on a pinnacle of 6 the temple, ' and saith unto him, If thou be the Son of God, cast thyself down: for it is written,ᵃ He shall give his angels charge concerning thee: and in *their* hands they shall bear thee up, lest at any time thou dash thy foot against a 7 stone. Jesus said unto him, It is written again,ᵇ	alone, but by every word of God. 9 —And he brought him to Jerusalem, and set him on a pinnacle of the temple, and said unto him, If thou be the Son of God, cast thyself 10 down from hence: ' for it is written,ᵃ He shall give his angels charge over thee, to keep thee: 11 ' and in *their* hands they shall bear thee up, lest at any time thou dash 12 thy foot against a stone. And Jesus answering, said unto him, It is said,ᵇ
Thou shalt not 8 tempt the Lord thy God. Again, the devil taketh him up into an exceeding high mountain, and sheweth him all the kingdoms of the 9 world, and the glory of them; ' and saith unto him, All these things will I give thee,	Thou shalt not tempt the Lord thy 5 God.—And the devil taking him up into an high mountain, shewed unto him all the kingdoms of the world 6 in a moment of time. And the devil said unto him, All this power will I give thee, and the glory of them: for that is delivered unto me, and to whomsoever I will, I give it.
if thou wilt fall 10 down and worship me. Then saith Jesus unto him, Get thee hence, Satan: for it is written,ᶜ Thou shalt worship the Lord thy God, and him only shalt thou serve. 11 Then the devil leaveth him, and behold, angels came and ministered unto him.	7 If thou therefore wilt worship me, 8 all shall be thine. And Jesus answered and said unto him, Get thee behind me, Satan: for it is written,ᶜ Thou shalt worship the Lord thy God, and him only shalt thou serve. 13 —And when the devil had ended the temptation, he departed from him for a season.

§ 17. *Preface to John's Gospel.*

JOHN I. 1—18.

1   In the beginning was the Word, and the Word was with God, and the
2 3 Word was God.   The same was in the beginning with God.   All things
were made by him; and without him was not any thing made that was
4 5 made.   In him was life; and the life was the light of men.   And the
light shineth in darkness; and the darkness comprehended it not.
6 7   There was a man sent from God, whose name *was* John.   The same
came for a witness, to bear witness of the Light, that all *men* through him
8 might believe.   He was not that Light, but *was sent* to bear witness of that
9 Light.   *That* was the true Light, which lighteth every man that cometh
10 into the world.   He was in the world, and the world was made by him,
11 and the world knew him not.   He came unto his own, and his own re-
12 ceived him not.   But to as many as received him, to them gave he power
13 to become the sons of God, *even* to them that believe on his name: ' which
were born, not of blood, nor of the will of the flesh, nor of the will of man,
14 but of God.   And the Word was made flesh, and dwelt among us, (and
we beheld his glory, the glory as of the only begotten of the Father,) full
of grace and truth.

ᵃ **6** etc. Ps. 91, 11.   ᵇ **7** etc. Deut. 6, 16.   ᶜ **10** etc. Deut. 6, 13.

2

JOHN I.

15   John bare witness of him, and cried, saying, This was he of whom I spake, He that cometh after me, is preferred before me ; for he was before 16 17 me. And of his fulness have all we received, and grace for grace. For the law was given by Moses, *but* grace and truth came by Jesus Christ. 18 No man hath seen God at any time ; the only begotten Son, which is in the bosom of the Father, he hath declared *him*.

§ 18. *Testimony of John the Baptist to Jesus.*—BETHABARA BEYOND JORDAN.

JOHN I. 19—34.

19   And this is the record of John, when the Jews sent priests and Levites 20 from Jerusalem, to ask him, Who art thou ? And he confessed, and denied 21 not ; but confessed, I am not the Christ. And they asked him, What then ? Art thou Elias ? And he saith, I am not. Art thou that prophet ? And 22 he answered, No. Then said they unto him, Who art thou ? that we may 23 give an answer to them that sent us. What sayest thou of thyself ? ¹ He said, I *am* the voice of one crying in the wilderness, Make straight the way 24 of the Lord, as said the prophet Esaias.ᵃ And they which were sent 25 were of the Pharisees. And they asked him, and said unto him, Why baptizest thou then, if thou be not that Christ, nor Elias, neither that 26 prophet ? John answered them, saying, I baptize with water : but there 27 standeth one among you, whom ye know not : ¹ he it is, who coming after me, is preferred before me, whose shoe's latchet I am not worthy to unloose. 28 These things were done in Bethabara beyond Jordan, where John was baptizing. 29 The next day John seeth Jesus coming unto him, and saith, Behold the 30 Lamb of God, which taketh away the sin of the world ! This is he of whom I said, After me cometh a man which is preferred before me ; for he 31 was before me. And I knew him not ; but that he should be made mani- 32 fest to Israel, therefore am I come baptizing with water. And John bare record, saying, I saw the Spirit descending from heaven like a dove, and it 33 abode upon him. - And I knew him not : but he that sent me to baptize with water, the same said unto me, Upon whom thou shalt see the Spirit descending and remaining on him, the same is he which baptizeth with the 34 Holy Ghost. And I saw and bare record, that this is the Son of God.

§ 19. *Jesus gains Disciples.*—THE JORDAN. GALILEE ?

JOHN I. 35—51.

35 36   Again the next day after, John stood, and two of his disciples ; ¹ and 37 looking upon Jesus as he walked, he saith, Behold the Lamb of God ! And 38 the two disciples heard him speak, and they followed Jesus. Then Jesus turned, and saw them following, and saith unto them, What seek ye ? They said unto him, Rabbi, (which is to say, being interpreted, Master,) where 39 dwellest thou ? ¹ He saith unto them, Come and see. They came and saw where he dwelt, and abode with him that day : for it was about the tenth 40 hour. One of the two which heard John *speak*, and followed him, was 41 Andrew, Simon Peter's brother. He first findeth his own brother Simon, and

ᵃ **23**. Is. 40, 3.

JOHN I.

saith unto him, We have found the Messias; which is, being interpreted,
42 the Christ. ' And he brought him to Jesus. And when Jesus beheld him,
he said, Thou art Simon the son of Jona: thou shalt be called Cephas;
which is, by interpretation, a stone.
43 The day following Jesus would go forth into Galilee, and findeth Philip,
44 and saith unto him, Follow me. Now Philip was of Bethsaida, the city of
45 Andrew and Peter. Philip findeth Nathanael, and saith unto him, We have
found him of whom Moses in the law, and the prophets, did write, Jesus of
46 Nazareth, the son of Joseph. And Nathanael said unto him, Can there any
good thing come out of Nazareth? Philip saith unto him, Come and see.
47 Jesus saw Nathanael coming to him, and saith of him, Behold an Israelite
48 indeed, in whom is no guile! Nathanael saith unto him, Whence knowest thou me? Jesus answered and said unto him, Before that Philip called
49 thee, when thou wast under the fig-tree, I saw thee. Nathanael answered
and said unto him, Rabbi, thou art the Son of God; thou art the King of
50 Israel. Jesus answered and said unto him, Because I said unto thee, I saw
thee under the fig-tree, believest thou? thou shalt see greater things than
51 these. And he saith unto him, Verily, verily, I say unto you, Hereafter ye
shall see heaven open, and the angels of God ascending and descending
upon the Son of man.[a]

§ 20. *The Marriage at Cana of Galilee.*

JOHN II. 1—12.

1 And the third day there was a marriage in Cana of Galilee; and the mother
2 of Jesus was there. And both Jesus was called, and his disciples, to the
3 marriage. And when they wanted wine, the mother of Jesus saith unto
4 him, They have no wine. Jesus saith unto her, Woman, what have I to
5 do with thee? mine hour is not yet come. His mother saith unto the ser-
6 vants, Whatsoever he saith unto you do *it.* And there were set there six
water-pots of stone, after the manner of the purifying of the Jews, contain-
7 ing two or three firkins apiece. Jesus saith unto them, Fill the water-pots
8 with water. And they filled them up to the brim. ' And he saith unto
them, Draw out now, and bear unto the governor of the feast. And they
9 bare *it.* When the ruler of the feast had tasted the water that was made
wine, and knew not whence it was, (but the servants which drew the water
10 knew,) the governor of the feast called the bridegroom, ' and saith unto
him, Every man at the beginning doth set forth good wine; and when men
have well drunk, then that which is worse: *but* thou hast kept the good
11 wine until now. This beginning of miracles did Jesus in Cana of Galilee,
and manifested forth his glory; and his disciples believed on him.
12 After this he went down to Capernaum, he, and his mother, and his
brethren, and his disciples; and they continued there not many days.

a 51. Comp. Gen. 28, 12.

PART III.

TIME: *One year*

§ 21. *At the Passover Jesus drives the Traders out of the Temple.*—JERUSALEM.

JOHN II. 13—25.

13 AND the Jews' passover was at hand, and Jesus went up to Jerusalem,
14 'and found in the temple those that sold oxen, and sheep, and doves, and
15 the changers of money, sitting. And when he had made a scourge of small
cords, he drove them all out of the temple, and the sheep, and the oxen ;
16 and poured out the changers' money, and overthrew the tables ; ' and said
unto them that sold doves, Take these things hence : make not my Father's
17 house an house of merchandise. And his disciples remembered that it was
written, The zeal of thine house hath eaten me up. *
18 Then answered the Jews, and said unto him, What sign shewest thou unto
19 us, seeing that thou doest these things? Jesus answered and said unto
20 them, Destroy this temple, and in three days I will raise it up. Then said
the Jews, Forty and six years was this temple in building, and wilt thou
21 22 rear it up in three days? But he spake of the temple of his body. When
therefore he was risen from the dead, his disciples remembered that he had
said this unto them: and they believed the scripture, and the word which
Jesus had said.
23 Now when he was in Jerusalem at the passover, in the feast-*day*, many
24 believed in his name, when they saw the miracles which he did. But Jesus
25 did not commit himself unto them, because he knew all *men*, ' and needed
not that any should testify of man: for he knew what was in man.

§ 22. *Our Lord's discourse with Nicodemus.*—JERUSALEM.

JOHN III. 1—21.

1 There was a man of the Pharisees named Nicodemus, a ruler of the Jews:
2 'the same came to Jesus by night, and said unto him, Rabbi, we know that

---

* 17. Ps. 69, 9.

JOHN III.

thou art a teacher come from God: for no man can do these miracles that
3 thou doest, except God be with him.   Jesus answered and said unto him,
Verily, verily, I say unto thee, Except a man be born again, he cannot see
4 the kingdom of God.   Nicodemus saith unto him, How can a man be born
when he is old? can he enter the second time into his mother's womb,
5 and be born?   Jesus answered, Verily, verily, I say unto thee, Except a
man be born of water, and *of* the Spirit, he cannot enter into the kingdom
6 of God.   That which is born of the flesh, is flesh; and that which is born
7 of the Spirit, is spirit.   Marvel not that I said unto thee, Ye must be born
8 again.   The wind bloweth where it listeth, and thou hearest the sound
thereof, but canst not tell whence it cometh, and whither it goeth: so is
9 every one that is born of the Spirit.   Nicodemus answered and said unto
10 him, How can these things be?   Jesus answered and said unto him, Art
11 thou a master of Israel, and knowest not these things?   Verily, verily, I
say unto thee, We speak that we do know, and testify that we have seen;
12 and ye receive not our witness.   If I have told you earthly things, and ye
13 believe not, how shall ye believe if I tell you *of* heavenly things?   And
no man hath ascended up to heaven, but he that came down from heaven,
even the Son of man which is in heaven.
14   And as Moses lifted up the serpent in the wilderness,ª even so must the
15 Son of man be lifted up: ' that whosoever believeth in him should not
16 perish, but have eternal life.   For God so loved the world, that he gave his
only begotten Son, that whosoever believeth in him, should not perish, but
17 have everlasting life.   For God sent not his Son into the world to con-
18 demn the world, but that the world through him might be saved.   He that
believeth on him, is not condemned: but he that believeth not, is condemned
already, because he hath not believed in the name of the only begotten Son
19 of God.   And this is the condemnation, that light is come into the world,
and men loved darkness rather than light, because their deeds were evil.
20 For every one that doeth evil hateth the light, neither cometh to the light,
21 lest his deeds should be reproved.   But he that doeth truth, cometh to
the light, that his deeds may be made manifest, that they are wrought in
God.

§ 23. *Jesus remains in Judea and baptizes.   Further testimony of John the
Baptist.*

JOHN III. 22—36.

22   After these things came Jesus and his disciples into the land of Judea;
23 and there he tarried with them, and baptized.   And John also was baptizing
in Ænon, near to Salim, because there was much water there: and they
24 came, and were baptized.   For John was not yet cast into prison.
25   Then there arose a question between *some* of John's disciples and the
26 Jews, about purifying.   And they came unto John, and said unto him, Rabbi,
he that was with thee beyond Jordan, to whom thou barest witness, be-
27 hold the same baptizeth, and all *men* come to him.   John answered and
28 said, A man can receive nothing, except it be given him from heaven.   Ye
yourselves bear me witness, that I said, I am not the Christ, but that I am
29 sent before him.   He that hath the bride, is the bridegroom: but the friend

ª 14. Comp. Num. 21, 8 sq.

2*

JOHN III.

of the bridegroom, which standeth and heareth him, rejoiceth greatly, be-
30 cause of the bridegroom's voice : this my joy therefore is fulfilled.   He must
31 increase, but I *must* decrease.   He that cometh from above is above all : he
that is of the earth is earthly, and speaketh of the earth : he that com^eth
32 from heaven is above all.   And what he hath seen and heard, that he testi-
33 fieth ; and no man receiveth his testimony.·   He that hath received his testi-
34 mony, hath set to his seal that God is true.   For he whom God hath sent,
speaketh the words of God : for God giveth not the Spirit by measure *unto*
35 *him.*   The Father loveth the Son and hath given all things into his hand.
36 He that believeth on the Son hath everlasting life : and he that believeth
not the Son, shall not see life ; but the wrath of God abideth on him.

§ 24. *Jesus departs into Galilee after John's imprisonment.*

MATTH. IV. 12.	MARK I. 14.	LUKE IV. 14.
12 Now, when Jesus had heard that John was cast into prison, he departed into Galilee.	14 Now after that John was put in prison, Jesus came into Galilee.—	And Jesus returned in the power of the Spirit into Galilee.—
MATTH. XIV. 3—5.	MARK VI. 17—20.	LUKE III. 19, 20.
3 For Herod had laid hold on John, and bound him, and put *him* in prison for Herodias' sake, his brother Philip's wife.	17 For Herod himself had sent forth and laid hold upon John, and bound him in prison for Herodias' sake, his brother Philip's wife : for he had married her.	19 But Herod the tetrarch, being reproved by him for Herodias his brother Philip's wife, and for all the evils which Herod had
4 For John said unto him, It is not lawful for thee to have 5 her. And when he would have put him to death, he feared the multitude, because they counted him as a prophet.	18 For John had said unto Herod, It is not lawful for thee to have thy 19 brother's wife. Therefore against him, and would have killed him ; but she 20 could not : ' for Herod feared John, knowing that he was a just man and an holy, and observed him : and when he heard him, he did many things, and heard him gladly.	20 done, ' added yet this above all, that he shut up John in prison. Herodias had a quarrel

JOHN IV. 1—3.

1 When therefore the Lord knew how the Pharisees had heard that Jesus
2 made and baptized more disciples than John, ' (though Jesus himself bap-
3 tized not, but his disciples,) ' he left Judea and departed again into Galilee.

, 25. *Our Lord's discourse with the Samaritan woman.   Many of the Samaritans believe on him.*—SHECHEM *or* NEAPOLIS.

JOHN IV. 4—42.

4 5 And he must needs go through Samaria.   Then cometh he to a city of
Samaria, which is called Sychar, near to the parcel of ground that Jacob
6 gave to his son Joseph.   Now Jacob's well was there.   Jesus therefore
being wearied with *his* journey, sat thus on the well : *and* it was about the

JOHN IV.

7 sixth hour. There cometh a woman of Samaria to draw water: Jesus
8 saith unto her, Give me to drink. (For his disciples were gone away unto
9 the city to buy meat.) Then saith the woman of Samaria unto him, How
is it that thou, being a Jew, askest drink of me, which am a woman of
10 Samaria? for the Jews have no dealings with the Samaritans. Jesus answered and said unto her, If thou knewest the gift of God, and who it is
that saith to thee, Give me to drink ; thou wouldest have asked of him, and
11 he would have given thee living water. The woman saith unto him, Sir, thou
hast nothing to draw with, and the well is deep: from whence then hast
12 thou that living water? Art thou greater than our father Jacob, which
gave us the well, and drank thereof himself, and his children, and his cattle?
13 Jesus answered and said unto her, Whosoever drinketh of this water shall
14 thirst again:¹ but whosoever drinketh of the water that I shall give him,
shall never thirst; but the water that I shall give him, shall be in him a
15 well of water springing up into everlasting life. The woman saith unto
him, Sir, give me this water, that I thirst not, neither come hither to draw.
16 17 Jesus saith unto her, Go call thy husband, and come hither. The woman
answered and said, I have no husband. Jesus said unto her, Thou hast
18 well said, I have no husband:¹ for thou hast had five husbands, and he
whom thou now hast, is not thy husband: in that saidst thou truly.
19 20 The woman saith unto him, Sir, I perceive that thou art a prophet. Our
fathers worshipped in this mountain ; and ye say, that in Jerusalem is the
21 place where men ought to worship. Jesus saith unto her, Woman, believe me, the hour cometh, when ye shall neither in this mountain, nor
22 yet at Jerusalem, worship the Father. Ye worship ye know not what: we
23 know what we worship, for salvation is of the Jews. But the hour cometh,
and now is, when the true worshippers shall worship the Father in spirit
24 and in truth: for the Father seeketh such to worship him. God is a Spirit:
25 and they that worship him, must worship him in spirit and in truth. The
woman saith unto him, I know that Messias cometh, which is called Christ ;
26 when he is come, he will tell us all things. Jesus saith unto her, I that
speak unto thee am he.
27   And upon this came his disciples, and marvelled that he talked with the
woman: yet no man said, What seekest thou? or, Why talkest thou with
28 her? The woman then left her water-pot, and went her way into the city,
29 and saith to the men, Come, see a man which told me all things that ever
30 I did: is not this the Christ? Then went they out of the city, and came
unto him.
31 32 In the mean while his disciples prayed him, saying, Master, eat. But
33 he said unto them, I have meat to eat that ye know not of. Therefore said
the disciples one to another, Hath any man brought him aught to eat?
34 Jesus saith unto them, My meat is to do the will of him that sent me, and to
35 finish his work. Say not ye, There are yet four months, and then cometh
harvest? behold, I say unto you, Lift up your eyes, and look on the fields ;
36 for they are white already to harvest. And he that reapeth receiveth
wages, and gathereth fruit unto life eternal : that both he that soweth, and
37 he that reapeth, may rejoice together. And herein is that saying true, One
38 soweth, and another reapeth. I sent you to reap that whereon ye bestowed
no labour: other men laboured, and ye are entered into their labours.
39   And many of the Samaritans of that city believed on him for the saying
40 of the woman, which testified, He told me all that ever I did. So when
the Samaritans were come unto him, they besought him that he would tarry
41 with them: and he abode there two days. And many more believed be-

JOHN IV.

¹² cause of his own word; ¹ and said unto the woman, Now we believe, not because of thy saying: for we have heard *him* ourselves,'and know that this is indeed the Christ, the Saviour of the world.

§ 26. *Jesus teaches publicly in Galilee.*

JOHN IV. 43—45.

⁴³ ⁴⁴ Now, after two days he departed thence, and went into Galilee. For Jesus himself testified, that a prophet hath no honour in his own country. ⁴⁵ Then when he was come into Galilee, the Galileans received him, having seen all the things that he did at Jerusalem at the feast: for they also went unto the feast.

MATTH. IV. 17.	MARK I. 14, 15.	LUKE IV. 14, 15.
¹⁷ From that time Jesus began to preach, and to say, Repent; for the kingdom of heaven is at hand.	¹⁴ —Preaching the gospel of the kingdom of God, ¹⁵ ¹ and saying, The time is fulfilled, and the kingdom of God is at hand: repent ye, and believe the gospel.	¹⁴ —And there went out a fame of him through all the region round ¹⁵ about. And he taught in their synagogues, being glorified of all.

§ 27. *Jesus again at Cana, where he heals the son of a Nobleman lying ill at Capernaum.*—CANA OF GALILEE.

JOHN IV. 46—54.

⁴⁶ So Jesus came again into Cana of Galilee, where he made the water wine. And there was a certain nobleman, whose son was sick at Caper- ⁴⁷ naum. When he heard that Jesus was come out of Judea into Galilee, he went unto him, and besought him that he would come down, and heal his ⁴⁸ son: for he was at the point of death. Then said Jesus unto him, Except ⁴⁹ ye see signs and wonders, ye will not believe. The nobleman saith unto ⁵⁰ him, Sir, come down ere my child die. Jesus saith unto him, Go thy way; thy son liveth. And the man believed the word that Jesus had spoken unto ⁵· him, and he went his way. And as he was now going down, his servants ⁵² met him, and told *him*, saying, Thy son liveth. Then inquired he of them the hour when he began to amend. And they said unto him, Yesterday at ⁵³ the seventh hour the fever left him. So the father knew that *it was* at the same hour, in the which Jesus said unto him, Thy son liveth: and himself ⁵⁴ believed, and his whole house. This *is* again the second miracle *that* Jesus did, when he was come out of Judea into Galilee.

§ 28. *Jesus at Nazareth; he is there rejected; and fixes his abode at Caper-naum.*

LUKE IV. 16—31.

¹⁶ And he came to Nazareth, where he had been brought up: and, as his custom was, he went into the synagogue on the sabbath-day, and stood up ·¹ for to read. And there was delivered unto him the book of the prophet Esaias. And when he had opened the book, he found the place where it

LUKE IV.

18 was written,[a] The Spirit of the Lord *is* upon me, because he hath anointed me to preach the gospel to the poor; he hath sent me to heal the broken-hearted, to preach deliverance to the captives, and recovering of 19 sight to the blind, to set at liberty them that are bruised, ' to preach the 20 acceptable year of the Lord. And he closed the book, and he gave *it* again to the minister, and sat down. And the eyes of all them that were in the 21 synagogue were fastened on him. And he began to say unto them, This day is this scripture fulfilled in your ears.

22 And all bare him witness, and wondered at the gracious words which proceeded out of his mouth. And they said, Is not this Joseph's son? 23 And he said unto them, Ye will surely say unto me this proverb, Physician, heal thyself: whatsoever we have heard done in Capernaum, do also here in 24 thy country. And he said, Verily I say unto you, No prophet is accepted 25 in his own country. But I tell you of a truth, many widows were in Israel in the days of Elias, when the heaven was shut up three years and six 26 months, when great famine was throughout all the land: ' but unto none of them was Elias sent, save unto Sarepta, *a city* of Sidon, unto a woman 27 *that was* a widow. [b] And many lepers were in Israel in the time of Eliseus the prophet; and none of them was cleansed, saving Naaman the Syrian. [c] 28 And all they in the synagogue, when they heard these things, were filled 29 with wrath, ' and rose up, and thrust him out of the city, and led him unto the brow of the hill, whereon their city was built, that they might cast him down 30 headlong. But he, passing through the midst of them, went his way,

MATTH. IV. 13—16.	31 ' and came down to Capernaum, a
13 And leaving Nazareth, he came and dwelt in Capernaum, which is upon the sea-coast, in the borders of 14 Zabulon and Nephthalim ; ' that it might be fulfilled which was spoken by 15 Esaias the prophet, saying, [d] ' The land of Zabulon, and the land of Nephthalim, *by* the way of the sea, beyond Jordan, Galilee of the Gentiles: 16 ' the people which sat in darkness, saw great light; and to them which sat in the region and shadow of death, light is sprung up.	city of Galilee.—

§ 29. *The call of Simon Peter and Andrew, and of James and John, with the miraculous draught of fishes.*—NEAR CAPERNAUM.

LUKE V. 1—11.

1 And it came to pass, that as the people pressed upon him to hear the 2 word of God, he stood by the lake of Gennesaret, ' and saw two ships standing by the lake: but the fishermen were gone out of them, and were 3 washing *their* nets. And he entered into one of the ships, which was Simon's, and prayed him that he would thrust out a little from the land. 4 And he sat down, and taught the people out of the ship. ' Now, when he had left speaking, he said unto Simon, Launch out into the deep, and let 5 down your nets for a draught. And Simon answering, said unto him, Master, we have toiled all the night, and have taken nothing; nevertheless, at thy word I will 6 let down the net. And when they had this done, they inclosed ɑ

MATT. IV. 18—22.	MARK 1. 16—20.
18 And Jesus, walking by the sea of Galilee,	16 Now as he walked by the sea of Galilee, he

---

a **17, 18.** Is. 61, 1. Comp. Is. 58, 6.   c **27.** 2 K. 5, 14.
b **25, 26** 1 K. 17, 1. 9.   d **14** sq. Is. 9, 1. 2.

MATTH. IV.	MARK I.	LUKE V.

saw two brethren, Simon called Peter, and Andrew his brother, casting a net into the sea ; for they were fishers.

saw Simon, and Andrew his brother, casting a net into the sea : for they were fishers.

great multitude of fishes: and their net brake. 7 And they beckoned unto *their* partners, which were in the other ship, that they should come and help them. And they came, and filled 8 both the ships, so that they began to sink. When Simon Peter saw *it*, he fell down at Jesus' knees, saying, Depart from me ; for I am a sinful man, O Lord. 9 For he was astonished, and all that were with him, at 10 the draught of the fishes which they had taken: 1 and so *was* also James and John the sons of Zebedee, which were partners with Simon.

MARK I.

19 And he saith unto them, Follow me, and I will make you fishers 20 of men. And they straightway left *their* nets, and followed him. 21 And going on from thence, he saw other two brethren, James *the son* of Zebedee, and John his brother, in a ship with Zebedee their father, mending their nets: and he 22 called them. And they immediately left the ship, and their father, and followed him.

MARK I.

17 And Jesus said unto them, Come ye after me, and I will make you to become fishers 18 of men. And straightway they forsook their nets, and 19 followed him. And when he had gone a little further thence, he saw James the *son* of Zebedee, and John his brother, who also were in the 20 ship mending their nets. And straightway he called them: and they left their father Zebedee in the ship with the hired servants, and went after him.

And Jesus said unto Simon, Fear not: from henceforth thou shalt catch men.

LUKE V.

11 And when they had brought their ships to land, they forsook all, and followed him.

§ 30. *The healing of a Demoniac in the Synagogue.*—CAPERNAUM.

MARK I. 21—28.	LUKE IV. 31—37.

21 And they went into Capernaum ; and straightway on the sabbath-day he entered into the synagogue and 22 taught. And they were astonished at his doctrine: for he taught them as one that had authority, and not 23 as the scribes. And there was in their synagogue a man with an unclean spirit ; and he cried out, 24 1 saying, Let *us* alone ; what have we to do with thee, Jesus of Nazareth? art thou come to destroy us? I know thee who thou art, the 25 Holy One of God. And Jesus rebuked him, saying, Hold thy peace, 26 and come out of him. And when the unclean spirit had torn him, and cried with a loud voice, he came

31 —And taught them on the sabbath-32 days. And they were astonished at his doctrine: for his word was with power. 33 And in the synagogue there was a man which had a spirit of an unclean devil ; and he cried out with 34 a loud voice, 1 saying, Let *us* alone ; what have we to do with thee, Jesus of Nazareth? art thou come to destroy us? I know thee who thou art, the Holy One of God. 35 And Jesus rebuked him, saying, Hold thy peace, and come out of him. And when the devil had thrown him in the midst, he came

MARK I.	LUKE IV.
27 out of him. And they were all amazed, insomuch that they questioned among themselves, saying, What thing is this? what new doctrine is this? for with authority commandeth he even the unclean 28 spirits, and they do obey him. And immediately his fame spread abroad throughout all the region round about Galilee.	36 out of him, and hurt him not. And they were all amazed, and spake among themselves, saying, What a word is this! for with authority and power he commandeth the unclean spirits, and they come out. 37 And the fame of him went out into every place of the country round about.

§ 31. *The healing of Peter's wife's mother, and many others.*—CAPERNAUM.

MATTH. VIII. 14—17.	MARK I. 29—34.	LUKE IV. 38—41.
14 And when Jesus was come into Peter's house,	29 And forthwith, when they were come out of the synagogue, they entered into the house of Simon and Andrew, with James and John.	38 Aud he arose out of the synagogue, and entered into Simon's house.
he saw his wife's mother laid, and sick of a fever.	30 But Simon's wife's mother lay sick of a fever; and anon they tell him 31 of her. And he came	And Simon's wife's mother was taken with a great fever; and they besought him 39 for her. And he stood
15 And he touched her hand, and the fever left her: and she arose, and ministered unto them.	and took her by the hand, and lifted her up; and immediately the fever left her, and she ministered unto them.	over her, and rebuked the fever; and it left her: and immediately she arose and ministered unto them.
16 When the even was come, they brought unto him many that were possessed with devils: and he cast out the spirits with *his* word, and healed all that 17 were sick; ¹ that it might be fulfilled which was spoken by Esaias the prophet, saying,ᵃ Himself took *our* infirmities, and bare *our* sicknesses.	32 And at even when the sun did set, they brought unto him all that were diseased, and them that were possessed with devils. 33 And all the city was gathered together at 34 the door. And he healed many that were sick of divers diseases, and cast out many devils; and suffered not the devils to speak, because they knew him.	40 Now when the sun was setting, all they that had any sick with divers diseases, brought them unto him: and he laid his hands on every one of them, and 41 healed them. And devils also came out of many, crying out, and saying, Thou art Christ the Son of God. And he, rebuking *them*, suffered them not to speak: for they knew that he was Christ.

§ 32. *Jesus with his Disciples goes from Capernaum throughout Galilee.*

MARK I. 35—39.	LUKE IV. 42—44.
35 And in the morning, rising up a great while before day, he went out	42 And when it was day, he departed, and went into a desert place;

ᵃ 17. Is. 53, 4.

MARK I.	LUKE IV.
and departed into a solitary place, **36** and there prayed. And Simon, and they that were with him, followed **37** after him. And when they had found him, they said unto him, All **38** men seek for thee. And he said unto them, Let us go into the next towns, that I may preach there also: for therefore came I forth. **39** And he preached in their synagogues throughout all Galilee, and cast out devils.	and the people sought him, and came unto him, and stayed him, that he should not depart from **43** them. And he said unto them, I must preach the kingdom of God to other cities also, for therefore am I **44** sent. And he preached in the synagogues of Galilee.

MATTH. IV. 23—25.

23 And Jesus went about all Galilee, teaching in their synagogues, and preaching the gospel of the kingdom, and healing all manner of sickness, and **24** all manner of disease among the people. And his fame went throughout all Syria: and they brought unto him all sick people that were taken with divers diseases and torments, and those which were possessed with devils, and those which were lunatic, and those that had the palsy; and he healed them. **25** And there followed him great multitudes of people from Galilee, and *from* Decapolis, and *from* Jerusalem, and *from* Judea, and *from* beyond Jordan.

§ 33. *The healing of a Leper.*—GALILEE.

MATTH. VIII. 2—4.	MARK I. 40—45.	LUKE V. 12—16.
2 And behold, there came a leper and worshipped him, saying,	**40** And there came a leper to him, beeseeching him, and kneeling down to him, and saying unto him, If thou	**12** And it came to pass, when he was in a certain city, behold, a man full of leprosy: who seeing Jesus, fell on *his*
Lord, if thou wilt, thou canst make me clean.	wilt, thou canst make **41** me clean. And Jesus, moved with compassion, put forth *his* hand,	face, and besought him, saying, Lord, if thou wilt, thou canst make **13** me clean. And he put
3 And Jesus put forth *his* hand, and touched him, saying, I will; be thou clean.	and touched him, and saith unto him, I will; **42** be thou clean. And as soon as he had spoken,	forth *his* hand and touched him, saying, I will; be thou clean.
And immediately his leprosy was cleansed.	immediately the leprosy departed from him, and he was cleansed.	And immediately the leprosy departed from him.
	43 And he straitly charged him, and forthwith sent **44** him away; ' and saith	
· And Jesus saith unto him, See thou tell no man; but go thy way, shew thyself to the priest, and offer the gift that Moses commanded, for a testimony unto them.ª	unto him, See thou say nothing to any man; but go thy way, shew thyself to the priest, and offer for thy cleansing those things which Moses commanded, for a testimony unto them.ª	**14** And he charged him to tell no man: but go, and shew thyself to the priest, and offer for thy cleansing, according as Moses commanded, for a testimony unto them.ª

MARK 1.

15 But he went out, and began to publish it much, and to blaze abroad the matter, insomuch that Jesus could no more openly enter into the city, but was without in desert places: and they came to him from every quarter.

LUKE V.

15 But so much the more went there a fame abroad of him: and great multitudes came together to hear and to be healed by him of their infirmities. 16 And he withdrew himself into the wilderness, and prayed.

§ 34. The healing of a Paralytic.—CAPERNAUM.

MARK II. 1—12.

1 And again he entered into Capernaum, after some days; and it was noised that he was in the house. 2 And straightway many were gathered together, insomuch that there was no room to receive them, no, not so much as about the door:

MATTH. IX. 2—8.

2 And behold, they brought to him a man sick of the palsy, lying on a bed.

and he preached the 3 word unto them. And they come unto him, bringing one sick of the palsy, which was 4 borne of four. And when they could not come nigh unto him for the press, they uncovered the roof where he was: and when they had broken it up, they let down the bed wherein the sick of the

And Jesus, seeing their faith, said unto the sick of the palsy, Son, be of good cheer; thy sins be forgiven thee. And behold, certain of the scribes said within themselves, This man blasphemeth.

5 palsy lay. When Jesus saw their faith, he said unto the sick of the palsy, Son, thy sins 6 be forgiven thee. But there were certain of the scribes sitting there, and reasoning in their 7 hearts, Why doth this man thus speak blasphemies? Who can forgive sins but God on8 ly? And immediately, when Jesus perceived in his spirit that they so reasoned within themselves, he said unto them, Why reason ye these things in

And Jesus, knowing their thoughts, said,

Wherefore think ye evil in your hearts?

LUKE V. 17—26.

17 And it came to pass on a certain day, as he was teaching, that there were Pharisees and doctors of the law sitting by, which were come out of every town of Galilee, and Judea, and Jerusalem: and the power of the Lord was present 18 to heal them. And behold, men brought in a bed a man which was taken with a palsy: and they sought to bring him in, and to lay 19 him before him. And when they could not find by what way they might bring him in, because of the multitude, they went upon the house-top, and let him down through the tiling with his couch, into the midst 20 before Jesus. And when he saw their faith, he said unto him,

Man, thy sins are forgiven thee.

21 And the scribes and the Pharisees began to reason, saying, Who is this which speaketh blasphemies? Who can forgive sins but God 22 alone? But when Jesus perceived their thoughts, he answering, said unto them,

What reason ye in your hearts?

3

MATTH. IX.	MARK II.	LUKE V.
⁶ For whether is easier, to say, Thy sins be forgiven thee ; or to say, Arise, and walk ?	⁹ your hearts ? Whether is it easier to say to the sick of the palsy, *Thy* sins be forgiven thee; or to say, Arise, and take up thy	²³ Whether is easier, to say, Thy sins be forgiven thee ; or to say, Rise up and walk ?
But that ye may know that the Son of man hath power on earth to forgive sins, (then saith he to the sick of the palsy,) Arise, take up thy bed, and go unto thine house.	¹⁰ bed, and walk ? But that ye may know that the Son of man hath power on earth to forgive sins, (he saith to the sick of the palsy,) ¹¹ I say unto thee, Arise, and take up thy bed, and go thy way into ¹² thine house. And im-	²⁴ But that ye may know that the Son of man hath power upon earth to forgive sins, (he said unto the sick of the palsy,) I say unto thee, Arise, and take up thy couch, and go unto ²⁵ thine house. And im-mediately he rose up before them, and took
And he ⁷ arose, and depart-ed to his house. ⁸ But when the multi-tude saw *it*, they mar-velled, and glorified God, which had given such power unto men.	mediately he arose, took up the bed, and went forth before them all ; insomuch that they were all amazed, and glorified God, saying, We never saw it on this fashion.	up that whereon he lay, and departed to his own house, glorify-²⁶ ing God. And they were all amazed, and they glorified God, and were filled with fear, saying, We have seen strange things to-day.

§ 35. *The call of Matthew.*—CAPERNAUM.

MATTH. IX. 9.	MARK II. 13, 14.	LUKE V. 27, 28.
	¹³ And he went forth again by the sea-side ; and all the multitude	
And as Jesus passed forth from thence, he saw a man named Matthew, sitting at the receipt of custom : and he saith unto him, Follow me. And he arose, and followed him.	resorted unto him, and ¹⁴ he taught them. And as he passed by, he saw Levi the *son* of Alpheus, sitting at the receipt of custom, and said unto him, Follow me. And he arose, and followed him.	²⁷ And after these things he went forth, and saw a publican named Levi, sitting at the receipt of custom : and he said unto him, ²⁸ Follow me. And he left all, rose up, and followed him.

PART IV.

TIME: *One year.*

---

§ 36. *The Pool of Bethesda; the healing of the infirm man; and our Lord's
subsequent discourse.*—JERUSALEM.

JOHN V. 1—47.

1 AFTER this there was a feast of the Jews: and Jesus went up to Jeru-
2 salem. · Now there is at Jerusalem, by the sheep *gate,* a pool, which
3 is called in the Hebrew tongue, Bethesda, having five porches. In these
lay a great multitude of impotent folk, of blind, halt, withered, waiting for
4 the moving of the water. For an angel went down at a certain season
into the pool, and troubled the water: whosoever then first after the troub-
ling of the water stepped in, was made whole of whatsoever disease he had.
5 And a certain man was there, which had an infirmity thirty and eight
6 years. When Jesus saw him lie, and knew that he had been now a long
7 time *in that case,* he saith unto him, Wilt thou be made whole? The impotent man answered him, Sir, I have no man, when the water is troubled,
to put me into the pool: but while I am coming, another steppeth down
8 before me. Jesus saith unto him, Rise, take up thy bed, and walk.
9 And immediately the man was made whole, and took up his bed, and
walked: and on the same day was the sabbath.
10 The Jews therefore said unto him that was cured, It is the sabbath-day;
11 it is not lawful for thee to carry *thy* bed. He answered them, He that
made me whole, the same said unto me, Take up thy bed, and walk.
12 Then asked they him, What man is that which said unto thee, Take up
13 thy bed, and walk? And he that was healed wist not who it was: for
14 Jesus had conveyed himself away, a multitude being in *that* place. Afterward Jesus findeth him in the temple, and said unto him, Behold, thou art
15 made whole: sin no more, lest a worse thing come unto thee. The man
departed, and told the Jews that it was Jesus which had made him whole.
16 And therefore did the Jews persecute Jesus, and sought to slay him, because he had done these things on the sabbath-day.

JOHN V.

17 But Jesus answered them, My Father worketh hitherto, and I work
18 Therefore the Jews sought the more to kill him, because he not only had
broken the sabbath, but said also, that God was his Father, making himself
19 equal with God.   Then answered Jesus, and said unto them, Verily, verily
I say unto you, The Son can do nothing of himself, but what he seeth the
Father do : for what things soever he doeth, these also doeth the Son like-
20 wise.   For the Father loveth the Son, and sheweth him all things that
himself doeth : and he will shew him greater works than these, that ye may
21 marvel.   For as the Father raiseth up the dead, and quickeneth *them*,
22 even so the Son quickeneth whom he will.   For the Father judgeth no
23 man ; but hath committed all judgment unto the Son : ' that all *men* should
honour the Son, even as they honour the Father.   He that honoureth not
24 the Son, honoureth not the Father which hath sent him.   Verily, verily, I
say unto you, He that heareth my word, and believeth on him that sent me,
hath everlasting life, and shall not come into condemnation ; but is passed
25 from death unto life.   Verily, verily, I say unto you, The hour is coming;
and now is, when the dead shall hear the voice of the Son of God : and
26 they that hear shall live.   For as the Father hath life in himself, so hath
27 he given to the Son to have life in himself; ' and hath given him authority
28 to execute judgment also, because he is the Son of man.   Marvel not at
this : for the hour is coming, in the which all that are in the graves shall hear
29 his voice, ' and shall come forth ; they that have done good, unto the resurrection of life ; and they that have done evil, unto the resurrection of dam-
30 nation.ª   I can of mine own self do nothing : as I hear, I judge : and my
judgment is just ; because I seek not mine own will, but the will of the
Father which hath sent me.
31 32 If I bear witness of myself, my witness is not true.   There is another
that beareth witness of me, and I know that the witness which he witness-
33 eth of me is true.   Ye sent unto John, and he bare witness unto the truth.
34 But I receive not testimony from man : but these things I say, that ye
35 might be saved.   He was a burning and a shining light : and ye were willing for a season to rejoice in his light.
36 But I have greater witness than *that* of John : for the works which the
Father hath given me to finish, the same works that I do, bear witness of
37 me, that the Father hath sent me.   And the Father himself which hath
sent me, hath borne witness of me.   Ye have neither heard his voice at
38 any time, nor seen his shape.   And ye have not his word abiding in you :
39 for whom he hath sent, him ye believe not.   Search the scriptures ; for in
them ye think ye have eternal life : and they are they which testify of me.
40 And ye will not come to me, that ye might have life.
41 42 I receive not honour from men.   But I know you, that ye have not the
43 love of God in you.   I am come in my Father's name, and ye receive me
44 not : if another shall come in his own name, him ye will receive.   How
can ye believe, which receive honour one of another, and seek not the
45 honour that *cometh* from God only ?   Do not think that I will accuse you
to the Father : there is *one* that accuseth you, *even* Moses, in whom ye
46 trust.   For had ye believed Moses, ye would have believed me : for he
47 wrote of me.   But if ye believe not his writings, how shall ye believe my
words ?

ª 39 Comp. Dan. 12, 2.

§ 37. *The Disciples pluck ears of grain on the Sabbath.*—ON THE WAY TO
GALILEE?

MATTH. XII. 1—8.

MARK II. 23—28.

LUKE VI. 1—5.

1 At that time Jesus went on the sabbath-day through the corn, and his disciples were an hungered, and began to pluck the ears of corn, and to eat.[a] 2 But when the Pharisees saw it, they said unto him, Behold, thy disciples do that which is not lawful to do upon 3 the sabbath-day. [*] But he said unto them, Have ye not read what David did, when he was an hungered, and they that were with him;[b] 4 [*] how he entered into the house of God, and did eat the shew-bread, which was not lawful for him to eat, neither for them which were with him, but only for 5 the priests? Or have ye not read in the law [c] how that on the sabbath-days the priests in the temple profane the sabbath, and 6 are blameless? But I say unto you, that in this place is *one* greater 7 than the temple. But if ye had known what *this* meaneth, I will have mercy, and not sacrifice,[d] ye would not have condemned the guiltless. 8 For the Son of man is Lord even of the sabbath-day.

23 And it came to pass, that he went through the corn-fields on the sabbath-day; and his disciples began, as they went, to pluck the ears 24 of corn.[a] And the Pharisees said unto him, Behold, why do they on the sabbath-day that which is not lawful? 25 And he said unto them, Have ye never read what David did, when he had need, and was an hungered, he and they that were 26 with him;[b] [*] how he went into the house of God, in the days of Abiathar the high-priest, and did eat the shew-bread, which is not lawful to eat, but for the priests, and gave also to them which were with him? 27 And he said unto them, The sabbath was made for man, and not man 28 for the sabbath: [*] therefore the Son of man is Lord also of the sabbath.

1 And it came to pass on the second sabbath after the first, that he went through the corn-fields; and his disciples plucked the ears of corn, and did eat, rubbing *them* in *their* 2 hands.[a] And certain of the Pharisees said unto them, Why do ye that which is not lawful to do on the sab-3 bath-days? And Jesus answering them, said, Have ye not read so much as this, what David did, when himself was an hungered, and they which were 4 with him;[b] [*] how he went into the house of God, and did take and eat the shew-bread, and gave also to them that were with him, which it is not lawful to eat but for the priests alone?

5 And he said unto them, that the Son of man is Lord also of the sabbath.

- - - - - -

a 1 etc. Deut. 23, 25.   b 3 etc. 1 Sam. 21, 1—7.   c 5. Num. 28, 9. 10. 18. 19
d 7. Hos. 6, 6

3*

§ 38. *The healing of the withered hand on the Sabbath.*—GALILEE.

MATTH. XII. 9—14.	MARK III. 1—6.	LUKE VI. 6—11.
9 And when he was departed thence, he went into their synagogue. 10 And behold, there was a man which had *his* hand withered. And they asked him, saying, Is it lawful to heal on the sabbath-days? that they might accuse him.	1 And he entered again into the synagogue; and there was a man there which had a 2 withered hand. And they watched him, whether he would heal him on the sabbath-day; that they might accuse him.	6 And it came to pass also on another sabbath, that he entered into the synagogue, and taught: and there was a man whose right hand was withered: 7 and the scribes and Pharisees watched him, whether he would heal on the sabbath-day;

8 that they might find an accusation against him. But he knew their thoughts, and said to the man which had the withered hand, Rise up, and stand forth in the midst.

11 And he said unto them, What man shall there be among you, that shall have one sheep, and if it fall into a pit on the sabbath-day, will he not lay hold on it, and 12 lift *it* out? How much then is a man better than a sheep? Wherefore it is lawful to do well on the sabbath-days.	3 And he saith unto the man which had the withered hand, Stand 4 forth. And he saith unto them, Is it lawful to do good on the sabbath-days, or to do evil? to save life, or to kill? but they held 5 their peace. And when he had looked round about on them with anger, being grieved for the hardness of their hearts, he saith unto	And he arose, and stood forth. 9 Then said Jesus unto them, I will ask you one thing; Is it lawful on the sabbath-days to do good, or to do evil? to save life, or to de-10 stroy *it*? And looking round about upon them all,
13 Then saith he to the man, Stretch forth thine hand. And he stretched *it* forth; and *it* was restored whole, like as the other. 14 Then the Pharisees went out, and held a council against him, how they might destroy him.	the man, Stretch forth thine hand. And he stretched *it* out: and his hand was restored whole as the other. 6 And the Pharisees went forth, and straightway took counsel with the Herodians against him, how they might destroy him.	he said unto the man, Stretch forth thy hand. And he did so: and his hand was restored whole as the other. 11 And they were filled with madness; and communed one with another what they might do to Jesus.

§ 39. *Jesus arrives at the Sea of Tiberias, and is followed by multitudes.*— LAKE OF GALILEE.

MATTH. XII. 15—21.	MARK III. 7—12.
15 But when Jesus knew *it*, he withdrew himself from thence: and great multitudes followed him, and he healed them all.	7 But Jesus withdrew himself with his disciples to the sea: and a great multitude from Galilee fol-8 lowed him, and from Judea, 1 and

MARK III.

from Jerusalem, and from Idumea, and *from* beyond Jordan ; and they about Tyre and Sidon, a great multitude, when they had heard what great
9 things he did, came unto him. And he spake to his disciples, that a small ship should wait on him, because of the multitude, lest they should throng
10 him. For he had healed many ; insomuch that they pressed upon him
11 for to touch him, as many as had plagues. And unclean spirits, when they saw him, fell down before him, and cried saying, Thou art the

MATTH. XII.   Son of God.

16 And *he* charged them that they   12 And he straitly charged them that
17 should not make him known : ' that   they should not make him known.
it might be fulfilled which was
18 spoken by Esaias the prophet, saying,ª Behold my servant, whom I have chosen ; my beloved, in whom my soul is well pleased : I will put my Spirit
19 upon him, and he shall shew judgment to the Gentiles. He shall not strive
20 nor cry ; neither shall any man hear his voice in the streets. A bruised reed shall he not break, and smoking flax shall he not quench, till he send
21 forth judgment unto victory. And in his name shall the Gentiles trust.

§ 40. *Jesus withdraws to the Mountain, and chooses the Twelve ; the multi-tudes follow him.*—NEAR CAPERNAUM.

MARK III. 13—19.	LUKE VI. 12—19.
13 And he goeth up into a mountain, and calleth *unto him* whom he would: and they came unto him. 14 And he ordained twelve, that they should be with him, and that he might send them forth to	12 And it came to pass in those days, that he went out into a mountain to pray, and continued all night 13 in prayer to God. And when it was day, he called unto *him* his disciples: and of them he chose twelve, whom

MATTH. X. 2—4.	preach, ' and to have	also he named Apos-
2 Now the names of the twelve apostles are these ; The first, Simon, who is called Peter, and Andrew his brother ; James *the son* of Zebedee, and John his brother ; Philip, and Bartholomew ; Thomas, and Matthew the publican ; James *the son* of Alpheus, and Lebbeus, whose surname was Thaddeus ; Simon the Canaanite, and Judas Iscariot, who also betrayed him.	15 preach, ' and to have power to heal sicknesses, and to cast out devils. And Simon he 16 surnamed Peter. And 17 James the *son* of Zebedee, and John the brother of James, (and he surnamed them Boanerges, which is, The sons of thunder,) 18 ' and Andrew, and Philip, and Bartholomew, and Matthew, and Thomas, and James the *son* of Alpheus, and Thaddeus, and Simon 19 the Canaanite, ' and Judas Iscariot, which also betrayed him.—	tles ; ' Simon (whom he also named Peter) and Andrew his brother, James and John, Philip and Bartholo-15 mew, Matthew and Thomas, James the *son* of Alpheus, and Simon called Zelotes, 16 ' and Judas *the brother* of James, and Judas Iscariot, which also was the traitor. 17 And he came down with them, and stood in the plain ; and the company of his disciples, and a great mul-

titude of people out of all Judea and Jerusalem, and from the sea-coast of

[18] Tyre and Sidon, which came to hear him, and to be healed of their diseases; [1] and they that were vexed with unclean spirits: and they were
[9] healed. And the whole multitude sought to touch him; for there went
virtue out of him, and healed *them* all.

§ 41. *The Sermon on the Mount.*—NEAR CAPERNAUM.

MATTH. V. 1.—VIII. 1.   LUKE VI. 20—49.

[1]   And seeing the multitudes, he
went up into a mountain: and when
he was set, his disciples came unto
[2] him. And he opened his mouth,   [20]   And he lifted up his eyes on his
[3] and taught them, saying, [1] Blessed   disciples, and said, Blessed *be ye*
are the poor in spirit: for theirs is   poor; for yours is the kingdom of
[4] the kingdom of heaven. Blessed   [21] God. Blessed *are ye* that hunger
are they that mourn: for they shall   now: for ye shall be filled. Blessed
[5] be comforted. Blessed *are* the   *are ye* that weep now: for ye shall
meek: for they shall inherit the   laugh.
[6] earth.[a]   Blessed *are* they which
do hunger and thirst after righteousness: for they shall be filled.
[7] [8] Blessed *are* the merciful: for they shall obtain mercy. Blessed
[9] *are* the pure in heart: for they shall see God. Blessed are the
[10] peace-makers: for they shall be called the children of God. Blessed *are* they which are persecuted for righteousness' sake: for
theirs is the kingdom of heaven.
[11] Blessed are ye when *men* shall re- [22] Blessed are ye when men shall hate
vile you, and persecute *you*, and   you, and when they shall separate
shall say all manner of evil against   you *from their company*, and shall
[12] you falsely, for my sake. Rejoice,   reproach *you*, and cast out your
and be exceeding glad: for great *is*   name as evil, for the Son of man's
your reward in heaven: for so per- [23] sake. Rejoice ye in that day, and
secuted they the prophets which   leap for joy: for behold, your re-
were before you.   ward *is* great in heaven: for in the
like manner did their fathers unto
[24] the prophets. But wo unto you that are rich! for ye have received your
[25] consolation. Wo unto you that are full! for ye shall hunger. Wo unto
[26] you that laugh now! for ye shall mourn and weep.[*] Wo unto you, when
all men shall speak well of you! for so did their fathers to the false prophets.

[13]   Ye are the salt of the earth: but if the salt have lost his savour, wherewith shall it be salted? it is thenceforth good for nothing, but to be cast
[14] out, and to be trodden under foot of men. Ye are the light of the world.
[15] A city that is set on an hill cannot be hid. [1] Neither do men light a candle,
and put it under a bushel, but on a candlestick: and it giveth light unto all
[16] that are in the house. Let your light so shine before men, that they may
see your good works, and glorify your Father which is in heaven.
[17]   Think not that I am come to destroy the law, or the prophets: I am not
[18] come to destroy, but to fulfil. For verily, I say unto you, Till heaven and
earth pass, one jot or one tittle shall in no wise pass from the law, till all be

[a] 5. Comp. Ps. 37, 11. 22. 29. 34.

MATTH. V.

⁹ fulfilled. Whosoever therefore shall break one of these least command-ments, and shall teach men so, he shall be called the least in the kingdom of heaven: but whosoever shall do, and teach *them*, the same shall be called ²⁰ great in the kingdom of heaven. For I say unto you, that except your righteousness shall exceed *the righteousness* of the scribes and Pharisees, ye shall in no case enter into the kingdom of heaven.

²¹ Ye have heard that it was said by them of old time,ᵃ Thou shalt not ²² kill; and whosoever shall kill, shall be in danger of the judgment. But I say unto you, That whosoever is angry with his brother without a cause, shall be in danger of the judgment: and whosoever shall say to his brother, Raca, shall be in danger of the council: but whosoever shall say, *Thou* ²³ fool, shall be in danger of hell-fire. Therefore, if thou bring thy gift to the altar, and there rememberest that thy brother hath aught against thee, ²⁴ ' leave there thy gift before the altar, and go thy way; first be reconciled to ²⁵ thy brother, and then come and offer thy gift. Agree with thine adversary quickly, while thou art in ιe way with him; lest at any time the adversary deliver thee to the judge, and the judge deliver thee to the officer, and ²⁶ thou be cast into prison. Verily, I say unto thee, Thou shalt by no means come out thence, till thou hast paid the uttermost farthing.

²⁷ Ye have heard that it was said by them of old time,ᵇ Thou shalt not ²⁸ commit adultery. But I say unto you, That whosoever looketh on a woman ²⁹ to lust after her, hath committed adultery with her already in his heart. And if thy right eye offend thee, pluck it out, and cast *it* from thee: for it is profit-able for thee that one of thy members should perish, and not *that* thy whole ³⁰ body should be cast into hell. And if thy right hand offend thee, cut it off, and cast *it* from thee: for it is profitable for thee that one of thy mem-bers should perish, and not *that* thy whole body should be cast into hell.

³¹ It hath been said,ᶜ Whosoever shall put away his wife, let him give her ³² a writing of divorcement. But I say unto you, That whosoever shall put away his wife, saving for the cause of fornication, causeth her to commit adultery: and whosoever shall marry her that is divorced, committeth adultery.

³³ Again, ye have heard that it hath been said by them of old time,ᵈ Thou ³⁴ shalt not forswear thyself, but shalt perform unto the Lord thine oaths. But I say unto you, Swear not at all: neither by heaven; for it is God's throne: ³⁵ ' nor by the earth; for it is his footstool: neither by Jerusalem; for it is ³⁶ the city of the great King: ' neither shalt thou swear by thy head, because ³⁷ thou canst not make one hair white or black. But let your communication be, Yea, yea; Nay, nay: for whatsoever *is* more than these cometh of evil.

³⁸ Ye have heard that it hath been said,ᵉ An eye for an eye, and a tooth ³⁹ for a tooth. But I say unto you, That ye resist not evil: but whoso-ever shall smite thee on thy right cheek, turn to him the other also.

⁴⁰ And if any man will sue thee at the law, and take away thy coat, let him ⁴¹ have *thy* cloak also. And whoso-ever shall compel thee to go a mile, ⁴² go with him twain. Give to him that asketh thee, and from him that	LUKE VI. ²⁹ And unto him that smiteth thee on the *one* cheek, offer also the other; and him that taketh away thy cloak, forbid not *to take thy* coat ³⁰ also. Give to every man that ask-eth of thee; and of him that

ᵃ 21. Ex. 20, 13. Lev. 24, 21.   ᵇ 27. Ex. 20, 14.   ᶜ 31. Deut. 24, 1.
ᵈ 33. Ex. 20, 7. Lev. 19, 12. Deut. 23, 21.   ᵉ 38. Ex. 21, 24. Lev. 24, 20.

MATTH. V.	LUKE VI.

would borrow of thee, turn not thou away.

43 Ye have heard that it hath been said,[a] Thou shalt love thy neighbour, and hate thine enemy. **44** But I say unto you, Love your enemies, bless them that curse you, do good to them that hate you, and pray for them which despitefully use **45** you, and persecute you;[1] that ye may be the children of your Father which is in heaven: for he maketh his sun to rise on the evil and on the good, and sendeth rain on the **46** just and on the unjust. For if ye love them which love you, what reward have ye? do not even the **47** publicans the same? And if ye salute your brethren only, what do ye more *than others?* do not even the publicans so?

taketh away thy goods, ask *them* not again.

27 —But I say unto you which hear, Love your enemies, do good to then **28** which hate you,[1] bless them tha curse you, and pray for them which despitefully use you.—

32   For if ye love them which love you, what thank have ye? for sinners also love those **33** that love them. And if ye do good to them which do good to you, what thank have ye? for sinners also dc **34** even the same. And if ye lend *to then* of whom ye hope to receive, what thank have ye? for sinners also lend **35** to sinners, to receive as much again. But love ye your enemies, and do good, and lend, hoping for nothing again; and your reward shall be great, and ye shall be the children of the Highest: for he is kind unto the unthankful and *to* the evil.

46 Be ye therefore perfect, even as your Father which is in heaven is perfect.

36 Be ye therefore merciful, as your Father also is merciful.

VI. **1** Take heed that ye do not your righteousness before men, to be seen of them: otherwise ye have no reward of your Father which is in heaven. **2** Therefore, when thou doest *thine* alms, do not sound a trumpet before thee, as the hypocrites do, in the synagogues, and in the streets, that they may have glory of men. Verily, I say unto you, They have their reward. **3** But when thou doest alms, let not thy left hand know what thy right hand **4** doeth;[1] that thine alms may be in secret: and thy Father which seeth in secret, himself shall reward thee openly.

5 And when thou prayest, thou shalt not be as the hypocrites *are:* for they love to pray standing in the synagogues, and in the corners of the streets, that they may be seen of men. Verily, I say unto you, They have their **6** reward. But thou, when thou prayest, enter into thy closet, and when thou hast shut thy door, pray to thy Father, which is in secret; and thy **7** Father, which seeth in secret, shall reward thee openly. But when ye pray, use not vain repetitions, as the heathen *do:* for they think that they **8** shall be heard for their much speaking. Be not ye therefore like unto them: for your Father knoweth what things ye have need of before ye ask **9** him. After this manner therefore pray ye: Our Father which art in **10** heaven, Hallowed be thy name. [1] Thy kingdom come. Thy will be done **11 12** in earth as *it is* in heaven. Give us this day our daily bread. [1] And for-**13** give us our debts, as we forgive our debtors. And lead us not into tempta-tion, but deliver us from evil. For thine is the kingdom, and the power,

MATTH. VI.

14 and the glory, for ever. Amen. For, if ye forgive men their trespasses,
15 your heavenly Father will also forgive you : ¹ but if ye forgive not men
their trespasses, neither will your Father forgive your trespasses.
16 　Moreover, when ye fast, be not as the hypocrites, of a sad countenance :
for they disfigure their faces, that they may appear unto men to fast. Verily,
17 I say unto you, They have their reward. But thou, when thou fastest,
18 anoint thine head, and wash thy face ; ¹ that thou appear not unto men to
fast, but unto thy Father, which is in secret : and thy Father, which seeth
in secret, shall reward thee openly.
19 　Lay not up for yourselves treasures upon earth, where moth and rust doth
20 corrupt, and where thieves break through and steal : ¹ but lay up for yourselves treasures in heaven, where neither moth nor rust doth corrupt, and
21 where thieves do not break through and steal. For where your treasure is,
22 there will your heart be also. The light of the body is the eye : if there-
23 fore thine eye be single, thy whole body shall be full of light. But if thine
eye be evil, thy whole body shall be full of darkness. If therefore the light
that is in thee be darkness, how great is that darkness !
24 　No man can serve two masters : for either he will hate the one, and love
the other ; or else he will hold to the one, and despise the other. Ye can-
25 not serve God and mammon. Therefore I say unto you, Take no thought
for your life, what ye shall eat, or what ye shall drink ; nor yet for your　·
body, what ye shall put on. Is not the life more than meat, and the body
26 than raiment ? Behold the fowls of the air : for they sow not, neither do
they reap, nor gather into barns ; yet your heavenly Father feedeth them.
27 Are ye not much better than they ? ¹ Which of you by taking thought can
28 add one cubit unto his stature ? And why take ye thought for raiment ?
Consider the lilies of the field how they grow ; they toil not, neither do
29 they spin ; ¹ and yet I say unto you, That even Solomon in all his glory
30 was not arrayed like one of these. Wherefore, if God so clothe the grass
of the field, which to-day is, and to-morrow is cast into the oven, *shall he*
31 not much more *clothe* you, O ye of little faith ? Therefore take no thought,
saying, What shall we eat ? or, What shall we drink ? or, Wherewithal shall
32 we be clothed ? ¹ (for after all these things do the Gentiles seek,) for your
33 heavenly Father knoweth that ye have need of all these things. But seek
ye first the kingdom of God, and his righteousness, and all these things
34 shall be added unto you. Take therefore no thought for the morrow : for
the morrow shall take thought for the things of itself. Sufficient unto the
day *is* the evil thereof.

LUKE VI.

VII. ¹ Judge not, that ye be not
2 judged. For with what judgment
ye judge, ye shall be judged : and
with what measure ye mete, it shall
be measured to you again.

37 　Judge not, and ye shall not be
judged : condemn not, and ye shall
not be condemned : forgive, and ye
38 shall be forgiven : ¹ give, and it shall
be given unto you ; good measure,
pressed down, and shaken together,
and running over, shall men give into your bosom. For with the
same measure that ye mete withal, it shall be measured to you
39 again. And he spake a parable unto them ; Can the blind lead the
40 blind ? shall they not both fall into the ditch ? The disciple is not
above his master : but every one that

3 And why beholdest thou the mote
that is in thy brother's eye, but con-
siderest not the beam that is in thine
4 own eye ? Or how wilt thou say to

41 is perfect, shall be as his master. And
why beholdest thou the mote that
is in thy brother's eye, but per-
ceivest not the beam that is in thine

MATTH. VII.

LUKE VI.

thy brother, Let me pull out the mote out of thine eye; and behold, 5 a beam *is* in thine own eye? Thou hypocrite, first cast out the beam out of thine own eye; and then shalt thou see clearly to cast out the mote out of thy brother's eye. 6 Give not that which is holy unto the dogs, neither cast ye your pearls before swine, lest they trample 7 them under their feet, and turn again

42 own eye? Either how canst thou say to thy brother, Brother, let me pull out the mote that is in thine eye, when thou thyself beholdest not the beam that is in thine own eye? Thou hypocrite, cast out first the beam out of thine own eye, and then shalt thou see clearly to pull out the mote that is in thy brother's eye.—

and rend you. Ask, and it shall be given you; seek, and ye shall find; knock, and 8 it shall be opened unto you: I for every one that asketh, receiveth; and he that seeketh, findeth; and to him that knocketh, 9 it shall be opened. Or what man is there of you, whom if his son 10 ask bread, will he give him a stone? Or if he ask a fish, will he 11 give him a serpent? If ye then being evil know how to give good gifts unto your children, how much more shall your Father which is in heaven give good things to them that ask him? 12 Therefore all things whatsoever ye would that men should do to you, do 31 And as ye would that men should do ye even so to them: for this is the to you, do ye also to them likewise.— law and the prophets.

I Enter ye in at the strait gate; for wide *is* the gate, and broad *is* the way, that leadeth to destruction, and many there be which 14 go in thereat: I because, strait *is* the gate, and narrow *is* the way, which leadeth unto life, and few there be that find it.

15 Beware of false prophets, which come to you in sheep's clothing, but inwardly they are ravening 16 wolves. Ye shall know them by 44 For every tree is known by his their fruits: Do men gather grapes of own fruit: for of thorns men do not 17 thorns, or figs of thistles? Even so gather figs, nor of a bramble-bush every good tree bringeth forth good 43 gather they grapes.—For a good tree fruit; but a corrupt tree bringeth bringeth not forth corrupt fruit; 18 forth evil fruit. A good tree can- neither doth a corrupt tree bring not bring forth evil fruit, neither *can* 45 forth good fruit.—A good man out a corrupt tree bring forth good fruit. of the good treasure of his heart, 19 Every tree that bringeth not forth bringeth forth that which is good; good fruit is hewn down, and cast and an evil man out of the evil trea- 20 into the fire. Wherefore, by their sure of his heart, bringeth forth that fruits ye shall know them. which is evil: for of the abundance 21 Not every one that saith unto me, of the heart his mouth speaketh. Lord, Lord, shall enter into the kingdom of heaven; but he that doeth the will of my Father which 22 is in heaven. Many will say to me in that day, Lord, Lord, have we not prophesied in thy name? and in thy name have cast out devils? and in thy name done many 23 wonderful works? And then will I 46 And why call ye me Lord, Lord, profess unto them, I never knew you: and do not the things which I say? depart from me, ye that work iniquity. 47 Whosoever cometh to me, and hear- 24 Therefore, whosoever heareth eth my sayings, and doeth them, I these sayings of mine, and doeth will shew you to whom he is like. them, I will liken him unto a wise 48 He is like a man which built an

MATTH. VII.	LUKE VI.
man, which built his house upon a ²⁵ rock : ' and the rain descended, and the floods came, and the winds blew, and beat upon that house ; and it fell not : for it was founded upon a ²⁶ rock. And every one that heareth these sayings of mine, and doeth them not, shall be likened unto a foolish man, which built his house upon the ²⁷ sand : ' and the rain descended, and the floods came, and the winds blew, and beat upon that house ; and it fell : and great was the fall of it.	house, and digged deep, and laid the foundation on a rock : and when the flood arose, the stream beat vehemently upon that house, and could not shake it : for it was founded ⁴⁹ upon a rock. But he that heareth and doeth not, is like a man that without a foundation built an house upon the earth, against which the stream did beat vehemently, and immediately it fell, and the ruin of that house was great.

²⁸ And it came to pass when Jesus had ended these sayings, the people were ²⁹ astonished at his doctrine. For he taught them as *one* having authority, and not as the scribes.

VIII. ¹ When he was come down from the mountain, great multitudes followed him.

§ 42. *The healing of the Centurion's servant.*—CAPERNAUM.

MATTH. VIII. 5—13.	LUKE VII. 1—10.
⁵ And when Jesus was entered into Capernaum, there came unto him a ⁶ centurion, beseeching him, ' and saying, Lord, my servant lieth at home sick of the palsy, grievously tormented.	¹ Now when he had ended all his sayings in the audience of the people, he entered into Capernaum. ² And a certain centurion's servant, who was dear unto him, was sick, ³ and ready to die. And when he heard of Jesus, he sent unto him the elders of the Jews, beseeching him that he would come and heal ⁴ his servant. And when they came to Jesus, they besought him in⁵ stantly, saying, That he was worthy for whom he should do this : ' for ⁶ he loveth our nation, and he hath built us a synagogue. Then Jesus went with them. And when he was now not far from the house, the centurion sent friends to him, saying unto him, Lord, trouble not thyself : for I am not worthy that thou shouldest enter ⁷ under my roof ; ' wherefore neither thought I myself worthy to come unto thee ; but say in a word, and ⁸ my servant shall be healed. For I also am a man set under authority, having under me soldiers, and I say unto one, Go, and he goeth ; and to another, Come, and he cometh ; and to my servant, Do this, and he doeth ⁹ *it.* When Jesus heard these things, he marvelled at him, and turned him about and said unto the people that followed him, I say unto you, I have not found so great faith, no, not in Israel.
⁷ And Jesus saith unto him, I will come and heal him. ⁸ The centurion answered and said, Lord, I am not worthy that thou shouldest come under my roof : but speak the word only, and my ser⁹ vant shall be healed. For I am a man under authority, having soldiers under me : and I say to this *man*, Go, and he goeth ; and to another, Come, and he cometh ; and to my servant, ¹⁰ Do this, and he doeth *it.* When Jesus heard *it*, he marvelled, and said to them that followed, Verily, I say unto you, I have not found so ¹¹ great faith, no, not in Israel. And I say unto you, That many shall	

4

MATTH. VIII.

come from the east and west, and shall sit down with Abraham, and
[12] Isaac, and Jacob, in the kingdom of heaven : ' but the children of the
kingdom shall be cast out into outer darkness: there shall be weeping and
[13] gnashing of teeth. And Jesus said
unto the centurion, Go thy way;
and as thou hast believed, so be it
done unto thee. And his servant
was healed in the self-same hour.

LUKE VII.

[20] And they that were sent, returning
to the house, found the servant whole
that had been sick.

§ 43. *The raising of the Widow's son.*—NAIN.

LUKE VII. 11—17.

[11]   And it came to pass the day after, that he went into a city called Nain :
[12] and many of his disciples went with him, and much people. Now when
he came nigh to the gate of the city, behold, there was a dead man carried
out, the only son of his mother, and she was a widow: and much people
[13] of the city was with her. And when the Lord saw her, he had compas-
[14] sion on her, and said unto her, Weep not. And he came and touched the
bier: and they that bare *him* stood still. And he said, Young man, I say
[15] unto thee, Arise. And he that was dead sat up, and began to speak : and
[16] he delivered him to his mother. And there came a fear on all: and they
glorified God, saying, That a great prophet is risen up among us ; and,
[17] That God hath visited his people. And this rumour of him went forth
throughout all Judea, and throughout all the region round about.

§ 44. *John the Baptist in prison sends Disciples to Jesus.*—GALILEE: CAPERNAUM ?

MATTH. XI. 2—19.

[2]   Now when John had heard in the
prison the works of Christ, he sent
[3] two of his disciples, ' and said unto
him, Art thou he that should come,
or do we look for another ?

LUKE VII. 18—35.

[18]   And the disciples of John shewed
[19] him of all these things. And John,
calling *unto him* two of his disciples, sent *them* to Jesus, saying, Art
thou he that should come ? or look
[20] we for another ? When the men
were come unto him, they said, John Baptist hath sent us unto
thee, saying, Art thou he that should come ? or look we for
[21] another ? And in that same hour he cured many of *their* infirmities, and plagues, and of evil spirits ; and unto many *that were*
[22] blind he gave sight. Then Jesus

[4] Jesus answered and said unto them,
Go and shew John again those things
[5] which ye do hear and see : ' the
blind receive their sight, and the
lame walk, the lepers are cleansed,
and the deaf hear, the dead are raised up, and the poor have the gospel
[6] preached to them.ª And blessed is *he*,
whosoever shall not be offended in me.

answering, said unto them, Go your
way, and tell John what things ye
have seen and heard ; how that the
blind see, the lame walk, the lepers
are cleansed, the deaf hear, the
dead are raised, to the poor the gos-
[23] pel is preached.ª And blessed is
he, whosoever shall not be offended
in me.

ª 5 etc. Comp Is. 35, 5 sq.

MATTH. XI.	LUKE VII.

And as they departed, Jesus began to say unto the multitudes concerning John, What went ye out into the wilderness to see? A reed shaken [8] with the wind? But what went ye out for to see? A man clothed in soft raiment? Behold, they that wear soft *clothing* are in kings' houses.

[9] But what went ye out for to see? A prophet? yea, I say unto you, and [10] more than a prophet. For this is *he*, of whom it is written,[a] Behold, I send my messenger before thy face, which shall prepare thy way before [11] thee. Verily, I say unto you, Among them that are born of women, there hath not risen a greater than John the Baptist: notwithstanding, he that is least in the kingdom of [12] heaven, is greater than he. And from the days of John the Baptist, until now, the kingdom of heaven suffereth violence, and the violent [13] take it by force. For all the prophets and the law prophesied until [14] John. And if ye will receive *it*, this is Elias which was for to come.[b] [15] He that hath ears to hear, let him hear.

[16] But whereunto shall I liken this generation? It is like unto children sitting in the markets, and [17] calling unto their fellows, ' and saying, We have piped unto you, and ye have not danced ; we have mourned unto you, and ye have not lamented. [18] For John came neither eating nor drinking, and they say, He hath a devil.

[19] The Son of man came eating and drinking, and they say, Behold, a man gluttonous, and a winebibber, a friend of publicans and sinners. But wisdom is justified of her children.

[24] And when the messengers of John were departed, he began to speak unto the people concerning John, What went ye out into the wilderness for to see? A reed shaken [25] with the wind? But what went ye out for to see? A man clothed in soft raiment? Behold, they which are gorgeously apparelled, and live delicately, are in kings' courts. [26] But what went ye out for to see? A prophet? Yea, I say unto you, and much more than a prophet. [27] This is *he*, of whom it is written,[a] Behold, I send my messenger before thy face, which shall prepare thy [28] way before thee. For I say unto you, Among those that are born of women, there is not a greater prophet than John the Baptist : but he that is least in the kingdom of God, [29] is greater than he. (And all the people that heard *him*, and the publicans, justified God, being baptized [30] with the baptism of John. But the Pharisees and lawyers rejected the counsel of God against themselves, being not baptized of him.)

[31] And the Lord said, Whereunto then shall I liken the men of this generation? and to what are they [32] like? They are like unto children sitting in the market-place, and calling one to another, and saying, We have piped unto you, and ye have [33] not danced ; we have mourned to you, and ye have not wept. For John the Baptist came neither eating bread, nor drinking wine, and [34] ye say, He hath a devil. The Son of man is come eating and drinking ; and ye say, Behold a gluttonous man, and a wine-bibber, a friend of [35] publicans and sinners ! But wisdom is justified of all her children.

---

a **10 etc** Mal. 3, 1.   b **14.** Mal. 4, 5

§ 45. *Reflections of Jesus on appealing to his mighty Works.*—CAPERNAUM?

MATTH. XI. 20—30.

20 Then began he to upbraid the cities wherein most of his mighty works
21 were done, because they repented not. Wo unto thee, Chorazin! wo
unto thee, Bethsaida! for if the mighty works which were done in you
had been done in Tyre and Sidon, they would have repented long ago in
22 sackcloth and ashes. But I say unto you, It shall be more tolerable for
23 Tyre and Sidon at the day of judgment, than for you. And thou, Capernaum, which art exalted unto heaven, shalt be brought down to hell: for
if the mighty works which have been done in thee, had been done in Sod-
24 om, it would have remained until this day. But I say unto you, that it
shall be more tolerable for the land of Sodom, in the day of judgment, than
for thee.
25 At that time Jesus answered and said, I thank thee, O Father, Lord of
heaven and earth, because thou hast hid these things from the wise and
26 prudent, and hast revealed them unto babes. Even so, Father, for so it
seemed good in thy sight. All things are delivered unto me of my Father;
and no man knoweth the Son, but the Father; neither knoweth any man
the Father, save the Son, and *he* to whomsoever the Son will reveal *him*.
28 Come unto me, all ye that labour, and are heavy laden, and I will give you
29 rest. Take my yoke upon you, and learn of me: for I am meek and lowly
30 in heart; and ye shall find rest unto your souls. For my yoke *is* easy, and
my burden is light.

§ 46. *While sitting at meat with a Pharisee, Jesus is anointed by a woman
who had been a sinner.*—CAPERNAUM?

LUKE VII. 36—50.

36 And one of the Pharisees desired him that he would eat with him. And
37 he went into the Pharisee's house, and sat down to meat. And behold, a
woman in the city, which was a sinner, when she knew that *Jesus* sat at
38 meat in the Pharisee's house, brought an alabaster-box of ointment, and
stood at his feet behind *him* weeping, and began to wash his feet with tears,
and did wipe *them* with the hairs of her head, and kissed his feet, and
anointed *them* with the ointment.
39 Now, when the Pharisee which had bidden him, saw *it*, he spake within
himself, saying, This man, if he were a prophet, would have known who,
and what manner of woman *this is* that toucheth him: for she is a sinner.
40 And Jesus answering, said unto him, Simon, I have somewhat to say unto
41 thee. And he saith, Master, say on. There was a certain creditor,
which had two debtors: the one owed five hundred pence, and the other
42 fifty. And when they had nothing to pay, he frankly forgave them both.
43 Tell me therefore, which of them will love him most? Simon answered
and said, I suppose that *he*, to whom he forgave most. And he said unto
44 him, Thou hast rightly judged. And he turned to the woman, and said
unto Simon, Seest thou this woman? I entered into thine house, thou
gavest me no water for my feet: but she hath washed my feet with tears,
45 and wiped *them* with the hairs of her head. Thou gavest me no kiss: but
this woman, since the time I came in, hath not ceased to kiss my feet.
46 Mine head with oil thou didst not anoint: but this woman hath anointed
47 my feet with ointment. Wherefore, I say unto thee, Her sins, which are

LUKE VII.

many, are forgiven; for she loved much: but to whom little is forgiven,
18 *the same* loveth little. And he said unto her, Thy sins are forgiven.
19 And they that sat at meat with him, began to say within themselves,
50 Who is this that forgiveth sins also? And he said to the woman, Thy
faith hath saved thee; go in peace.

§ 47. *Jesus, with the Twelve, makes a second circuit in Galilee.*

LUKE VIII. 1—3.

1 And it came to pass afterward, that he went throughout every city and
village, preaching and shewing the glad tidings of the kingdom of God:
2 and the twelve *were* with him, ' and certain women, which had been
healed of evil spirits and infirmities, Mary called Magdalene, out of whom
3 went seven devils, ' and Joanna the wife of Chuza, Herod's steward, and
Susanna, and many others, which ministered unto him of their substance.

§ 48. *The healing of a Demoniac.   The Scribes and Pharisees blaspheme.—*
GALILEE.

MARK III. 19—30.

19 20 —And they went into an house. And the multitude cometh together
21 again, so that they could not so much as eat bread. And when his
friends heard *of it*, they went out to lay hold on him: for they said,
He is beside himself.

MATTH. XII. 22—37.		LUKE XI. 14, 15, 17—23.
22 Then was brought unto him one possessed with a devil, blind and dumb; and he healed him, insomuch that the blind and dumb both spake		
		14 And he was casting out a devil, and it was dumb. And it came to pass when the devil was gone out, the
23 and saw. And all the people were amazed, and said, Is not this the son of David?	MARK III.	dumb spake; and the
24 But when the Phari-	22 And the scribes which	15 people wondered. But
sees heard *it*, they said, This *fellow* doth not cast out devils, but by Beelzebub the prince of the devils.	came down from Jerusalem, said, He hath Beelzebub, and by the prince of the devils cast-	some of them said, He casteth out devils through Beelzebub, the chief of the devils.—
25 And Jesus knew their thoughts, and said unto them, Every kingdom divided against itself, is brought to desolation; and every city or house divided against itself, shall not stand.	23 eth he out devils. And he called them *unto him*, and said unto them in parables, How can Satan cast out Sa-	17 But he, knowing their thoughts, said unto them, Every kingdom divided against itself, is brought to desolation; and a house *divided* against a house,
26 And if Satan cast out Satan, he is divided against himself; how shall ther his kingdom	24 tan? And if a kingdom be divided against itself, that kingdom 25 cannot stand. And if an house be divided against itself,that house 26 cannot stand. And if Satan arise up against	18 falleth. If Satan also be divided against himself, how shall his kingdom stand? because ye say that I cast out devils through Beel-

4*

MATTH. XII.	MARK III.	LUKE XI.

37 stand? And if I by Beelzebub cast out devils, by whom do your children cast *them* out? therefore they shall be your judges. **24** But if I cast out devils by the Spirit of God, then the kingdom of God is come unto you. Or else, how can one enter into a strong man's house, and spoil his goods, except he first bind the strong man? and then he will spoil his house.

himself, and be divided, he cannot stand, but hath an end.

therefore they shall be your judges. **20** But if I with the finger of God cast out devils, no doubt the kingdom of God is come upon you.

MARK III.

27 No man can enter into a strong man's house, and spoil his goods, except he will first bind the strong man; and then he will spoil his house.

19 zebub. And if I by Beelzebub cast out devils, by whom do your sons cast *them* out? therefore shall they be your judges.

21 When a strong man armed keepeth his palace, his goods are in **22** peace: but when a stronger than he shall come upon him, and overcome him, he taketh from him all his armour wherein he trusted, and divideth his spoils.

30 He that is not with me, is against me; and he that gathereth not with me, scattereth abroad.

23 He that is not with me is against me: and he that gathereth not with me scattereth.

MARK III.

31 Wherefore I say unto you, All manner of sin and blasphemy shall be forgiven unto men: but the blasphemy *against* the *Holy* Ghost shall **32** not be forgiven unto men. And whosoever speaketh a word against the Son of man, it shall be forgiven him: but whosoever speaketh against the Holy Ghost, it shall not be forgiven him, neither in this world, neither in the *world* to come.

28 Verily I say unto you, All sins shall be forgiven unto the sons of men, and blasphemies wherewith soever they **29** shall blaspheme: but he that shall blaspheme against the Holy Ghost hath never forgiveness, but is in **30** danger of eternal damnation. Because they said, He hath an unclean spirit.

33 Either make the tree good, and his fruit good; or else make the tree **34** corrupt, and his fruit corrupt: for the tree is known by *his* fruit. O generation of vipers, how can ye, being evil, speak good things? for out of **35** the abundance of the heart, the mouth speaketh. A good man, out of the good treasure of the heart, bringeth forth good things: and an evil man, **36** out of the evil treasure, bringeth forth evil things. But I say unto you, That every idle word that men shall speak, they shall give account thereof **37** in the day of judgment. For by thy words thou shalt be justified, and by thy words thou shalt be condemned.

§ 49. *The Scribes and Pharisees seek a sign. Our Lord's reflections.*—
GALILEE.

MATTH. XII. 38—45.	LUKE XI. 16, 24—36.

38 Then certain of the scribes and of the Pharisees answered, saying, Master, we would see a sign from **39** thee. But he answered and said to them, An evil and adulterous generation seeketh after a sign, and

16 And others tempting *him*, sought of him a sign from heaven.—

29 And when the people were gathered thick together, he began to say, This is an evil generation: they

| MATTH. XII. | LUKE XI. . |

there shall no sign be given to it, but the sign of the prophet Jonas. **40** For as Jonas was three days and three nights in the whale's belly;[a] so shall the Son of man be three days and three nights in the heart **41** of the earth. The men of Nineveh shall rise in judgment with this generation, and shall condemn it: because they repented at the preaching of Jonas;[b] and behold, a great- **42** er than Jonas *is* here. The queen of the south shall rise up in the judgment with this generation, and shall condemn it: for she came from the uttermost parts of the earth to hear the wisdom of Solomon;[c] and behold, a greater than Solomon is here.

seek a sign; and there shall no sign **50** be given it, but the sign of Jonas the prophet. For as Jonas was a sign unto the Ninevites,[a] so shall also the Son of man be to this gene- ration.— **32** The men of Nineveh shall rise up in the judgment with this generation, and shall condemn it: for they repented at the preaching of Jo- nas;[b] and behold, a greater than **31** Jonas *is* here.—The queen of the south shall rise up in the judgment with the men of this generation, and condemn them: for she came from the uttermost parts of the earth to hear the wisdom of Solo- mon;[c] and behold, a greater than Solomon *is* here.—

33 No man when he hath lighted a candle, putteth *it* in a secret place, neither under a bushel, but on **34** a candlestick, that they which come in may see the light. The light of the body is the eye: therefore when thine eye is single, thy whole body also is full of light; but when *thine eye* is evil, **35** thy body also *is* full of darkness. Take heed therefore, that **36** the light which is in thee be not darkness. If thy whole body therefore *be* full of light, having no part dark, the whole shall be full of light; as when the bright shining of a candle doth give thee light.—

43 When the unclean spirit is gone out of a man, he walketh through dry places, seeking rest, and findeth **44** none. Then he saith, I will return into mine house from whence I came out; and when he is come, he find- eth *it* empty, swept, and garnished. **45** Then goeth he, and taketh with himself seven other spirits more wicked than himself, and they enter in and dwell there: and the last *state* of that man is worse than the first. Even so shall it be also unto this wicked generation.

24 When the unclean spirit is gone out of a man, he walketh through dry places, seeking rest: and finding none, he saith, I will return unto my house whence I came out. **25** And when he cometh, he findeth *it* **26** swept and garnished. Then goeth he, and taketh *to him* seven other spirits more wicked than himself; and they enter in, and dwell there: and the last *state* of that man is worse than the first. **27** And it came to pass, as he spake these things, a certain woman of the company lifted up her voice,

and said unto him, Blessed *is* the womb that bare thee, and the paps which **28** thou hast sucked. But he said, Yea, rather blessed *are* they that hear the word of God, and keep it.

---

[a] **40** etc. Jon. 1, 17.   [b] **41** etc. Jon. 3, 4. 5.   [c] **42** etc. 1 K. 10, 1 sq.

§ 50. *The true Disciples of Christ his nearest relatives.*—GALILEE.

MATTH. XII. 46—50.	MARK III. 31—35.	LUKE VIII. 19—21.
46 While he yet talked to the people, behold, *his* mother and his brethren stood without, desiring to speak 47 with him. Then one said unto him, Behold, thy mother and thy brethren stand without, desiring to speak 48 with thee. But he answered and said unto him that told him, Who is my mother? and who are my brethren? 49 And he stretched forth his hand toward his disciples, and said, Behold my mother and 50 my brethren! For whosoever shall do the will of my Father which is in heaven, the same is my brother, and sister, and mother.	31 There came then his brethren and his mother, and standing without, sent unto him, 32 calling him. And the multitude sat about him; and they said unto him, Behold, thy mother and thy brethren without seek for 33 thee. And he answered them, saying, Who is my mother, or my 34 brethren? And he looked round about on them which sat about him, and said, Behold my mother and my 35 brethren! For whosoever shall do the will of God, the same is my brother, and my sister, and mother.	19 Then came to him *his* mother and his brethren, and could not come at him for the press. 20 And it was told him *by certain*, which said, Thy mother and thy brethren stand without, desiring to 21 see thee. And he answered and said unto them, My mother and my brethren are these which hear the word of God, and do it.

§ 51. *At a Pharisee's table, Jesus denounces woes against the Pharisees and others.*—GALILEE.

LUKE XI. 37—54.

37 And as he spake, a certain Pharisee besought him to dine with him: and 38 he went in and sat down to meat. And when the Pharisee saw *it*, he mar- 39 velled that he had not first washed before dinner. And the Lord said unto him, Now do ye Pharisees make clean the outside of the cup and the platter; 40 but your inward part is full of ravening and wickedness. Ye fools, did not he that made that which is without, make that which is within also? 41 But rather give alms of such things as ye have; and behold, all things are 42 clean unto you. But wo unto you, Pharisees! for ye tithe mint, and rue, and all manner of herbs, and pass over judgment and the love of God: 43 these ought ye to have done, and not to leave the other undone. Wo unto you, Pharisees! for ye love the uppermost seats in the synagogues, and 44 greetings in the markets. Wo unto you, scribes and Pharisees, hypocrites! for ye are as graves which appear not, and the men that walk over *them* are not aware *of them*. 45 Then answered one of the lawyers, and said unto him, Master, thus say- 46 ing, thou reproachest us also. And he said, Wo unto you also, *ye* lawyers! for ye lade men with burdens grievous to be borne, and ye yourselves touch 47 not the burdens with one of your fingers. Wo unto you! for ye build the 48 sepulchres of the prophets, and your fathers killed them. Truly ye bear

LUKE XI.

witness, that ye allow the deeds of your fathers: for they indeed killed
⁹ them, and ye build their sepulchres.   Therefore also said the wisdom of
God, I will send them prophets and apostles, and *some* of them they shall
⁵⁰ slay and persecute : ¹ that the blood of all the prophets, which was shed from
⁵¹ the foundation of the world, may be required of this generation ; ¹ from the
blood of Abel unto the blood of Zacharias, which perished between the
altar and the temple : ª verily I say unto you, It shall be required of this
⁵² generation.   Wo unto you, lawyers ! for ye have taken away the key of
knowledge : ye entered not in yourselves, and them that were entering in
⁵³ ye hindered.   And as he said these things unto them, the scribes and the
Pharisees began to urge *him* vehemently, and to provoke him to speak of
⁵⁴ many things ; ¹ laying wait for him, and seeking to catch something out of
his mouth, that they might accuse him.

§ 52. *Jesus discourses to his Disciples and the multitude.—*GALILEE.

LUKE XII. 1—59.

¹   In the mean time, when there were gathered together an innumerable
multitude of people, insomuch that they trode one upon another, he began
to say unto his disciples first of all, Beware ye of the leaven of the Pharisees,
² which is hypocrisy.   For there is nothing covered, that shall not be re-
³ vealed ; neither hi ¹, that shall not be known.   Therefore, whatsoever ye
have spoken in darkness, shall be heard in the light ; and that which ye
have spoken in the ear in closets, shall be proclaimed upon the house-tops.
⁴ And I say unto you, my friends, Be not afraid of them that kill the body,
⁵ and after that, have no more that they can do.   But I will forewarn you
whom ye shall fear : Fear him, which after he hath killed, hath power to
⁶ cast into hell ; yea, I say unto you, Fear him.   Are not five sparrows sold
⁷ for two farthings, and not one of them is forgotten before God ?   But even
the very hairs of your head are all numbered.   Fear not therefore : ye
⁸ are of more value than many sparrows.   Also I say unto you, Whosoever
shall confess me before men, him shall the Son of man also confess before
⁹ the angels of God.   But he that denieth me before men, shall be denied
¹⁰ before the angels of God.   And whosoever shall speak a word against the
Son of man, it shall be forgiven him : but unto him that blasphemeth
¹¹ against the Holy Ghost, it shall not be forgiven.   And when they bring
you unto the synagogues, and *unto* magistrates, and powers, take ye
¹² no thought how or what thing ye shall answer, or what ye shall say : ¹ for
the Holy Ghost shall teach you in the same hour what ye ought to say.
¹³   And one of the company said unto him, Master, speak to my brother,
¹⁴ that he divide the inheritance with me.   And he said unto him, Man, who
¹⁵ made me a judge, or a divider over you ?   And he said unto them, Take
heed, and beware of covetousness : for a man's life consisteth not in the
¹⁶ abundance of the things which he possesseth.   And he spake a parable
unto them, saying, The ground of a certain rich man brought forth plenti-
¹⁷ fully : ¹ and he thought within himself, saying, What shall I do, because I
¹⁸ have no room where to bestow my fruits ?   And he said, This will I do : I
will pull down my barns, and build greater ; and there will I bestow all my
⁹ fruits and my goods.   And I will say to my soul, Soul, thou hast much
goods laid up for many years ; take thine ease, eat, drink, *and* be merry.

ª 51 Gen. 4, 8. 2 Chr. 24, 20 sq.

LUKE XII.

²⁰ But God said unto him, *Thou* fool, this night thy soul shall be required of ²¹ thee: then whose shall those things be which thou hast provided? So *is* he that layeth up treasure for himself, and is not rich toward God.

²² And he said unto his disciples, Therefore I say unto you, Take no thought for your life, what ye shall eat; neither for the body, what ye shall ²³ put on. The life is more than meat, and the body *is more* than raiment. ²⁴ Consider the ravens: for they neither sow nor reap: which neither have store-house, nor barn; and God feedeth them. How much more are ye ²⁵ better than the fowls? And which of you with taking thought can add to ²⁶ his stature one cubit? If ye then be not able to do that thing which is least, ²⁷ why take ye thought for the rest? Consider the lilies how they grow: they toil not, they spin not: and yet I say unto you, that Solomon in all ²⁸ his glory was not arrayed like one of these. If then God so clothe the grass, which is to-day in the field, and to-morrow is cast into the oven; how ²⁹ much more *will he clothe* you, O ye of little faith? And seek not ye what ³⁰ ye shall eat, or what ye shall drink, neither be ye of doubtful mind. For all these things do the nations of the world seek after: and your Father ³¹ knoweth that ye have need of these things. But rather seek ye the kingdom of God, and all these things shall be added unto you.

³² Fear not, little flock; for it is your Father's good pleasure to give you ³³ the kingdom. Sell that ye have, and give alms: provide yourselves bags which wax not old, a treasure in the heavens that faileth not, where no ³⁴ thief approacheth, neither moth corrupteth. For where your treasure is, ³⁵ there will your heart be also. Let your loins be girded about, and *your* ³⁶ lights burning; ' and ye yourselves like unto men that wait for their lord, when he will return from the wedding; that,.when he cometh and knock- ³⁷ eth, they may open unto him immediately. Blessed *are* those servants, whom the lord when he cometh shall find watching: verily, I say unto you, that he shall gird himself, and make them to sit down to meat, and ³⁸ will come forth and serve them. And if he shall come in the second watch, or come in the third watch, and find *them* so, blessed are those servants. ³⁹ And this know, that if the good man of the house had known what hour the thief would come, he would have watched, and not have suffered his ⁴⁰ house to be broken through. Be ye therefore ready also: for the Son of man cometh at an hour when ye think not.

⁴¹ Then Peter said unto him, Lord, speakest thou this parable unto us, or ⁴² even to all? And the Lord said, Who then is that faithful and wise stew- ard, whom *his* lord shall make ruler over his household, to give *them their* ⁴³ portion of meat in due season? Blessed *is* that servant, whom his lord ⁴⁴ when he cometh shall find so doing. Of a truth I say unto you, that he ⁴⁵ will make him ruler over all that he hath. But and if that servant say in his heart, My lord delayeth his coming; and shall begin to beat the men- ⁴⁶ servants, and maidens, and to eat and drink, and to be drunken; ' the lord of that servant will come in a day when he looketh not for *him*, and at an hour when he is not aware, and will cut him in sunder, and will appoint ⁴⁷ him his portion with the unbelievers. And that servant which knew his lord's will, and prepared-not *himself*, neither did according to his will, ⁴⁸ shall be beaten with many *stripes*. But he that knew not, and did commit things worthy of stripes, shall be beaten with few *stripes*. For unto whom-soever much is given, of him shall be much required; and to whom men have committed much, of him they will ask the more.

⁴⁹ I am come to send fire on the earth, and what will I, if it be already ⁵⁰ kindled? But I have a baptism to be baptized with; and how am I strait-

LUKE XII.

⁵¹ ened till it be accomplished! Suppose ye that I am come to give peace on
⁵² earth? I tell you, Nay; but rather division: ¹ for from henceforth there
shall be five in one house divided, three against two, and two against three.
⁵³ The father shall be divided against the son, and the son against the father;
the mother against the daughter, and the daughter against the mother; the
mother-in-law against her daughter-in-law, and the daughter-in-law against
her mother-in-law.
⁵⁴ And he said also to the people, When ye see a cloud rise out of the west,
⁵⁵ straightway ye say, There cometh a shower; and so it is. And when ye
see the south wind blow, ye say, There will be heat; and it cometh to
⁵⁶ pass. Ye hypocrites, ye can discern the face of the sky, and of the earth;
⁵⁷ but how is it, that ye do not discern this time? Yea, and why even of
⁵⁸ yourselves judge ye not what is right? When thou goest with thine adversary to the magistrate, as thou art in the way, give diligence that thou
mayest be delivered from him; lest he hale thee to the judge, and the
⁵⁹ judge deliver thee to the officer, and the officer cast thee into prison. I
tell thee, thou shalt not depart thence, till thou hast paid the very last
mite.

§ 53. *The slaughter of certain Galileans. Parable of the barren Fig-tree.—*
GALILEE.

LUKE XIII. 1—9.

¹ There were present at that season some that told him of the Galileans,
² whose blood Pilate had mingled with their sacrifices. And Jesus answering, said unto them, Suppose ye that these Galileans were sinners above
³ all the Galileans, because they suffered such things? I tell you, Nay; but
⁴ except ye repent, ye shall all likewise perish. Or those eighteen, upon
whom the tower in Siloam fell, and slew them, think ye that they were
⁵ sinners above all men that dwelt in Jerusalem? I tell you, Nay; but except ye repent, ye shall all likewise perish.
⁶ He spake also this parable: A certain *man* had a fig-tree planted in his
⁷ vineyard; and he came and sought fruit thereon, and found none. Then said
he unto the dresser of his vineyard, Behold, these three years I come seeking fruit on this fig-tree, and find none: cut it down; why cumbereth it
⁸ the ground? And he answering, said unto him, Lord, let it alone this
⁹ year also, till I shall dig about it, and dung *it:* ¹ and if it bear fruit, *well:*
and if not, *then* after that thou shalt cut it down.

§ 54. *Parable of the Sower.*—LAKE OF GALILEE: NEAR CAPERNAUM?

MATTH. XIII. 1—23.	MARK IV. 1—25.	
¹ The same day went Jesus out of the house, and sat by the seaside. ² And great multitudes were gathered toge- ther unto him, so that he went into a ship, and sat; and the whole multitude stood on the shore. ³ And he spake many	¹ And he began again to teach by the seaside: and there was gathered unto him a great multitude, so that he entered into a ship, and sat in the sea; and the whole multitude was by the sea, on the land. ² And he taught them many things by para-	LUKE VIII. 4—18. ⁴ And when much peo- ple were gathered toge- ther, and were come to

MATTH. XIII.	MARK IV.	LUKE VIII.
things unto them in parables, saying, Behold, a sower went forth to sow. ⁴ And when he sowed, some *seeds* fell by the way-side, and the fowls came and devoured ⁵ them up. Some fell upon stony places, where they had not much earth; and forth-with they sprang up, because they had no ⁶ deepness of earth: ¹ and when the sun was up, they were scorched; and because they had no root, they withered ⁷ away. And some fell among thorns; and the thorns sprang up, and choked them. ⁸ But other fell into good ground, and brought forth fruit, some an hundred-fold, some sixty-fold, some thirty-fold.	bles, and said unto them in his doctrine, ³ ¹ Hearken; Behold, there went out a sower ⁴ to sow. And it came to pass as he sowed, some fell by the way-side, and the fowls of the air came and de-⁵ voured it up. And some fell on stony ground, where it had not much earth; and immediately it sprang up, because it had no ⁶ depth of earth: ¹ but when the sun was up, it was scorched; and because it had no root, ⁷ it withered away. And some fell among thorns, and the thorns grew up, and choked it, and it yielded no fruit. ⁸ And other fell on good ground, and did yield fruit that sprang up, and increased, and brought forth, some thirty, and some sixty, and some an hundred.	him out of every city, he spake by a parable: ⁵ A sower went out to sow his seed: and as he sowed, some fell by the way-side; and it was trodden down, and the fowls of the air de-voured it. ⁶ And some fell upon a rock; and as soon as it was sprung up, it withered away, because it lacked mois-ture. ⁷ And some fell among thorns, and the thorns sprang up with it, and choked it. ⁸ And other fell on good ground, and sprang up, and bare fruit an hun-dred-fold.
⁹ Who hath ears to hear, let him hear. ¹⁰ And the disciples came, and said unto him, Why speakest thou unto them in para-¹ bles? He answered and said unto them, Because it is given unto you to know the mysteries of the kingdom of heaven, but to them it is not ⁸ given. For whosoever hath, to him shall be given, and he shall have more abundance:	⁹ And he said unto them, He that hath ears to hear, let him hear. ¹⁰ And when he was alone, they that were about him, with the twelve, asked of him ¹¹ the parable. And he said unto them, Unto you it is given to know the mystery of the kingdom of God: but unto them that are without, all *these* things are done in parables: but whosoever hath	And when he had said these things, he cried, He that hath ears to hear, let him hear. ⁹ And his disciples asked him, saying, What might this para-ble be? ¹⁰ And he said, Unto you it is given to know the mysteries of the kingdom of God: but to others in para-bles; not, from Therefore
⁸ him shall be taken away even that he hath. ¹² ¹ that seeing they may speak I to them in para-bles: because they see-ing, see not; and hear-	¹² ¹ that seeing they may see, and not perceive;	that seeing they might not see, and hear-

MATTH. XIII.	MARK IV.	LUKE VIII.

ing, they hear not; neither do they under- **14** stand. And in them is fulfilled the prophecy of Esaias, which saith,[a] By hearing ye shall hear, and shall not understand; and seeing ye shall see, **15** and shall not perceive: ' for this people's heart is waxed gross, and *their* ears are dull of hearing, and their eyes they have closed; lest at any time they should see with *their* eyes, and hear with *their* ears, and should understand with **16** *their* heart, and should be converted, and I should heal them. But blessed *are* your eyes, for they see: and your ears, for they hear. **17** For verily I say unto you, That many prophets and righteous *men* have desired to see *those things* which ye see, and have not seen *them;* and to hear *those things* which ye hear, and have not heard *them.* **18** Hear ye therefore the parable of the sower. **19** When any one heareth the word of the king- dom, and understand- eth *it* not, then cometh the wicked *one,* and catcheth away that which was sown in his heart. This is he which received seed by **20** the way-side. But he into received the seed that stony places, the same is he that heareth the word, and anon with joy receiveth it; **21** ' yet hath he not root in himself, but dureth for a while: for when tri- bulation or persecution ariseth because of the word, by and by he is offended.

[22] He also that received seed among the thorns is he that heareth the word; and the care of this world, and the deceitfulness

and hearing they may hear, and not under- stand;[a] lest at any time they should be converted, and *their* sins should be forgiven them.

MARK IV.

13 And he said unto them, Know ye not this para- ble? and how then will ye know all para- bles? **14** The sower soweth **15** the word. And these are they by the way- side, where the word is sown; but when they have heard, Satan com- eth immediately, and taketh away the word that was sown in their hearts. **16** And these are they likewise which are sown on stony ground; who, when they have heard the word, immediately re- ceive it with gladness; **17** ' and have no root in themselves, and so en- dure but for a time: afterward, when afflic- tion or persecution ari- seth for the word's sake, immediately they **18** are offended. And these are they which are sown among thorns; such as hear the word, **19** ' and the cares of this world, and the deceit-

ing they might not understand.[a]

LUKE VIII.

11 Now the parable is this: The seed is the **12** word of God. Those by the way-side, are they that hear; then cometh the devil, and taketh away the word out of their hearts, lest they should believe and be saved. **13** They on the rock *are they,* which, when they hear, receive the word with joy; and these have no root, which for a while believe, and in time of temptation fall away.

14 And that which fell among thorns, are they, which, when they have heard, go forth, and are choked with cares, and riches, and plea-

---

MATTH. XIII.	MARK IV.	LUKE VIII.
of riches choke the word, and he becometh unfruitful.	fulness of riches, and the lusts of other things entering in, choke the word, and it becometh	sures of *this* life, and bring no fruit to perfection.
23 But he that received seed into the good ground is he that heareth the word, and understandeth *it;* which also beareth fruit, and bringeth forth, some an hundred-fold, some sixty, some thirty.	**20** unfruitful. And these are they which are sown on good ground; such as hear the word, and receive *it*, and bring forth fruit, some thirty-fold, some sixty, and some an hundred.	**15** But that on the good ground are they, which in an honest and good heart, having heard the word, keep *it*, and bring forth fruit with patience.

MARK IV.	LUKE VIII.
21 And he said unto them, Is a candle brought to be put under a bushel, or under a bed? and not to be set on a **22** candlestick? For there is nothing hid, which shall not be manifested; neither was any thing kept secret, **23** but that it should come abroad. If any man have ears to hear, let him **24** hear. And he said unto them, Take heed what ye hear: with what measure ye mete, it shall be measured to you: and unto you that hear, shall **25** more be given. For he that hath, to him shall be given: and he that hath not, from him shall be taken even that which he hath.	**16** No man, when he hath lighted a candle, covereth it with a vessel, or putteth *it* under a bed; but setteth *it* on a candlestick, that they which **17** enter in may see the light. For nothing is secret, that shall not be made manifest; neither *any thing* hid, that shall not be known, and **18** come abroad. Take heed therefore how ye hear: for whosoever hath, to him shall be given; and whosoever hath not, from him shall be taken even that which he seemeth to have.

§ 55. *Parable of the Tares. Other Parables.*—NEAR CAPERNAUM?

MATTH. XIII. 24—53.

24 Another parable put he forth unto them, saying, The kingdom of heaven **25** is likened unto a man which sowed good seed in his field: ' but while men slept, his enemy came and sowed tares among the wheat, and went his **26** way. But when the blade was sprung up, and brought forth fruit, then ap- **27** peared the tares also. So the servants of the householder came and said unto him, Sir, didst thou not sow good seed in thy field? from whence then **28** hath it tares? ' He said unto them, An enemy hath done this. The ser- **29** vants said unto him, Wilt thou then that we go and gather them up? But he said, Nay; lest while ye gather up the tares, ye root up also the wheat **30** with them. Let both grow together until the harvest: and in the time of harvest I will say to the reapers, Gather ye together first the tares, and bind them in bundles to burn them: but gather the wheat into my barn.

MARK IV. 26—34.

26 And he said, So is the kingdom of God, as if a man should cast seed **27** into the ground; ' and should sleep, and rise night and day, and the seed **28** should spring and grow up, he knoweth not how. For the earth bringeth

MARK IV.

forth fruit of herself; first the blade, then the ear, after that the full corn in
²⁰ the ear. But when the fruit is brought forth, immediately he putteth in the

MATTH. XIII.

²¹ Another parable put he forth unto
them, saying, The kingdom of
heaven is like to a grain of mustard-
seed, which a man took, and sowed
²² in his field: ' which indeed is the
least of all seeds: but when it is
grown, it is the greatest among
herbs, and becometh a tree, so that
the birds of the air come and lodge
in the branches thereof.

²³ Another parable spake he unto
them: The kingdom of heaven is
like unto leaven, which a woman
took, and hid in three measures of
meal, till the whole was leavened.

²⁴ All these things spake Jesus unto
the multitude in parables; and without a parable spake he not unto
²⁵ them: ' that it might be fulfilled
which was spoken by the prophet,
saying,ᵃ I will open my mouth in
parables; I will utter things which
have been kept secret from the
foundation of the world.

sickle, because the harvest is come.
³⁰ And he said, Whereunto shall we
liken the kingdom of God? or with
what comparison shall we compare
³¹ it? It is like a grain of mustard-
seed, which, when it is sown in the
earth, is less than all the seeds that
³² be in the earth: ' but when it is
sown, it groweth up, and becometh
greater than all herbs, and shooteth
out great branches; so that the
fowls of the air may lodge under the
shadow of it.

³³ And with many such parables
spake he the word unto them, as
³⁴ they were able to hear it. But
without a parable spake he not unto
them: and when they were alone,
he expounded all things to his
disciples.

²⁶ Then Jesus sent the multitude away, and went into the house: and his
disciples came unto him, saying, Declare unto us the parable of the tares
²⁷ of the field. He answered and said unto them, He that soweth the good
²⁸ seed is the Son of man; ' the field is the world; the good seed are the children of the kingdom; but the tares are the children of the wicked one;
²⁹ ' the enemy that sowed them is the devil; the harvest is the end of the
⁴⁰ world; and the reapers are the angels. As therefore the tares are gathered
⁴¹ and burned in the fire; so shall it be in the end of this world. The Son
of man shall send forth his angels, and they shall gather out of his kingdom
⁴² all things that offend, and them which do iniquity; ' and shall cast them
⁴³ into a furnace of fire: there shall be wailing and gnashing of teeth. Then
shall the righteous shine forth as the sun in the kingdom of their Father.
Who hath ears to hear, let him hear.

⁴⁴ Again, the kingdom of heaven is like unto treasure hid in a field; the
which when a man hath found, he hideth, and for joy thereof goeth and
selleth all that he hath, and buyeth that field.

⁴⁵ Again, the kingdom of heaven is like unto a merchant-man seeking goodly
⁴⁶ pearls: ' who, when he had found one pearl of great price, went and sold
all that he had, and bought it.

⁴⁷ Again, the kingdom of heaven is like unto a net, that was cast into the
⁴⁸ sea, and gathered of every kind: ' which, when it was full, they drew to
shore, and sat down, and gathered the good into vessels, but cast the bad
⁴⁹ away. So shall it be at the end of the world: the angels shall come forth,

---

ᵃ 35. Ps. 78, 2

MATTH. XIII.

50 and sever the wicked from among the just, ' and shall cast them into the furnace of fire : there shall be wailing and gnashing of teeth.
51 Jesus saith unto them, Have ye understood all these things? They say
52 unto him, Yea, Lord. Then said he unto them, Therefore every scribe *which is* instructed unto the kingdom of heaven, is like unto a man *that is* an householder, which bringeth forth out of his treasure *things* new and old.
53 And it came to pass, *that* when Jesus had finished these parables, he departed thence.

§ 56. *Jesus directs to cross the Lake. Incidents. The tempest stilled.*—
LAKE OF GALILEE.

MATTH. VIII. 18—27.   MARK IV. 35—41.   LUKE VIII. 22—25. IX. 57—62.

18 Now when Jesus saw great multitudes about him, he gave commandment to depart unto the other side.

35 And the same day, when the even was come, he saith unto them, Let us pass over unto the other side.

22 Now it came to pass on a certain day, that he went into a ship with his disciples : and he said unto them, Let us go over unto the other side of the lake.—

MATTH. VIII.

19 And a certain scribe came, and said unto him, Master, I will fol-low thee whithersoever thou go-
20 est. And Jesus saith unto him, The foxes have holes, and the birds of the air *have* nests ; but the Son of man hath not where to lay *his*
21 head. And another of his disciples said unto him, Lord, suffer me first
22 to go and bury my father. But Je-sus said unto him, Follow me ; and let the dead bury their dead.

IX. **57** And it came to pass, that as they went in the way, a certain *man* said unto him, Lord, I will follow
58 thee whithersoever thou goest. And Jesus said unto him, Foxes have holes, and birds of the air *have* nests ; but the Son of man hath not
59 where to lay *his* head. And he said unto another, Follow me. But he said, Lord, suffer me first to go and
60 bury my father. Jesus said unto him, Let the dead bury their dead : but go thou and preach the king-
61 dom of God. And another also said, Lord, I will follow thee ; but let me first go bid them farewell which are at home at my
62 house. And Jesus said unto him, No man having put his hand to the plough, and looking back, is fit for the kingdom of God.

MARK IV.

36 And when they had sent away the multi-tude, they took him even as he was in the ship. And there were
37 also with him other little ships. And there arose a great storm of wind, and the waves beat into the ship, so that it was now full.
38 And he was in the hinder part of the ship,

MATTH. VIII.

23 And when he was entered into a ship, his disciples followed him.
24 And behold, there arose a great tempest in the sea, insomuch that the ship was covered with the waves ; but he was
25 asleep. And his disci-ples came to *him*, and

LUKE VIII.

23 —And they launch-ed forth. But as they sailed, he fell asleep : and there came down a storm of wind on the lake ; and they were filled *with water*, and were in jeopardy.
24 And they came to him, and

MATTH. VIII.	MARK IV.	LUKE VIII.
awoke him, saying, Lord, save us: we per- [16] ish. And he saith unto them, Why are ye fearful, O ye of little faith? Then he arose, and rebuked the winds and the sea; and there was a great calm.	asleep on a pillow: and they awake him, and say unto him, Master, carest thou not [39] that we perish? And he arose, and rebuked the wind, and said unto the sea, Peace, be still. And the wind ceased, and there was	awoke him, saying, Master, master, we perish. Then he arose, and rebuked the wind, and the raging of the water: and they ceased, and there was a calm.
[40] a great calm. Why are ye [27] But the men marvelled, saying, What manner of man is this, that even the winds and the sea obey him!	And he said unto them, so fearful? how is it that ye have no faith? [41] And they feared exceedingly, and said one to another, What manner of man is this, that even the wind and the sea obey him?	[25] And he said unto them, Where is your faith? And they being afraid, wondered, saying one to another, What manner of man is this! for he commandeth even the winds and water, and they obey him.

§ 57. *The two Demoniacs of Gadara.*—S. E. COAST OF THE LAKE OF GALILEE.

MATTH. VIII. 28–34. IX. 1.	MARK V. 1—21.	LUKE VIII. 26—40.
[28] And when he was come to the other side, into the country of the Gergesenes, there met him two possessed with devils, coming out of the tombs, exceeding fierce, so that no man might pass by that way.	[1] And they came over unto the other side of the sea, into the country of the Gadarenes. [2] And when he was come out of the ship, immediately there met him out of the tombs a man with an unclean spirit, [3] ¹ who had *his* dwelling	[26] And they arrived at the country of the Gadarenes, which is over against Galilee. [27] And when he went forth to land, there met him out of the city a certain man, which had devils long time, and ware no clothes, neither abode in *any* house, but in the tombs.
	among the tombs; and no man could [4] bind him, no, not with chains: ¹ because that he had been often bound with fetters and chains, and the chains had been plucked asunder by him, and the fetters broken in [5] pieces: neither could any *man* tame him. And always, night and day, he was in the mountains, and in the tombs, crying, and cutting him- [6] self with stones. But when he saw Je-	
[29] And behold, they cried out, saying, What have we to do with thee, Jesus, thou Son of God? art thou come hither to torment us before the time?	sus afar off, he ran and [7] worshipped him, ¹ and cried with a loud voice, and said, What have I to do with thee, Jesus, *thou* Son of the Most High God? I adjure thee by God, that thou torment me not.	[28] When he saw Jesus, he cried out, and fell down before him, and with a loud voice said, What have I to do with thee, Jesus, *thou* Son of God most high? I beseech thee torment me not.

MARK V.

⁸ For he said unto him, Come out of the man, *thou* unclean spirit.

⁹ And he asked him, What *is* thy name? And he answered, saying, My name *is* Legion: for we are ¹⁰ many. And he besought him much that he would not send them away out of the country.

MATTH. VIII.

³⁰ And there was a good way off from them an herd of many ³¹ swine, feeding. So the devils besought him, saying, If thou cast us out, suffer us to go away into the herd of ³² swine. And he said unto them, Go. And when they were come out, they went into the herd of swine: and behold, the whole herd of swine ran violently down a steep place into the sea, and perished in the waters.

³³ And they that kept them, fled, and went their ways into the city, and told every thing; and what was befallen to the possessed of the ³⁴ devils. And behold, the whole city came out to meet Jesus:

LUKE VIII.

²⁹ For he had commanded the unclean spirit to come out of the man. For oftentimes it had caught him: and he was kept bound with chains, and in fetters; and he brake the bands, and was driven of the ³⁰ devil into the wilderness. And Jesus asked him, saying, What is thy name? And he said, Legion: because many devils were entered into ³¹ him. And they besought him, that he would not command them to go out into the deep.

MARK V.

¹¹ Now there was there nigh unto the mountains a great herd of ¹² swine feeding. And all the devils besought him, saying, Send us into the swine, that we may ¹³ enter into them. And forthwith Jesus gave them leave. And the unclean spirits went out, and entered into the swine: and the herd ran violently down a steep place into the sea, (they were about two thousand,) and were choked in the sea.

¹⁴ And they that fed the swine fled, and told *it* in the city, and in the country. And they went out to see what it was that was ¹⁵ done. And they come to Jesus, and see him that was possessed with the devil, and had the

LUKE VIII.

³² And there was there an herd of many swine feeding on the mountain: and they besought him that he would suffer them to enter into them. And he suffered them.

³³ Then went the devils out of the man, and entered into the swine: and the herd ran violently down a steep place into the lake, and were choked.

³⁴ When they that fed *them* saw what was done, they fled, and went and told *it* in the city and in the country. ³⁵ Then they went out to see what was done; and came to Jesus, and found the man out of whom the devils were departed, sitting at the feet of Jesus, clothed, and in his right ³⁶ mind: and they were afraid. They also which saw *it*, told them by what means he that was possessed of the devils was healed. ³⁷ Then the whole multitude of the country of the Gadarenes round about, besought him to depart from them; for they were taken with great fear. And he went up into the ship, and

legion, sitting, and clothed, and in his right mind: and ¹⁶ they were afraid. And they that saw *it* told them how it befell to him that was possessed with the devil, and *also* concerning the swine.

and when they ¹⁷ saw him, they besought *him* that he would depart out of their coasts.

MARK V.

And they began to pray him to depart out of their coasts.

MARK V.

And when he was come into the ship,

MARK V.

he that had been possessed with the devil prayed him that he might be [10] with him. Howbeit Jesus suffered him not, but saith unto him, Go home to thy friends, and tell them how great things the Lord hath done for thee, and hath had compassion on thee. [20] And he departed, and began to publish in Decapolis how great things Jesus had done for him. And all men

MATTH. IX.

[1] And he entered into a ship, and passed over, and came into his own city.

LUKE VIII.

[38] returned back again. Now the man out of whom the devils were departed, besought him that he might be with him. But Jesus sent him away, [39] saying, Return to thine own house, and shew how great things God hath done unto thee. And he went his way and published throughout the whole city, how great things Jesus had done unto [40] him. And it came to pass, that, when Jesus was returned, the people gladly received him: for they were all waiting for him.

[21] did marvel. And when Jesus was passed over again by ship unto the other side, much people gathered unto him: and he was nigh unto the sea.

§ 58. Levi's Feast.—CAPERNAUM.

MATTH. IX. 10—17.

[10] And it came to pass, as Jesus sat at meat in the house, behold, many publicans and sinners came and sat down with him and his disciples.

[11] And when the Pharisees saw it, they said unto his disciples, Why eateth your Master with publicans and sinners?

[12] But when Jesus heard that, he said unto them, They that be whole need not a physician, but they that are sick. [13] But go ye and learn what that meaneth, I will have mercy, and not sacrifice:[a] for I am not come to call the righteous, but sinners to repentance.

MARK II. 15—22.

[15] And it came to pass, that as Jesus sat at meat in his house, many publicans and sinners sat also together with Jesus and his disciples; for there were many, and they [16] followed him. And when the scribes and Pharisees saw him eat with publicans and sinners, they said unto his disciples, How is it that he eateth and drinketh with publicans and sinners? When Jesus [17] heard it, he saith unto them, They that are whole, have no need of the physician, but they that are sick: I came not to call the righteous, but sinners, to repentance.

LUKE V. 29—39.

[29] And Levi made him a great feast in his own house; and there was a great company of publicans, and of others that sat down with them.

[30] But their scribes and Pharisees murmured against his disciples, saying, Why do ye eat and drink with publicans and sinners?

[31] And Jesus answering, said unto them, They that are whole need not a physician; but [32] they that are sick. I came not to call the righteous, but sinners to repentance.

---

a 13. Hos 6, 6. Comp. 1 Sam. 15, 22.

MATTH. IX.	MARK II.	LUKE V.
¹⁴ Then came to him the disciples of John, saying, Why do we and the Pharisees fast oft, but thy disciples fast not?	¹⁸ And the disciples of John, and of the Pharisees, used to fast: and they come, and say unto him, Why do the disciples of John, and of the Pharisees fast, but thy disciples fast not? And Jesus said unto them, Can the children of the bride-chamber fast, while the bridegroom is with them? As long as they have the bridegroom with them, they cannot fast. But the days will come, when the bridegroom shall be taken away from them, and then shall they fast in those days.	³³ And they said unto him, Why do the disciples of John fast often, and make prayers, and likewise *the disciples* of the Pharisees; but thine eat and drink?
¹⁵ And Jesus said unto them, Can the children of the bride-chamber mourn, as long as the bridegroom is with them?		³⁴ And he said unto them, Can ye make the children of the bride-chamber fast while the bridegroom is with them?
But the days will come, when the bridegroom shall be taken from them, and then shall they fast.	²⁰	³⁵ But the days will come, when the bridegroom shall be taken away from them, and then shall they fast in those days.
		³⁶ And he spake also a parable unto them: No man putteth a piece of a new garment upon an old: if otherwise, then both the new maketh a rent, and the piece that was *taken* out of the new, agreeth
¹⁶ No man putteth a piece of new cloth unto an old garment: for that which is put in to fill it up, taketh from the garment, and the rent is made worse.	²¹ No man also seweth a piece of new cloth on an old garment: else the new piece that filled it up, taketh away from the old, and the rent is made worse.	
¹⁷ Neither do men put new wine into old bottles: else the bottles break, and the wine runneth out, and the bottles perish: but they put new wine into new bottles, and both are preserved.	²² And no man putteth new wine into old bottles: else the new wine doth burst the bottles, and the wine is spilled, and the bottles will be marred: but new wine must be put into new bottles.	³⁷ not with the old. And no man putteth new wine into old bottles; else the new wine will burst the bottles, and be spilled, and the bottles shall perish. But ³⁸ new wine must be put into new bottles, and both are preserved.

³⁹ No man also having drunk old *wine*, straightway desireth new: for he saith, The old is better.

§ 59. *The raising of Jairus' daughter. The woman with a bloody flux.*—
CAPERNAUM.

MATTH. IX. 18—26.	MARK V. 22—43.	LUKE VIII. 41—56.
¹⁸ While he spake these things unto them, behold, there came a cer-	²² And behold, there cometh one of the rulers of the synagogue,	⁴¹ And behold, there came a man named Jairus, and he was a

MATTH. IX.	MARK V.	LUKE VIII.

tain ruler, ånd worshipped him, saying, My daughter is even now dead: but come and lay thy hand upon her, and she shall live.

¹⁹ And Jesus arose, and followed him, and so did his disciples.

²⁰ And behold, a woman which was diseased with an issue of blood twelve years,

came behind him, and touched the hem of his gar²¹ ment: ' for she said within herself, If I may but touch his garment, I shall be whole.—
²² And the woman was made whole from that hour.—

Jairus by name; and when he saw him, he ²³ fell at his feet, ' and besought him greatly, saying, My little daughter lieth at the point of death: I pray thee, come and lay thy hands on her, that she may be healed; and she shall live.
²⁴ And Jesus went with him; and much people followed him and thronged him.

²⁵ And a certain woman which had an issue of blood twelve years, ²⁶ ' and had suffered many things of many physicians, and had spent all that she had, and was nothing bettered, but rather ²⁷ grew worse, ' when she had heard of Jesus, came in the press behind, and touched ²⁸ his garment: ' for she said, If I may touch but his clothes, I shall ²⁹ be whole. And straightway the fountain of her blood was dried up; and she felt in her body that she was healed of that plague.

---

ruler of the synagogue: and he fell down at Jesus' feet, and besought him that he would come into his ⁴² house: ' for he had one only daughter, about twelve years of age, and she lay a dying. But as he went, the people thronged him.

⁴³ And a woman having an issue of blood twelve years, which had spent all her living upon physicians, neither could be healed of any,

⁴⁴ ' came behind him and touched the border of his garment: and immediately her issue of blood stanched.

MARK V.	LUKE VIII.

³⁰ And Jesus, immediately knowing in himself that virtue had gone out of him, turned him about in the press, and said, Who touched my clothes? ³¹ And his disciples said unto him, Thou seest the multitude thronging thee, and sayest thou, Who touched ³² me? And he looked round about to see her that had done this thing. ³³ But the woman, fearing and trembling, knowing what was done in her, came and fell down before him, and told him all the truth.

---

⁴⁵ And Jesus said, Who touched me? When all denied, Peter, and they that were with him, said, Master, the multitude throng thee, and press ⁴⁶ thee, and sayest thou, Who touched me? And Jesus said, Somebody ⁴⁷ hath touched me: for I perceive that virtue is gone out of me. And when the woman saw that she was not hid, she came trembling, and falling down before him, she declared unto him before all the people for what cause she had touched him, and how she was healed immediately.

MATTH. IX.	MARK V.	LUKE VIII.

²² But Jesus turned him about, and when he saw her, he said, Daughter, be of good comfort: thy faith hath made thee whole.—

---

³⁴ And he said unto her, Daughter, thy faith hath made thee whole; go in peace, and be whole of thy plague.

---

⁴⁸ And he said unto her, Daughter, be of good comfort: thy faith hath made thee whole; go in peace.

MARK V.	LUKE VIII.
35 While he yet spake, there came from the ruler of the synagogue's *house certain* which said, Thy daughter is dead: why troublest **36** thou the Master any further? As soon as Jesus heard the word that was spoken, he saith unto the ruler of the synagogue, Be not afraid, only believe.—	**49** While he yet spake, there cometh one from the ruler of the synagogue's *house*, saying to him, Thy daughter is dead: trouble not the **50** Master. But when Jesus heard *it*, he answered him, saying, Fear not: believe only, and she shall be made whole.

MATTH. IX.	MARK V.	LUKE VIII.
23 And when Jesus came into the ruler's house,	**38** And he cometh to the house of the ruler of the synagogue.—	**51** And when he came into the house, he suffered no man to go in, save Peter, and James,
37 And he suffered no man to follow him, save Peter, and James, and John the **38** brother of James.—And he seeth the tumult, and	And *he* seeth the them that wept and **39** wailed greatly. And when he was come in,	and John, and the father and the mother **52** of the maiden. And all wept and bewailed
and saw the minstrels and the people making a noise, **24** he said unto them, Give place: for the maid is not dead, but sleepeth. And they laughed him to scorn.	he saith unto them, Why make ye this ado, and weep? the damsel is not dead, but **40** sleepeth. And they laughed him to scorn.	her: but he said, Weep not: she is not dead, **53** but sleepeth. And they laughed him to scorn, knowing that she was **54** dead. And he put them all out,
25 But when the people were put forth, he went in, and took her by the hand, and the maid **26** arose. And the fame hereof went abroad into all that land.	But when he had put them all out, he taketh the mother of the damsel, and with him, and entereth **41** damsel was lying. And he took the damsel by the hand, and said unto her, Talitha-cumi: which is, being inter- preted, Damsel, (I say **42** unto thee) arise. And straightway the damsel	the father and the mother of the damsel, and them that were in where the and took her by the hand, and called, saying, Maid, **55** arise. And her spirit came again, and she arose straightway: and he commanded to
arose, and walked; for she was *of the age* of twelve years. And they were astonished with a great aston- ishment. And he charged them straitly that no man should know it; and commanded that something should be given her to eat.		**56** give her meat. And her parents were astonished: but he charged them that they should tell no man what was done.

§ 60. *Two blind men healed, and a dumb spirit cast out.*—CAPERNAUM?

MATTH. IX. 27—34.

27 And when Jesus departed thence, two blind men followed him, crying,
28 and saying, *Thou* son of David, have mercy on us. And when he was come into the house, the blind men came to him: and Jesus saith unto them, Believe ye that I am able to do this? They said unto him, Yea,
29 Lord. Then touched he their eyes, saying, According to your faith be it

MATTH. IX.

[30] unto you.   And their eyes were opened; and Jesus straitly charged them, [31] saying, See *that* no man know *it.*   But they, when they were departed, spread abroad his fame in all that country.
[32]   As they went out, behold, they brought to him a dumb man possessed [33] with a devil.   And when the devil was cast out, the dumb spake : and the [34] multitudes marvelled, saying, It was never so seen in Israel.   But the Pharisees said, He casteth out devils, through the prince of the devils.

§ 61. *Jesus again at Nazareth, and again rejected.*

MATTH. XIII. 54—58.

[54]   And when he was come into his own country, he taught them in their synagogue, insomuch that they were astonished, and said, Whence hath this *man* this wisdom, and *these* mighty works?

[55] Is not this the carpenter's son? is not his mother called Mary? and his brethren, James, and Joses, and [56] Simon, and Judas? And his sisters, are they not all with us? Whence then hath this *man* all [57] these things? And they were offended in him.   But Jesus said unto them, A prophet is not without honour, save in his own country, [58] and in his own house.   And he did not many mighty works there, because of their unbelief.

MARK VI. 1—6.

[1]   And he went out from thence, and came into his own country; and [2] his disciples follow him.   And when the sabbath-day was come, he began to teach in the synagogue: and many hearing *him* were astonished, saying, From whence hath this *man* these things? and what wisdom *is* this which is given unto him, that even such mighty works are wrought by his hands? [3] Is not this the carpenter, the son of Mary, the brother of James, and Joses, and of Juda, and Simon? and are not his sisters here with us? And they were offended at him. [4] But Jesus said unto them, A prophet is not without honour, but in his own country, and among his own [5] kin, and in his own house.   And he could there do no mighty work, save that he laid his hands upon a few [6] sick folk, and healed *them.*   And he marvelled because of their unbelief.—

§ 62. *A third circuit in Galilee.   The Twelve instructed and sent forth.—*
GALILEE.

MATTH. IX. 35—38. X. 1, 5—42. XI. 1.

[35]   And Jesus went about all the cities and villages, teaching in their synagogues, and preaching the gospel of the kingdom, and healing every sick [36] ness, and every disease among the people.   But when he saw the multitudes, he was moved with compassion on them, because they fainted, and were scattered abroad, as sheep having no shepherd. [37] Then saith he unto his disciples, the harvest truly *is* plenteous, but the la [38] bourers *are* few.   Pray ye therefore the Lord of the harvest, that he will send forth labourers into his harvest.
X. [1]   And when he had called unto him his

MARK VI. 6—13.

[6] —And he went round about the villages teaching.

MARK VI.

[7]   And he called *unto* him the twelve, and

LUKE IX. 1—6.

[1]   Then he called his twelve disciples toge-

MATTH. X.	MARK VI.	LUKE IX.
twelve disciples, he gave them power *against* unclean spirits, to cast them out, and to heal all manner of sickness, and all manner of disease.—	began to send them forth by two and two; and gave them power over unclean spirits.	ther, and gave them power and authority over all devils, and to ² cure diseases. And he sent them to preach the kingdom of God, and to heal the sick.

⁵ These twelve Jesus sent forth, and commanded
them, saying, Go not into the way of the Gentiles, and into *any*
⁶ city of the Samaritans enter ye not. But go rather to the lost
⁷ sheep of the house of Israel. And as ye go, preach, saying, The
⁸ kingdom of heaven is at hand. Heal the sick, cleanse the
lepers, raise the dead, cast out devils: freely ye have received,
⁹ freely give. Provide

	MARK VI.	LUKE IX.
neither gold, nor silver, nor brass in your ¹⁰ purses; ¹ nor scrip for *your* journey, neither two coats, neither shoes, nor yet staves: for the workman is worthy of his meat. ¹¹ And into whatsoever city or town ye shall enter, inquire who in it is worthy; and there abide till ye go thence. ¹² And when ye come into an house, salute it.	⁸ And commanded them that they should take nothing for *their* journey, save a staff only; no scrip, no bread, no money in *their* purse: ⁹ ¹ but *be* shod with sandals; and not put on ¹⁰ two coats. And he said unto them, In what place soever ye enter into an house, there abide till ye depart from that place.	³ And he said unto them, Take nothing for *your* journey, neither staves, nor scrip, neither bread, neither money; neither have two coats apiece. ⁴ And whatsoever house ye enter into, there abide, and thence depart.

¹³ And if the house be worthy, let your peace
come upon it: but if it be not worthy, let your
peace return to you.

| ¹⁴ And whosoever shall not receive you, nor hear your words, when ye depart out of that house, or city, shake off the dust of your ¹⁵ feet. Verily, I say unto you, It shall be more tolerable for the land of Sodom and Gomorrah, in the day of judgment, than for that city. | ¹¹ And whosoever shall not receive you, nor hear you, when ye depart thence, shake off the dust under your feet, for a testimony against them. Verily, I say unto you, It shall be more tolerable for Sodom and Gomorrah in the day of judgment, than for that city. | ⁵ And whosoever will not receive you, when ye go out of that city, shake off the very dust from your feet for a testimony against them. |

¹⁶ Behold, I send you forth as sheep in the midst of wolves: be ye there-
¹⁷ fore wise as serpents, and harmless as doves. But beware of men: for they
will deliver you up to the councils, and they will scourge you in their syna-
¹⁸ gogues. And ye shall be brought before governors and kings for my sake,
¹⁹ for a testimony against them and the Gentiles. But when they deliver you
up, take no thought how or what ye shall speak, for it shall be given you in
⁰ that same hour what ye shall speak. For it is not ye that speak, but the

MATTH. X.

[21] Spirit of your Father which speaketh in you. And the brother shall deliver up the brother to death, and the father the child : and the children shall [22] rise up against *their* parents, and cause them to be put to death. And ye shall be hated of all *men* for my name's sake : but he that endureth to the [23] end shall be saved. But when they persecute you in this city, flee ye into another : for verily I say unto you, Ye shall not have gone over the cities of Israel till the Son of man be come.

[24] The disciple is not above *his* master, nor the servant above his lord. [25] It is enough for the disciple that he be as his master, and the servant as his lord : if they have called the master of the house Beelzebub, how much [26] more *shall they call* them of his household ? Fear them not therefore : for there is nothing covered, that shall not be revealed ; and hid, that shall not [27] be known. What I tell you in darkness, *that* speak ye in light : and what [28] ye hear in the ear, *that* preach ye upon the house-tops. And fear not them which kill the body, but are not able to kill the soul : but rather fear him [29] which is able to destroy both soul and body in hell. Are not two sparrows sold for a farthing ? and one of them shall not fall on the ground without [30] [31] your Father. But the very hairs of your head are all numbered. Fear [32] ye not therefore, ye are of more value than many sparrows. Whosoever therefore shall confess me before men, him will I confess also before my [33] Father which is heaven. But whosoever shall deny me before men, him will [34] I also deny before my Father which is in heaven. Think not that I am come to [35] send peace on earth ; I came not to send peace, but a sword. For I am come to set a man at variance against his father, and the daughter against [36] her mother, and the daughter-in-law against her mother-in-law. And a [37] man's foes *shall be* they of his own household.[a] He that loveth father or mother more than me, is not worthy of me : and he that loveth son or [38] daughter more than me, is not worthy of me. And he that taketh not his [39] cross, and followeth after me, is not worthy of me. He that findeth his life shall lose it : and he that loseth his life for my sake, shall find it.

[40] He that receiveth you, receiveth me ; and he that receiveth me, receiveth [41] him that sent me. He that receiveth a prophet in the name of a prophet, shall receive a prophet's reward ; and he that receiveth a righteous man in the name of a righteous man, shall receive a righteous man's reward. [42] And whosoever shall give to drink unto one of these little ones, a cup of cold *water* only, in the name of a disciple, verily, I say unto you, he shall in no wise lose his reward.

XI. [1] And it came to pass when Jesus had made an end of commanding his twelve disciples, he departed thence to teach and to preach in their cities.

MARK VI.	LUKE IX.
[12] And they went out, and preached [13] that men should repent. And they cast out many devils, and anointed with oil many that were sick, and healed *them.*	[6] And they departed, and went through the towns, preaching the gospel, and healing every where.

---

a **36.** Comp. Mic. 7, 6.

6

§ 63. *Herod holds Jesus to be John the Baptist, whom he had just before beheaded* —GALILEE? PEREA.

MATTH. XIV. 1, 2, 6—12.   MARK VI. 14—16, 21—29.   LUKE IX. 7—9.

[1] At that time Herod the tetrarch heard of [2] the fame of Jesus, [1] and said unto his servants, This is John the Baptist; he is risen from the dead; and therefore mighty works do shew forth themselves in him.—

[14] And king Herod heard *of him*, (for his name was spread abroad,) and he said, That John the Baptist was risen from the dead, and therefore mighty works do shew forth themselves in [15] him. Others said, That it is Elias. And others said, That it is a prophet, [16] or as one of the prophets. But when Herod heard *thereof*, he said, It is John, whom I beheaded.: he is risen from the dead.—

[7] Now Herod the tetrarch heard of all that was done by him: and he was perplexed, because that it was said of some, that John was risen from the dead; [8] [1] and of some, that Elias had appeared; and of others, that one of the old prophets was [9] risen again. And Herod said, John have I beheaded; but who is this of whom I hear such things? And he desired to see him.

MARK VI.

[6] But when Herod's birth-day was kept, the daughter of Herodias danced before them, and pleased Herod. [7] Whereupon he promised with an oath to give her whatsoever she would ask. [8] And she, being before instructed of her mother, said, Give me here John Baptist's head in [9] a charger. And the king was sorry: nevertheless for the oath's sake, and them which sat with him at meat, he commanded *it* to be [10] given *her*. And he sent, and beheaded [11] John in the prison. And his head was brought in a charger, and given to the damsel: and she brought *it* [12] to her mother. And his disciples came, and took up the body, and buried it, and went and told Jesus.

[21] And when a convenient day was come, that Herod on his birth-day made a supper to his lords, high captains, and chief *estates* of Galilee; [22] [1] and when the daughter of the said Herodias came in, and danced, and pleased Herod, and the king said unto the damsel, Ask of me whatsoever thou wilt, and I [23] will give *it* thee. And he sware unto her, Whatsoever thou shalt ask of me, I will give *it* thee, [24] unto the half of my kingdom. And she went forth, and said unto her mother, What shall I ask? And she said, The head of John the Baptist. [25] And she came in straightway with haste unto the king, and asked, saying, I will that thou give me, by and by, in a charger, the head of [26] John the Baptist. And the king was exceeding sorry; *yet* for his oath's sake, and for their sakes which sat with him, he would not reject her. [27] And immediately the king sent an executioner, and commanded his head to be brought: and he went and beheaded him in the prison; [28] on; [1] and brought his head in a charger, and gave it to the damsel; and the damsel gave it to her mother. [29] And when his disciples heard *of it*, they came and took up his corpse, and laid it in a tomb.

§ 64. *The Twelve return, and Jesus retires with them across the Lake. Five thousand are fed.*—CAPERNAUM.   N. E. COAST OF THE LAKE OF GALILEE.

MARK VI. 30—44.	LUKE IX. 10—17.
[30] And the apostles gathered themselves together unto Jesus, and told him all things, both what they had done, and what they had taught.	[10] And the apostles, when they were returned, told him all that they had done.—

[31] And he said unto them, Come ye yourselves apart into a desert place, and rest a while: for there were many coming and going, and they had no leisure so much as to eat.

MATTH. XIV. 13—21.	MARK VI.	LUKE IX.	JOHN VI. 1—14.
[13] When Jesus heard *of it*, he departed thence by ship into a desert place apart: and when the people had heard *thereof*, they followed him on foot out of the cities. [14] And Jesus went forth, and saw a great multitude, and was moved with compassion toward them, and he healed their sick.	[32] And they departed into a desert place by ship privately. And the people saw them departing, and many knew him, and ran afoot thither out of all cities, and outwent them, and came together unto him. [34] And Jesus, when he came out, saw much people, and was moved with compassion toward them, because they were as sheep not having a shepherd: and he began to teach them many things.	[10] —And he took them, and went aside privately into a desert place, belonging to the city called Beth- saida. And the people, when they knew *it*, followed him: and he received them, and spake unto them of the kingdom of God, and heal- ed them that had need of healing.	[1] After these things Jesus went over the sea of Galilee, which is *the sea* [2] of Tiberias. And a great multitude followed him, be- cause they saw his miracles which he did on them that were diseas- [3] ed. And Jesus went up into a mountain, and there he sat with [4] his disciples. And the passover, a feast of the Jews, was nigh. [5] When Jesus then lifted up *his* eyes, and saw a great company come unto him,
[15] And when it was evening, his disciples came to him, saying, This is a desert place, and the time is now past; send the multitude away, that they may go into the villages, and buy themselves vict- uals.	[35] And when the day was now far spent, his disci- ples came unto him, and said, This a desert place, and now the time *is* far passed: [36] send them away, that they may go into the country round about, and into the villages, and buy themselves bread: for they have nothing to	[12] And when the day began to wear away, then came the twelve, and said unto him, Send the multi- tude away, that they may go into the towns and country round about, and lodge, and get victuals: for we are here in a desert place.	he saith unto Philip, Whence shall we buy bread that these may [6] eat? (And this he said to prove him: for he him- self knew what he would do.) [7] Philip answered him, Two hun- dred pennyworth of bread is not
[16] But Jesus said unto them,	[37] eat. He answer- ed and said unto	[13] But he said unto them, Give ye	

MATTH. XIV.	MARK VI.	LUKE IX.	JOHN VI.
They need not depart; give ye them to eat. 17 And they say un-to him, We have here but five loaves, and two 18 fishes. He said, Bring them hith-19 er to me. And he commanded the multitude to sit down on the grass, and took the five loaves, and the two fish-es, and looking up to heaven, he blessed, and brake, and gave the loaves to *his* disciples, and the disciples to the multitude.	them, Give ye them to eat. And they say unto him, Shall we go and buy two hundred pennyworth of bread, and 37 give them to eat? He saith unto them, How many loaves have ye? go and see. And when they say, Five, and 38 es. And he com-manded them to make all sit down by companies up-on the green 40 grass. And they sat down in ranks, by hundreds, and 41 by fifties. And when he had tak-en the five loaves, and the two fish-es, he looked up to heaven, and blessed, and brake the loaves, and gave *them* to his disciples to set before them; and the two fishes di-vided he among 42 them all. And	them to eat. And they said, We have no more but five loaves and two fishes; ex-cept we should go and buy meat for all this people.— 13 —And he said to his disciples, Make them sit 14 down by fifties in 15 a company. And they did so, and made them all sit 16 down. Then he took the five loaves, and the two fishes, and looking up to heaven, he bless-ed them, and brake, and gave to the disciples to set before the multitude.	sufficient for them, that every one of them may 8 take a little. One of his disciples, Andrew, Simon Peter's brother, saith unto him, 9 There is a lad here, which hath five barley-loaves, and two small fishes: but what are they among 10 so many? And Jesus said, Make the men sit down. (Now there was much grass in 11 the place.)—And Jesus took the loaves; and when he had given thanks, he distri-buted to the dis-ciples, and the disciples to them that were set down; and like-wise of the fishes, as much as they would.
20 And they did all eat, and were filled: and they took up of the fragments that remained twelve baskets full.	they did all eat, and were filled. 43 And they took up twelve baskets full of the frag-ments, and of the fishes.	17 And they did eat, and were all filled: and there was taken up of fragments that remained to them twelve bas-kets.	12 When they were filled, he said unto his disciples, Gather up the fragments that remain, that nothing be lost. 13 Therefore they gathered *them*

together, and filled twelve baskets with
the fragments of the five barley-loaves,
which remained over and above unto them
that had eaten.

MATTH. XIV.	MARK VI.	LUKE IX.	JOHN VI.
21 And they that had eaten were about five thou-sand men, beside women and chil-dren.	44 And they that did eat of the loaves, were about five thousand men.	14 —For they were about five thou-sand men.—	10 —So the men sat down in number about five thou-14 sand.—Then those men, when they

had seen the miracle that Jesus did, said, This is of a
truth that Prophet that should come into the world

§ 65. *Jesus walks upon the water.*—LAKE OF GALILEE. GENNESARETH.

MATTH. XIV. 22—36.

²² And straightway Jesus constrained his disciples to get into a ship, and to go before him unto the other side, while he sent the multitudes ²³ away. And when he had sent the multitudes away, he went up into a mountain apart to pray.

MARK VI. 45—56.

⁴⁵ And straightway he constrained his disciples to get into the ship, and to go to the other side before unto Bethsaida, while he sent away ⁴⁶ the people. And when he had sent them away, he departed into a mountain to pray.

JOHN VI. 15—21.

When Jesus therefore perceived that they would come and take him by force, to make him a king, he departed again into a mountain himself alone.

MATTH. XIV.

And when the evening was come, he was ²⁴ there alone. But the ship was now in the midst of the sea, tossed with waves: for the wind was contrary. ²⁵ And in the fourth watch of the night Jesus went unto them, walking on the sea. ²⁶ And when the disciples saw him walking on the sea, they were troubled, saying, It is a spirit; and they cri- ²⁷ ed out for fear. But straightway Jesus spake unto them, saying, Be of good cheer; it is I; be not afraid.

²⁸ And Peter answered him and said, Lord, if it be thou, bid me come unto thee on the water. ²⁹ ' And he said, Come.

MARK VI.

⁴⁷ And when even was come, the ship was in the midst of the sea, and he alone on ⁴⁸ the land. And he saw them toiling in rowing; for the wind was contrary unto them; and about the fourth watch of the night he cometh unto them, walking upon the sea, and would have passed ⁴⁹ by them. But when they saw him walking upon the sea, they supposed it had been a spirit, and cried out. ⁵⁰ (For they all saw him, and were troubled.) And immediately he talked with them, and saith unto them, Be of good cheer; it is I; be not afraid.

¹⁶ And when even was *now* come, his disciples went down unto the ¹⁷ sea, ' and entered into a ship, and went over the sea toward Capernaum. And it was now dark, and Jesus was not come to them. ¹⁸ And the sea arose by reason of a great wind ¹⁹ that blew. So when they had rowed about five and twenty or thirty furlongs, they see Jesus walking on the sea, and drawing nigh unto the ship: and they were afraid. ²⁰ But he saith unto them, It is I; be not afraid.

³⁰ ship, he walked on the water, to go to Jesus. But when he saw the wind boisterous, he was afraid; and beginning to sink, he cried, ³¹ saying, Lord, save me. And immediately Jesus stretched forth *his* hand, and caught him, and said unto him, O thou of little faith, wherefore didst thou ³² doubt? And when they were come into the ship, the wind ceased. ³³ Then they that were in the ship came and worshipped him, saying, Of a truth thou art the Son of God.

⁵¹ And he went up unto them into the ship; and the wind ceased: and they were sore amazed in themselves beyond measure, and wonder- ⁵² ed. For they considered not *the miracle* of the loaves; for their heart was hardened.

²¹ Then they willingly received him into the ship: and immediately the ship was at the land whither they went.

6*

MATTH. XIV.	MARK VI.

54 And when they were gone over, they came into the land of Genne-**56** saret. And when the men of that place had knowledge of him, they sent out into all that country round about, and brought unto him all that **36** were diseased; ' and besought him that they might only touch the hem of his garment: and as many as touched were made perfectly whole.

53 And when they had passed over, they came into the land of Genne-**54** saret, and drew to the shore. And when they were come out of the ship, straightway they knew him, **55** ' and ran through that whole region round about, and began to carry about in beds those that were sick, **66** where they heard he was. And whithersoever he entered, into villages, or cities, or country, they laid the sick in the streets, and besought him that they might touch, if it were but the border of his garment: and as many as touched him, were made whole.

§ 66. *Our Lord's discourse to the multitude in the Synagogue at Capernaum. Many disciples turn back. Peter's profession of faith.*—CAPERNAUM.

JOHN VI. 22—71. VII. 1.

22 The day following, when the people which stood on the other side of the sea saw that there was none other boat there, save that one whereinto his disciples were entered, and that Jesus went not with his disciples into the **23** boat, but *that* his disciples were gone away alone; ' (howbeit there came other boats from Tiberias nigh unto the place where they did eat bread, **24** after the Lord had given thanks ;) ' when the people therefore saw that Jesus was not there, neither his disciples, they also took shipping, and came to **25** Capernaum, seeking for Jesus. And when they had found him on the other side of the sea, they said unto him, Rabbi, when camest thou hither? **26** Jesus answered them and said, Verily, verily, I say unto you, Ye seek me, not because ye saw the miracles, but because ye did eat of the loaves, and **27** were filled. Labour not for the meat which perisheth, but for that meat which endureth unto everlasting life, which the Son of man shall give unto **28** you: for him hath God the Father sealed. Then said they unto him, What **29** shall we do, that we might work the works of God. Jesus answered and said unto them, This is the work of God, that ye believe on him whom he **30** hath sent. They said therefore unto him, What sign shewest thou then, **31** that we may see, and believe thee? what dost thou work? Our fathers did eat manna in the desert ; as it is written,* He gave them bread from **32** heaven to eat. Then Jesus said unto them, Verily, verily, I say unto you, Moses gave you not that bread from heaven ; but my Father giveth you **33** the true bread from heaven. For the bread of God is he which cometh **34** down from heaven, and giveth life unto the world. Then said they unto **35** him, Lord, evermore give us this bread. And Jesus said unto them, I am the bread of life : he that cometh to me, shall never hunger ; and he that be-**36** lieveth on me, shall never thirst. But I said unto you, that ye also have **37** seen me, and believe not. All that the Father giveth me, shall come to **38** me ; and him that cometh to me, I will in no wise cast out. For I came down from heaven, not to do mine own will, but the will of him that sent **39** me. And this is the Father's will which hath sent me, that of all which he hath given me, I should lose nothing, but should raise it up again at the **40** last day. And this is the will of him that sent me; that every one which

---

* 3 1. Ps. 78, 24. Comp. Ex. 16, 15

JOHN VI.

seeth the Son, and believeth on him, may have everlasting life: and I will
raise him up at the last day.
41 The Jews then murmured at him, because he said, I am the bread which
42 came down from heaven. And they said, Is not this Jesus the son of
Joseph, whose father and mother we know? how is it then that he saith,
43 I came down from heaven? Jesus therefore answered and said unto them,
44 Murmur not among yourselves. No man can come to me, except the
Father which hath sent me draw him: and I will raise him up at the last
45 day. It is written in the prophets,[a] And they shall be all taught of God.
Every man therefore that hath heard, and hath learned of the Father,
46 cometh unto me. Not that any man hath seen the Father, save he which is
47 of God, he hath seen the Father. Verily, verily, I say unto you, He that
48 49 believeth on me hath everlasting life. I am that bread of life. Your
50 fathers did eat manna in the wilderness, and are dead.[b] This is the bread
which cometh down from heaven, that a man may eat thereof, and not die.
51 I am the living bread which came down from heaven: if any man eat of
this bread, he shall live for ever: and the bread that I will give is my flesh,
which I will give for the life of the world.
52 The Jews therefore strove among themselves, saying, How can this man
53 give us his flesh to eat? Then Jesus said unto them, Verily, verily, I say
unto you, Except ye eat the flesh of the Son of man, and drink his blood,
54 ye have no life in you. Whoso eateth my flesh, and drinketh my blood,
55 hath eternal life: and I will raise him up at the last day. For my flesh is
56 meat indeed, and my blood is drink indeed. He that eateth my flesh, and
57 drinketh my blood, dwelleth in me, and I in him. As the living Father
hath sent me, and I live by the Father: so he that eateth me, even he shall
58 live by me. This is that bread which came down from heaven: not as your
fathers did eat manna, and are dead: he that eateth of this bread shall live
59 for ever. These things said he in the synagogue, as he taught in Capernaum.
60 Many therefore of his disciples, when they had heard this, said, This is
61 an hard saying; who can hear it? When Jesus knew in himself that his
62 disciples murmured at it, he said unto them, Doth this offend you? What
63 and if ye shall see the Son of man ascend up where he was before? It is
the Spirit that quickeneth; the flesh profiteth nothing: the words that I
64 speak unto you, they are spirit, and they are life. But there are some of
you that believe not. For Jesus knew from the beginning who they were
65 that believed not, and who should betray him. And he said, Therefore said
I unto you, that no man can come unto me, except it were given unto him
of my Father.
66 From that time many of his disciples went back, and walked no more
67 with him. Then said Jesus unto the twelve, Will ye also go away?
68 Then Simon Peter answered him, Lord, to whom shall we go? thou hast
69 the words of eternal life. And we believe, and are sure that thou art that
70 Christ, the Son of the living God. Jesus answered them, Have not I
71 chosen you twelve, and one of you is a devil? He spake of Judas Iscariot
the son of Simon: for he it was that should betray him, being one of the
twelve.
VII. 1 After these things Jesus walked in Galilee: for he would not walk
in Jewry, because the Jews sought to kill him.

---

a **45.** Is. 54, 13. Comp. Jer. 31, 33 sq.   b **49.** Comp. Ex. 16, 15

PART V.

FROM OUR LORD'S THIRD PASSOVER UNTIL HIS FINAL DEPARTURE FROM GALILEE AT THE FESTIVAL OF TABERNACLES.

TIME: *Six Months.*

§ 67. *Our Lord justifies his Disciples for eating with unwashen hands. Pharisaic Traditions.*—CAPERNAUM.

MATTH. XV. 1—20.

¹ THEN came to Jesus scribes and Pharisees, which were of Jerusalem,

² saying, 'Why do thy disciples transgress the tradition of the elders? for they wash not their hands when ³ they eat bread. But he answered ⁷ and said unto them,— ' *Ye* hypocrites, well did Esaias prophesy of ⁸ you, saying, ᵃ This people draweth nigh unto me with their mouth, and honoureth me with *their* lips; but ⁹ their heart is far from me. But in vain they do worship me, teaching *for* doctrines the commandments of men.

MARK VII. 1—23.

¹ Then came together unto him the Pharisees, and certain of the scribes, ² which came from Jerusalem. And when they saw some of his disciples eat bread with defiled ³ (that is to say, with unwashen) hands, they found fault. For the Pharisees, and all the Jews, except they wash *their* hands ⁴ oft, eat not, holding the tradition of the elders. And *when they come* from the market, except they wash, they eat not. And many other things there be, which they have received to hold, *as* the washing of cups, and pots, and brazen vessels, and ⁵ tables. Then the Pharisees and scribes asked him, Why walk not thy disciples according to the tradition of the elders, but eat bread with unwash- ⁶ en hands? He answered and said unto them, Well hath Esaias prophesied of you hypocrites, as it is written,ᵃ This people honoureth me with *their* lips, but their heart is far from me. ⁷ Howbeit, in vain do they worship me, teaching *for* doctrines the com- ⁸ mandments of men. For laying aside the commandments of God, ye hold the tradition of men, *as* the washing of pots and cups: and many other such like things ye do.

ᵃ 7 etc. Is 29, 13.

MATTH. XV.

¹ —Why do ye also transgress the commandment of God by your tradi- ⁴ tion? For God commanded, say- ing,ª Honour thy father and mother: and, He that curseth father or ⁵ mother, let him die the death. But ye say, Whosoever shall say to *his* father or *his* mother, *It is* a gift, by whatsoever thou mightest be profited ⁶ by me ; ¹ and honour not his father or his mother, *he shall be free.*

Thus have ye made the command- ment of God of none effect by your tradition.

¹⁰   And he called the multitude, and said unto them, Hear, and under- ¹¹ stand : Not that which goeth into the mouth defileth a man ; but that which cometh out of the mouth, this defileth a man.

MARK VII.

⁹ And he said unto them, Full well ye reject the commandment of God, that ye may keep your own tradi- ¹⁰ tion. For Moses said,ª Honour thy father and thy mother ; and, Whoso curseth father or mother, let him die ¹¹ the death. But ye say, If a man shall say to his father or mother, *It is* Corban, that is to say, a gift, by whatsoever thou mightest be profit- ¹² ed by me ; *he shall be free.* And ye suffer him no more to do aught ¹³ for his father or his mother ; ¹ making the word of God of none effect through your tradition, which ye have delivered : and many such like things do ye.

¹⁴   And when he had called all the people *unto him*, he said unto them, Hearken unto me every one *of you*, ¹⁵ and understand. There is nothing from without a man, that entering into him, can defile him : but the things which come out of him, those

¹⁶ are they that defile the man. If any man have ears to hear, let him hear.

MATTH. XV.

¹² Then came his disciples, and said unto him, Knowest thou that the Pharisees ¹³ were offended after they heard this saying ? But he answered and said, Every ¹⁴ plant, which my heavenly Father hath not planted, shall be rooted up. Let them alone : they be blind leaders of the blind. And if the blind lead the blind, both shall fall into the ditch.

¹⁵   Then answered Peter and said unto him, Declare unto us this ¹⁶ parable. And Jesus said, Are ye also yet without understanding ? ¹⁷ Do not ye yet understand, that what- soever entereth in at the mouth goeth into the belly, and is cast out into the draught ?

¹⁸   But those things which proceed out of the mouth, come forth from the heart ; and they ¹⁹ defile the man. For out of the heart proceed evil thoughts, mur- ders, adulteries, fornications, thefts, ²⁰ false witness, blasphemies : ¹ these are *the things* which defile a man : but to eat with unwashen hands defileth not a man.

MARK VII.

¹⁷   And when he was entered into the house from the people, his disci- ples asked him concerning the para- ¹⁸ ble. And he saith unto them, Are ye so without understanding also ? Do ye not perceive, that whatsoever thing from without entereth into the ¹⁹ man, *it* cannot defile him : ¹ because it entereth not into his heart, but into the belly, and goeth out into the draught, purging all ²⁰ meats ? And he said, That which cometh out of the man, that defileth ²¹ the man. For from within, out of the heart of men, proceed evil thoughts, adulteries, fornications, ²² murders, ¹ thefts, covetousness, wick- edness, deceit, lasciviousness, an evil eye, blasphemy, pride, foolishness ; ²³ ¹ all these evils things come from within, and defile the man.

ª 4 etc. Ex. 20, 12. 21, 17. Comp. Deut. 5, 16.

§ 68. *The daughter of a Syrophenician woman is healed.*—REGION OF TYRE
AND SIDON

MATTH. XV. 21—28.	MARK VII. 24—30.
21 Then Jesus went thence, and departed into the coasts of Tyre and 22 Sidon. And behold, a woman of Canaan came out of the same coasts, and cried unto him, saying, Have mercy on me, O Lord, *thou* son of David ; my daughter is grievously 23 vexed with a devil. But he answered her not a word. And his disciples came and besought him, saying, Send her away ; for she crieth after us. 24 But he answered and said, I am not sent but unto the lost sheep of 25 the house of Israel. Then came she and worshipped him, say- 26 ing, Lord, help me. But he answered and said, It is not meet to take the children's bread and to cast *it* 27 to dogs. And she said, Truth, Lord : yet the dogs eat of the crumbs which fall from their mas- 28 ters' table. Then Jesus answered and said unto her, O woman, great *is* thy faith : be it unto thee even as thou wilt. And her daughter was made whole from that very hour.	24 And from thence he arose, and went into the borders of Tyre and Sidon, and entered into an house, and would have no man know *it* : but he 25 could not be hid. For a *certain* woman, whose young daughter had an unclean spirit, heard of him, and 26 came and fell at his feet ; ' (the woman was a Greek, a Syrophenician by nation ;) and she besought him that he would cast forth the devil out of her daughter. 27 But Jesus said unto her, Let the children first be filled : for it is not meet to take the children's bread, 28 and to cast *it* unto the dogs. And she answered and said unto him, Yes, Lord : yet the dogs under the table eat of the children's crumbs 29 And he said unto her, For this saying, go thy way ; the devil is gone 30 out of thy daughter. And when she was come to her house, she found the devil gone out, and her daughter laid upon the bed.

§ 69. *A deaf and dumb man healed; also many others. Four thousand are
fed.*—THE DECAPOLIS.

MATTH. XV. 29—38.	MARK VII. 31—37. VIII. 1—9.
29 And Jesus departed from thence, and came nigh unto the sea of Galilee ; and went up into a mountain, and sat down there.	31 And again, departing from the coasts of Tyre and Sidon, he came unto the sea of Galilee, through the midst of the coasts of Decapolis.

32 And they bring unto him one that
was deaf, and had an impediment in his speech ; and they beseech him to
33 put his hand upon him. And he took him aside from the multitude, and
34 put his fingers into his ears, and he spit, and touched his tongue : ' and
looking up to heaven, he sighed, and saith unto him, Ephphatha, that is,
35 Be opened. And straightway his ears were opened, and the string of his
36 tongue was loosed, and he spake plain. And he charged them that they
should tell no man : but the more he charged them, so much the more a
37 great deal they published *it* : ' and were beyond measure astonished, saying, He hath done all things well ; he maketh both the deaf to hear, and
the dumb to speak.

MATTH. XV.

30 And great multitudes came unto him, having with them *those that were* lame, blind, dumb, maimed, and many others, and cast them down at Jesus' 51 feet; and he healed them: [1] insomuch that the multitude wondered, when they saw the dumb to speak, the maimed to be whole, the lame to walk, and the blind to see; and they glorified the God of Israel.

MARK VIII.

1 In those days the multitude being very great, and having nothing to eat,

MATTH. XV.	Jesus called his disciples *unto him*,
52 Then Jesus called his disciples *unto him*, and said, I have compassion on the multitude, because they continue with me now three days, and have nothing to eat: and I will not send them away fasting, lest 28 they faint in the way. And his disciples say unto him, Whence should we have so much bread in the wilderness, as to fill so great a multi- 54 tude? And Jesus saith unto them, How many loaves have ye? And they said, Seven, and a few little 55 fishes. And he commanded the multitude to sit down on the ground. 56 And he took the seven loaves and the fishes, and gave thanks, and brake *them*, and gave to his disciples, and the disciples to the multitude.	2 and saith unto them, [1] I have compassion on the multitude, because they have now been with me three days, and have nothing to eat: 3 [1] and if I send them away fasting to their own houses, they will faint by the way: for divers of them came 4 from far. And his disciples answered him, From whence can a man satisfy these *men* with bread 5 here in the wilderness? And he asked them, How many loaves have 6 ye? and they said, Seven. And he commanded the people to sit down on the ground: and he took the seven loaves, and gave thanks, and brake, and gave to his disciples to set before *them;* and they did set 7 *them* before the people. And they had a few small fishes: and he

blessed, and commanded to set them also before *them.*

8 So they did eat, and were filled:
37 And they did all eat, and were filled: and they took up of the broken *meat* 38 that was left seven baskets full. And they that did eat were four thousand men, beside women and children. | and they took up of the broken *meat* that was left, seven baskets. 9 And they that had eaten were about four thousand: and he sent them away.

§ 70. *The Pharisees and Sadducees again require a sign.* [*See* § 49.]—NEAR MAGDALA.

MATTH. XV. 39. XVI. 1—4.	MARK VIII. 10—12.
39 And he sent away the multitude, and took ship, and came into the XVI. 1 coasts of Magdala. The Pharisees also with the Sadducees came, and, tempting, desired him that he would shew them a sign from 2 heaven. He answered and said	10 And straightway he entered into a ship with his disciples, and came 11 into the parts of Dalmanutha. And the Pharisees came forth, and began to question with him, seeking of him a sign from heaven, tempting him.

unto them, When it is evening, ye say, *It will be* fair weather: 3 for the sky is red. And in the morning, *It will be* foul weather to-day: for the sky is red and lowering. O *ye* hypocrites, ye can discern the face of the sky; but can ye not *discern* the signs of 12 And he sighed deeply in his spirit, 4 the times? A wicked and adul and saith, Why doth this generation

MATTH. XV.

terous generation seeketh after a sign; and there shall no sign be given unto it, but the sign of the prophet Jonas.—

MARK VIII.

seek after a sign? Verily I say unto you, there shall no sign be given unto this generation.

§ 71. *The Disciples cautioned against the leaven of the Pharisees.*—N. E. COAST OF THE LAKE OF GALILEE.

MATTH. XVI. 4—12.

4   —And he left them, and departed.

5   And when his disciples were come to the other side, they had forgotten 6 to take bread. Then Jesus said unto them, Take heed and beware of the leaven of the Pharisees and of the Sadducees.
7   And they reasoned among themselves, saying, *It is* because we have taken no bread. 8 *Which* when Jesus perceived, he said unto them, O ye of little faith, why reason ye among yourselves, because ye have brought no bread? 9 Do ye not yet understand, neither remember the five loaves of the five thousand, and how many baskets ye took up?

10 Neither the seven loaves of the four thousand, and how many baskets ye 11 took up? How is it that ye do not understand that I spake *it* not to you concerning bread, that ye should beware of the leaven of the Phari-12 sees and of the Sadducees? Then understood they how that he bade *them* not beware of the leaven of bread, but of the doctrine of the Pharisees and of the Sadducees.

MARK VIII. 13—21.

13   And he left them, and entering into the ship again, departed to the other side. 14 Now *the disciples* had forgotten to take bread, neither had they in the ship with them more than one loaf. 15 And he charged them, saying, Take heed, beware of the leaven of the Pharisees, and *of* the leaven of 16 Herod. And they reasoned among themselves, saying, *It is* because we 17 have no bread. And when Jesus knew *it*, he saith unto them, Why reason ye, because ye have no bread? perceive ye not yet, neither understand? have ye your heart yet hard-18 ened? ! having eyes, see ye not? and having ears, hear ye not? and 19 do ye not remember? When I brake the five loaves among five thousand, how many baskets full of fragments took ye up? They say unto him, 20 Twelve. And when the seven among four thousand, how many baskets full of fragments took ye up? And 21 they said, Seven. And he said unto them, How is it that ye do not understand?

§ 72. *A blind man healed.*—BETHSAIDA (JULIAS).

MARK VIII. 22—26.

22   And he cometh to Bethsaida; and they bring a blind man unto him, 23 and besought him to touch him. And he took the blind man by the hand, and led him out of the town; and when he had spit on his eyes, and put 24 his hands upon him, he asked him if he saw aught. And he looked up, 25 and said, I see men as trees walking. After that, he put *his* hands again upon his eyes, and made him look up: and he was restored, and saw every 26 man clearly. And he sent him away to his house, saying, Neither go into the town, nor tell *it* to any in the town.

§ 73. *Peter and the rest again profess their faith in Christ.* [*See* § 66.]—
REGION OF CESAREA PHILIPPI.

MATTH. XVI. 13—20.	MARK VIII. 27—30.	LUKE IX. 18—21.
13 When Jesus came into the coasts of Cesarea Philippi, he asked his disciples, saying, Whom do men say that I, the Son of man, am ? 14 And they said, Some *say that thou art* John the Baptist ; some, Elias ; and others, Jeremias, or one of the 15 prophets. He saith unto them, But whom say 16 ye that I am ? And Simon Peter answered and said, Thou art the Christ, the Son of the 17 living God. And Jesus answered and said	27 And Jesus went out, and his disciples, into the towns of Cesarea Philippi : and by the way he asked his disciples, saying unto them, Whom do men say that 28 I am ? And they answered, John the Baptist ; and some *say*, Elias ; and others, One of 29 the prophets. And he saith unto them, But whom say ye that I am ? And Peter answereth and saith unto him, Thou art the . Christ.	18 And it came to pass, as he was alone praying, his disciples were with him ; and he asked them, saying, Whom say the people that I 19 am ? They answering, said, John the Baptist ; but some *say*, Elias ; others *say*, that one of the old prophets is risen again. He said un- 20 to them, But whom say ye that I am ? Peter answering, said, The Christ of God.

unto him, Blessed art thou, Simon Bar-jona : for flesh and blood hath not 18 revealed *it* unto thee, but my Father which is in heaven. And I say also unto thee, That thou art Peter, and on this rock I will build my church : 19 and the gates of hell shall not prevail against it. And I will give unto thee the keys of the kingdom of heaven : and whatsoever thou shalt bind on earth, shall be bound in heaven ; and whatsoever thou shalt loose on earth, shall be loos-

| 20 ed in heaven. Then charged he his disciples that they should tell no man that he was Jesus the Christ. | MARK VIII. 30 And he charged them that they should tell no man of him. | LUKE IX. 21 And he straitly charged them, and commanded *them* to tell no man that thing. |

§ 74. *Our Lord foretells his own death and resurrection, and the trials of his followers.*—REGION OF CESAREA PHILIPPI.

MATTH. XVI. 21—28.	MARK VIII. 31—38. IX. 1.	LUKE IX. 22—27.
21 From that time forth began Jesus to shew unto his disciples, how that he must go unto Jerusalem, and suffer many things of the elders, and chief priests, and scribes, and be killed, and be raised 22 again the third day. Then Peter took him, and began to	31 And he began to teach them, that the Son of man must suffer many things, and be rejected of the elders, and of the chief priests, and scribes, and be killed, and after three 32 days rise again. And he spake that saying openly. And Peter took 33 him, and began to rebuke him,	22 Saying, The Son of man must suffer many things, and be rejected of the elders, and chief priests, and scribes, and · be slain, and be raised the third day.

And Peter took him. But

7

MATTH. XVI.

saying, Be it far from thee, Lord:
23. this shall not be unto thee. But he turned, and said unto Peter, Get thee behind me, Satan; thou art an offence unto me: for thou savourest not the things that be of God, but those that be of men.

24 Then said Jesus unto his disciples, If any *man* will come after me, let him deny himself, and take up his cross, and follow me.

25 For whosoever will save his life, shall lose it: and whosoever will lose his life for my 26 sake, shall find it. For what is a man profited, if he shall gain the whole world, and lose his own soul? or what shall a man give in exchange for his soul? 27 For the Son of man shall come in the glory of his Father, with his angels; and then he shall reward every man according to his works.

28 Verily I say unto you, There be some standing here, which shall not taste of death, till they see the Son of man coming in his kingdom.

MARK VIII.

when he had turned about, and looked on his disciples, he rebuked Peter, saying, Get thee behind me, Satan: for thou savourest not the things that be of God, but the things that be of men.

MARK VIII.

34 And when he had called the people *unto him* with his disciples also, he said unto them, Whosoever will come after me, let him deny himself, and take up his cross, and follow 35 me. For whosoever will save his life, shall lose it; but whosoever shall lose his life for my sake and the gospel's, the same shall 36 save it. For what shall it profit a man, if he shall gain the whole world, and lose his 37 own soul? ¹ or what shall a man give in exchange for his soul? 38 Whosoever therefore shall be ashamed of me, and of my words, in this adulterous and sinful generation; of him also shall the Son of man be ashamed, when he cometh in the glory of his IX. ¹ Father with the holy angels. And he said unto them, Verily I say unto you, That there be some of them that stand here, which shall not taste of death, till they have seen the kingdom of God come with power.

LUKE IX.

23 And he said to *them* all, If any *man* will come after me, let him deny himself, and take up his cross daily, and follow me.

24 For whosoever will save his life, shall lose it: but whosoever will lose his life for my sake, the same shall save it. 25 For what is a man advantaged, if he gain the whole world, and lose himself, or be cast away?

26 For whosoever shall be ashamed of me, and of my words, of him shall the Son of man be ashamed, when he shall come in his own glory, and *in his* Father's, and of the holy angels.

27 But I tell you of a truth, that there be some standing here, which shall not taste of death, till they see the kingdom of God

§ 75. *The Transfiguration.   Our Lord's subsequent discourse with the three Disciples.*—REGION OF CESAREA PHILIPPI.

MATTH. XVII. 1—13.

1 And after six days, Jesus taketh Peter, James, and John his

MARK IX. 2—13.

² And after six days, Jesus taketh Peter, and James, and John, and

LUKE IX. 28—36.

28 And it came to pass, about an eight days after these sayings, he

MATTH. XVII.

brother, and bringeth them up into an high ¹ mountain apart, ¹ and was transfigured before them: and his face did shine as the sun, and his raiment was white as the light. ² And behold, there appeared unto them Moses and Elias talking with him.

MARK IX.

leadeth them up into an high mountain apart by themselves; and he was transfigured before ² them. And his raiment became shining, exceeding white as snow; so as no fuller on earth ⁴ can white them. And there appeared unto them Elias, with Moses: and they were talking with Jesus.

LUKE IX.

took Peter, and John, and James, and went up into a mountain to ²⁹ pray. And as he prayed, the fashion of his countenance was altered, and his raiment *was* white *and* glister- ³⁰ ing. And behold, there talked with him two men, which were Moses and Elias: ³¹ who appeared in glory, and spake of his decease

³² which he should accomplish at Jerusalem. But Peter and they that were with him were heavy with sleep: and when they were awake, they saw his glory, and the two men that stood with him.

⁴ Then answered Peter, and said unto Jesus, Lord, it is good for us to be here: if thou wilt, let us make here three tabernacles; one for, thee, and one for Moses, and one for Elias.

⁵ While he yet spake, behold, a bright cloud overshadowed them: and behold, a voice out of the cloud, which said,ª This is my beloved Son, in whom I am well pleased: hear ⁶ ye him. And when the disciples heard *it*, they fell on their face, and were sore afraid. ⁷ And Jesus came and touched them, and said, Arise, and be not afraid. ⁸ And when they had lifted up their eyes, they saw no man, save Jesus only.

⁹ And as they came down from the mountain, Jesus charged them, saying, Tell the vision to no man, until the Son of man be risen again from the dead.

⁵ And Peter answered and said to Jesus, Master, it is good for us to be here: and let us make three tabernacles; one for thee, and one for Moses, ⁶ and one for Elias. For he wist not what to say: for they were sore ⁷ afraid. And there was a cloud that overshadowed them: and a voice came out of the cloud, saying,ª This is my beloved Son: hear him.

³⁰

⁸ And suddenly, when they had looked round about, they saw no man any more, save Jesus only with themselves.

MARK IX.

⁹ And as they came down from the mountain, he charged them that they should tell no man what things they had seen, till the Son of man were ¹⁰ risen from the dead. And they

³³ And it came to pass, as they departed from him, Peter said unto Jesus, Master, it is good for us to be here: and let us make three tabernacles; one for thee, and one for Moses, and one for Elias: not knowing what he ³⁴ said. While he thus spake, there came a cloud, and overshadowed them: and they feared as they entered ³⁵ into the cloud. And there came a voice out of the cloud, saying,ª This is my beloved Son: hear him. And when the voice was past, Jesus was found alone. And they kept *it* close, and told no man in those days any of those things which they had seen.

MARK IX.

kept that saying with themselves, questioning one with another what the

MATTH. XVII.	
¹⁰ And his disciples asked him, saying, Why then say the scribes, that **¹¹** Elias must first come? And Jesus answered and said unto them, Elias truly shall first come, and restore all **¹²** things: ¹ but I say unto you, that Elias is come already, and they knew him not, but have done unto him whatsoever they listed: likewise shall also the Son of man suffer **¹³** of them. Then the disciples understood that he spake unto them of John the Baptist.	rising from the dead should mean. **¹¹** And they asked him, saying, Why say the scribes that Elias must first **¹²** come? And he answered and told them, Elias verily cometh first, and restoreth all things; and how it is written of the Son of man, that he must suffer many things, and be set **¹³** at nought. But I say unto you, That Elias is indeed come, and they have done unto him whatsoever they listed, as it is written of him.

§ 76. *The healing of a Demoniac, whom the Disciples could not heal.—* REGION OF CESAREA PHILIPPI.

MATTH. XVII. 14—21.	MARK IX. 14—29.	LUKE IX. 37—43.
¹⁴ And when they were come to the multitude,	**¹⁴** And when he came to *his* disciples, he saw a great multitude about them, and the scribes questioning with them. **¹⁵** And straightway all the people, when they beheld him, were greatly amazed, and running to **¹⁶** *him*, saluted him. And he asked the scribes, What question ye with **¹⁷** them? And one of the multitude answered and said, Master, I have brought unto thee my son, which hath a dumb **¹⁸** spirit; ¹ and wheresoever he taketh him, he teareth him; and he foameth and gnasheth with his teeth, and pineth away; and I spake to thy disciples **¹⁹** that they should cast him out, and they could not. He answereth him, and saith, O faithless generation, how long shall I be with you? how long shall I suffer you? Bring him **⁴²** son hither, coming, the devil threw him down and tare *him.—*	**³⁷** And it came to pass, that on the next day, when they were come down from the hill, much people met him.
there came to him a *certain* man kneeling down to him, **¹⁵** and saying, ¹ Lord, have mercy on my son; for he is a lunatic, and sore vexed; for ofttimes he falleth into the fire, and oft into the **¹⁶** water. And I brought him to thy disciples, and they could not cure him. **¹⁷** Then Jesus answered and said, O faithless and perverse generation, how long shall I be with you, how long shall I suffer you? Bring him hither to me. **²⁰** unto me. And they brought him unto him: and when he saw him, straightway the spirit tare him; and he fell on the ground, and wallowed,		**³⁸** And behold, a man of the company cried out, saying, Master, I beseech thee look upon my son: for he is mine **³⁹** only child. And lo, a spirit taketh him, and he suddenly crieth out; and it teareth him that he foameth again, and bruising him, hardly departeth from him. **⁴⁰** And I besought thy disciples to cast him out, and they could **⁴¹** not. And Jesus answering said, O faithless and perverse generation, how long shall I be with you, and suffer you? Bring thy son hither. And as he was yet a

MARK IX.

[21] foaming. And he asked his father, How long is it ago since this came unto [22] him? And he said, Of a child. [1] And oft-times it hath cast him into the fire, and into the waters to destroy him: but if thou canst do any thing, have com- [23] passión on us, and help us. Jesus said unto him, If thou canst believe, all [24] things *are* possible to him that believeth. And straightway the father of the child cried out, and said with tears, Lord, I believe; help thou mine unbe-

MATTH. XVII.	[25] lief. When Jesus saw	LUKE IX.
[18] And Jesus rebuked the devil, and he departed out of him: and the child was cured from [19] that very hour. Then came the disciples to Jesus apart, and said, Why could not we cast [20] him out? And Jesus said unto them, Because of your unbelief: for verily I say unto you, If ye have faith as a grain of mustard-seed, ye shall say unto this mountain, Remove hence to yonder place; and it shall remove; and nothing shall be [21] impossible unto you. Howbeit, this kind goeth not out, but by prayer and fasting.	that the people came running together, he rebuked the foul spirit, saying unto him, *Thou* dumb and deaf spirit, I charge thee, come out of him, and enter no [26] more into him. And *the spirit* cried, and rent him sore, and came out of him: and he was as one dead; insomuch that many [27] said, He is dead. But Jesus took him by the hand, and lifted him up; [28] and he arose. And when he was come into the house, his disciples asked him privately, Why could not [29] we cast him out? And he said unto them, This kind can come forth by nothing, but by prayer and fasting.	[42] —And Jesus rebuked the unclean spirit, and healed the child, and delivered him again to his father. [43] And they were all amazed at the mighty power of God.—

§ 77. *Jesus again foretells his own Death and Resurrection.* [See § 74.]— GALILEE.

MATTH. XVII. 22, 23.	MARK IX. 30—32.	LUKE IX. 43—45.
[22] And while they abode in Galilee, [31] Jesus said unto them, The Son of man shall be betrayed into the hands of men, [23] and they shall kill him; and the third day he shall be raised again. And they were exceeding sorry.	[30] And they departed thence, and passed through Galilee; and he would not that any man should know it. For he taught his disciples, and said unto them, The Son of man is delivered into the hands of men, and they shall kill him; and after that he is killed, he shall [32] rise the third day. But they understood not that saying, and were afraid to ask him	[43] —But while they wondered every one at all things which Jesus did, he said unto his disci- [44] ples, Let these sayings sink down into your ears: for the Son of man shall be delivered into the hands of men. [45] But they understood not this saying, and it was hid from them, that they perceived it not: and they feared to ask him of that saying.

7*

§ 78. *The Tribute-money miraculously provided.*—CAPERNAUM.

MATTH. XVII. 24—27.	MARK IX. 33.

24 And when they were come to 33 And he came to Capernaum.—
Capernaum, they that received
tribute-*money*, came to Peter, and said, Doth not your Master pay tribute?
25 ' He saith, Yes. And when he was come into the house, Jesus prevented
him, saying, What thinkest thou, Simon? of whom do the kings of the
earth take custom or tribute? of their own children, or of strangers?
26 ' Peter saith unto him, Of strangers. Jesus saith unto him, Then are the
27 children free. Notwithstanding, lest we should offend them, go thou to the
sea, and cast an hook, and take up the fish that first cometh up: and when
thou hast opened his mouth, thou shalt find a piece of money: that take,
and give unto them for me and thee.

§ 79. *The Disciples contend who should be the greatest. Jesus exhorts to
humility, forbearance, and brotherly love.*—CAPERNAUM.

MATTH. XVIII. 1—35.	MARK IX. 33—50.	LUKE IX. 46—50.

1 At the same time 33 —And being in the 46 Then there arose
came the disciples unto house, he asked them, a reasoning among
Jesus, saying, Who is What was it that ye them, which of them
the greatest in the disputed among your- should be greatest.
kingdom of heaven? selves by the way? 47 And Jesus perceiving
34 But they held their the thought of their
peace: for by the heart,
way they had disputed
35 among themselves, who *should be* the greatest. And he
sat down, and called the twelve, and saith unto them, If
any man desire to be first, *the same* shall be last of
all, and servant of all.

2 And Jesus called a little 36 And he took a child, took a
child unto him, and set and set him in the child, and set him by
him in the midst of midst of them; and 48 him, ' and said unto
3 them, ' and said, Verily when he had taken them, Whosoever shall
I say unto you, Except him in his arms, he receive this child in my
ye be converted, and 37 said unto them, ' Who- name, receiveth me;
become as little chil- soever shall receive and whosoever shall
dren, ye shall not enter one of such children in receive me, receiveth
into the kingdom of my name, receiveth him that sent me: for
4 heaven. Whosoever me: and whosoever he that is least among
therefore shall humble shall receive me, re- you all, the same shall
himself as this little ceiveth not me, but him be great.
child, the same is great- that sent me.
est in the kingdom of
5 heaven. And whoso shall receive one such
little child in my name, receiveth me.

MARK IX.
36 And John answered him, saying, Master, we 49 And John answered
saw one casting out devils in thy name, and and said, Master, we
he followeth not us; and we forbade him, be- saw one casting out

MARK IX.

[39] cause he followeth not us. But Jesus said, For-bid him not: for there is no man which shall do a miracle in my name, that can lightly speak evil of [40] me. For he that is not against us, is on our part. [41] For whosoever shall give you a cup of water to drink in my name, because ye belong to Christ, verily I say unto you, he shall not lose his re-ward.

LUKE IX.

devils in thy name; and we forbade him, because he followeth [50] not with us. And Jesus said unto him, Forbid *him* not: for he that is not against us, is for us.

MATTH. XVIII.

[6] But, whoso shall offend one of these little ones which believe in me, it were better for him that a millstone were hanged about his neck, and *that* he were drowned in the depth [7] of the sea. Wo unto the world be-cause of offences! for it must needs be that offences come; but wo to that man by whom the offence com-[8] eth! Wherefore, if thine hand or thy foot offend thee, cut them off, and cast *them* from thee; it is bet-ter for thee to enter into life halt or maimed, rather than having two hands or two feet, to be cast into everlasting fire.

[9] And if thine eye offend thee, pluck it out, and cast *it* from thee: it is better for thee to enter into life with one eye, rather than having two eyes, to be cast into hell-fire.

MARK IX.

[42] And whosoever shall offend one of *these* little ones that believe in me, it is better for him that a millstone were hanged about his neck, and he were [43] cast into the sea. And if thy hand offend thee, cut it off: it is better for thee to enter into life maimed, than having two hands to go into hell, into the fire that never shall be [44] quenched: [ ] where their worm dieth not, and the fire is not quenched.[a] [45] And if thy foot offend thee, cut it off: it is better for thee to enter halt into life, than having two feet to be cast into hell, into the fire that [46] never shall be quenched: [ ] where their worm dieth not, and the fire [47] is not quenched. And if thine eye offend thee, pluck it out: it is better for thee to enter into the kingdom [ ] of God with one eye, than having two eyes, to be cast into hell-fire: [48] [ ] where their worm dieth not, and [49] the fire is not quenched. For every one shall be salted with [50] fire, and every sacrifice shall be salted with salt. Salt *is* good: but if the salt have lost its saltness, wherewith will ye season it? Have salt in yourselves, and have peace one with another.

MATTH. XVIII.

[ ] Take heed that ye despise not one of these little ones: for I say unto you, that in heaven their angels do always behold the face of my Father [11] which is in heaven. For the Son of man is come to save that which was [12] lost. How think ye? If a man have an hundred sheep, and one of them be gone astray, doth he not leave the ninety and nine, and goeth into [13] the mountains, and seeketh that which is gone astray? And if so be that he find it, verily I say unto you, he rejoiceth more of that *sheep*, [14] than of the ninety and nine which went not astray. Even so it is not the will of your Father which is in heaven, that one of these little ones should perish. [15] Moreover, if thy brother shall trespass against thee, go and tell him his fault between thee and him alone; [b] if he shall hear thee, thou hast gained [16] thy brother. But if he will not hear *thee, then* take with thee one or two more, that in the mouth of two or three witnesses every word may be

---

MATTH. XVIII.

[17] established.[a] And if he shall neglect to hear them, tell it unto the church:
but if he neglect to hear the church, let him be unto thee as an heathen
[18] man and a publican. Verily, I say unto you, Whatsoéver ye shall bind on
earth, shall be bound in heaven: and whatsoever ye shall loose on earth,
[19] shall be loosed in heaven. Again I say unto you, That if two of you shall
agree on earth, as touching any thing that they shall ask, it shall be done
[20] for them of my Father which is in heaven. For where two or three are
gathered together in my name, there am I in the midst of them.
[21]   Then came Peter to him, and said, Lord, how oft shall my brother sin
[22] against me, and I forgive him? till seven times? Jesus saith unto him, I
say not unto thee, Until seven times; but, Until seventy times seven.
[23] Therefore is the kingdom of heaven likened unto a certain king, which
[24] would take account of his servants. And when he had begun to reckon,
[25] one was brought unto him which owed him ten thousand talents. But
forasmuch as he had not to pay, his lord commanded him to be sold, and
his wife and children, and all that he had, and payment to be made. The
servant therefore fell down, and worshipped him, saying, Lord, have pa-
[27] tience with me, and I will pay thee all. Then the lord of that servant was
[28] moved with compassion, and loosed him, and forgave him the debt. But
the same servant went out, and found one of his fellow-servants, which
owed him an hundred pence: and he laid hands on him, and took him by
[29] the throat, saying, Pay me that thou owest. And his fellow-servant fell
down at his feet, and besought him, saying, Have patience with me, and I
[30] will pay thee all. And he would not: but went and cast him into prison,
[31] till he should pay the debt. So when his fellow-servants saw what was
done, they were very sorry, and came and told unto their lord all that was
[32] done. Then his lord, after that he had called him, said unto him, O thou
wicked servant, I forgave thee all that debt, because thou desiredst me:
[33] I shouldest not thou also have had compassion on thy fellow-servant, even
[34] as I had pity on thee? And his lord was wroth, and delivered him to the
[35] tormentors, till he should pay all that was due unto him. So likewise
shall my heavenly Father do also unto you, if ye from your hearts forgive
not every one his brother their trespasses.

§ 80. *The Seventy instructed and sent out.*—CAPERNAUM.

LUKE X. 1—16.

[1]   After these things, the Lord appointed other seventy also, and sent them
two and two before his face into every city, and place, whither he himself
[2] would come. Therefore said he unto them, The harvest truly is great, but
the labourers are few: pray ye therefore the Lord of the harvest, that he
[3] would send forth labourers into his harvest. Go your ways: behold, I
[4] send you forth as lambs among wolves. Carry neither purse, nor scrip,
[5] nor shoes: and salute no man by the way.[b] And into whatsoever house
[6] ye enter, first say, Peace be to this house. And if the son of peace be
there, your peace shall rest upon it: if not, it shall turn to you again.
[7] And in the same house remain, eating and drinking such things as they
give: for the labourer is worthy of his hire. Go not from house to house.
[8] And into whatsoever city ye enter, and they receive you, eat such things
[9] as are set before you. And heal the sick that are therein, and say unto

---

[a] **16.** Deut. 19, 15.   [b] **4.** Comp. 2 K. 4, 29.

LUKE X.

¹⁰ them, The kingdom of God is come nigh unto you. But into whatsoever city ye enter, and they receive you not, go your ways out into the streets ¹¹ of the same, and say, ' Even the very dust of your city which cleaveth on us, we do wipe off against you: notwithstanding, be ye sure of this, that ¹² the kingdom of God is come nigh unto you. But I say unto you, That it ¹³ shall be more tolerable in that day for Sodom than for that city. Wo unto thee, Chorazin! wo unto thee, Bethsaida! for if the mighty works had been done in Tyre and Sidon, which have been done in you, they had a ¹⁴ great while ago repented, sitting in sackcloth and ashes. But it shall be ¹⁵ more tolerable for Tyre and Sidon at the judgment, than for you. And thou, Capernaum, which art exalted to heaven, shalt be thrust down to hell. ¹⁶ He that heareth you, heareth me ; and he that despiseth you, despiseth me ; and he that despiseth me, despiseth him that sent me.

§ 81. *Jesus goes up to the Festival of Tabernacles. His final departure from Galilee. Incidents in Samaria.*

JOHN VII. 2—10.

² ³ Now the Jews' feast of tabernacles was at hand. His brethren there-fore said unto him, Depart hence, and go into Judea, that thy disciples also ⁴ may see the works that thou doest. For *there is* no man *that* doeth any thing in secret, and he himself seeketh to be known openly. If thou do ⁵ these things, shew thyself to the world. (For neither did his brethren ⁶ believe in him.) Then Jesus said unto them, My time is not yet come : ⁷ but your time is always ready. The world cannot hate you ; but me it ⁸ hateth, because I testify of it, that the works thereof are evil. Go ye up unto this feast: I go not up yet unto this feast ; for my time is not yet full ⁹ come. When he had said these words unto them, he abode *still* in Gali- ¹⁰ lee. But when his brethren were gone up, then went he also up unto the feast, not openly, but as it were in secret.

LUKE IX. 51—56.

⁵¹ And it came to pass, when the time was come that he should be received ⁵² up, he steadfastly set his face to go to Jerusalem, ' and sent messengers before his face : and they went and entered into a village of the Samari- ⁵³ tans, to make ready for him. And they did not receive him, because his ⁵⁴ face was as though he would go to Jerusalem. And when his disciples James and John saw *this*, they said, Lord, wilt thou that we command fire ⁵⁵ to come down from heaven, and consume them, even as Elias did ? But he turned, and rebuked them, and said, Ye know not what manner of ⁵⁶ spirit ye are of. For the Son of man is not come to destroy men's lives, but to save *them*. And they went to another village.

§ 82. *Ten Lepers cleansed.*—SAMARIA.

LUKE XVII. 11—19.

¹¹ And it came to pass, as he went to Jerusalem, that he passed through ¹² the midst of Samaria and Galilee. And as he entered into a certain vil- ¹³ lage, there met him ten men that were lepers, which stood afar off: ' and they lifted up *their* voices, and said, Jesus, Master, have mercy on us. ¹⁴ And when he saw *them*, he said unto them, Go shew yourselves unto the

LUKE XVII.

priests. And it came to pass, that, as they went, they were cleansed.
[15] And one of them, when he saw that he was healed, turned back, and with
[16] a loud voice glorified God, ' and fell down on *his* face at his feet, giving
[17] him thanks: and he was a Samaritan. And Jesus answering, said, Were
[18] there not ten cleansed? but where *are* the nine? There are not found tha·
[19] returned to give glory to God, save this stranger. And he said unto him,
Arise, go thy way: thy faith hath made thee whole.

PART VI.

THE FESTIVAL OF TABERNACLES, AND THE SUBSEQUENT TRANSACTIONS
UNTIL OUR LORD'S ARRIVAL AT BETHANY SIX DAYS
BEFORE THE FOURTH PASSOVER.

TIME : *Six months, less six days.*

§ 83. *Jesus at the Festival of Tabernacles. His public teaching.*—JERU-
SALEM.

JOHN VII. 11—53. VIII. 1.

¹¹ THEN the Jews sought him at the feast, and said, Where is he?
¹² And there was much murmuring among the people concerning him:
for some said, He is a good man: others said, Nay; but he deceiveth the
¹³ people. Howbeit, no man spake openly of him, for fear of the Jews.
¹⁴ Now about the midst of the feast, Jesus went up into the temple, and
¹⁵ taught. And the Jews marvelled, saying, How knoweth this man letters,
¹⁶ having never learned? Jesus answered them, and said, My doctrine is
¹⁷ not mine, but his that sent me. If any man will do his will, he shall know
¹⁸ of the doctrine, whether it be of God, or *whether* I speak of myself. He
that speaketh of himself, seeketh his own glory: but he that seeketh his
glory that sent him, the same is true, and no unrighteousness is in him.
¹⁹ Did not Moses give you the law, and *yet* none of you keepeth the law?
²⁰ Why go ye about to kill me? The people answered and said, Thou hast
²¹ a devil: who goeth about to kill thee? Jesus answered and said unto
²² them, I have done one work, and ye all marvel. Moses therefore gave
unto you circumcision, (not because it is of Moses, but of the fathers,) and
²³ ye on the sabbath-day circumcise a man.ᵃ If a man on the sabbath-day
receive circumcision, that the law of Moses should not be broken; are ye
angry at me, because I have made a man every whit whole on the sabbath-
²⁴ day? Judge not according to the appearance, but judge righteous judg-
²⁵ ment. Then said some of them of Jerusalem, Is not this he whom they
²⁶ seek to kill? But lo, he speaketh boldly, and they say nothing unto him.
²⁷ Do the rulers know indeed that this is the very Christ? ‖ Howbeit, we know
this man, whence he is: but when Christ cometh, no man knoweth whence
²⁸ he is. Then cried Jesus in the temple, as he taught, saying, Ye both know

---

ᵃ **22.** Lev. 12, 3.

JOHN VII.

me, and ye know whence I am: and I am not come of myself, but he that
[29] sent me is true, whom ye know not. But I know him; for I am from
[30] him, and he hath sent me. Then they sought to take him: but no man
[31] laid hands on him, because his hour was not yet come. And many of the
people believed on him, and said, When Christ cometh, will he do more
miracles than these which this *man* hath done?
[32] The Pharisees heard that the people murmured such things concerning
him: and the Pharisees and the chief priests sent officers to take him.
[33] Then said Jesus unto them, Yet a little while am I with you, and *then* I go
[34] unto him that sent me. Ye shall seek me, and shall not find *me:* and
[35] where I am, *thither* ye cannot come. Then said the Jews amóng themselves, Whither will he go, that we shall not find him? will he go unto the
[36] dispersed among the Gentiles, and teach the Gentiles? What *manner of*
saying is this that he said, Ye shall seek me, and shall not find *me:* and
[37] where I am, *thither* ye cannot come? In the last day, that great *day* of
the feast, Jesus stood and cried, saying, If any man thirst, let him come
[38] unto me, and drink. He that believeth on me, as the scripture hath said,
[39] out of his belly shall flow rivers of living water.[a] But this spake he of the
Spirit, which they that believe on him should receive; for the Holy Ghost
was not yet *given*, because that Jesus was not yet glorified.
[40] Many of the people therefore, when they heard this saying, said, Of a
[41] truth this is the Prophet. ¹ Others said, This is the Christ. But some said,
[42] Shall Christ come out of Galilee? Hath not the scripture said, That
Christ cometh of the seed of David, and out of the town of Bethlehem,
[43] where David was?[b] So there was a division among the people because of
[44] him. And some of them would have taken him; but no man laid hands
on him.
[45] Then came the officers to the chief priests and Pharisees; and they said
[46] unto them, Why have ye not brought him? The officers answered, Never
[47] man spake like this man. Then answered them the Pharisees, Are ye
[48] also deceived? Have any of the rulers, or of the Pharisees believed on
[49][50] him? But this people who knoweth not the law are cursed. Nicodemus saith unto them, (he that came to Jesus by night, being one of them,)
[51] Doth our law judge *any* man before it hear him, and know what he doeth?
[52] ¹ They answered and said unto him, Art thou also of Galilee? Search, and
look: for out of Galilee ariseth no prophet.
[53] VIII. ¹ And every man went unto his own house. But Jesus went unto
the mount of Olives.

§ 84. *The Woman taken in Adultery.*—JERUSALEM.

JOHN VIII. 2—11.

[2] And early in the morning he came again into the temple, and all the
[3] people came unto him; and he sat down and taught them. And the
scribes and Pharisees brought unto him a woman taken in adultery: and
[4] when they had set her in the midst, ¹ they say unto him, Master, this woman
[5] was taken in adultery, in the very act. Now Moses in the law commanded
[6] us, that such should be stoned:[c] but what sayest thou? This they said,
tempting him, that they might have to accuse him. But Jesus stooped down,

---

[a] 38. In. 55, l. 58, 11. Comp. In. 44, 3. Zech. 13, l. 14, 8.
[b] 42. Comp. Ps. 89, 3. 4. 132, 11. Mic. 5, 2.   [c] 5. Lev. 20, 10. Comp. Deut. 22, 21.

JOHN VIII.

[7] and with *his* finger wrote on the ground, *as though he heard them not.* So when they continued asking him, he lifted up himself, and said unto them, [8] He that is without sin among you, let him first cast a stone at her. And [9] again he stooped down, and wrote on the ground. And they which heard *it*, being convicted by *their own* conscience, went out one by one, beginning at the eldest, *even* unto the last: and Jesus was left alone, and the [10] woman standing in the midst. When Jesus had lifted up himself, and saw none but the woman, he said unto her, Woman, where are those thine [11] accusers? hath no man condemned thee? She said, No man, Lord. And Jesus said unto her, Neither do I condemn thee: go, and sin no more.

§ 85. *Further public teaching of our Lord. He reproves the unbelieving Jews, and escapes from their hands.*—JERUSALEM.

JOHN VIII. 12—59.

[12] Then spake Jesus again unto them, saying, I am the light of the world: he that followeth me shall not walk in darkness, but shall have the light of [13] life. The Pharisees therefore said unto him, Thou bearest record of thy-[14] self; thy record is not true. Jesus answered and said unto them, Though I bear record of myself, *yet* my record is true: for I know whence I came, and whither I go: but ye cannot tell whence I come, and whither I go. [15] [16] Ye judge after the flesh, I judge no man. And yet if I judge, my judg-[17] ment is true: for I am not alone, but I and the Father that sent me. It is [18] also written in your law,[b] that the testimony of two men is true. I am one that beareth witness of myself; and the Father that sent me, beareth [19] witness of me. ' Then said they unto him, Where is thy Father? Jesus answered, Ye neither know me, nor my Father: if ye had known me, ye [20] should have known my Father also. These words spake Jesus in the treasury, as he taught in the temple: and no man laid hands on him, for his hour was not yet come.

[21] Then said Jesus again unto them, I go my way, and ye shall seek me, [22] and shall die in your sins: whither I go, ye cannot come. Then said the Jews, Will he kill himself? because he saith, Whither I go, ye cannot [23] come. And he said unto them, Ye are from beneath; I am from above: [24] ye are of this world; I am not of this world. I said therefore unto you, that ye shall die in your sins: for if ye believe not that I am *he*, ye shall [25] die in your sins. ' Then said they unto him, Who art thou? And Jesus saith unto them, Even *the same* that I said unto you from the beginning. [26] I have many things to say, and to judge of you: but he that sent me, is true; and I speak to the world those things which I have heard of him. [27] [28] They understood not that he spake to them of the Father. Then said Jesus unto them, When ye have lifted up the Son of man, then shall ye know that I am *he*, and *that* I do nothing of myself; but as my Father [29] hath taught me, I speak these things. And he that sent me is with me: the Father hath not left me alone; for I do always those things that please [30] him. As he spake these words, many believed on him. [31] Then said Jesus to those Jews which believed on him, If ye continue in [32] my word, *then* are ye my disciples indeed; ' and ye shall know the truth, [33] and the truth shall make you free. They answered him, We be Abra·ham's seed, and were never in bondage to any man: how sayest thou, Ye

---

8

[a] **17.** Deut. 17, 6. Comp. Deut. 19, 15.

JOHN VIII.

[34] shall be made free? Jesus answered them, Verily, verily, I say unto you,
[35] Whosoever committeth sin, is the servant of sin. And the servant abideth
[36] not in the house for ever, *but* the Son abideth ever. If the Son therefore
[37] shall make you free, ye shall be free indeed. I know that ye are Abraham's seed; but ye seek to kill me, because my word hath no place in
[38] you. I speak that which I have seen with my Father; and ye do that
[39] which ye have seen with your father. They answered and said unto him,
Abraham is our father. Jesus saith unto them, If ye were Abraham's
[40] children, ye would do the works of Abraham. But now ye seek to kill me,
a man that hath told you the truth, which I have heard of God: this did
[41] not Abraham. ' Ye do the deeds of your father. Then said they to him,
[42] We be not born of fornication; we have one Father, *even* God. Jesus said
unto them, If God were your Father, ye would love me: for I proceeded
[43] forth and came from God; neither came I of myself, but he sent me. Why
do ye not understand my speech? *even* because ye cannot hear my word.
[44] Ye are of *your* father the devil, and the lusts of your father ye will do: he
was a murderer from the beginning, and abode not in the truth; because
there is no truth in him. When he speaketh a lie, he speaketh of his own:
[45] for he is a liar, and the father of it. And because I tell *you* the truth, ye
[46] believe me not. ' Which of you convinceth me of sin? And if I say the
[47] truth, why do ye not believe me? He that is of God, heareth God's words:
ye therefore hear *them* not, because ye are not of God.
[48] Then answered the Jews, and said unto him, Say we not well that thou
[49] art a Samaritan, and hast a devil? Jesus answered, I have not a devil;
[50] but I honour my Father, and ye do dishonour me. And I seek not mine
[51] own glory: there is one that seeketh and judgeth. Verily, verily, I say
[52] unto you, If a man keep my saying, he shall never see death. Then said
the Jews unto him, Now we know that thou hast a devil. Abraham is
dead, and the prophets; and thou sayest, If a man keep my saying, he shall
[53] never taste of death. Art thou greater than our father Abraham, which is
[54] dead? and the prophets are dead: whom makest thou thyself? Jesus answered, If I honour myself, my honour is nothing: it is my Father that
[55] honoureth me, of whom ye say, that he is your God. Yet ye have not
known him; but I know him: and if I should say, I know him not, I shall
[56] be a liar like unto you: but I know him, and keep his saying. Your father
[57] Abraham rejoiced to see my day: and he saw *it*, and was glad. Then said
the Jews unto him, Thou art not yet fifty years old, and hast thou seen
[58] Abraham? Jesus said unto them, Verily, verily, I say unto you, Before
Abraham was, I am.
[59] Then took they up stones to cast at him: but Jesus hid himself, and
went out of the temple, going through the midst of them, and so passed by.

§ 86. *A Lawyer instructed. Love to our neighbour defined. Parable of the
good Samaritan.*—NEAR JERUSALEM.

LUKE X. 25—37.

[25] And behold, a certain lawyer stood up, and tempted him, saying, Master,
[26] what shall I do to inherit eternal life? He said unto him, What is written
[27] in the law? how readest thou? And he answering said,* Thou shalt love
the Lord thy God with all thy heart, and with all thy soul, and with all thy

---

* 27. Deut. 6, 5. Lev. 19, 18. Comp. Lev 18, 5.

LUKE X.

[28] strength, and with all thy mind ; and thy neighbour as thyself. And he said unto him, Thou hast answered right: this do, and thou shalt live.
[29] But he, willing to justify himself, said unto Jesus, And who is my neigh-
[30] bour ? And Jesus answering, said, A certain *man* went down from Jerusalem to Jericho, and fell among thieves, which stripped him of his raiment,
[31] and wounded *him*, and departed, leaving *him* half dead. And by chance there came down a certain priest that way ; and when he saw him, he
[32] passed by on the other side. And likewise a Levite, when he was at the
[33] place, came and looked *on him*, and passed by on the other side. But a certain Samaritan, as he journeyed, came where he was : and when he
[34] saw him, he had compassion *on him*, ' and went to *him*, and bound up his wounds, pouring in oil and wine, and set him on his own beast, and brought
[35] him to an inn, and took care of him. And on the morrow, when he departed, he took out two pence, and gave *them* to the host, and said unto him, Take care of him : and whatsoever thou spendest more, when I come
[36] again, I will repay thee. Which now of these three, thinkest thou, was
[37] neighbour unto him that fell among the thieves? And he said, He that shewed mercy on him. Then said Jesus unto him, Go, and do thou likewise.

§ 87. *Jesus in the house of Martha and Mary.*—BETHANY.

LUKE X. 38—42.

[38] Now it came to pass, as they went, that he entered into a certain village :
[39] and a certain woman, named Martha, received him into her house. And she had a sister called Mary, which also sat at Jesus' feet, and heard his
[40] word. But Martha was cumbered about much serving, and came to him, and said, Lord, dost thou not care that my sister hath left me to serve
[41] alone ? bid her therefore that she help me. And Jesus answered, and said unto her, Martha, Martha, thou art careful, and troubled about many things ;
[42] ' but one thing is needful ; and Mary hath chosen that good part, which shall not be taken away from her.

§ 88. *The Disciples again taught how to pray.*—NEAR JERUSALEM.

LUKE XI. 1—13.

[1] And it came to pass, that as he was praying in a certain place, when he ceased, one of his disciples said unto him, Lord, teach us to pray, as John
[2] also taught his disciples. And he said unto them, When ye pray, say, Our Father which art in heaven, Hallowed be thy name. Thy kingdom come.
[3] Thy will be done, as in heaven, so in earth. ' Give us day by day our daily
[4] bread. And forgive us our sins ; for we also forgive every one that is indebted to us. And lead us not into temptation ; but deliver us from evil.
[5] And he said unto them, Which of you shall have a friend, and shall go
[6] unto him at midnight, and say unto him, Friend, lend me three loaves : ' for a friend of mine in his journey is come to me, and I have nothing to set be-
[7] fore him ? And he from within shall answer and say, Trouble me not : the door is now shut, and my children are with me in bed ; I cannot rise and
[8] give thee. I say unto you, Though he will not rise and give him, because he is his friend, yet because of his importunity he will rise and give him
[9] as many as he needeth. And I say unto you, Ask, and it shall be given

LUKE XI.

[10] you ; seek, and ye shall find ; knock, and it shall be opened unto you. For
every one that asketh, receiveth ; and he that seeketh, findeth ; and to him
[11] that knocketh, it shall be opened. If a son shall ask bread of any of
you that is a father, will he give him a stone? or if *he ask* a fish, will he
[2] for a fish give him a serpent? Or if he shall ask an egg, will he offer him
[13] a scorpion? If ye then, being evil, know how to give good gifts unto your
children : how much more shall *your* heavenly Father give the Holy Spirit
to them that ask him?

§ 89. *The Seventy return.*—JERUSALEM?

LUKE X. 17—24.

[17]   And the seventy returned again with joy, saying, Lord, even the devils
[18] are subject unto us through thy name. And he said unto them, I beheld
[19] Satan as lightning fall from heaven. Behold, I give unto you power to
tread on serpents and scorpions, and over all the power of the enemy : and
[20] nothing shall by any means hurt you. Notwithstanding, in this rejoice not,
that the spirits are subject unto you ; but rather rejoice, because your names
are written in heaven.
[21]   In that hour Jesus rejoiced in spirit, and said, I thank thee, O Father,
Lord of heaven and earth, that thou hast hid these things from the wise
and prudent, and hast revealed them unto babes ; even so, Father ; for so
[22] it seemed good in thy sight. All things are delivered to me of my Father :
and no man knoweth who the Son is, but the Father ; and who the Father
is, but the Son, and *he* to whom the Son will reveal *him.*
[23]   And he turned him unto *his* disciples, and said privately, Blessed *are* the
[24] eyes which see the things that ye see. For I tell you, that many prophets
and kings have desired to see those things which ye see, and have not seen
them; and to hear those things which ye hear, and have not heard *them.*

§ 90. *A man born blind is healed on the Sabbath. Our Lord's subsequent
discourses.*—JERUSALEM.

JOHN IX. 1—41. X. 1—21.

[1]   And as *Jesus* passed by, he saw a man which was blind from *his* birth.
[2] And his disciples asked him, saying, Master, who did sin, this man or his
[3] parents, that he was born blind? Jesus answered, Neither hath this man
sinned, nor his parents : but that the works of God should be made mani-
[4] fest in him. I must work the works of him that sent me while it is day :
[5] the night cometh when no man can work. As long as I am in the world,
[6] I am the light of the world. When he had thus spoken, he spat on the
ground, and made clay of the spittle, and he anointed the eyes of the blind
[7] man with the clay, ' and said unto him, Go, wash in the pool of Siloam,
which is by interpretation, Sent. He went his way therefore, and washed,
and came seeing.
[8]   The neighbours, therefore, and they which before had seen him that he
[9] was blind, said, Is not this he that sat and begged? Some said, This is
[10] he : others *said,* He is like him : *but* he said, I am *he.* Therefore said
[11] they unto him, How were thine eyes opened? He answered and said, A
man that is called Jesus, made clay, and anointed mine eyes, and said unto
me, Go to the pool of Siloam, and wash : and I went and washed, and I

JOHN IX.

[12] received sight. Then said they unto him, Where is he? He said, I know not.
[13] [14] They brought to the Pharisees him that aforetime was blind. And it was the sabbath-day when Jesus made the clay, and opened his eyes.
[15] Then again the Pharisees also asked him how he had received his sight. He said unto them, He put clay upon mine eyes, and I washed, and do see.
[16] Therefore said some of the Pharisees, This man is not of God, because he keepeth not the sabbath-day. Others said, How can a man that is a sin-
[17] ner do such miracles? And there was a division among them. ' They say unto the blind man again, What sayest thou of him, that he hath opened
[18] thine eyes? He said, He is a prophet.'' But the Jews did not believe con- cerning him, that he had been blind, and received his sight, until they called
[19] the parents of him that had received his sight. And they asked them, say- ing, Is this your son, who ye say was born blind? How then doth he now
[20] see? His parents answered them and said, We know that this is our son,
[21] and that he was born blind: ' but by what means he now seeth, we know not; or who hath opened his eyes, we know not: he is of age; ask him:
[22] he shall speak for himself. These *words* spake his parents, because they feared the Jews: for the Jews had agreed already, that if any man did con-
[23] fess that he was Christ, he should be put out of the synagogue. Therefore said his parents, He is of age; ask him.
[24] Then again called they the man that was blind, and said unto him, Give
[25] God the praise: we know that this man is a sinner. He answered and said, Whether he be a sinner *or no*, I know not: one thing I know, that,
[26] whereas I was blind, now I see. Then said they to him again, What did
[27] he to thee? how opened he thine eyes? He answered them, I have told you already, and ye did not hear: wherefore would ye hear *it* again? will
[28] ye also be his disciples? Then they reviled him, and said, Thou art his
[29] disciple; but we are Moses' disciples. We know that God spake unto
[30] Moses; *as for* this *fellow*, we know not from whence he is. The man an- swered and said unto them, Why, herein is a marvellous thing, that ye
[31] know not from whence he is, and *yet* he hath opened mine eyes. Now we know that God heareth not sinners; [a] but if any man be a worshipper of
[32] God, and doeth his will, him he heareth. Since the world began was it
[33] not heard that any man opened the eyes of one that was born blind. If
[34] this man were not of God, he could do nothing. They answered and said unto him, Thou wast altogether born in sins, and dost thou teach us? And they cast him out.
[35] Jesus heard that they had cast him out: and when he had found him, he
[36] said unto him, Dost thou believe on the Son of God? He answered and
[37] said, Who is he, Lord, that I might believe on him? And Jesus said unto
[38] him, Thou hast both seen him, and it is he that talketh with thee. And
[39] he said, Lord, I believe. And he worshipped him. ' And Jesus said, For judgment I am come into this world; that they which see not might see,
[40] and that they which see, might be made blind. And *some* of the Pharisees which were with him heard these words, and said unto him, Are we blind
[41] also? Jesus said unto them, If ye were blind, ye should have no sin: but now ye say, We see; therefore your sin remaineth.
X. [1] Verily, verily, I say unto you, He that entereth not by the door into the sheepfold, but climbeth up some other way, the same is a thief and a rob-
[2] ber. But he that entereth in by the door, is the shepherd of the sheep.

[a] **31.** Comp. Prov. 28, 9.

8*

³ To him the porter openeth ; and the sheep hear his voice : and he calleth
⁴ his own sheep by name, and leadeth them out. And when he putteth forth
his own sheep, he goeth before them, and the sheep follow him : for they
⁵ know his voice. And a stranger will they not follow, but will flee from
⁶ him : for they know not the voice of strangers. This parable spake Jesus
unto them : but they understood not what things they were which he spake
unto them.
⁷   Then said Jesus unto them again, Verily, verily, I say unto you, I am tho
⁸ door of the sheep. All that ever came before me are thieves and robbers :
⁹ but the sheep did not hear them. I am the door : by me if any man enter
¹⁰ in, he shall be saved, and shall go in and out, and find pasture. The thief
cometh not, but for to steal, and to kill, and to destroy : I am come that they
¹¹ might have life, and that they might have *it* more abundantly. I am the
¹² good shepherd : the good shepherd giveth his life for the sheep. But he
that is an hireling, and not the shepherd, whose own the sheep are not,
seeth the wolf coming, and leaveth the sheep, and fleeth ; and the wolf
¹³ catcheth them, and scattereth the sheep. The hireling fleeth, because he is
¹⁴ an hireling, and careth not for the sheep. I am the good shepherd, and
¹⁵ know my *sheep*, and am known of mine. As the Father knoweth me, even
¹⁶ so know I the Father : and I lay down my life for the sheep. And other
sheep I have, which are not of this fold : them also I must bring, and they
shall hear my voice ; and there shall be one fold, *and* one shepherd.
¹⁷ Therefore doth my Father love me, because I lay down my life, that I might
¹⁸ take it again. ' No man taketh it from me, but I lay it down of myself. I
have power to lay it down, and I have power to take it again. This commandment have I received of my Father.
¹⁹   There was a division therefore again among the Jews for these sayings.
²⁰ And many of them said, He hath a devil, and is mad ; why hear ye him ?
²¹ Others said, These are not the words of him that hath a devil. Can a
devil open the eyes of the blind ?

§ 91. *Jesus in Jerusalem at the Festival of Dedication. He retires beyond
Jordan.*—JERUSALEM. BETHABARA BEYOND JORDAN.

JOHN X. 22—42.
²²   And it was at Jerusalem the feast of the dedication, and it was winter.
²³ ²⁴ And Jesus walked in the temple in Solomon's porch. Then came the Jews
round about him, and said unto him, How long dost thou make us to doubt ?
²⁵ If thou be the Christ, tell us plainly. ' Jesus answered them, I told you, and
ye believed not : the works that I do in my Father's name, they bear wit-
²⁶ ness of me. But ye believe not, because ye are not of my sheep, as I said
²⁷ unto you. My sheep hear my voice, and I know them, and they follow me :
²⁸ ' and I give unto them eternal life ; and they shall never perish, neither
²⁹ shall any man pluck them out of my hand. My Father, which gave *them*
me, is greater than all ; and no man is able to pluck *them* out of my Father's
³⁰ hand. I and *my* Father are one.
³¹ ³² Then the Jews took up stones again to stone him. Jesus answered
them, Many good works have I shewed you from my Father ; for which of
³³ those works do ye stone me ? The Jews answered him, saying, For a good
work we stone thee not ; but for blasphemy, and because that thou, being
³⁴ a man, makest thyself God. Jesus answered them, Is it not written in

JOHN X.

[35] your law,[a] I said, Ye are gods? If he called them gods, unto whom the [36] word of God came, and the scripture cannot be broken; I say ye of him whom the Father hath sanctified, and sent into the world, Thou blasphe- [37] mest; because I said, I am the Son of God? If I do not the works of my [38] Father, believe me not. But if I do, though ye believe not me, believe the works: that ye may know and believe that the Father is in me, and I in him.

[39] Therefore they sought again to take him; but he escaped out of their [40] hand, I and went away again beyond Jordan, into the place where John at [41] first baptized; and there he abode. And many resorted unto him, and said, John did no miracle; but all things that John spake of this man were true. [42] And many believed on him there.

§ 92. The raising of Lazarus.—BETHANY.

JOHN XI. 1—46.

Now a certain man was sick, named Lazarus, of Bethany, the town of Mary and her sister Martha. It was that Mary which anointed the Lord with ointment, and wiped his feet with her hair, whose brother Lazarus was [3] sick. Therefore his sisters sent unto him, saying, Lord, behold, he whom [4] thou lovest is sick. When Jesus heard that, he said, This sickness is not unto death, but for the glory of God, that the Son of God might be glorified [5][6] thereby. Now Jesus loved Martha, and her sister, and Lazarus. When he had heard therefore that he was sick, he abode two days still in the same [7] place where he was. Then after that saith he to his disciples, Let us go [8] into Judea again. His disciples say·unto him, Master, the Jews of late [9] sought to stone thee; and goest thou thither again? Jesus answered, Are there not twelve hours in the day? If any man walk in the day, he stum- [10] bleth not, because he seeth the light of this world. But if a man walk in the night, he stumbleth, because there is no light in him.

[11] These things said he: and after that he saith unto them, Our friend Lazarus [12] sleepeth; but I go that I may awake him out of sleep. Then said his dis- [13] ciples, Lord, if he sleep, he shall do well. Howbeit, Jesus spake of his [14] death: but they thought that he had spoken of taking of rest in sleep. Then [15] said Jesus unto them plainly, Lazarus is dead. And I am glad for your sakes that I was not there, to the intent ye may believe; nevertheless, let [16] us go unto him. Then said Thomas, which is called Didymus, unto his fel- low-disciples, Let us also go, that we may die with him.

[17] Then when Jesus came, he found that he had lain in the grave four [18] days already. Now Bethany was nigh unto Jerusalem, about fifteen fur- [19] longs off: I and many of the Jews came to Martha and Mary, to comfort [20] them concerning their brother. Then Martha, as soon as she heard that Jesus was coming, went and met him: but Mary sat still in the house. [21] Then said Martha unto Jesus, Lord, if thou hadst been here, my brother [22] had not died. But I know that even now, whatsoever thou wilt ask of God, [23] God will give it thee. Jesus saith unto her, Thy brother shall rise again. [24] Martha saith unto him, I know that he shall rise again in the resurrection [25] at the last day. Jesus said unto her, I am the resurrection, and the life: [26] he that believeth in me, though he were dead, yet shall he live: I and who- soever liveth, and believeth in me, shall never die. Believest thou this?

JOHN XI.

[27] She saith unto him, Yea, Lord : I believe that thou art the Christ, the Son of [28] God, which should come into the world. And when she had so said, she went her way, and called Mary her sister secretly, saying, The Master is [29] come, and calleth for thee. As soon as she heard *that*, she arose quickly, and came unto him.

[30] Now Jesus was not yet come into the town, but was in that place where [31] Martha met him. The Jews then which were with her in the house, and comforted her, when they saw Mary that she rose up hastily, and went out, [32] followed her, saying, She goeth unto the grave to weep there. Then when Mary was come where Jesus was, and saw him, she fell down at his feet, saying unto him, Lord, if thou hadst been here, my brother had not died. [33] When Jesus therefore saw her weeping, and the Jews also weeping which [34] came with her, he groaned in the spirit, and was troubled. And said, Where have ye laid him ? They say unto him, Lord, come and see. [35] [36] [37] Jesus wept. Then said the Jews, Behold how he loved him ! And some of them said, Could not this man, which opened the eyes of the blind, have caused that even this man should not have died ?

[38] Jesus therefore again groaning in himself, cometh to the grave. It was [39] a cave, and a stone lay upon it. Jesus said, Take ye away the stone. Martha, the sister of him that was dead, saith unto him, Lord, by this time [40] he stinketh : for he hath been *dead* four days. Jesus saith unto her, Said I not unto thee, that if thou wouldest believe, thou shouldest see the glory [41] of God ? Then they took away the stone *from the place* where the dead was laid. And Jesus lifted up *his* eyes, and said, Father, I thank thee that [42] thou hast heard me : [1] and I knew that thou hearest me always : but because of the people which stand by, I said *it ;* that they may believe that thou [43] hast sent me. And when he thus had spoken, he cried with a loud voice, [44] Lazarus, come forth. And he that was dead came forth, bound hand and foot with grave-clothes : and his face was bound about with a napkin. Jesus saith unto them, Loose him, and let him go. [45] Then many of the Jews which came to Mary, and had seen the things [46] which Jesus did, believed on him. But some of them went their ways to the Pharisees, and told them what things Jesus had done.

§ 93. *The counsel of Caiaphas against Jesus. He retires from Jerusalem.—* JERUSALEM. EPHRAIM.

JOHN XI. 47—54.

[47] Then gathered the chief priests and the Pharisees a council, and said, [48] What do we ? for this man doeth many miracles. If we let him thus alone, all *men* will believe on him : and the Romans shall come, and take away [49] both our place and nation. And one of them, *named* Caiaphas, being the [50] high priest that same year, said unto them, Ye know nothing at all, [1] nor consider that it is expedient for us, that one man should die for the people, [51] and that the whole nation perish not. And this spake he not of himself : but being high priest that year, he prophesied that Jesus should die for that [52] nation ; [1] and not for that nation only, but that also he should gather together [53] in one the children of God that were scattered abroad. Then from that day forth they took counsel together for to put him to death. [54] Jesus therefore walked no more openly among the Jews ; but went thence into a country near to the wilderness, into a city called Ephraim, and there continued with his disciples.

§ 94. *Jesus beyond Jordan is followed by multitudes. The healing of the infirm Woman on the Sabbath.*—VALLEY OF JORDAN ? PEREA.

MATTH. XIX. 1, 2.	MARK X. 1.
[1] And it came to pass, *that* when Jesus had finished these sayings, he departed from Galilee, and came into the coasts of Judea, beyond [2] Jordan : ' and great multitudes followed him, and he healed them there.	[1] And he arose from thence, and cometh into the coasts of Judea, by the farther side of Jordan : and the people resort unto him again ; and, as he was wont, he taught them again.

LUKE XIII. 10—21.

[10] [11] And he was teaching in one of the synagogues on the sabbath. And behold, there was a woman which had a spirit of infirmity eighteen [12] years, and was bowed together, and could in no wise lift up *herself.* And when Jesus saw her, he called *her to him,* and said unto her, Woman, thou [13] art loosed from thine infirmity. And he laid *his* hands on her : and imme- [14] diately she was made straight, and glorified God. And the ruler of the synagogue answered with indignation, because that Jesus had healed on the sabbath-day, and said unto the people, There are six days in which men ought to work : in them therefore come and be healed, and not on the [15] sabbath-day. The Lord then answered him, and said, *Thou* hypocrite, doth not each one of you on the sabbath loose *his* ox or *his* ass from the [16] stall, and lead h*im* away to watering ? And ought not this woman, being a daughter of Abraham, whom Satan hath bound, lo, these eighteen years, be [17] loosed from this bond on the sabbath-day ? And when he had said these things, all his adversaries were ashamed : and all the people rejoiced for all the glorious things that were done by him.

[18] Then said he, Unto what is the kingdom of God like ? and whereunto [19] shall I resemble it ? It is like a grain of mustard-seed, which a man took, and cast into his garden, and it grew, and waxed a great tree ; and the fowls [20] of the air lodged in the branches of it. And again he said, Whereunto [21] shall I liken the kingdom of God ? It is like leaven, which a woman took and hid in three measures of meal, till the whole was leavened.

§ 95. *Our Lord goes teaching and journeying towards Jerusalem. He is warned against Herod.*—PEREA.

LUKE XIII. 22—35.

[22] And he went through the cities and villages, teaching, and journeying toward Jerusalem.
[23] Then said one unto him, Lord, are there few that be saved ? And he [24] said unto them, ' Strive to enter in at the strait gate : for many, I say unto [25] you, will seek to enter in, and shall not be able. When once the Master of the house is risen up, and hath shut to the door, and ye begin to stand without, and to knock at the door, saying, Lord, Lord, open unto us ; and [26] he shall answer and say unto you, I know you not whence ye are : ' then shall ye begin to say, We have eaten and drunk in thy presence, and thou [27] hast taught in our streets. But he shall say, I tell you, I know you not [28] whence ye are ; depart from me, all *ye* workers of iniquity. There shall be weeping and gnashing of teeth, when ye shall see Abraham, and Isaac, and Jacob, and all the prophets, in the kingdom of God, and you *yourselves* [29] thrust out. And they shall come from the east, and *from* the west, and

LUKE XIII.

from the north, and *from* the south, and shall sit down in the kingdom of
³⁰ God.   And behold, there are last, which shall be first ; and there are first,
which shall be last.   .
³¹   The same day there came certain of the Pharisees, saying unto him, Get
³² thee out, and depart hence ; for Herod will kill thee.   And he said unto
them, Go ye and tell that fox, Behold, I cast out devils, and I do cures
³³ to-day and to-morrow, and the third *day* I shall be perfected.   Nevertheless, I must walk to-day and to-morrow, and the *day* following : for it
³⁴ cannot be that a prophet perish out of Jerusalem.   O Jerusalem, Jerusalem,
which killest the prophets, and stonest them that are sent unto thee ; how
often would I have gathered thy children together, as a hen *doth gather* her
³⁵ brood under *her* wings, and ye would not !   Behold, your house is left unto
you desolate ᵃ   And verily, I say unto you, Ye shall not see me, until *the
time* come when ye shall say, Blessed *is* he that cometh in the name of
the Lord.

§ 96. *Our Lord dines with a chief Pharisee on the Sabbath.   Incidents.*—
PEREA.

LUKE XIV. 1—24.

¹   And it came to pass, as he went into the house of one of the chief Phari-
² sees to eat bread on the sabbath-day, that they watched him.   And behold,
³ there was a certain man before him which had the dropsy.   And Jesus
answering, spake unto the lawyers and Pharisees, saying, Is it lawful to
⁴ heal on the sabbath-day ?   And they held their peace.   And he took *him*,
⁵ and healed him, and let him go : ¹ and answered them, saying, Which of
you shall have an ass or an ox fallen into a pit, and will not straightway
⁶ pull him out on the sabbath-day ?   And they could not answer him again
to these things.
⁷   And he put forth a parable to those which were bidden, when he marked
⁸ how they chose out the chief rooms ; saying unto them, ¹ When thou art
bidden of any *man* to a wedding, sit not down in the highest room,ᵇ lest a
⁹ more honourable man than thou be bidden of him ; ¹ and he that bade thee
and him come and say to thee, Give this man place ; and thou begin with
¹⁰ shame to take the lowest room.   But when thou art bidden, go and sit
down in the lowest room ; that when he that bade thee cometh, he may
say unto thee, Friend, go up higher : then shalt thou have worship in the
¹¹ presence of them that sit at meat with thee.   For whosoever exalteth himself shall be abased, and he that humbleth himself shall be exalted.
¹²   Then said he also to him that bade him, When thou makest a dinner or
a supper, call not thy friends, nor thy brethren, neither thy kinsmen, nor
thy rich neighbours ; lest they also bid thee again, and a recompense be
¹³ made thee.   But when thou makest a feast, call the poor, the maimed, the
¹⁴ lame, the blind ; ¹ and thou shalt be blessed : for they cannot recompense
thee : for thou shalt be recompensed at the resurrection of the just.
¹⁵   And when one of them that sat at meat with him heard these things, he
said unto him, Blessed *is* he that shall eat bread in the kingdom of God.
¹⁶ Then said he unto him, A certain man made a great supper, and bade
¹⁷ many : ¹ and sent his servant at supper-time, to say to them that were bid-
¹⁸ den, Come, for all things are now ready.   And they all with one *consent*

ᵃ **35.** Comp. Ps. 69, 25. Jer. 12, 7. 22, 5.   ᵇ **8.** Comp. Prov. 25, 6

LUKE XIV.

began to make excuse. The first said unto him, I have bought a piece of ground, and I must needs go and see it: I pray thee have me excused.
[19] And another said, I have bought five yoke of oxen, and I go to prove them:
[20] I pray thee have me excused. And another said, I have married a wife:
[21] and therefore I cannot come. So that servant came, and shewed his lord these things. Then the master of the house being angry, said to his servant, Go out quickly into the streets and lanes of the city, and bring in
[22] hither the poor, and the maimed, and the halt, and the blind. And the servant said, Lord, it is done as thou hast commanded, and yet there is
[23] room. And the lord said unto the servant, Go out into the highways and
[24] hedges, and compel them to come in, that my house may be filled. For I say unto you, that none of those men which were bidden, shall taste of my supper.

§ 97. *What is required of true Disciples.*—PEREA.

LUKE XIV. 25—35.

[25]   And there went great multitudes with him: and he turned, and said unto
[26] them, ' If any man come to me, and hate not his father, and mother, and wife, and children, and brethren, and sisters, yea, and his own life also, he
[27] cannot be my disciple. And whosoever doth not bear his cross, and come
[28] after me, cannot be my disciple. For which of you intending to build a tower, sitteth not down first, and counteth the cost, whether he have *suffi-*
[29] *cient* to finish *it?* Lest haply after he hath laid the foundation, and is not
[30] able to finish *it*, all that behold *it* begin to mock him, ' saying, This man
[31] began to build, and was not able to finish. Or what king going to make war against another king, sitteth not down first, and consulteth whether he be able with ten thousand to meet him that cometh against him with twenty
[32] thousand? Or else, while the other is yet a great way off, he sendeth an
[33] ambassage, and desireth conditions of peace. So likewise, whosoever he be of you that forsaketh not all that he hath, he cannot be my disciple.
[34] Salt *is* good: but if the salt have lost his savour, wherewith shall it be
[35] seasoned? It is neither fit for the land, nor yet for the dunghill; *but* men cast it out. He that hath ears to hear, let him hear.

§ 98. *Parable of the Lost Sheep, etc. Parable of the Prodigal Son.*—PEREA

LUKE XV. 1—32.

[1]   Then drew near unto him all the publicans and sinners for to hear him.
[2] And the Pharisees and scribes murmured, saying, This man receiveth sinners, and eateth with them.
[3][4]   And he spake this parable unto them, saying, ' What man of you having an hundred sheep, if he lose one of them, doth not leave the ninety and nine in the wilderness, and go after that which is lost, until he find it?
[5][6] And when he hath found *it*, he layeth *it* on his shoulders, rejoicing. And when he cometh home, he called together *his* friends and neighbours, saying unto them, Rejoice with me ; for I have found my sheep which was lost.
[7] I say unto you, that likewise joy shall be in heaven over one sinner that repenteth, more than over ninety and nine just persons which need no repentance.
[8]   Either what woman having ten pieces of silver, if she lose one piece, doth not light a candle, and sweep the house, and seek diligently till she find

LUKE XV.

⁹ *it?* And when she hath found *it,* she calleth *her* friends and *her* neighbours together, saying, Rejoice with me ; for I have found the piece which
¹⁰ I had lost. Likewise, I say unto you, There is joy in the presence of the
angels of God over one sinner that repenteth.
¹¹ ¹² And he said, A certain man had two sons: ' and the younger of them
said to *his* father, Father, give me the portion of goods that falleth *to me.*
¹³ And he divided unto them *his* living. ' And not many days after, the
younger son gathered all together, and took his journey into a far country,
¹⁴ and there wasted his substance with riotous living. And when he had spent
all, there arose a mighty famine in that land ; and he began to be in want.
¹⁵ And he went and joined himself to a citizen of that country ; and he sent
¹⁶ him into his fields to feed swine. And he would fain have filled his belly
with the husks that the swine did eat ; and no man gave unto him.
¹⁷ And when he came to himself, he said, How many hired servants of my
¹⁸ father's have bread enough and to spare, and I·perish with hunger! I will
arise and go to my father, and will say unto him, Father, I have sinned
¹⁹ against heaven, and before thee, ' and am no more worthy to be called thy
²⁰ son: make me as one of thy hired servants. And he arose, and came to
his father. But when he was yet a great way off, his father saw him, and
²¹ had compassion, and ran, and fell on his neck, and kissed him. And the
son said unto him, Father, I have sinned against heaven, and in thy sight,
²² and am no more worthy to be called thy son. But the father said to his
servants, Bring forth the best robe, and put *it* on him ; and put a ring on his
²³ hand, and shoes on *his* feet: ' and bring hither the fatted calf, and kill *it ;*
²⁴·and let us eat, and be merry : ' for this my son was dead, and is alive again ;
²⁵ he was lost, and is found. And they began to be merry. ' Now his elder
son was in the field : and as he came and drew nigh to the house, he heard
²⁶ music and dancing. And he called one of the servants, and asked what
²⁷ these things meant. And he said unto him, Thy brother is come ; and thy
father hath killed the fatted calf, because he hath received him safe and
²⁸ sound. And he was angry, and would not go in ; therefore came his father
²⁹ out, and entreated him. And he answering, said to *his* father, Lo, these
many years do I serve thee, neither transgressed I at any time thy commandment ; and yet thou never gavest me a kid, that I might make merry
³⁰ with my friends : ' but as soon as this thy son was come, which hath de-
³¹ voured thy living with harlots, thou hast killed for him the fatted calf. And
he said unto him, Son, thou art ever with me ; and all that I have is thine
³² It was meet that we should make merry, and be glad : for this thy brother
was dead, and is alive again ; and was lost, and is found.

§ 99. *Parable of the Unjust Steward.*—PEREA.

LUKE XVI. 1—13.

¹ And he said also unto his disciples, There was a certain rich man which
had a steward ; and the same was accused unto him that he had wasted·
² his goods. And he called him, and said unto him, How is it that I hear
this of thee ? give an account of thy stewardship: for thou mayest be no
³ longer steward. Then the steward said within himself, What shall I do ?
for my lord taketh away from me the stewardship: I cannot dig ; to beg I
⁴ am ashamed. I am resolved what to do, that when I am put out of the
⁵ stewardship, they may receive me into their houses. So he called every
one of his lord's debtors *unto him,* and said unto the first, How much owest

LUKE XVI.

⁶ thou unto my lord? ' And he said, An hundred measures of oil. And he
⁷ said unto him, Take thy bill, and sit down quickly, and write fifty. Then
said he to another, And how much owest thou? And he said, An hundred
measures of wheat. And he said unto him, Take thy bill, and write four-
⁸ score. And the lord commended the unjust steward, because he had done
wisely: for the children of this world are in their generation wiser than the
children of light.
⁹ And I say unto you, Make to yourselves friends of the mammon of
unrighteousness; that when ye fail, they may receive you into everlasting
¹⁰ habitations. He that is faithful in that which is least, is faithful also in
¹¹ much; and he that is unjust in the least, is unjust also in much. If therefore ye have not been faithful in the unrighteous mammon, who will commit
¹² to your trust the true *riches*? And if ye have not been faithful in that
¹³ which is another man's, who shall give you that which is your own? No
servant can serve two masters; for either he will hate the one, and love
the other; or else he will hold to the one, and despise the other. Ye can-
nôt serve God and mammon.

§ 100. *The Pharisees reproved. Parable of the Rich Man and Lazarus.—*
PEREA.

LUKE XVI. 14—31.

¹⁴ And the Pharisees also, who were covetous, heard all these things, and
¹⁵ they derided him. And he said unto them, Ye are they which justify yourselves before men; but God knoweth your hearts: for that which is highly
¹⁶ esteemed among men, is abomination in the sight of God. The law and
the prophets *were* until John: since that time the kingdom of God is
¹⁷ preached, and every man presseth into it. And it is easier for heaven and
¹⁸ earth to pass, than one tittle of the law to fail. Whosoever putteth away
his wife, and marrieth another, committeth adultery; and whosoever marrieth her that is put away from *her* husband, committeth adultery.
¹⁹ There was a certain rich man, which was clothed in purple and fine
²⁰ linen, and fared sumptuously every day: ' and there was a certain beggar
²¹ named Lazarus, which was laid at his gate, full of sores, ' and desiring to
be fed with the crumbs which fell from the rich man's table: moreover, the
²² dogs came and licked his sores. And it came to pass, that the beggar died,
and was carried by the angels into Abraham's bosom. The rich man also
²³ died, and was buried: ' and in hell he lifted up his eyes, being in torments,
²⁴ and seeth Abraham afar off, and Lazarus in his bosom. And he cried, and
said, Father Abraham, have mercy on me, and send Lazarus, that he may
dip the tip of his finger in water, and cool my tongue: for I am tormented
²⁵ in this flame. But Abraham said, Son, remember that thou in thy lifetime
receivedst thy good things, and likewise Lazarus evil things: but now he
²⁶ is comforted, and thou art tormented. And besides all this, between us
and you there is a great gulf fixed: so that they which would pass from
hence to you, cannot; neither can they pass to us, that *would come* from
²⁷ thence. Then he said, I pray thee therefore, father, that thou wouldest
²⁸ send him to my father's house: ' for I have five brethren; that he may
²⁹ testify unto them, lest they also come into this place of torment. Abraham
saith unto him, They have Moses and the prophets; let them hear them.
³⁰ And he said, Nay, father Abraham: but if one went unto them from the
³¹ dead, they will repent. And he said unto him, If they hear not Moses and
the prophets, neither will they be persuaded, though one rose from the dead.

§ 101. *Jesus inculcates forbearance, faith, humility.*—PEREA.

LUKE XVII. 1—10.

[1] Then said he unto the disciples, It is impossible but that offences will
[2] come : but wo *unto him* through whom they come ! It were better for him
that a millstone were hanged about his neck, and he cast into the sea, than
[3] that he should offend one of these little ones. Take heed to yourselves : if
thy brother trespass against thee, rebuke him ; and if he repent, forgive him.
[4] And if he trespass against thee seven times in a day, and seven times in a
day turn again to thee, saying, I repent ; thou shalt forgive him.[a]
[5][6] And the apostles said unto the Lord, Increase our faith. And the Lord
said, If ye had faith as a grain of mustard-seed, ye might say unto this
sycamine-tree, Be thou plucked up by the root, and be thou planted in the
[7] sea ; and it should obey you. But which of you having a servant plough-
ing, or feeding cattle, will say unto him by and by, when he is come out of
[8] the field, Go and sit down to meat ? ¹ and will not rather say unto him,
Make ready wherewith I may sup, and gird thyself, and serve me, till I
[9] have eaten and drunken ; and afterward thou shalt eat and drink ? Doth
he thank that servant, because he did the things that were commanded him ?
[10] I trow not. ¹ So likewise ye, when ye shall have done all those things which
are commanded you, say, We are unprofitable servants : we have done
that which was our duty to do.

§ 102. *Christ's coming will be sudden.*—PEREA.

LUKE XVII. 20—37.

[20] And when he was demanded of the Pharisees, when the kingdom of God
should come, he answered them and said, The kingdom of God cometh
[21] not with observation. Neither shall they say, Lo here ! or, Lo there ! for
[22] behold, the kingdom of God is within you. And he said unto the disciples,
The days will come, when ye shall desire to see one of the days of the
[23] Son of man, and ye shall not see *it*. And they shall say to you, See here !
[24] or, See there ! go not after *them*, nor follow *them*. For as the lightning
that lighteneth out of the one *part* under heaven, shineth unto the other
[25] *part* under heaven ; so shall also the Son of man be in his day. But first
[26] must he suffer many things, and be rejected of this generation. And as it
was in the days of Noe, so shall it be also in the days of the Son of man.
[27] They did eat, they drank, they married wives, they were given in marriage,
until the day that Noe entered into the ark, and the flood came, and
[28] destroyed them all.[b] Likewise also as it was in the days of Lot : they did
[29] eat, they drank, they bought, they sold, they planted, they builded ; ¹ but
the same day that Lot went out of Sodom, it rained fire and brimstone from
[30] heaven, and destroyed *them* all : [c] ¹ even thus shall it be in the day when
[31] the Son of man is revealed. In that day, he which shall be upon the
house-top, and his stuff in the house, let him not come down to take it
[32] away : and he that is in the field, let him likewise not return back. Re-
[33] member Lot's wife.[d] Whosoever shall seek to save his life, shall lose it ;
[34] and whosoever shall lose his life, shall preserve it. I tell you, in that night
there shall be two *men* in one bed ; the one shall be taken, and the other

---

a **4.** Comp. Lev. 19, 17. 18.　　　　b **27.** Gen. 7, 4. 7
c **29.** Gen. 19, 15 sq.　　　　　　　d **33.** Gen. 19, 26.

LUKE XVII.

¹⁵ shall be left. Two *women* shall be grinding together; the one shall be *¹⁶* taken, and the other left. Two *men* shall be in the field; the one shall be *¹⁷* taken, and the other left. And they answered and said unto him, Where, Lord? And he said unto them, Wheresoever the body *is*, thither will the eagles be gathered together.

§ 103. *Parables: The Importunate Widow. The Pharisee and Publican.*—PEREA.

LUKE XVIII. 1—14.

¹ And he spake a parable unto them *to this end*, that men ought always ² to pray, and not to faint; ' saying, There was in a city a judge, which ³ feared not God, neither regarded man. And there was a widow in that ⁴ city; and she came unto him, saying, Avenge me of mine adversary. And he would not for a while: but afterward he said within himself, Though I ⁵ fear not God, nor regard man, ' yet, because this widow troubleth me, I ⁶ will avenge her, lest by her continual coming she weary me. And the ⁷ Lord said, Hear what the unjust judge saith. And shall not God avenge his own elect, which cry day and night unto him, though he bear long with ⁸ them? ' I tell you that he will avenge them speedily. Nevertheless, when the Son of man cometh, shall he find faith on the earth? ⁹ And he spake this parable unto certain which trusted in themselves ¹⁰ that they were righteous, and despised others: Two men went up into the ¹¹ temple to pray; the one a Pharisee, and the other a publican. The Pharisee stood and prayed thus with himself, God, I thank thee, that I am not as other men *are*, extortioners, unjust, adulterers, or even as this publican. ¹² ¹³ I fast twice in the week, I give tithes of all that I possess. And the publican, standing afar off, would not lift up so much as *his* eyes unto heaven, ⁴ but smote upon his breast, saying, God be merciful to me a sinner. I tell you, this man went down to his house justified *rather* than the other: for every one that exalteth himself shall be abased; and he that humbleth himself shall be exalted.

§ 104. *Precepts respecting Divorce.*—PEREA.

MATTH. XIX. 3—12.	MARK X. 2—12.
³ The Pharisees also came unto him, tempting him, and saying unto him, Is it lawful for a man to put away his wife for every cause?	² And the Pharisees came to him, and asked him, Is it lawful for a man to put away *his* wife? tempt- ³ ing him. And he answered and said unto them, What did Moses ⁴ command you? And they said, Moses suffered to write a bill of divorcement, and to put *her* away.* ⁵ And Jesus answered and said unto
⁴ And he answered and said unto them, Have ye not read, that he which made *them* at the beginning, ⁵ made them male and female,ᵇ ' and said, For this cause shall a man	them, For the hardness of your heart he wrote you this precept: ⁶ ' but from the beginning of the creation, God made them male and fe- ⁷ male.ᵇ For this cause shall a man

ᵃ 4. Deut. 24 1. ᵇ 4 etc. Gen. 1, 27

MATTH. XIX.	MARK X.

leave father and mother, and shall cleave to his wife: and they twain [a] shall be one flesh ? [a] Wherefore they are no more twain, but one flesh. What therefore God hath joined together, let not man put [7] asunder. They say unto him, Why did Moses then command to give a writing of divorcement, and to put [8] her away? [b] He saith unto them, Moses, because of the hardness of your hearts, suffered you to put away your wives; but from the beginning it was not so. [9] And I say unto you, whosoever shall put away his wife, except it be for fornication, and shall marry another, committeth adultery: and whoso marrieth her which is put away, doth commit adultery.

leave his father and mother, and [8] cleave to his wife; [7] and they twain shall be one flesh: [a] so then they are no more twain, but one flesh. [9] What therefore, God hath joined together, let not man put asunder. [10] And in the house his disciples asked him again of the same matter.

[11] And he saith unto them, Whosoever shall put away his wife, and marry another, committeth adultery against [12] her. And if a woman shall put away her husband, and be married to another, she committeth adultery.

[10] His disciples say unto him, If the [11] case of the man be so with his wife, it is not good to marry. But he said unto them, All men cannot receive this saying, save they to whom it is [12] given. For there are some eunuchs, which were so born from their mother's womb: and there are some eunuchs, which were made eunuchs of men: and there be eunuchs, which have made themselves eunuchs for the kingdom of heaven's sake. He that is able to receive it, let him receive it.

§ 105. *Jesus receives and blesses little children.*—PEREA.

MATTH. XIX. 13—15.	MARK X. 13—16.	LUKE XVIII. 15—17.

[13] Then were there brought unto him little children, that he should put his hands on them, and pray: and the disciples rebuked them. [14] But Jesus said, Suffer little children, and forbid them not, to come unto me: for of such is the kingdom of [15] heaven. And he laid his hands on them, and departed thence.

[13] And they brought young children to him, that he should touch them; and his disciples rebuked those that [14] brought them. But when Jesus saw it, he was much displeased, and said unto them, Suffer little children to come unto me, and forbid them not: for of such is the [15] kingdom of God. Verily I say unto you, Whosoever shall not receive the kingdom of God [16] as a little child, he shall not enter therein. And he took them up in his arms, put his hands upon them, and blessed them.

[15] And they brought unto him also infants, that he would touch them: but when his disciples saw it, they [16] rebuked them. But Jesus called them unto him, and said, Suffer little children to come unto me, and forbid them not: for of such is the kingdom of God. [17] Verily I say unto you, Whosoever shall not receive the kingdom of God as a little child, shall in no wise enter therein.

---

a 5 etc. Gen. 2, 24.   b 7. Deut. 24, 1.

§ 106. *The rich Young Man. Parable of the Labourers in the Vineyard.—*
PEREA.

MATTH. XIX. 16—30. XX. 1—16.	MARK X. 17—31.	LUKE XVIII. 18—30.
16 And behold, one came and said unto him, Good Master, what good thing shall I do that I may have 17 eternal life? And he said unto him, Why callest thou me good? *there is* none good but one, *that is*, God: but if thou wilt enter into life, keep the com- 18 mandments. He saith unto him, Which? Jesus said,ᵃ Thou shalt do no murder, Thou shalt not commit adul- tery, Thou shalt not steal, Thou shalt not bear false witness, 19 ᵗ Honour thy father and *thy* mother: and, Thou shalt love thy neigh- 20 bour as thyself. The young man saith unto him, All these things have I kept from my youth up: what lack I 21 yet? Jesus said unto him, If thou wilt be perfect, go *and* sell that thou hast, and give to the poor, and thou shalt have treasure in hea- ven: and come, fol- low me.	17 And when he was gone forth into the way, there came one run- ning, and kneeled to him, and asked him, Good Master, what shall I do that I may inherit eternal life? 18 And Jesus said unto him, Why callest thou me good? *there is* none good, but one, 19 *that is*, God. Thou knowest the command- ments,ᵃ Do not commit adultery, Do not kill, Do not steal, Do not bear false witness, De- fraud not, Honour thy father and mother. 20 And he answered and said unto him, Master, all these have I ob- served from my youth	18 And a certain ruler asked him, saying, Good Master, what shall I do to inherit eternal life? 19 And Jesus said unto him, Why callest thou me good? none *is* good, save one, *that is*, God. 20 Thou knowest the commandments,ᵃ Do not commit adul- tery, Do not kill, Do not steal, Do not bear false witness, Honour thy father and thy mother.
	21 Then Jesus beholding him loved him, and said unto him, One thing thou lackest: go thy way, sell whatso- ever thou hast, and give to the poor, and thou shalt have trea- sure in heaven; and come, take up the cross,	21 And he said, All these have I kept from my youth up. 22 Now when Jesus heard these things, he said unto him, Yet lackest thou one thing: sell all that thou hast, and dis- tribute unto the poor, and thou shalt have treasure in heaven: and come, follow me.
22 But when the young man heard that saying, he went away sorrowful: for he had great possessions. 23 Then said Jesus unto his disciples, Verily I say unto you, that a rich man shall hardly	22 and follow me. And he was sad at that saying, and went away griev- ed: for he had great 23 possessions. And Jesus looked round about, and saith unto his dis- ciples, How hardly shall they that have	23 And when he had heard this, he was very sorrowful: for he was very rich. 24 And when Jesus saw that he was very sor- rowful, he said, How hardly shall they that

18 etc. Ex. 20, 12 sq. Deut. 5, 16 sq. Lev. 19, 18.
9*

MATTH. XIX.	MARK X.	LUKE XVIII.
enter into the kingdom of heaven.	riches enter into the ²⁴ kingdom of God! And	have riches enter into the kingdom of God!

the disciples were astonished at his words. But Jesus answereth again, and saith unto them, Children, how hard is it for them that trust in riches to enter into the kingdom of

²⁴ And again I say unto you, It is easier for a camel to go through the eye of a needle, than for a rich man to enter into the kingdom ²⁵ of God. When his disciples heard *it*, they were exceedingly amazed, saying, Who then can be saved? ²⁶ But Jesus beheld *them*, and said unto them, With men this is impossible, but with God all things are possible. ²⁷ Then answered Peter, and said unto him, Behold, we have forsaken all, and followed thee; what shall we have ²⁸ therefore? And Jesus said unto them, Verily I say unto you, That ye which have followed me in the regeneration, when the Son of man shall sit in the throne of his glory, ye also shall sit upon twelve thrones, judging the twelve tribes of Israel. ²⁹ And every one that hath forsaken houses, or brethren, or sisters, or father, or mother, or wife, or children, or lands, for my name's sake, shall receive an hundred-fold, and shall inherit everlasting life. ³⁰ But many *that are* first shall be last; and the last first.	²⁵ God! It is easier for a camel to go through the eye of a needle, than for a rich man to enter into the kingdom ²⁶ of God. And they were astonished out of measure, saying among themselves, Who then ²⁷ can be saved? And Jesus looking upon them, saith, With men *it is* impossible, but not with God: for with God all things are possible. ²⁸ Then Peter began to say unto him, Lo, we have left all, and have ²⁹ followed thee. And Jesus answered and said, Verily I say unto you, There is no man that hath left house, or brethren, or sisters, or father, or mother, or wife, or children, or lands, for my sake, and the gos- ³⁰ pel's, ' but he shall receive an hundred-fold now in this time, houses, and brethren, and sisters, and mothers, and children, and lands, with persecutions; and in the world to come, eternal life. ³¹ But many *that are* first shall be last; and the last first.	²⁵ For it is easier for a camel to go through a needle's eye, than for a rich man to enter into the kingdom of God. ²⁶ And they that heard *it*, said, Who then can be saved? ²⁷ And he said, The things which are impossible with men, are possible with God. ²⁸ Then Peter said, Lo, we have left all, and ²⁹ followed thee. And he said unto them, Verily I say unto you, There is no man that hath left house, or parents, or brethren, or wife, or children, for the kingdom of God's sake, ³⁰ ' who shall not receive manifold more in this present time, and in the world to come life everlasting.

MATTH. XX.

¹   For the kingdom of heaven is like unto a man *that is* an householder, which
² went out early in the morning to hire labourers into his vineyard. And when he

MATTH. XX.

had agreed with the labourers for a penny a day, he sent them into his vine-
³ yard. And he went out about the third hour, and saw others standing idle in
⁴ the market-place,¹ and said unto them, Go ye also into the vineyard ; and what-
⁵ soever is right, I will give you. And they went their way. ¹ Again he went
⁶ out about the sixth and ninth hour, and did likewise. And about the
eleventh hour he went out, and found others standing idle, and saith unto
⁷ them, Why stand ye here all the day idle ? They say unto him, Because
no man hath hired us. He saith unto them, Go ye also into the vineyard
⁸ and whatsoever is right, *that* shall ye receive. So when even was come,
the lord of the vineyard saith unto his steward, Call the labourers, and give
⁹ them *their* hire, beginning from the last unto the first. And when they
came that *were hired* about the eleventh hour, they received every man a
¹⁰ penny. But when the first came, they supposed that they should have re-
¹¹ ceived more ; and they likewise received every man a penny. And when
they had received *it*, they murmured against the good man of the house,
¹² ¹ saying, These last have wrought *but* one hour, and thou hast made them
¹³ equal unto us, which have borne the burden and heat of the day. But
he answered one of them, and said, Friend, I do thee no wrong : didst not
¹⁴ thou agree with me for a penny ? Take *that* thine *is*, and go thy way : I
¹⁵ will give unto this last, even as unto thee. Is it not lawful for me to do
¹⁶ what I will with mine own ? is thine eye evil because I am good ? So the
last shall be first, and the first last : for many be called, but few chosen.

§ 107. *Jesus a third time foretells his Death and Resurrection.*
[See §§ 74, 77.]—PEREA.

MATTH. XX. 17—19.	MARK X. 32—34.	LUKE XVIII. 31—34.
¹⁷ And Jesus going up to Jerusalem, took the twelve disciples apart in the way, and said unto them,	³² And they were in the way, going up to Jerusalem ; and Jesus went before them : and they were amazed ; and as they followed, they were afraid. And he took again the twelve, and began to tell them what things should happen unto	³¹ Then he toook *unto him* the twelve, and said unto them,
¹⁸ Behold, we go up to Jerusalem ; and the Son of man shall be betrayed unto the chief priests, and unto the scribes, and they shall condemn him to death, ¹⁹ ¹ and shall deliver him to the Gentiles to mock, and to scourge, and to crucify *him :* and the third day he shall rise again.	³³ him, ¹ *saying*, Behold, we go up to Jerusalem ; and the Son of man shall be delivered unto the chief priests, and unto the scribes ; and they shall condemn him to death, and shall deliver him to the Gentiles ; ³⁴ ¹ and they shall mock him, and shall scourge him, and shall spit upon him, and shall kill him : and the third day he shall rise again.	Behold, we go up to Jerusalem, and all things that are written by the prophets concerning the Son of man shall be accom- ³² plished. For he shall be delivered unto the Gentiles, and shall be mocked, and spitefully entreated, and spitted ³³ on ; ¹ and they shall scourge *him*, and put him to death ; and the third day he shall rise

³⁴ again. And they understood none of these things : and this saying
was hid from them, neither knew they the things which were spoken.

§ 108. *James and John prefer their ambitious request.*—PEREA.

MATTH. XX. 20—28.	MARK X. 35—45.

[20] Then came to him the mother of Zebedee's children, with her sons, worshipping *him*, and desiring a certain thing of him. [21] And he said unto her, What wilt thou? She saith unto him, Grant that these my two sons may sit, the one on thy right hand, and the other on the left, in thy kingdom. [22] But Jesus answered and said, Ye know not what ye ask. Are ye able to drink of the cup that I shall drink of, and to be baptized with the baptism that I am baptized with? They [23] say unto him, We are able. And he saith unto them, Ye shall drink indeed of my cup, and be baptized with the baptism that I am baptized with: but, to sit on my right hand, and on my left, is not mine to give, but *it shall be given to them* for whom it is prepared of my Father. [24] And when the ten heard *it*, they were moved with indignation against [25] the two brethren. But Jesus called them *unto him*, and said, Ye know that the princes of the Gentiles exercise dominion over them, and they that are great exercise authority upon them. [26] But it shall not be so among you: but whosoever will be great among you, let him be your [27] minister;¹ and whosoever will be chief among you, let him be your [28] servant:¹ even as the Son of man came not to be ministered unto, but to minister, and to give his life a ransom for many.

[35] And James and John, tne sons of Zebedee, come unto him, saying, Master, we would that thou shouldest do for us whatsoever we shall desire. [36] And he said unto them, What would ye that I should do for you? [37] They said unto him, Grant unto us that we may sit, one on thy right hand, and the other on thy left hand, in thy glory. [38] But Jesus said unto them, Ye know not what ye ask: can ye drink of the cup that I drink of? and be baptized with the baptism that I am baptized with? [39] And they said unto him, We can. And Jesus said unto them, Ye shall drink of the cup that I drink of; and with the baptism that I am baptized withal shall ye [40] be baptized:¹ but to sit on my right hand and on my left hand, is not mine to give, but *it shall be given to them* for whom it is prepared. [41] And when the ten heard *it*, they began to be much displeased with [42] James and John. But Jesus calleth them *to him*, and saith unto them, Ye know that they which are accounted to rule over the Gentiles, exercise lordship over them; and their great ones exercise authority [43] upon them. But so shall it not be among you: but whosoever will be great among you, shall be your min- [44] ister;¹ and whosoever of you will be the chiefest, shall be servant of [45] all. For even the Son of man came not to be ministered unto, but to minister, and to give his life a ransom for many.

§ 109. *The healing of two blind men near Jericho.*

MATTH. XX. 29—34.	MARK X. 46—52.	LUKE XVIII. 35—43. XIX. 1.

[29] And as they departed from Jericho, a great multitude followed [30] him. And behold, two

[46] And they came to Jericho: and as he went out of Jericho with his disciples, and

[35] And it came to pass, that as he was come nigh unto Jericho, a certain blind man sat

MATTH. XX.	MARK X.	LUKE XVIII.

blind men sitting by the way-side, when [47] they heard that Jesus passed by, cried out, saying, Have mercy on us, O Lord, *thou* [31] son of David. And the multitude rebuked them, because they should hold their peace: but they cried the more, saying, Have mercy on us, O Lord, *thou* son of David. [32] And Jesus stood still, and called them,

a great number of people, blind Bartimeus, [36] the son of Timeus, sat by the highway side begging. And when he heard that it was Jesus of Nazareth, he began to cry out, and say, Jesus, *thou* son of David, have mercy on [48] me. And many charged him that he should hold his peace: but he cried the more a great deal, *Thou* son of David, have mercy on me. [49] And Jesus stood still, and commanded him to be called: and they call the blind man, saying unto him, Be of good comfort, rise; he calleth [50] thee. And he, casting away his garment, [51] rose, and came to Jesus. And Jesus answered and said unto

by the way-side begging; [1] and hearing the multitude pass by, he asked what it meant. [37] And they told him, that Jesus of Nazareth passeth by. And he cried, saying, Jesus, *thou* son of David, have mercy [39] on me. And they which went before rebuked him, that he should hold his peace: but he cried so much the more, *Thou* son of David, have mercy on me. [40] And Jesus stood and commanded him to be brought unto him:

and said, What will ye that I shall do unto [33] you? They say to him, Lord, that our eyes may be opened. [34] So Jesus had compassion *on them*, and touched their eyes: and immediately their eyes received sight, and they followed him.

him, What wilt thou that I should do unto thee? The blind man said unto him, Lord, [52] that I might receive my sight. And Jesus said unto him, Go thy way; thy faith hath made thee whole. And immediately he received his sight, and followed Jesus in the way.

and when he was come near, he asked [41] him, saying, What wilt thou that I shall do unto thee? And he said, Lord, that I may re- [42] ceive my sight. And Jesus said unto him, Receive thy sight: thy faith hath saved thee. [43] And immediately he received his sight, and followed him, glorifying God: and all the people, when they saw *it*, gave praise unto God.

XIX. [1] And *Jesus* entered and passed through Jericho.

§ 110. *The visit to Zaccheus.   Parable of the ten Pounds.*—JERICHO.

LUKE XIX. 2—28.

[2] And behold, *there was* a man named Zaccheus, which was the chief [3] among the publicans, and he was rich. And he sought to see Jesus who [4] he was; and could not for the press, because he was little of stature. And he ran before, and climbed up into a sycamore-tree to see him; for he was [5] to pass that *way*. And when Jesus came to the place, he looked up, and saw him, and said unto him, Zaccheus, make haste, and come down: for [6] to-day I must abide at thy house. And he made haste, and came down, [7] and received him joyfully. And when they saw *it*, they all murmured, saying, That he was gone to be guest with a man that is a sinner. And Zac-

LUKE XIX.

cheus stood, and said unto the Lord ; Behold, Lord, the half of my goods I give to the poor ; and if I have taken any thing from any man by false ac-
⁹ cusation, I restore *him* four-fold.   And Jesus said unto him, This day is salvation come to this house, forasmuch as he also is a son of Abraham.
¹⁰ For the Son of man is come to seek and to save that which was lost.
·¹ And as they heard these things, he added and spake a parable, because he was nigh to Jerusalem, and because they thought that the kingdom of
¹² God should immediately appear.   He said therefore, A certain nobleman went into a far country to receive for himself a kingdom, and to return.
¹³ And he called his ten servants, and delivered them ten pounds, and said un-
¹⁴ to them, Occupy till I come.   But his citizens hated him, and sent a mes-
¹⁵ sage after him, saying, We will not have this *man* to reign over us.   And it came to pass, that when he was returned, having received the kingdom, then he commanded these servants to be called unto him, to whom he had given the money, that he might know how much every man had gained by
¹⁶ trading.   Then came the first, saying, Lord, thy pound hath gained ten
¹⁷ pounds.   And he said unto him, Well, thou good servant : because thou
¹⁸ hast been faithful in a very little, have thou authority over ten cities.   And
¹⁹ the second came, saying, Lord, thy pound hath gained five pounds. And he said
²⁰ likewise to him, Be thou also over five cities.   And another came, saying, Lord, behold, *here is* thy pound, which I have kept laid up in a napkin :
²¹ ' for I feared thee, because thou art an austere man : thou takest up that
²² thou layedst not down, and reapest that thou didst not sow.   And he saith unto him, Out of thine own mouth will I judge thee, *thou* wicked servant. Thou knewest that I was an austere man, taking up that I laid not down,
²³ and reaping that I did not sow : ' wherefore then gavest not thou my money into the bank, that at my coming I might have required mine own with usury ?
²⁴ And he said unto them that stood by, Take from him the pound, and give
²⁵ *it* to him that hath ten pounds.   (And they said unto him, Lord, he hath
²⁶ ten pounds.)   For I say unto you, That unto every one which hath, shall be given ; and from him that hath not, even that he hath shall be taken
²⁷ away from him.   But those mine enemies, which would not that I should reign over them, bring hither, and slay *them* before me.
²⁸ And when he had thus spoken, he went before, ascending up to Jerusalem.

§ 111. *Jesus arrives at Bethany six days before the Passover.*—BETHANY.

JOHN XI. 55—57. XII. 1, 9—11.

⁵⁵ And the Jews' passover was nigh at hand : and many went out of the
⁵⁶ country up to Jerusalem before the passover, to purify themselves.   Then sought they for Jesus, and spake among themselves, as they stood in the
⁵⁷ temple, What think ye, that he will not come to the feast ?   Now both the chief priests and the Pharisees had given a commandment, that, if any man knew where he were, he should shew *it*, that they might take him.
XII. ¹   Then Jesus, six days before the passover, came to Bethany, where
⁹ Lazarus was which had been dead, whom he raised from the dead.—Much people of the Jews therefore knew that he was there : and they came, not for Jesus' sake only, but that they might see Lazarus also, whom he had
¹⁰ raised from the dead.   But the chief priests consulted that they might put
¹¹ Lazarus also to death ; ' because that by reason of him many of the Jews went away, and believed on Jesus.

PART VII.

OUR LORD'S PUBLIC ENTRY INTO JERUSALEM, AND THE SUBSEQUENT
TRANSACTIONS BEFORE THE FOURTH PASSOVER.

Time: *Four days.*

§ 112. *Our Lord's public Entry into Jerusalem.*—Bethany, Jerusalem.

Second Day of the Week.

JOHN XII. 12—19.

[12] ON the next day, much people that were come to the feast, when they heard that Jesus was coming to Jerusalem,—

MATTH. XXI. 1–11. 14–17.	MARK XI. 1—11.	LUKE XIX. 29—44.
[1] And when they drew nigh unto Jerusalem, and were come to Bethphage unto the mount of Olives, then sent Je- [2] sus two disciples, [1] saying unto them, Go into the village over against you, and straightway ye shall find an ass tied, and a colt with her: loose *them,* and bring *them* unto me.	[1] And when they came nigh to Jerusalem, unto Bethphage, and Bethany, at the mount of Olives, he sendeth forth two of his disci- [2] ples, [1] and saith unto them, Go your way into the village over against you:[·] and as soon as ye be entered into it, ye shall find a colt tied, whereon never man sat: loose him, and	[29] And it came to pass, when he was come nigh to Bethphage and Bethany, at the mount called *the mount* of Olives, he sent two of his disciples, [1] saying, Go ye into the village over against *you;* in the which at your en- tering ye shall find a colt tied, whereon yet never man sat: loose him, and bring *him*
And if any *man* say aught unto you, ye shall say, The Lord hath need of them: and straightway he will send them.— And the disciples went, and did as Jesus com- manded them.	[3] bring *him.* And if any man say unto you, Why do ye this? say ye that the Lord hath need of him; and straightway he will send him hither. [4] And they went their way, and found the colt tied by the door without, in a place where two	[31] *hither.* And if any man ask you, Why do ye loose *him?* thus shall ye say unto him, Because the Lord hath need of him. [32] And they that were sent went their way, and found even as he had said unto them.

MARK XI.

ways met; and they loose him. And certain of them that stood there said unto them, What do ye, loosing the colt? And they said unto them even as Jesus had commanded:

LUKE XIX.

33 And as they were loosing the colt, the owners thereof said unto them, 34 Why loose ye the colt? And they said, The Lord hath need of him.

MATTH. XXI.

7 And *they* brought the ass and the colt, and put on them their clothes, and they set *him* thereon.

and they let them go. 7 And they brought the colt to Jesus, and cast their garments on him; and he sat upon him.

LUKE XIX.

35 And they brought him to Jesus: and they cast their garments upon the colt, and they set Jesus thereon.

MATTH. XXI.

4 All this was done, that it might be fulfilled which was spoken by the 5 prophet, saying,ᵃ | Tell ye the daughter of Sion, Behold, thy King cometh unto thee, meek, and sitting upon an ass, and a colt the foal of an ass.—

JOHN XII.

14 And Jesus, when he had found a young ass, sat thereon; as it is 15 written,ᵃ Fear not, daughter of Sion: behold, thy King cometh, sitting on an ass's colt.—

8 And a very great multitude spread their garments in the way; others cut down branches from the trees, and strewed *them* in 9 the way. And the multitudes that went before, and that followed, cried, saying, Hosanna to the Son of David: Blessed *is* he that cometh in the name of the Lord: Hosanna in the highest.

MARK XI.

8 And many spread their garments in the way: and others cut down branches off the trees, and strewed *them* in 9 way. And they that went before, and they that followed, cried, saying, Hosanna: Blessed *is* he that cometh in the name of the Lord. 10 Blessed *be* the kingdom of our father David, that cometh in the name of the Lord: Hosanna in the highest.

LUKE XIX.

36 And as he went, they spread their clothes in the 37 way. And when he was come nigh, even now at the descent of the mount of Olives, the whole multitude of the disciples began to rejoice and praise God with a loud voice, for all the mighty works that they had seen; 38 saying, Blessed *be* the King that cometh in the name of the Lord: Peace in heaven, and glory in the highest.

JOHN XII.

13 I took branches of palm-trees, and went forth to meet him, and cried, Hosanna; Blessed *is* the King of Israel that cometh in the name of the Lord.ᵇ—

JOHN XII.

16 These things understood not his disciples at the first: but when Jesus was glorified, then remembered they that these things were written of him, 17 and *that* they had done these things unto him. The people therefore that was with him when he called Lazarus out of his grave, and raised him from 18 the dead, bare record. For this cause the people also met him, for that 19 they heard that he had done this miracle. The Pharisees therefore said among themselves, Perceive ye how ye prevail nothing? behold, the world is gone after him.

ᵃ **5** etc. Zech. 9, 9.   ᵇ **13.** Comp. Ps. 118, 26.

LUKE XIX.

39 And some of the Pharisees from among the multitude said unto him,
40 Master, rebuke thy disciples. And he answered and said unto them, I tell
you, that if these should hold their peace, the stones would immediately cry
41 out. And when he was come near, he beheld the city, and wept over it,
42 ' saying, If thou hadst known, even thou, at least in this thy day, the things
43 *which belong* unto thy peace! but now they are hid from thine eyes. For
the days shall come upon thee, that thine enemies shall cast a trench about
44 thee, and compass thee round, and keep thee in on every side, ' and shall
lay thee even with the ground, and thy children within thee: and they shall
not leave in thee one stone upon another: because thou knewest not the
time of thy visitation.

<table>
<tr><td>MATTH. XXI.</td><td>MARK XI.</td></tr>
</table>

10 And when he was come into Jeru-   **11** And Jesus entered into Jerusalem,
salem, all the city was moved, say-   and into the temple: and when he
11 ing, Who is this? And the multi-   had looked round about upon all
tude said, This is Jesus the prophet   things,—
14 of Nazareth of Galilee.—And the
15 blind and the lame came to him in the temple ; and he healed them. And
when the chief priests and scribes saw the wonderful things that he did,
and the children crying in the temple, and saying, Hosanna to the Son of
16 David ; they were sore displeased, ' and said unto him, Hearest thou what
these say? And Jesus saith unto them, Yea: have ye never read,[a] Out
of the mouth of babes and sucklings
thou hast perfected praise?   MARK XI.
17 And he left them, and went out   **11** —and now the even-tide was come,
of the city into Bethany, and he   he went out unto Bethany, with tho
lodged there.   twelve.

§ 113. *The barren Fig-tree.   The cleansing of the Temple.*—BETHANY, JERU-
•   SALEM.

Third Day of the Week.

MATTH. XXI. 12, 13. 18, 19.   MARK XI. 12—19.

18 Now in the morning, as he re-   **12** And on the morrow, when they
turned into the city, he hungered.   were come from Bethany, he was
19 And when he saw a fig-tree in the   **13** hungry. And seeing a fig-tree afar
way, he came to it, and found no-   off, having leaves, he came, if haply
thing thereon, but leaves only, and·   he might find any thing thereon :
said unto it, Let no fruit grow on   and when he came to it, he found
thee henceforward for ever. And   nothing but leaves; for the time
presently the fig-tree withered   **14** of figs was not *yet*. And Jesus
away.—   answered and said unto it, No
man eat fruit of thee hereafter for ever. And
his disciples heard it.

<table>
<tr><td>MATTH. XXI.</td><td>**15** And they come to</td><td>LUKE XIX. 45—48.</td></tr>
</table>

12 And Jesus went into   Jerusalem: and Jesus   **45** And he went into the
the temple of God,   went into the temple,   temple, and began to
and cast out all them   and began to cast out   cast out them that sold
that sold and bought in   them that sold and   therein, and them that
the temple, and over-   bought in the temple,   bought,

MATTH. XXI.	MARK XI.
threw the tables of the money-changers, and the seats of them that sold doves.	and overthrew the tables of the money-changers, and the seats of [16] them that sold doves; [?] and would not suffer that any man should carry any vessel through the temple.

LUKE XIX.

[13] And said unto them, It is written,[a] My house shall be called the house of prayer, but ye have made it a den of thieves. [18] made it a den of thieves. And the scribes and chief priests heard it, and sought how they might destroy him: for they feared him, because all the people was astonished at his [19] doctrine. And when even was come, he went out of the city.	[17] And he taught, saying unto them, Is it not written,[a] My house shall be called, of all nations, the house of prayer? but ye have [46] Saying unto them, It is written,[a] My house is the house of prayer, but ye have made it a [47] den of thieves. And he taught daily in the temple. But the chief priests, and the scribes, and the chief of the people sought to destroy him, [48] [?] and could not find what they might do: for all the people were very attentive to hear him.	

LUKE XXI. 37, 38.

[37] And in the day-time he was teaching in the temple; and at night he [38] went out, and abode in the mount that is called *the mount* of Olives. And all the people came early in the morning to him in the temple, for to hear him.

§ 114. *The barren Fig-tree withers away.*—BETWEEN BETHANY AND JERUSALEM.

Fourth Day of the Week.

MATTH. XXI. 20—22.	MARK XI. 20—26.
	[20] And in the morning, as they passed by, they saw the fig-tree [21] dried up from the roots. And Peter
[20] And when the disciples saw it, they marvelled, saying, How soon is the fig-tree withered away! [21] Jesus answered and said unto them, Verily I say unto you, If ye have faith, and doubt not, ye shall not only do this which is done to the fig-tree, but also, if ye shall say unto this mountain, Be thou removed, and be thou cast into the [22] sea; it shall be done. And all things whatsoever ye shall ask in prayer, believing, ye shall receive.	calling to remembrance, saith unto him, Master, behold, the fig-tree which thou cursedst is withered [22] away. And Jesus answering, saith [23] unto them, Have faith in God. For verily I say unto you, That whosoever shall say unto this mountain, Be thou removed, and be thou cast into the sea; and shall not doubt in his heart, but shall believe that those things which he saith shall come to pass; he shall have whatsoever he [24] saith. Therefore I say unto you, What things soever ye desire when

[25] ye pray, believe that ye receive *them*, and ye shall have *them*. And when ye stand praying, forgive, if ye have aught against any: that your Father [26] also which is in heaven may forgive you your trespasses. But if ye do not forgive, neither will your Father which is in heaven forgive you your trespasses.

---

[a] **13** etc. Is. 56, 7. Comp. Jer. 7, 11.

§ 115. *Christ's authority questioned. Parable of the Two Sons.*—JERUSALEM

Fourth Day of the Week.

MATTH. XXI. 23—32. | MARK XI. 27—33. | LUKE XX. 1—8.

²⁷ And they come again to Jerusalem: and as he was walking in the temple, there come to him the chief priests, and the scribes, and ²⁸ the elders, ¹ and say unto him, By what authority doest thou these things? and who gave thee this authority to ²⁹ do these things? And Jesus answered and said unto them, I will also ask of you one question, and answer me, and I will tell you ³⁰ by what authority I do these things. The baptism of John, was *it* from heaven, or of ³¹ men? answer me. And they reasoned with themselves, saying, If we shall say, From heaven; he will say, ³² Why then did ye not believe him? But if we shall say, Of men; they feared the people: for all *men* counted ³³ John, that he was a prophet indeed. And they answered and said unto Jesus, We cannot tell. And Jesus answering saith unto them, Neither do I tell you by what authority I do these things.

²³ And when he was come into the temple, the chief priests and the elders of the people came unto him as he was teaching, and said, By what authority doest thou these things? ²⁴ and who gave thee this authority? And Jesus answered and said unto them, I also will ask you one thing, which, if ye tell me, I in like wise will tell you by what authority I do ²⁵ these things. The baptism of John, whence was it? from heaven, or of men? And they reasoned with themselves, saying, If we shall say, From heaven; he will say unto us, Why did ye not ²⁶ then believe him? But if we shall say, Of men; we fear the people: for all hold John ²⁷ as a prophet. And they answered Jesus, and said, We cannot tell. And he said unto them, Neither tell I you by what authority I do these things.

¹ And it came to pass, *that* on one of those days, as he taught the people in the temple, and preached the gospel, the chief priests and the scribes came upon *him*, with the el-² ders, ¹ and spake unto him, saying, Tell us, by what authority doest thou these things? or who is he that gave thee this authority? ³ And he answered and said unto them, I will also ask you one thing; and answer me:

⁴ The baptism of John, was it from heaven, or of ⁵ men? And they reasoned with themselves, saying, If we shall say, From heaven; he will say, Why then believed ⁶ ye him not? But and if we say, Of men; all the people will stone us: for they be persuaded that John was a prophet. And they ⁷ answered, that they could not tell whence ⁸ *it was*. And Jesus said unto them, Neither tell I you by what authority I do these things.

²⁸ But what think ye? A *certain* man had two ²⁹ sons; and he came to the first, and said, Son, go work to-day in my vineyard. He answered and said, I will not; but afterward he repented, and ³⁰ went. ¹ And he came to the second, and said likewise. And he answered ³¹ and said, I *go*, sir: and went not. Whether of them twain did the will of *his* father? They say unto him, The first. Jesus saith unto them, Verily I say unto you, That the publicans and the harlots go into the kingdom of ³² God before you. For John came unto you in the way of righteousness, and

MATTH. XXI.

ye believed him not: but the publicans and the harlots believed him: and ye, when ye had seen *it*, repented not afterward, that ye might believe him

§ 116. *Parable of the wicked Husbandmen* —JERUSALEM.

Fourth Day of the Week.

MATTH. XXI. 33—46.	MARK XII. 1—12.	LUKE XX. 9—19.
³³ Hear another parable: There was a certain householder, which planted a vineyard, and hedged it round about, and digged a winepress in it, and built a tower, and let it out to husbandmen, and went into a far country. ³⁴ And when the time of the fruit drew near, he sent his servants to the husbandmen, that they might receive the fruits ³⁵ of it. And the husbandmen took his servants, and beat one, and killed another, and ³⁶ stoned another. Again he sent other servants more than the first: and they did unto them likewise.	¹ And he began to speak unto them by parables: A *certain* man planted a vineyard, and set an hedge about *it*, and digged *a place for* the wine-fat, and built a tower, and let it out to husbandmen, and went into a ² far country. And at the season he sent to the husbandmen a servant, that he might receive from the husbandmen of the fruit ³ of the vineyard. And they caught *him*, and beat him, and sent ⁴ *him* away empty. And again he sent unto them another servant: and at him they cast stones, and wounded *him* in the head, and sent *him* away shamefully handled. ⁵ And again he sent another; and him they killed, and many others; beating some, and killing some.	⁹ Then began he to speak to the people this parable: A certain man planted a vineyard, and let it forth to husbandmen, and went into a far country for a long time. ¹⁰ And at the season he sent a servant to the husbandmen, that they should give him of the fruit of the vineyard: but the husbandmen beat him, and sent *him* away empty. ¹¹ And again he sent another servant: and they beat him also, and entreated *him* shamefully, and sent *him* away empty. ¹² And again he sent a third: and they wounded him also, and cast ¹³ *him* out. Then said the lord of the vineyard, What shall I do? I will send my beloved son: it may be they will reverence *him* when they see him. ¹⁴ But when the husbandmen saw him, they reasoned among themselves, saying, This is the heir: come, let us kill him, that the inheritance may be ours.
³⁷ But last of all, he sent unto them his son, saying, They will rever- ³⁸ ence my son. But when the husbandmen saw the son, they said among themselves, This is the heir; come, let us kill him, and let us seize on his inheritance.	⁶ Having yet therefore one son, his well-beloved, he sent him also last unto them, saying, They will reverence ⁷ my son. But those husbandmen said among themselves, This is the heir; come, let us kill him, and the inheritance shall be ours.	
³⁹ And they caught him, and cast *him* out of	⁸ And they took him, and killed *him*, and	¹⁵ So they cast him out of the vineyard, and

MATTH. XXI.	MARK XII.	LUKE XX.
the vineyard, and slew **⁴⁰** him. When the lord therefore of the vineyard cometh, what will he do unto those hus-**⁴¹** bandmen? They say unto him, He will miserably destroy those wicked men, and will let out *his* vineyard unto other husbandmen, which shall render him the fruits in their seasons.	cast *him* out of the **⁹** vineyard. What shall therefore the lord of the vineyard do? He will come and destroy the husbandmen, and will give the vineyard unto others.	killed *him*. What therefore shall the lord of the vineyard do unto **¹⁶** them? He shall come and destroy these husbandmen, and shall give the vineyard to others. And when they heard *it*, they said, God forbid.
⁴² Jesus saith unto them, Did ye never read in the scriptures,ᵃ The stone which the builders rejected, the same is become the head of the corner: this is the Lord's doing, and it is marvellous in our eyes?	**¹⁰** And have ye not read this scripture,ᵃ The stone which the builders rejected is become the head of the **¹¹** corner: this was the Lord's doing, and it is marvellous in our eyes?	**¹⁷** And he beheld them, and said, What is this then that is written,ᵃ The stone which the builders rejected, the same is become the head of the corner?
⁴³ Therefore say I unto you, The kingdom of God shall be taken from you, and given to a nation bringing forth the fruits thereof.		
⁴⁴ And whosoever shall fall on this stone, shall be broken: but on whomsoever it shall fall, it will **⁴⁵** grind him to powder. And when the chief priests and Pharisees had heard his parables, they perceived that he **⁴⁶** spake of them. But when they sought to lay hands on him, they feared the multitude, because they took him for a prophet.		LUKE XX. **¹⁸** Whosoever shall fall upon that stone, shall be broken: but on whomsoever it shall fall, it will grind him to powder.ᵇ
	¹² And they sought to lay hold on him, but feared the people; for they knew that he had spoken the parable against them: and they left him, and went their way.	**¹⁹** And the chief priests and the scribes the same hour sought to lay hands on him; and they feared the people: for they perceived that he had spoken this parable against them.

§ 117. *Parable of the Marriage of the King's Son.*—JERUSALEM.

Fourth Day of the Week.

MATTH. XXII. 1—14.

¹ And Jesus answered and spake unto them again by parables, and said,
² The kingdom of heaven is like unto a certain king, which made a marriage
³ for his son, ¹ and sent forth his servants to call them that were bidden to the wedding: and they would not come. Again, he sent forth other servants, saying, Tell them which are bidden, Behold, I have prepared my dinner: my oxen and *my* fatlings *are* killed, and all things *are* ready: come unto the marriage. But they made light of *it*, and went their ways, one to his farm, another to his merchandise. And the remnant took his servants,

ᵃ **42** etc. Ps. 118, 22.   ᵇ **44** etc. Comp. Is. 8, 14 sq. Zech. 12, 3. Dan. 2, 34 sq. 44 sq.
10*

MATTH. XXII.

7 and entreated *them* spitefully, and slew *them*. But when the king heard
thereof, he was wroth : and he sent forth his armies, and destroyed those
8 murderers, and burnēd up *their* city. Then saith he to his servants, The
9 wedding is ready, but they which were bidden were not worthy. Go ye
therefore into the highways, and as many as ye shall find, bid to the mar-
10 riage. So those servants went out into the highways, and gathered together all as many as they found, both bad and good : and the wedding was
furnished with guests.
11   And when the king came in to see the guests, he saw there a man which
12 had not on a wedding garment : ' and he saith unto him, Friend, how camest
thou in hither, not having a wedding-garment ? And he was speechless.
13 Then said the king to the servants, Bind him hand and foot, and take him
away, and cast *him* into outer darkness : there shall be weeping and gnash-
14 ing of teeth. For many are called, but few *are* chosen.

§ 118. *Insidious question of the Pharisees: Tribute to Cesar.*—JERUSALEM.

Fourth Day of the Week.

MATTH. XXII. 15—22.	MARK XII. 13—17.	LUKE XX. 20—26.
15 Then went the Pha-risees, and took coun-sel how they might en-tangle him in *his* talk. 16 And they sent out unto him their disciples, with the Herodians, saying, Master, we know that thou art true, and teachest the way of God in truth, neither carest thou for any *man :* for thou re-gardest not the person 17 of men. Tell us there-fore, What thinkest thou ? Is it lawful to give tribute unto Cesar, 18 or not ? But Jesus per-ceived their wicked-ness, and said, Why tempt ye me, *ye* hypo-19 crites ? Shew me the tribute-money. And they brought unto him 20 a penny. And he saith unto them, Whose *is* this image and super-21 scription ? They say unto him, Cesar's. Then saith he unto them, Render therefore unto Cesar, the things which	13 And they send unto him certain of the Pha-risees, and of the Hero-dians, to catch him in 14 *his* words. And when they were come, they say unto him, Master, we know that thou art true, and carest for no man : for thou regard-est not the person of men, but teachest the way of God in truth : Is it lawful to give tri-bute to Cesar, or not ? 15 Shall we give, or shall we not give ? But he, knowing their hypo-crisy, said unto them, Why tempt ye me ? bring me a penny, that 16 I may see *it*. And they brought *it*. And he saith unto them, Whose *is* this image and superscription ? And they said unto 17 him, Cesar's. And Jesus answering, said unto them, Render to Cesar the things that	20 And they watched *him*, and sent forth spies, which should feign themselves just men, that they might take hold of his words, that so they might de-liver him unto the power and authority of 21 the governor. And they asked him, saying, Master, we know that thou sayest and teach-est rightly, neither ac-ceptest thou the person *of any*, but teachest the 22 way of God truly : Is it lawful for us to give tribute unto Cesar, or 23 no ? But he perceived their craftiness, and said unto them, Why 24 tempt ye me ? Shew me a penny. Whose image and superscrip-tion hath it ? They answered and said, 25 Cesar's. And he said unto them, Render therefore unto Cesar the things which be Cesar's, and unto God the things which be

MATTH. XXII.	MARK XII.	LUKE XX.
are Cesar's ; and unto God, the things that [22] are God's. When they had heard *these words,* they marvelled, and left him, and went their way.	are Cesar's, and to God the things that are God's. And they marvelled at him.	[26] God's. And they could not take hold of his words before the people : and they marvelled at his answer, and held their peace.

§ 119. *Insidious question of the Sadducees : The Resurrection.*—JERUSALEM.

Fourth Day of the Week.

MATTH. XXII. 23—33.	MARK XII. 18—27.	LUKE XX. 27—40.
[23] The same day came to him the Sadducees, which say that there is no resurrection, and asked him,	[18] Then come unto him the Sadducees, which say there is no resurrection ; and they asked him, saying,	[27] Then came to *him* certain of the Sadducees, (which deny that there is any resurrection,) and they asked
[24] ' saying, Master, Moses said,ª If a man die, having no children, his brother shall marry his wife, and raise up seed unto his brother.	[19] Master, Moses wrote unto us,ª If a man's brother die, and leave *his* wife *behind him,* and leave no children, that his brother should take his wife, and raise up seed unto his brother. Now	[28] him, ' saying, Master, Moses wrote unto us,ª If any man's brother die, having a wife, and he die without children, that his brother should take his wife, and raise up seed unto his brother. There
[25] Now there were with us seven brethren : and the first, when he had married a wife, deceased ; and having no issue, left his wife unto his [26] brother. Likewise the second also, and the third, unto the se- [27] venth. And last of all the woman died also.	[20] unto his brother. Now there were seven brethren : and the first took a wife, and dying left [21] no seed. And the second took her, and died, neither left he any seed : and the [22] third likewise. And the seven had her, and left no seed : last of all the woman died also.	were therefore seven brethren : and the first took a wife, and died [30] without children. And the second took her to wife, and he died child- [31] less. And the third took her ; and in like manner the seven also : and they left no chil- [32] dren, and died. Last of all the woman died also.
[28] Therefore, in the resurrection, whose wife shall she be of the seven ? for they all had [29] her. Jesus answered and said unto them, Ye do err, not knowing the scriptures, nor the pow- e.' of God.	[23] In the resurrection therefore, when they shall rise, whose wife shall she be of them ? for the seven had her to [24] wife. And Jesus answering, said unto them, Do ye not therefore err, because ye know not the scriptures, neither the pow- [25] er of God ? For when they shall rise from the	[33] Therefore in the resurrection, whose wife of them is she ? for seven had her to wife. [34] And Jesus answering, said unto them, The children of this world marry, and are given [35] in marriage : ' but they which shall be account- ed worthy to obtain that world, and the re- surrection from the
[30] For in the resurrection they nei-	[25]	

ª **24** etc. **Deut. 25, 5**

MATTH. XXII.	MARK XII.	LUKE XX.

ther marry, nor are given in marriage, but are the angels of God in heaven.

dead, they neither marry, nor are given in marriage; but are as [36] the angels which are in heaven.

dead, neither marry, nor are given in marriage: [36] ' neither can they die any more : for they are equal unto the angels ; and are the children of God, being the children of the resurrection.

[31] But, as touching the resurrection of the dead, have ye not read that which was spoken unto you by [32] God, saying,[a] ' I am the God of Abraham, and the God of Isaac, and the God of Jacob? God is not the God of the dead, but of the [33] living. And when the multitude heard *this*, they were astonished at his doctrine.

[26] And as touching the dead, that they rise ; [27] have ye not read in the book of Moses, how in the bush God spake unto him, saying,[a] I *am* the God of Abraham, and the God of Isaac, and the God of Jacob? He is not the God of the dead, but the God of the living: ye therefore do greatly err.

Now that the dead are raised, even Moses shewed at the bush,[a] when he calleth the Lord the God of Abraham, and the God of Isaac, and the God of Jacob.

[38] For he is not a God of the dead, but of the living: for all live unto him. [39] Then certain of the scribes answering, said,

[40] Master, thou hast well said. And after that they durst not ask him any *question at all.*

§ 120. *A Lawyer questions Jesus.   The two great Commandments.—* JERUSALEM.

Fourth Day of the Week

MATTH. XXII. 34—40.	MARK XII. 28—34.

[34] But when the Pharisees had heard that he had put the Sadducees to silence, they were gathered together. [35] Then one of them *which was* a lawyer, asked *him a question*, tempting [36] him, and saying, ' Master, which *is* the great commandment in the law? [37] Jesus said unto him,[a] Thou shalt love the Lord thy God with all thy heart, and with all thy soul, and [38] with all thy mind. This is the first [39] and great commandment. And the second *is* like unto it,[b] Thou shalt [40] love thy neighbour as thyself. On these two commandments hang all the law and the prophets.

[28] And one of the scribes came, and having heard them reasoning together, and perceiving that he had answered them well, asked him, Which is the first commandment of all? [29] And Jesus answered him, The first of all the commandments *is*,[a] Hear, O Israel ; The Lord our God is one [30] Lord : ' and thou shalt love the Lord thy God with all thy heart, and with all thy soul, and with all thy mind, and with all thy strength: this *is* the [31] first commandment. And the second *is* like, *namely* this,[b] Thou shalt love thy neighbour as thyself: there is none other com- [32] mandment greater than these. And

the scribe said unto him, Well, Master, thou hast said the truth : [33] for there is one God ; and there is none other but he : ' and to love him with all the heart, and with all the understanding, and with all the soul,

a 31 etc Ex. 3, 6   b 37 etc. Deut 6, 4. 5.   c 39 etc. Lev. 19, 18

MARK XII.

and with all the strength, and to love *his* neighbour as himself, is more than
³⁴ all whole burnt-offerings and sacrifices. And when Jesus saw that he answered discreetly, he said unto him, Thou art not far from the kingdom of
God. And no man after that durst ask him *any question.*

§ 121. *How is Christ the Son of David?*—JERUSALEM.

Fourth Day of the Week.

MATTH. XXII. 41—46.	MARK XII. 35—37.	LUKE XX. 41—44.
⁴¹ While the Pharisees were gathered toge-ther, Jesus asked them. ⁴² ' saying, What think ye of Christ? whose son is he? They say unto him, *The son* of ⁴³ David. He saith unto them, How then doth David in spirit call him ⁴⁴ Lord, saying,ᵃ ' The LORD said unto my Lord, Sit thou on my right hand, till I make thine enemies thy foot- ⁴⁵ stool? If David then call him Lord, how is ⁴⁶ he his son? And no man was able to an-swer him a word, nei-ther durst any *man,* from that day forth, ask	³⁵ And Jesus answered and said, while he taught in the temple, How say the scribes that Christ is the son of David? ³⁶ For David himself said by the Holy Ghost,ᶜ The LORD said unto my Lord, Sit thou on my right hand, ³⁷ till I make thine ene-mies thy footstool. Da-vid therefore himself calleth him Lord, and whence is he *then* his son? And the com-mon people heard him gladly.	⁴¹ And he said unto them, How say they that Christ is David's son? ⁴² And David him-self saith in the book of Psalms,ᵉ The LORD said unto my Lord, Sit thou on my right hand, ⁴³ ' till I make thine ene-mies thy footstool. ⁴⁴ David therefore calleth him Lord, how is he then his son?

him any more *questions.*

§ 122. *Warnings against the evil example of the Scribes and Pharisees.*—
JERUSALEM.

Fourth Day of the Week.

MARK XII. 38, 39.	LUKE XX. 45, 46.
³⁸ And he said unto them in his doc-trine, Beware of the scribes, which love to go in long clothing, and *love* salutations in the market-places, ³⁹ ' and the chief seats in the syna-gogues, and the uppermost rooms at feasts.	⁴⁵ Then in the audience of all the people, he said unto his disciples, ⁴⁶ ' Beware of the scribes, which de-sire to walk in long robes, and love greetings in the markets, and the highest seats in the synagogues, and the chief rooms at feasts.

MATTH. XXIII. 1—12.

¹ ² Then spake Jesus to the multitude, and to his disciples, ' saying, The
³ scribes and the Pharisees sit in Moses' seat: ' all therefore whatsoeve'
they bid you observe, *that* observe and do: but do not ye after their works:
⁴ for they say, and do not. For they bind heavy burdens, and grievous to b€

ᵃ 44 etc. Ps. 110, 1

MATTH. XXIII.

borne, and lay *them* on men's shoulders; but they *themselves* will not move
⁴ them with one of their fingers.   But all their works they do for to be seen of
men: they make broad their phylacteries, and enlarge the borders of their
⁶ garments, ' and love the uppermost rooms at feasts, and the chief seats in
⁷ the synagogues, ' and greetings in the markets, and to be called of men,
⁸ Rabbi, Rabbi.   But be not ye called Rabbi: for one is your Master, *even*
⁹ Christ; and all ye are brethren.   And call no *man* your father upon the
¹⁰ earth: for one is your Father which is in heaven.   Neither be ye called
¹¹ masters: for one is your Master, *even* Christ. But he that is greatest among
¹² you, shall be your servant.   And whosoever shall exalt himself, shall be
abased; and he that shall humble himself, shall be exalted.

§ 123. *Woes against the Scribes and Pharisees.   Lamentation over Jeru-*
salem.—JERUSALEM.

Fourth Day of the Week.

MATTH. XXIII. 13—39.   MARK XII. 40.   LUKE XX. 47.

¹⁴   Wo unto you, scribes
and Pharisees, hypo-
crites! for ye devour ⁴⁰   Which devour wi- ⁴⁷   Which devour wi-
widows' houses, and dows' houses, and for dows' houses, and for a
for a pretence make a pretence make long shew make long pray-
long prayers: there- prayers: these shall re- ers: the same shall re-
fore ye shall receive ceive greater damna- ceive greater damna-
the greater damnation. tion. tion.
¹⁵ But   wo   unto   you,
scribes and Pharisees, hypocrites! for ye shut up the kingdom of heaven
against men: for ye neither go in *yourselves*, neither suffer ye them that
¹⁶ are entering to go in.   Wo unto you, scribes and Pharisees, hypocrites! for
ye compass sea and land to make one proselyte; and when he is made, ve
make him two-fold more the child of hell than yourselves.
¹⁶   Wo unto you, *ye* blind guides! which say, Whosoever shall swear by the
temple, it is nothing; but whosoever shall swear by the gold of the temple,
¹⁷ he is a debtor.   *Ye* fools, and blind! for whether is greater, the gold, or the
¹⁸ temple that sanctifieth the gold?   And whosoever shall swear by the altar,
it is nothing; but whosoever sweareth by the gift that is upon it, he is
¹⁹ guilty.   *Ye* fools, and blind! for whether *is* greater, the gift, or the altar
²⁰ that sanctifieth the gift?   Whoso therefore shall swear by the altar, swear-
²¹ eth by it, and by all things thereon.   And whoso shall swear by the tem-
²² ple, sweareth by it, and by him that dwelleth therein.   And he that shall
swear by heaven, sweareth by the throne of God, and by him that sitteth
thereon.
²³   Wo unto you, scribes and Pharisees, hypocrites! for ye pay tithe of mint,
and anise, and cummin, and have omitted the weightier *matters* of the law,
judgment, mercy, and faith: these ought ye to have done, and not to leave
²⁴ the other undone.   *Ye* blind guides, which strain at a gnat, and swallow a
²⁵ camel.   Wo unto you, scribes and Pharisees, hypocrites! for ye make clean
the outside of the cup and of the platter, but within they are full of extor-
²⁶ tion and excess.   *Thou* blind Pharisee, cleanse first that *which is* within
the cup and platter, that the outside of them may be clean also.
²⁷   Wo unto you, scribes and Pharisees, hypocrites! for ye are like unto
whited **sepulchres**, which indeed appear beautiful outward, but are within

MATTH. XXIII.

[28] full of dead *men's* bones, and of all uncleanness. Even so ye also outwardly appear righteous unto men, but within ye are full of hypocrisy and iniquity. [29] Wo unto you, scribes and Pharisees, hypocrites! because ye build the [30] tombs of the prophets, and garnish the sepulchres of the righteous. And say, If we had been in the days of our fathers, we would not have been par- [31] takers with them in the blood of the prophets. Wherefore, ye be witnesses unto yourselves, that ye are the children of them which killed the prophets. [32] [33] Fill ye up then the measure of your fathers. *Ye* serpents, *ye* generation [34] of vipers, how can ye escape the damnation of hell? Wherefore, behold, I send you prophets, and wise men, and scribes; and *some* of them ye shall kill and crucify, and *some* of them shall ye scourge in your synagogues, and [35] persecute *them* from city to city: [a] that upon you may come all the righteous blood shed upon the earth, from the blood of righteous Abel, unto the blood of Zacharias, son of Barachias, whom ye slew between the temple [36] and the altar.[a] Verily, I say unto you, All these things shall come upon this generation. [37] O Jerusalem, Jerusalem, *thou* that killest the prophets, and stonest them which are sent unto thee, how often would I have gathered thy children together, even as a hen gathereth her chickens under *her* wings, and ye would [38] [39] not! Behold, your house is left unto you desolate.[b] For I say unto you, Ye shall not see me henceforth, till ye shall say, Blessed *is* he that cometh in the name of the Lord.[c]

§ 124. *The Widow's mite.*—JERUSALEM.

Fourth Day of the Week.

MARK XII. 41—44.	LUKE XXI. 1—4.
[41] And Jesus sat over against the treasury, and beheld how the people cast money into the treasury: and many that were rich cast in much. [42] And there came a certain poor widow, and she threw in two [43] mites, which make a farthing. And he called *unto him* his disciples, and saith unto them, Verily, I say unto you, that this poor widow hath cast more in, than all they which have cast into [44] the treasury. For all *they* did cast in of their abundance: but she of her want did cast in all that she had, *even* all her living.	[1] And he looked up and saw the rich men casting their gifts into the [2] treasury. And he saw also a certain poor widow, casting in thither two mites. [3] And he said, Of a truth I say unto you, that this poor widow hath cast in more than they all. [4] For all these have of their abundance cast in unto the offerings of God: but she of her penury hath cast in all the living that she had.

[a] 35. Gen. 4, 8. 2 Chr. 24, 20—22.   [b] 38. Comp. Ps. 69, 25. Jer. 12, 7. 22, 5.
[c] 39. Comp. Ps. 118, 26.

§ 125. *Certain Greeks desire to see Jesus.*—JERUSALEM.

Fourth Day of the Week.

JOHN XII. 20—36.

20 And there were certain Greeks among them, that came up to worship at
21 the feast. The same came therefore to Philip, which was of Bethsaida of
22 Galilee, and desired him, saying, Sir, we would see Jesus. Philip cometh
and telleth Andrew: and again, Andrew and Philip tell Jesus.
23 And Jesus answered them, saying, The hour is come, that the Son of
24 man should be glorified. Verily, verily, I say unto you, Except a corn of
wheat fall into the ground and die, it abideth alone: but if it die, it bring-
25 eth forth much fruit. He that loveth his life shall lose it; and he that
26 hateth his life in this world, shall keep it unto life eternal. If any man
serve me, let him follow me; and where I am, there shall also my servant
27 be: if any man serve me, him will *my* Father honour. Now is my soul
troubled; and what shall I say? Father, save me from this hour: but for
28 this cause came I unto this hour. ¹ Father, glorify thy name. Then came
there a voice from heaven, *saying*, I have both glorified *it*, and will glorify
it again.
29 The people therefore that stood by and heard *it*, said that it thundered.
30 Others said, An angel spake to him. ¹ Jesus answered and said, This voice
31 came not because of me, but for your sakes. Now is the judgment of this
32 world: now shall the prince of this world be cast out. And I, if I be lifted
33 up from the earth, will draw all *men* unto me. (This he said, signifying
34 what death he should die.) The people answered him, We have heard out
of the law that Christ abideth forever; ⁴ and how sayest thou, The son of
35 man must be lifted up? Who is this Son of man? ¹ Then Jesus said unto
them, Yet a little while is the light with you. Walk while ye have the
light, lest darkness come upon you: for he that walketh in darkness know-
36 eth not whither he goeth. While ye have light, believe in the light, that ye
may be the children of light. These things spake Jesus, and departed, and
did hide himself from them.

§ 126. *Reflections upon the unbelief of the Jews* —JERUSALEM.

Fourth Day of the Week.

JOHN XII. 37—50.

37 But though he had done so many miracles before them, yet they believed
38 not on him: ¹ that the saying of Esaias the prophet might be fulfilled,
which he spake,ᵇ Lord, who hath believed our report? and to whom hath
39 the arm of the Lord been revealed? Therefore they could not believe, be-
40 cause that Esaias said again,ᶜ He hath blinded their eyes, and hardened
their heart; that they should not see with *their* eyes, nor understand with
41 *their* heart, and be converted, and I should heal them. These things said
42 Esaias, when he saw his glory, and spake of him.ᵈ Nevertheless, among
the chief rulers also many believed on him; but because of the Pharisees
they did not confess *him*, lest they should be put out of the synagogue:
43 ¹ for they loved the praise of men more than the praise of God.
44 Jesus cried, and said, He that believeth on me, believeth not on me, but

---

ᵃ 34. Comp. 2 Sam. 7, 13 sq. Ps. 89, 29 36. 110, 4.   ᵇ 38. Is. 53, 1.

ᶜ 39. Is. 6, 10.   ᵈ 41. Is. 6, 1 sq.

JOHN XII.

⁴⁶ ⁴⁶ on him that sent me : ¹ and he that seeth me, seeth him that sent me. I am come a light into the world, that whosoever believeth on me should not ⁴⁷ abide in darkness. And if any man hear my words, and believe not, I judge him not: for I came not to judge the world, but to save the world. ⁴⁸ He that rejecteth me, and receiveth not my words, hath one that judgeth him : the word that I have spoken, the same shall judge him in the last day. ⁴⁹ For I have not spoken of myself; but the Father which sent me, he gave ⁵⁰ me a commandment, what I should say, and what I should speak. And I know that his commandment is life everlasting : whatsoever I speak therefore, even as the Father said unto me, so I speak.

§ 127. *Jesus, on taking leave of the Temple, foretells its destruction and the persecution of his Disciples.*—JERUSALEM. MOUNT OF OLIVES.

Fourth Day of the Week.

MATTH. XXIV. 1—14.	MARK XIII. 1—13.	LUKE XXI. 5—19.
¹ And Jesus went out, and departed from the temple : and his disciples came to *him* for to shew him the buildings ² of the temple. And Jesus said unto them, See ye not all these things ? verily I say unto you, There shall not be left here one stone upon another, that shall not be thrown down. ³ And as he sat upon the mount of Olives, the disciples came unto him privately, saying, Tell us, when shall these things be ? and what *shall be* the sign of thy coming, and of the end of the world ? And Jesus answered and said unto them, Take heed that no man deceive you. For many shall come in my name, saying, I am Christ ; and shall deceive many. And ye shall hear of wars, and rumours of wars: see that ye be not troubled : for all *these things* must come	¹ And as he went out of the temple, one of his disciples saith unto him, Master, see what manner of stones, and what buildings *are* ² *here !* And Jesus answering, said unto him, Seest thou these great buildings ? there shall not be left one stone upon another, that shall not be thrown down. ³ And as he sat upon the mount of Olives, over against the temple, Peter, and James, and John, and Andrew, asked him privately, ⁴ ¹ Tell us, when shall these things be ? and what *shall be* the sign when all these things ⁵ shall be fulfilled ? And Jesus answering them, began to say, Take heed lest any *man* de- ⁶ ceive you: ¹ for many shall come in my name, saying, I am *Christ ;* and shall deceive many. ⁷ And when ye shall hear of wars, and rumours of wars, be ye not troubled: for *such things* must needs be ;	⁵ And as some spake of the temple, how it was adorned with goodly stones, and gifts, he said, ⁶ *As for* these things which ye behold, the days will come, in the which there shall not be left one stone upon another, that shall not be thrown down. ⁷ And they asked him, saying, Master, but when shall these things be ? and what sign *will there be* when these things shall come ⁸ to pass ? And he said, Take heed that ye be not deceived : for many shall come in my name, saying, I am *Christ ;* and the time draweth near: go ye not therefore after them. But ⁹ when ye shall hear of wars, and commotions, be not terrified: for these things must first

11

MATTH. XXIV.	MARK XIII.	LUKE XXI.
to pass, but the end is **7** not yet. For nation shall rise against nation, and kingdom against kingdom: and there shall be famines, and pestilences, and earthquakes in divers **8** places. All these *are* the beginning of sorrows.	but the end *is* **8** not yet. For nation shall rise against nation, and kingdom against kingdom : and there shall be earthquakes in *divers* places, and there shall be famines, and troubles: these *are* the beginnings of sorrows.	come to pass ; but the end *is* not by and by. **10** Then said he unto them, Nation shall rise against nation, and kingdom against kingdom : **11** and great earthquakes shall be in divers places, and famines, and pestilences: and fearful sights, and great signs shall there be from heaven.

MARK XIII.	LUKE XXI.
9 But take heed to yourselves: for they shall deliver you up to councils ; and in the synagogues ye shall be beaten : and ye shall be brought before rulers and kings for my sake, **11** for a testimony against them.—But when they shall lead *you*, and deliver you up, take no thought beforehand what ye shall speak, neither do ye premeditate : but whatsoever shall be given you in that hour, that speak ye ; for˙it is not ye that speak, but the Holy Ghost.	**12** But before all these they shall lay their hands on you, and persecute *you*, delivering *you* up to the synagogues, and into prisons, being brought before kings and rulers for **13** my name's sake. And it shall turn **14** to you for a testimony. Settle *it* therefore in your hearts, not to meditate before what ye shall answer. **15** For I will give you a mouth and wisdom, which all your adversaries shall not be able to gainsay nor resist.

MATTH. XXIV.	MARK XIII.	LUKE XXI.
9 Then shall they deliver you up to be afflicted, and shall kill you: and ye shall be hated of all nations for my name's **10** sake. And then shall many be offended, and shall betray one another, and shall hate one **11** another. And many false	betray the brother to death, and the father the son : and children shall rise up against *their* parents, and shall cause them to be put to **13** death. And ye shall be hated of all *men* for my name's sake.	**16** And ye shall be betrayed both by parents, and brethren, and kinsfolks, and friends ; and *some* of you shall they cause to be put to death.

	12 Now, the brother shall	
		17 And ye shall be hated of all *men* for my name's sake.

11 another. And many false prophets shall rise, and shall deceive many.
12 And because iniquity shall abound, the love of many shall wax cold.   .

MATTH. XXIV.	MARK XIII.	LUKE XXI.
13 But he that shall endure unto the end, the same shall be saved. **14** And this gospel of the kingdom shall be preached in all the world, for a witness	But he that shall endure unto the end, the same shall be saved.— **10** And the gospel must first be published among all nations.	**18** But there shall not an hair of your head perish. **19** In your patience possess ye your souls.

unto all nations ; and then shall the end come.

§ 128. *The signs of Christ's coming to destroy Jerusalem, and put an end to the Jewish State and Dispensation..—MOUNT OF OLIVES.*

Fourth Day of the Week.

MATTH. XXIV. 15—42.	MARK XIII. 14—37.	LUKE XXI. 20—36.

15 When ye, therefore, shall see the abomination of desolation, spoken of by Daniel the prophet,[a] stand in the holy place, (whoso readeth, let him under- 16 stand,) ' then let them which be in Judea flee into the mountains: 17 ' let him which is on the house-top not come down to take any thing 18 out of his house : ' neither let him which is in the field return back to take his clothes.

14 But when ye shall see the abomination of desolation, spoken of by Daniel the prophet,[a] standing where it ought not, (let him that read- eth understand,) then let them that be in Judea flee to the moun- 15 tains : ' and let him that is on the house-top not go down into the house, neither enter *therein,* to take any thing out of 16 his house : ' and let him that is in the field not turn back again for to take up his garment.

20 And when ye shall see Jerusalem com- passed with armies, then know that the desolation thereof is 21 nigh. Then let them which are in Judea flee to the mountains ; and let them which are in the midst of it depart out ; and let not them that are in the coun- tries enter thereinto. 22 For these be the days of vengeance, that all things which are writ- ten may be fulfilled.

19 And wo unto them that are with child, and to them that give suck in 20 those days ! But pray ye that your flight be not in the winter, nei- ther on the sabbath- 21 day : ' for then shall be great tribulation, such as was not since the beginning of the world to this time, no, nor 22 ever shall be. And ex- cept those days should be shortened, there should no flesh be saved : but for the elect's sake those days 23 shall be shortened. 24 Christ, or there ; believe *it* not. For there shall arise false Christs, and false prophets, and shall shew great signs and wonders ; insomuch that, if *it were* possible, they shall deceive 25 the very elect. Behold, I have told 26 you before. Wherefore, if they shall

17 But wo to them that are with child, and to them that give suck in 18 those days ! And pray ye that your flight be 19 not in the winter. For *in* those days shall be affliction, such as was not from the beginning of the creation which God created unto this time, neither shall be. 20 And except that the Lord had shortened those days, no flesh should be saved : but for the elect's sake, whom he hath chosen, he hath 21 shortened the days. Then, if any man shall say to you, Lo, here is Christ ; or lo, *he is* there ; believe 22 him not. For false Christs, and false prophets shall rise, and shall shew signs and wonders, to seduce, if *it* 23 *were* possible, even the elect. But take ye heed : behold, I have fore- told you all things.

23 But wo unto them that are with child, and to them that give suck in those days ! for there shall be great distress in the land, and wrath 24 upon this people. And they shall fall by the edge of the sword, and shall be led away cap- tive into all nations : and Jerusalem shall be trodden down of the Gentiles, until the times of the Gentiles be ful- filled.

And then, if any man shall say unto you, Lo, here is

MATTH. XXIV.

say unto you, Behold, he is in the desert; go not forth: behold, *he is* in [77] the secret chambers; believe *it* not. For as the lightning cometh out of the east, and shineth even unto the west; so shall also the coming of the [28] Son of man be. For wheresoever the carcass is, there will the eagles be gathered together.

MATTH. XXIV.	MARK XIII.	LUKE XXI.
[29] Immediately after the tribulation of those days, shall the sun be darkened, and the moon shall not give her light, and the stars shall fall from heaven, and the powers of the heavens [30] shall be shaken:ᵃ ' and then shall appear the sign of the Son of man in heaven: and then shall all the tribes of the earth mourn, and they shall see the Son of man coming in the clouds of heaven with power and great [31] glory. And he shall send his angels with a great sound of a trumpet, and they shall gather together his elect from the four winds, from one end of heaven to the other. [32] Now learn a parable of the fig-tree: When her branch is yet tender, and putteth forth leaves, ye know that summer *is* nigh. So likewise ye, when ye shall see all these things, know that it is near, *even* at the doors. [34] Verily I say unto you, This generation shall not pass, till all these things be fulfilled. [35] Heaven and earth shall pass away, but my words shall not pass [36] away. But of that day and hour knoweth no *man*, no, not the angels of heaven, but my Father only.	[24] But in those days, after that tribulation, the sun shall be darkened, and the moon shall not give her light, [25] ' and the stars of heaven shall fall, and the powers that are in heaven shall be shaken.ᵃ [26] And then shall they see the Son of man coming in the clouds with great power and [27] glory. And then shall he send his angels, and shall gather together his elect from the four winds, from the uttermost part of the earth to the uttermost part of heaven. [28] Now learn a parable of the fig-tree: When her branch is yet tender, and putteth forth leaves, ye know that [29] summer is near. So ye in like manner, when ye shall see these things come to pass, know that it is nigh, [30] *even* at the doors. Verily I say unto you, That this generation shall not pass, till all these [31] things be done. Heaven and earth shall pass away: but my words [32] shall not pass away. But of that day and *that* hour knoweth no man, no, not the angels which are in heaven, neither the Son, but the Father.	[25] And there shall be signs in the sun, and in the moon, and in the stars; and upon the earth distress of nations, with perplexity; the sea and the [26] waves roaring; ' men's hearts failing them for fear, and for looking after those things which are coming on the earth: for the powers of heaven shall be [27] shaken.ᵃ And then shall they see the Son of man coming in a cloud, with power and [28] great glory. And when these things begin to come to pass, then look up, and lift up your heads: for your redemption draweth nigh. [29] And he spake to them a parable; Behold the fig-tree, and all the [30] trees; ' when they now shoot forth, ye see and know of your own selves that summer is [31] now nigh at hand. So likewise ye, when ye see these things come to pass, know ye that the kingdom of God is nigh [32] at hand. Verily I say unto you, This generation shall not pass away, till all be fulfill-[33] ed. Heaven and earth shall pass away: but my words shall not pass away.

ᵃ 29 etc. Comp. Is. 13, 9. 10. Joel 2, 30. 31 3, 15. etc

MATTH. XXIV.

[37] But as the days of Noe *were*, so shall also the coming of the Son of [38] man be. For as in the days that were before the flood, they were eating and drinking, marrying and giving in marriage, until the day that Noe [39] entered into the ark,[a] [1] and knew not until the flood came, and took them [40] all away: so shall also the coming of the Son of man be. Then shall two [41] be in the field; the one shall be taken, and the other left. Two *women shall be* grinding at the mill; the one shall be taken, and the other left.

<table>
<tr><td> MARK XIII. </td><td> LUKE XXI. </td></tr>
<tr><td>

[33] Take ye heed, watch and pray: [34] *For the Son of man is* as a man taking a far journey, who left his house, and gave authority to his servants, and to every man his work;

MATTH. XXIV.

[42] Watch therefore: for ye know not what hour your Lord doth come.

</td><td>

[34] And take heed to yourselves, lest at any time your hearts be overcharged with surfeiting and drunkenness, and cares of this life, and *so* that day come upon you unawares. [35] For as a snare shall it come on all them that dwell on the face of the whole earth. Watch ye therefore, and pray always, that ye may be accounted worthy to escape all these things that shall come to pass, and to stand before the Son of man.

</td></tr>
</table>

when the time is.

[35] and commanded the porter to watch. Watch ye therefore: for ye know not when the master of the house cometh, at even, or at midnight, or at the cock-crowing, or in the [36] morning: [1] lest coming suddenly, he find [37] you sleeping. And what I say unto you, I say unto all, Watch.

§ 129. *Transition to Christ's final coming at the Day of Judgment. Exhortation to watchfulness. Parables: The Ten Virgins; The Five Talents.*—MOUNT OF OLIVES.

Fourth Day of the Week.

MATTH. XXIV. 43—51. XXV. 1—30.

[43] But know this, that if the good man of the house had known in what watch the thief would come, he would have watched, and would not have [44] suffered his house to be broken up. Therefore be ye also ready: for in [45] such an hour as ye think not, the Son of man cometh. Who then is a faithful and wise servant, whom his lord hath made ruler over his house- [46] hold, to give them meat in due season? Blessed *is* that servant, whom his [47] lord, when he cometh, shall find so doing. Verily I say unto you, that he [48] shall make him ruler over all his goods. But and if that evil servant shall [49] say in his heart, My Lord delayeth his coming; [1] and shall begin to smite [50] *his* fellow-servants, and to eat and drink with the drunken; [1] the lord of that servant shall come in a day when he looketh not for *him*, and in an [51] hour that he is not aware of, [1] and shall cut him asunder, and appoint *him* his portion with the hypocrites: there shall be weeping and gnashing of teeth.

XXV. [1] Then shall the kingdom of heaven be likened unto ten virgins, which [2] took their lamps, and went forth to meet the bridegroom. And five of them [3] were wise, and five *were* foolish. They that *were* foolish took their [4] lamps, and took no oil with them: [1] but the wise took oil in their vessels [5] with their lamps. While the bridegroom tarried, they all slumbered and

---

11*   a 38. Gen. 7, 1 sq.

MATTH. XXV.

⁶ slept.   And at midnight there was a cry made, Behold, the bridegroom
⁷ cometh ; go ye out to meet him.   Then all those virgins arose, and trimmed
⁸ their lamps.   And the foolish said unto the wise, Give us of your oil : for
⁹ our lamps are gone out.   But the wise answered, saying, Not so; lest there
be not enough for us and you : but go ye rather to them that sell, and buy
¹⁰ for yourselves.   And while they went to buy, the bridegroom came ; and
they that were ready, went in with him to the marriage : and the door was
¹¹ shut.   Afterward came also the other virgins, saying, Lord, Lord, open
¹² to us.   But he answered and said, Verily I say unto you, I know you
¹³ not.   Watch therefore, for ye know neither the day nor the hour when the
Son of man cometh.

¹⁴   For *the kingdom of heaven is* as a man travelling into a far country, *who*
¹⁵ called his own servants, and delivered unto them his goods.   And unto one
he gave five talents, to another two, and to another one ; to every man
¹⁶ according to his several ability ; and straightway took his journey.   Then
he that had received the five talents, went and traded with the same, and
¹⁷ made *them* other five talents.   And likewise he that *had received* two, he
¹⁸ also gained other two.   But he that had received one, went and digged in
¹⁹ the earth, and hid his lord's money.   After a long time the lord of those
²⁰ servants cometh, and reckoneth with them.   And so he that had received
five talents, came and brought other five talents, saying, Lord, thou deliveredst unto me five talents : behold, I have gained besides them five talents
²¹ more.   His lord said unto him, Well done, *thou* good and faithful servant ;
thou hast been faithful over a few things, I will make thee ruler over many
²² things : enter thou into the joy of thy lord.   He also that had received two
talents came, and said, Lord, thou deliveredst unto me two talents : behold,
²³ I have gained two other talents besides them.   His lord said unto him,
Well done, good and faithful servant ; thou hast been faithful over a few
things, I will make thee ruler over many things ; enter thou into the joy of
²⁴ thy lord.   Then he which had received the one talent came, and said, Lord,
I knew thee that thou art an hard man, reaping where thou hast not sown,
²⁵ and gathering where thou hast not strewed : ' and I was afraid, and went
²⁶ and hid thy talent in the earth : lo, *there* thou hast *that is* thine.   His lord
answered and said unto him, *Thou* wicked and slothful servant, thou knewest that I reap where I sowed not, and gather where I have not strewed :
²⁷ ' thou oughtest therefore to have put my money to the exchangers, and *then*
²⁸ at my coming I should have received mine own with usury.   Take therefore the talent from him, and give *it* unto him which hath ten talents.
²⁹ For unto every one that hath shall be given, and he shall have abundance :
but from him that hath not, shall be taken away even that which he hath.
³⁰ And cast ye the unprofitable servant into outer darkness : there shall be
weeping and gnashing of teeth.

§ 130. *Scenes of the Judgment Day.*—MOUNT OF OLIVES.

Fourth Day of the Week.

MATTH. XXV. 31—46.

³¹   When the Son of man shall come in his glory, and all the holy angels
³² with him, then shall he sit upon the throne of his glory : ' and before him
shall be gathered all nations : and he shall separate them one from another,
³³ as a shepherd divideth *his* sheep from the goats : ' and he shall set the sheep
on his right hand, but the goats on the left.

MATTH. XXV.

34 Then shall the King say unto them on his right hand, Come, ye blessed of my Father, inherit the kingdom prepared for you from the foundation of **35** the world: ¹ for I was an hungered, and ye gave me meat: I was thirsty, **36** and ye gave me drink: I was a stranger, and ye took me in: ¹ naked, and ye clothed me: I was sick, and ye visited me: I was in prison, and ye **37** came unto me. Then shall the righteous answer him, saying, Lord, when saw we thee an hungered, and fed *thee?* or thirsty, and gave *thee* drink? **38** When saw we thee a stranger, and took *thee* in? or naked, and clothed **39** *thee?* ¹ or when saw we thee sick, or in prison, and came unto thee? **40** And the King shall answer and say unto them, Verily I say unto you, Inasmuch as ye have done *it* unto one of the least of these my brethren, ye have done *it* unto me.

41 Then shall he say also unto them on the left hand, Depart from me, ye **42** cursed, into everlasting fire, prepared for the devil and his angels: ¹ for I was an hungered, and ye gave me no meat: I was thirsty, and ye gave me **43** no drink: ¹ I was a stranger, and ye took me not in: naked, and ye clothed **44** me not: sick, and in prison, and ye visited me not. Then shall they also answer him, saying, Lord, when saw we thee an hungered, or athirst, or a stranger, or naked, or sick, or in prison, and did not minister unto thee? **45** Then shall he answer them, saying, Verily I say unto you, Inasmuch as ye **46** did *it* not to one of the least of these, ye did *it* not to me. And these shall go away into everlasting punishment: but the righteous into life eternal.

§ 131. *The Rulers conspire. The Supper at Bethany. Treachery of Judas.—* JERUSALEM. BETHANY.

Fifth Day of the Week.

MATTH. XXVI. 1—16.   MARK XIV. 1—11.   LUKE XXII. 1—6.

¹ And it came to pass, when Jesus had finished all these sayings, he said unto his disciples, **2** Ye know that after two days is *the feast of* the passover, and the Son of man is betrayed to **3** be crucified. Then assembled together the chief priests, and the scribes, and the elders of the people, unto the palace of the high priest, who was called Caiaphas, **4** ¹ and consulted that they might take Jesus by subtilty, and **5** kill *him*. But they said, Not on the feast-*day*, lest there be an uproar among the people.

¹ After two days was *the feast of* the passover, and of unleavened bread. **2** put *him* to death. But they said, Not on the feast-*day*, lest there be an uproar of the people.

¹ Now the feast of unleavened bread drew nigh, which is called the Passover.

And the chief priests, and the scribes, sought how they might take him by craft, and

2 And the chief priests and scribes sought how they might kill him: for they feared the people.

6 Now when Jesus was in Bethany, in the house of Simon the leper

3 And being in Bethany, in the house of Simon the leper, as he sat at meat,

JOHN XII. 2—8.

2 There they made him a supper; and Martha served: but Lazarus was one of them that sat at the table with him.

MATTH. XXVI.	MARK XIV.	JOHN XII.

7 | there came unto him a woman having an alabaster-box of very precious ointment, and poured *it* on his head as he sat *at meat*. **8** But when his disciples saw *it*, they had indignation, saying, To what purpose *is* this **9** waste? | for this ointment might have been sold for much, and given to the poor.

there came a woman having an alabaster-box of spikenard, very precious; and she brake the box, **4** and poured *it* on his head. And there were some that had indignation within themselves, and said, Why was this waste of the oint- **5** ment made? | for it might have been sold for more than three hundred pence, and have been given to the poor. And they murmured against her.

3 Then took Mary a pound of ointment of spikenard, very costly and anointed the feet of Jesus, and wiped his feet with her hair: and the house was filled with the odour of the **4** ointment. Then saith one of his disciples, Judas Iscariot, Simon's *son*, which should be- **5** tray him, Why was not this ointment sold for three hundred pence, and given to the poor? **6** This he said, not that he cared for the poor; but because he was a thief, and had the bag, and bare what was put therein.

10 When Jesus understood *it*, he said unto them, Why trouble ye the woman? for she hath wrought a good work **11** upon me. For ye have the poor always with you; but me ye have **12** not always. For in that she hath poured this ointment on my body, she did *it* for my buri- **13** al. Verily I say unto you, Wheresoever this gospel shall be preached in the whole world, *there* shall also this, that this woman hath done, be told for a memorial of her.

6 And Jesus said, Let her alone; why trouble ye her? she hath wrought a good work **7** on me. For ye have the poor with you always, and whensoever ye will ye may do them good: **8** but me ye have not always. She hath done what she could: she is come aforehand to anoint my body **9** to the burying. Verily I say unto you, Wheresoever this gospel shall be preached throughout the whole world, *this* also that she hath done shall be spoken of, for a memorial of her.

7 Then said Jesus, Let her alone: against the day of my burying hath **8** she kept this. For the poor always ye have with you; but me ye have not always.

MARK XIV.	LUKE XXI.

14 Then one of the twelve, called Judas Iscariot, went unto the **15** chief priests, | and said *unto them*, What will ye give me, and I will deliver him unto you? And they covenanted with him for thirty pieces of silver. **16** And from that time he sought opportunity to betray him.

10 And Judas Iscariot, one of the twelve, went unto the chief priests, to betray him unto **11** them. And when they heard *it*, they were glad, and promised to give him money. And he sought how he might conveniently betray him.

3 Then entered Satan into Judas surnamed Iscariot, being of the number of the twelve. **4** And he went his way, and communed with the chief priests and captains, how he might betray him unto them. **5** And they were glad, and covenanted to give **6** him money. And he promised, and sought opportunity to betray him unto them in the absence of the multitude.

§ 132. *Preparation for the Passover.*—BETHANY. JERUSALEM.

Fifth Day of the Week.

MATTH. XXVI. 17—19.	MARK XIV. 12—16.	LUKE XXII. 7—13.
17 Now the first *day* of the *feast of* unleavened bread, the disciples came to Jesus, saying unto him, Where wilt thou that we prepare for thee to eat the passover?	12 And the first day of unleavened bread, when they killed the passover, his disciples said unto him, Where wilt thou that we go and prepare, that thou mayest eat the passover?	7 Then came the day of unleavened bread, when the passover must 8 be killed. And he sent Peter and John, saying, Go and prepare us the passover, that we may 9 eat. And they said unto him, Where wilt thou that we prepare?
18 And he said, Go into the city to such a man,	13 And he sendeth forth two of his disciples, and saith unto them, Go ye into the city, and there shall meet you a man bearing a pitcher of water: follow him. 14 And wheresoever he shall go in, say ye to	10 And he said unto them, Behold, when ye are entered into the city, there shall a man meet you, bearing a pitcher of water; follow him into the house where he entereth
and say unto him, The Master saith, My time is at hand; I will keep the passover at thy house with my disciples.	the good man of the house, The Master saith, Where is the guest-chamber, where I shall eat the passover with my disciples?	11 in. And ye shall say unto the good man of the house, The Master saith unto thee, Where is the guest-chamber, where I shall eat the passover with my disciples?
19 And the disciples did as Jesus had appointed them; and they made ready the passover.	15 And he will shew you a large upper room furnished *and* prepared: there make ready for us. 16 And his disciples went forth, and came into the city, and found as he had said unto them: and they made ready the passover.	12 And he shall shew you a large upper room furnished: there make 13 ready. And they went and found as he had said unto them: and they made ready the passover.

PART VIII.

THE FOURTH PASSOVER; OUR LORD'S PASSION; AND THE ACCOMPANY ING EVENTS UNTIL THE END OF THE JEWISH SABBATH.

TIME: *Two days.*

---

§ 133. *The Passover Meal. Contention among the Twelve.*—JERUSALEM.

Evening introducing the Sixth Day of the Week.

MATTH. XXVI. 20.	MARK XIV. 17.	LUKE XXII. 14–18. 24–30.
NOW when the even was come, he sat down with the twelve.	And in the evening he cometh with the twelve.	And when the hour was come, he sat down, and the twelve apostles with him.

And he said unto them, With desire I have desired to eat this passover with you before I suffer. For I say unto you, I will not any more eat thereof, until it be fulfilled in the kingdom of God. And he took the cup, and gave thanks, and said, Take this, and divide it among yourselves. For I say unto you, I will not drink of the fruit of the vine, until the kingdom of God shall come.—

And there was also a strife among them, which of them should be accounted the greatest. And he said unto them, The kings of the Gentiles exercise lordship over them; and they that exercise authority upon them are called benefactors. But ye *shall* not *be* so: but he that is greatest among you, let him be as the younger; and he that is chief, as he that doth serve. For whether *is* greater, he that sitteth at meat, or he that serveth? *is* not he that sitteth at meat? but I am among you as he that serveth. Ye are they which have continued with me in my temptations; ' and I appoint unto you a kingdom, as my Father hath appointed unto me; ' that ye may eat and drink at my table in my kingdom, and sit on thrones, judging the twelve tribes of Israel.

§ 134. *Jesus washes the feet of his Disciples.*—JERUSALEM.

Evening introducing the Sixth Day of the Week.

JOHN XIII. 1—20.

Now before the feast of the passover, when Jesus knew that his hour was come that he should depart out of this world unto the Father, having loved

JOHN XIII.

² his own which were in the world, he loved them unto the end.   And supper being ended, (the devil having now put into the heart of Judas Iscariot,
² Simon's *son*, to betray him,) ¹ Jesus knowing that the Father had given al.
things into his hands, and that he was come from God, and went to God
⁴ ¹ he riseth from supper, and laid aside his garments, and took a towel, and
⁶ girded himself.   After that, he poureth water into a basin, and began to
wash the disciples' feet, and to wipe *them* with the towel wherewith he was
⁶ girded.   Then cometh he to Simon Peter: and Peter saith unto him, Lord,
⁷ dost thou wash my feet?   Jesus answered and said unto him, What I do
⁸ thou knowest not now; but thou shalt know hereafter.   Peter saith unto
him, Thou shalt never wash my feet.   Jesus answered him, If I wash thee
⁹ not, thou hast no part with me.   Simon Peter saith unto him, Lord, not
¹⁰ my feet only, but also *my* hands and *my* head.   Jesus saith to him, He
that is washed needeth not save to wash *his* feet, but is clean every whit:
¹¹ and ye are clean, but not all.   For he knew who should betray him: therefore said he, Ye are not all clean.
¹² So after he had washed their feet, and had taken his garments, and was
set down again, he said unto them, Know ye what I have done to you?
¹³ ¹⁴ Ye call me Master, and Lord: and ye say well: for *so* I am.   If I then,
your Lord and Master, have washed your feet; ye also ought to wash one
¹⁵ another's feet.   For I have given you an example, that ye should do as I
¹⁶ have done to you.   Verily, verily, I say unto you, The servant is not greater
¹⁷ than his lord; neither he that is sent greater than he that sent him.   If
¹⁸ ye know these things, happy are ye if ye do them.   I speak not of you all;
I know whom I have chosen; but that the scripture may be fulfilled,ᵃ He
⁹ that eateth bread with me, hath lifted up his heel against me.   Now I tel¹
you before it come, that when it is come to pass, ye may believe that I am
²⁰ *he.*   Verily, verily, I say unto you, He that receiveth whomsoever I send,
receiveth me; and he that receiveth me, receiveth him that sent me.

§ 135. *Jesus points out the Traitor.   Judas withdraws.*—JERUSALEM.

Evening introducing the Sixth Day of the Week.

MATTH. XXVI. 21—25.	MARK XIV. 18—21.	LUKE XXII. 21--23.	JOHN XIII. 21—35.
²¹ And as they did eat, he said, Verily I say unto you, that one of you shall betray me.	¹⁸ And as they sat, and did eat, Jesus said, Verily I say unto you, One of you which eateth with me, shall	²¹ But behold, the hand of him that betrayeth me *is* with me on the table.—	²¹ When Jesus had thus said, he was troubled in spirit, and testified, and said, Verily, verily, I say unto you,
²² And they were exceeding sorrowful, and began every one of them to say unto him, Lord, is it I?	¹⁹ betray me. And ²⁰ they began to be sorrowful, and to say unto him one by one, *Is* it I? and another *said, Is* it I?	²³ And they began to inquire among them-selves, which of them it was that should do this thing.	that one of you shall betray me. ²² Then the dis-ciples looked one on ano-ther, d/ubting of whom he spake.

ᵃ 18. Ps. 41, 9.

JOHN XIII.

[23] Now there was leaning on Jesus' bosom, one of his disciples, whom Jesus [24] loved.   Simon Peter therefore beckoned to him, that he should ask who it [25] should be of whom he spake.   He then, lying on Jesus' breast, saith unto

MATTH. XXVI.	MARK XIV.	him, Lord, who is it ?
[23] And he answered and said, He that dippeth *his* hand with me in the dish, the same shall [24] betray me. The Son of man goeth, as it is written of him : but wo unto that man by whom the Son of man is betrayed! it had been good for that man if he had not been [25] born. Then Judas, which betrayed him, answered and said, Master, is it I ? him, Thou hast said.	[20] And he answered and said unto them, *It is* one of the twelve that dippeth with me in the [21] dish. The Son of man indeed goeth, as it is written of him : but wo to the man by whom the Son of man is betrayed! good were it for that man if he had never been born. He said unto	[26] Jesus answered, He it is to whom I shall give a sop, when I have dipped *it.*—
		LUKE XXII.
		[22] And truly the Son of man goeth as it was determined : but wo unto that man by whom he is betrayed !
		JOHN XIII.
		[26] —And when he had dipped the sop, he gave *it* to Judas Iscariot, *the son* of Simon. [27] And after the sop Satan entered into him. Then said Jesus unto him,

[28] That thou doest, do quickly.   Now no man at the table knew for what in- [29] tent he spake this unto him.   For some *of them* thought, because Judas had the bag, that Jesus had said unto him, Buy *those things* that we have need [30] of against the feast ; or, that he should give something to the poor.   He then, having received the sop, went immediately out : and it was night. [31] Therefore, when he was gone out, Jesus said, Now is the Son of man glo- [32] rified, and God is glorified in him.   If God be glorified in him, God shall [33] also glorify him in himself, and shall straightway glorify him.   Little children, yet a little while I am with you.   Ye shall seek me ; and, as I said [34] unto the Jews, Whither I go, ye cannot come, so now I say to you.   A new commandment I give unto you, that ye love one another ; as I have [35] loved you, that ye also love one another.   By this shall all *men* know that ye are my disciples, if ye have love one to another.

§ 136. *Jesus foretells the fall of Peter, and the dispersion of the Twelve.*— JERUSALEM.

Evening introducing the Sixth Day of the Week.

JOHN XIII. 36—38.

[36]   Simon Peter said unto him, Lord, whither goest thou ? Jesus answered him, Whither I go, thou canst not follow me now ; but thou shalt follow me [37] afterward.   Peter said unto him, Lord, why cannot I follow thee now ? I will lay down my life for thy sake.

MATTH. XXVI. 31—35.	MARK XIV. 27—31.
[31] Then saith Jesus unto them, All ye shall be offended because of me this night : for it is written,[a] I will smite the Shepherd, and the sheep of the flock shall be scattered abroad.	[27] And Jesus saith unto them, All ye shall be offended because of me this night : for it is written,[a] I will smite the Shepherd, and the sheep shall be [28] scattered. But after that I am risen,

[a] 31 etc. Zech. 13. 7.

MATTH. XXVI.	MARK XIV.
[32] But after I am risen again, I will go [33] before you into Galilee. Peter answered and said unto him, Though all *men* shall be offended because of thee, *yet* will I never be offended.	I will go before you into Galilee. [29] But Peter said unto him, Although all shall be offended, yet *will* not I.

Luke XXII. 31—38.

[31] And the Lord said, Simon, Simon, behold, Satan hath desired *to have* [32] you, that he may sift *you* as wheat: ' but I have prayed for thee, that thy [33] faith fail not: and when thou art converted, strengthen thy brethren. And he said unto him, Lord, I am ready to go with thee, both into prison, and to death.

MATTH. XXVI.	MARK XIV.	LUKE XXII.	JOHN XIII.
[34] Jesus said unto him, Verily I say unto thee, That this night, before the cock crow, thou shalt deny [35] me thrice. Peter said unto him, Though I should die with thee, yet will I not deny thee. Likewise also said all the disciples.	[30] And Jesus saith unto him, Verily I say unto thee, That this day, *even* in this night, before the cock crow twice, thou [31] shalt deny me thrice. But he spake the more vehemently, if I should die with thee, I will not deny thee in any wise. Likewise also said they all.	[34] And he said, I tell thee, Peter, the cock shall not crow this day, before that thou shalt thrice deny that thou knowest me.	[38] Jesus answered him, Wilt thou lay down thy life for my sake? Verily, verily, I say unto thee, The cock shall not crow, till thou hast denied me thrice.

LUKE XXII.

[35] And he said unto them, When I sent you without purse, and scrip, and [36] shoes, lacked ye any thing? And they said, Nothing. Then said he unto them, But now, he that hath a purse, let him take *it*, and likewise *his* scrip: [37] and he that hath no sword, let him sell his garment, and buy one. For I say unto you, that this that is written must yet be accomplished in me,[a] And he was reckoned among the transgressors: for the things concerning [38] me have an end. And they said, Lord, behold, here *are* two swords. And he said unto them, It is enough.

§ 137. *The Lord's Supper.*—JERUSALEM.

Evening introducing the Sixth Day of the Week.

MATTH. XXVI. 26—29.	MARK XIV. 22—25.	LUKE XXII. 19, 20.	1 COR. XI. 23—25.
[26] And as they were eating, Jesus took bread, and blessed *it*, and brake it, and gave *it* to the disciples, and said, Take, eat: this is my body.	[22] And as they did eat, Jesus took bread, and blessed, and brake *it*, and gave to them, and said, Take, eat: this is my body.	[19] And he took bread, and gave thanks, and brake *it*, and gave unto them, saying, This is my body which is given for you: this do in remembrance of me.	[23] The Lord Jesus—took bread, [24] and when he had given thanks, he brake *it*, and said, Take, eat: this is my body which is broken for you: this do in remembrance of me.

12   [a] 37. Is. 53, 12

MATTH. XXVI.	MARK XIV.	LUKE XXII.	1 COR. XI.

[27] And he took the cup, and gave thanks, and gave it to them, saying, Drink ye [28] all of it; [29] for this is my blood of the new testament, which is shed for many for the remission of sins. But I say unto you, I will not drink henceforth of this

[23] And he took the cup, and when he had given thanks, he gave it to them: and they all [24] drank of it. And he said unto them, This is my blood of the new [25] testament, which is shed for many. Verily I say unto you, I will drink no more of the fruit of the vine, until that day that I drink it new in the kingdom of God.

[20] Likewise also the cup after supper, saying, This cup is the new testament in my blood, which is shed for you.

[25] After the same manner also he took the cup, when he had supped, saying, This cup is the new testament in my blood: this do ye, as oft as ye drink it, in remembrance of me.

fruit of the vine, until that day when I drink it new with you in my Father's kingdom.

§ 138. *Jesus comforts his Disciples.   The Holy Spirit promised.*—JERUSALEM.

Evening introducing the Sixth Day of the Week

JOHN XIV. 1—31.

[1] Let not your heart be troubled: ye believe in God, believe also in me.
[2] In my Father's house are many mansions: if *it were* not *so*, I would have
[3] told you. I go to prepare a place for you. ' And *if* I go and prepare a place for you, I will come again and receive you unto myself; that where
[4] I am, *there* ye may be also. And whither I go ye know, and the way ye
[5] know. Thomas saith unto him, Lord, we know not whither thou goest;
[6] and how can we know the way? Jesus saith unto him, I am the way, and
[7] the truth, and the life: no man cometh unto the Father, but by me. If ye had known me, ye should have known my Father also: and from henceforth ye know him, and have seen him.
[8] Philip saith unto him, Lord, shew us the Father, and it sufficeth us.
[9] Jesus saith unto him, Have I been so long time with you, and yet hast thou not known me, Philip? he that hath seen me, hath seen the Father;
[10] and how sayest thou then, Shew us the Father? Believest thou not that I am in the Father, and the Father in me? the words that I speak unto you, I speak not of myself: but the Father, that dwelleth in me, he doeth the
[11] works. Believe me that I *am* in the Father, and the Father in me: or else
[12] believe me for the very works' sake. Verily, verily, I say unto you, He that believeth on me, the works that I do shall he do also; and greater
[13] *works* than these shall he do; because I go unto my Father. And whatsoever ye shall ask in my name, that will I do, that the Father may be glori-
[14] fied in the Son. If ye shall ask any thing in my name, I will do *it*.
[15] [16] If ye love me, keep my commandments: ' and I will pray the Father, and he shall give you another Comforter, that he may abide with you for
[17] ever; ' *even* the Spirit of truth; whom the world cannot receive, because it seeth him not, neither knoweth him: but ye know him; for he dwelleth
[18] with you, and shall be in you. I will not leave you comfortless: I will
[19] come to you. Yet a little while, and the world seeth me no more; but ye
[20] see me: because I live, ye shall live also. At that day ye shall know that
[21] I *am* in my Father, and ye in me, and I in you. He that hath my com

JOHN XIV.

mandments, and keepeth them, he it is that loveth me: and he that loveth me, shall be loved of my Father, and I will love him, and will manifest
¹² myself to him. Judas saith unto him, (not Iscariot,) Lord, how is it that
²³ thou wilt manifest thyself unto us, and not unto the world? Jesus answered and said unto him, If a man love me, he will keep my words: and my Father will love him, and we will come unto him, and make our abode
²⁴ with him. He that loveth me not, keepeth not my sayings: and the word which ye hear is not mine, but the Father's which sent me.
²⁵ ²⁶ These things have I spoken unto you, being *yet* present with you. But the Comforter, *which is* the Holy Ghost, whom the Father will send in'my name, he shall teach you all things, and bring all things to your remem-
²⁷ brance, whatsoever I have said unto you. Peace I leave with you, my peace I give unto you: not as the world giveth, give I unto you. Let not
²⁸ your heart be troubled, neither let it be afraid. Ye have heard how I said unto you, I go away, and come *again* unto you. If ye loved me, ye would rejoice, because I said, I go unto the Father: for my Father is greater than
²⁹ I. And now I have told you before it come to pass, that when it is come
³⁰ to pass, ye might believe. Hereafter I will not talk much with you: for
³¹ the prince of this world cometh, and hath nothing in me. But that the world may know that I love the Father; and as the Father gave me commandment, even so I do. Arise, let us go hence.

§ 139. *Christ the true Vine. His Disciples hated by the World.—*
JERUSALEM.

Evening introducing the Sixth Day of the Week.

JOHN XV. 1—27.

¹ ² I am the true vine, and my Father is the husbandman. Every branch in me that beareth not fruit, he taketh away: and every *branch* that bear-
³ eth fruit, he purgeth it, that it may bring forth more fruit. Now ye are
⁴ clean through the word which I have spoken unto you. Abide in me, and I in you. As the branch cannot bear fruit of itself, except it abide in the
⁵ vine; no more can ye, except ye abide in me. I am the vine, ye *are* the branches: he that abideth in me, and I in him, the same bringeth forth
⁶ much fruit: for without me ye can do nothing. If a man abide not in me, he is cast forth as a branch, and is withered; and men gather them, and
⁷ cast *them* into the fire, and they are burned. If ye abide in me, and my words abide in you, ye shall ask what ye will, and it shall be done unto
⁸ you. Herein is my Father glorified, that ye bear much fruit; so shall ye
⁹ be my disciples. As the Father hath loved me, so have I loved you: con-
¹⁰ tinue ye in my love. If ye keep my commandments, ye shall abide in my love; even as I have kept my Father's commandments, and abide in his
¹¹ love. These things have I spoken unto you, that my joy might remain in you, and *that* your joy might be full.
¹² This is my commandment, That ye love one another, as I have loved
¹³ you. Greater love hath no man than this, that a man lay down his life for
¹⁴ his friends. Ye are my friends, if ye do whatsoever I command you.
¹⁵ Henceforth I call you not servants; for the servant knoweth not what his lord doeth: but I have called you friends; for all things that I have heard of my Father, I have made known unto you. Ye have not chosen me, but I have chosen you, and ordained you, that ye should go and bring forth fruit, and *that* your fruit should remain: that whatsoever ye shall ask of the

JOHN XV.

[8] Father in my name, he may give it you. These things I command you, [9] That ye love one another. If the world hate you, ye know that it hated me [9] before it *hated* you. If ye were of the world, the world would love his own ; but because ye are not of the world, but I have chosen you out of the world, therefore the world hateth you.

[10] Remember the word that I said unto you, The servant is not greater than his lord. If they have persecuted me, they will also persecute you : if they [11] have kept my saying, they will keep yours also. But all these things will they do unto you for my name's sake, because they know not him that sent [12] me. If I had not come and spoken unto them, they had not had sin : but [13] now they have no cloak for their sin. He that hateth me, hateth my Father [14] also. If I had not done among them the works which none other man did, they had not had sin : but now have they both seen, and hated both me and [15] my Father. But *this cometh to pass*, that the word might be fulfilled that [16] is written in their law,[a] They hated me without a cause. But when the Comforter is come, whom I will send unto you from the Father, *even* the Spirit [17] of truth, which proceedeth from the Father, he shall testify of me. And ye also shall bear witness, because ye have been with me from the beginning.

§ 140. *Persecution foretold. Further promise of the Holy Spirit. Prayer in the name of Christ.*—JERUSALEM.

Evening introducing the Sixth Day of the Week.

JOHN XVI. 1—33.

[1] These things have I spoken unto you, that ye should not be offended. [2] They shall put you out of the synagogues : yea, the time cometh, that [3] whosoever killeth you, will think that he doeth God service. And these things will they do unto you, because they have not known the Father, nor [4] me. But these things have I told you, that when the time shall come, ye may remember that I told you of them. And these things I said not unto [5] you at the beginning because I was with you. But now I go my way to [6] him that sent me, and none of you asketh me, Whither goest thou ? But because I have said these things unto you, sorrow hath filled your heart. [7] Nevertheless, I tell you the truth : It is expedient for you that I go away : for if I go not away, the Comforter will not come unto you ; but if [8] I depart, I will send him unto you. And when he is come, he will reprove [9] the world of sin, and of righteousness, and of judgment : [1] of sin, because [10] they believe not on me ; [1] of righteousness, because I go to my Father, and [11] ye see me no more ; [1] of judgment, because the prince of this world is [12] judged. I have yet many things to say unto you, but ye cannot bear them [13] now. Howbeit, when he, the Spirit of truth, is come, he will guide you into all truth : for he shall not speak of himself ; but whatsoever he shall [14] hear, *that* shall he speak : and he will shew you things to come. He shall [15] glorify me : for he shall receive of mine, and shall shew *it* unto you. All things that the Father hath are mine : therefore said I, that he shall take [16] of mine, and shall shew *it* unto you. A little while, and ye shall not see me : and again, a little while, and ye shall see me, because I go to the Father.

[17] Then said *some* of his disciples among themselves, What is this that he saith unto us, A little while, and ye shall not see me : and again, a little

JOHN XVI.

¹⁸ while, and ye shall see me: and, Because I go to the Father? They said therefore, What is this that he saith, A little while? we cannot tell what ¹⁹ he saith. Now Jesus knew that they were desirous to ask him, and said unto them, Do ye inquire among yourselves of that I said, A little while, and ye shall not see me: and again, a little while, and ye shall see me? ²⁰ Verily, verily, I say unto you, that ye shall weep and lament, but the world shall rejoice: and ye shall be sorrowful, but your sorrow shall be turned ²¹ into joy. A woman when she is in travail hath sorrow, because her hour is come: but as soon as she is delivered of the child, she remembereth no ²² more the anguish, for joy that a man is born into the world. And ye now therefore have sorrow: but I will see you again, and your heart shall ²³ rejoice, and your joy no man taketh from you. And in that day ye shall ask me nothing. Verily, verily, I say unto you, Whatsoever ye shall ask ²⁴ the Father in my name, he will give it you. Hitherto have ye asked nothing in my name: ask, and ye shall receive, that your joy may be full. ²⁵ These things have I spoken unto you in proverbs: but the time cometh when I shall no more speak unto you in proverbs, but I shall shew you ²⁶ plainly of the Father. At that day ye shall ask in my name: and I say ²⁷ not unto you, that I will pray the Father for you: ' for the Father himself loveth you, because ye have loved me, and have believed that I came out ²⁸ from God. I came forth from the Father, and am come into the world: ²⁹ again, I leave the world, and go to the Father. His disciples said unto ³⁰ him, Lo, now speakest thou plainly, and speakest no proverb. Now are we sure that thou knowest all things, and needest not that any man should ³¹ ask thee: by this we believe that thou camest forth from God. Jesus an- ³² swered them, Do ye now believe? ' behold, the hour cometh, yea, is now come, that ye shall be scattered every man to his own, and shall leave me ³³ alone: and yet I am not alone, because the Father is with me. These things I have spoken unto you, that in me ye might have peace. In the world ye shall have tribulation, but be of good cheer: I have overcome the world. ┄

§ 141. *Christ's last prayer with his Disciples.*—JERUSALEM.

Evening introducing the Sixth Day of the Week.

JOHN XVII. 1—26.

¹ These words spake Jesus, and lifted up his eyes to heaven, and said, Father, the hour is come; glorify thy Son, that thy Son also may glorify ² thee: ' as thou hast given him power over all flesh, that he should give ³ eternal life to as many as thou hast given him. And this is life eternal, that they might know thee the only true God, and Jesus Christ whom thou ⁴ hast sent. I have glorified thee on the earth: I have finished the work ⁵ which thou gavest me to do. And now, O Father, glorify thou me with thine own self, with the glory which I had with thee before the world was. ⁶ I have manifested thy name unto the men which thou gavest me out of the world: thine they were, and thou gavest them me; and they have kept ⁷ thy word. Now they have known that all things whatsoever thou hast ⁸ given me are of thee: ' for I have given unto them the words which thou gavest me; and they have received *them*, and have known surely that I ⁹ came out from thee, and they have believed that thou didst send me. I pray for them: I pray not for the world, but for them which thou hast given ¹⁰ me; for they are thine. And all mine are thine, and thine are mine; and ¹¹ I am glorified in them. And now I am no more in the world, but these

12*

JOHN XVII.

are in the world, and I come to thee. Holy Father, keep through thine
own name those whom thou hast given me, that they may be one, as we
[12] *are.* While I was with them in the world, I kept them in thy name: those
that thou gavest me I have kept, and none of them is lost, but the son of
[13] perdition ; that the scripture might be fulfilled.[a] And now come I to thee,
and these things I speak in the world, that they might have my joy fulfilled
[14] in themselves. I have given them thy word ; and the world hath hated
[15] them, because they are not of the world, even as I am not of the world. I
pray not that thou shouldest take them out of the world, but that thou
[16] shouldest keep them from the evil. They are not of the world, even as I
[17] am not of the world. Sanctify them through thy truth: thy word is truth.
[18] As thou hast sent me into the world, even so have I also sent them into
[19] the world. And for their sakes I sanctify myself, that they also might
be sanctified through the truth.
[20]   Neither pray I for these alone ; but for them also which shall believe on
[21] me through their word: ' that they all may be one ; as thou, Father, *art* in
me, and I in thee, that they also may be one in us: that the world may
[22] believe that thou hast sent me. And the glory which thou gavest me, I
[23] have given them ; that they may be one, even as we are one ; ' I in them,
and thou in me, that they may be made perfect in one ; and that the world
may know that thou hast sent me, and hast loved them as thou hast
loved me.
[24]   Father, I will that they also whom thou hast given me be with me where
I am ; that they may behold my glory which thou hast given me: for thou
[25] lovedst me before the foundation of the world. O righteous Father, the
world hath not known thee: but I have known thee, and these have known
[26] that thou hast sent me. And I have declared unto them thy name, and
will declare *it :* that the love wherewith thou hast loved me, may be in
them, and I in them.

§ 142. *The agony in Gethsemane.*—MOUNT OF OLIVES.

Evening introducing the Sixth Day of the Week.

MATTH. XXVI. 30, 36—46.	MARK XIV. 26, 32—42.	LUKE XXII. 39–46.	JOHN XVIII. 1.
[30] And when they had sung an hymn, they went out into the mount of [36] Olives. — Then cometh Jesus with them unto a place called Gethsemane, and saith unto the disciples, Sit ye here, while I go and pray yonder.	[26] And when they had sung an hymn, they went out into the mount of [32] Olives. — And they came to a place which was named Gethsemane: and he saith to his disciples, Sit ye here, while I shall pray.	[39] And he came out, and went, as he was wont, to the mount of Olives; and his disciples also followed him. And [40] when he was at the place, he said unto them, Pray that ye enter not into temptation.	[1] When Jesus had spoken these words, he went forth with his disciples over the brook Cedron, where was a garden, into the which he entered, and his disciples.

[a] 12 Comp. Ps. 41, 9. 109, 8. 17

MATTH. XXVI.

7 And he took with him Peter, and the two sons of Zebedee, and began 38 to be sorrowful and very heavy. Then saith he unto them, My soul is exceeding sorrowful, even unto death: tarry ye here, and watch 39 with me. And he went a little further, and fell on his face, and prayed,

saying, O my Father, if it be possible, let this cup pass from me: nevertheless, not as I will, but as thou *wilt*.

MARK XIV.

33 And he taketh with him Peter, and James, and John, and began to be sore amazed, and to be very 34 heavy; 1 and saith unto them, My soul is exceeding sorrowful unto death: tarry ye here, and watch. 35 And he went forward a little, and fell on the ground, and prayed that, if it were possible, the hour might pass from 36 him. And he said, Abba, Father, all things *are* possible unto thee; take away this cup from me: nevertheless, not what I will, but what thou wilt.

LUKE XXII.

41 And he was withdrawn from them about a stone's cast, and kneeled down, and 42 prayed, 1 saying, Father, if thou be willing, remove this cup from me: nevertheless, not my will, but thine, be 43 done. And there appeared an angel unto 44 to him from heaven, strengthening him. And being in an agony, he prayed more earnestly: and his sweat was as it were great drops of blood falling down to the ground.

40 And he cometh unto the disciples, and findeth them asleep, and saith unto Peter, What! could ye not watch with me one hour? 41 Watch and pray, that ye enter not into temptation: the spirit indeed *is* willing, but the flesh 42 *is* weak. He went away again the second time, and prayed, saying, O my Father, if this cup may not pass away from me except I drink it, thy will be done. 43 And he came and found them asleep again: for their eyes were heavy. 44 And he left them, and went away again, and prayed the third time, saying the same words. 45 Then cometh he to his disciples, and saith unto them, Sleep on now, and take *your* rest: behold, the hour is at hand, and the Son of man is betrayed into the hands of sinners. 9 Rise, let us be going: behold, he is at hand that doth betray me.

37 And he cometh, and findeth them sleeping, and saith unto Peter, Simon, sleepest thou? couldest not thou watch 38 one hour? Watch ye and pray, lest ye enter into temptation. The spirit truly *is* ready, but 39 the flesh *is* weak. And again he went away, and prayed, 40 and spake the same words. And when he returned, he found them asleep again, for their eyes were heavy; neither wist they what to answer him.

45 And when he rose up from prayer, and was come to his disciples, he found them sleeping for sorrow, 46 1 and said unto them, Why sleep ye? rise and pray, lest ye enter into temptation.

41 And he cometh the third time, and saith unto them, Sleep on now, and take *your* rest: it is enough, the hour is come; behold, the Son of 42 man is betrayed into the hands of sinners. Rise up, let us go; lo, he that betrayeth me is at hand.

§ 143. *Jesus betrayed, and made prisoner.*—MOUNT OF OLIVES.

Evening introducing the Sixth Day of the Week.

JOHN XVIII. 2—12.

² And Judas also, which betrayed him, knew the place: for Jesus oft-
³ times resorted thither with his disciples. Judas then, having received a
band *of men* and officers from the chief priests and Pharisees, cometh thither
with lanterns, and torches, and weapons.

MATTH. XXVI. 47—56.	MARK XIV. 43—52.	LUKE XXII. 47—53.
⁴⁷ And while he yet spake, lo, Judas, one of the twelve, came, and with him a great multitude with swords and staves, from the chief priests and elders of the people.	⁴³ And immediately while he yet spake, cometh Judas, one of the twelve, and with him a great multitude with swords and staves, from the chief priests, and the scribes, and the elders.	⁴⁷ And while he yet spake, behold a multitude, and he that was called Judas, one of the twelve, went before them.—

JOHN XVIII.

⁴ Jesus therefore, knowing all things that should come upon him, went
⁵ forth, and said unto them, Whom seek ye? They answered him, Jesus of
Nazareth. Jesus saith unto them, I am *he.* And Judas also, which be-
⁶ trayed him, stood with them. As soon then as he had said unto them, I
⁷ am *he,* they went backward, and fell to the ground. Then asked he them
⁸ again, Whom seek ye? And they said, Jesus of Nazareth. ' Jesus answered, I have told you that I am *he.* If therefore ye seek me, let these
⁹ go their way: ' that the saying might be fulfilled which he spake, Of them
which thou gavest me, have I lost none.

MATTH. XXVI.	MARK XIV.	LUKE XXII.	JOHN XVIII.
⁴⁸ Now he that betrayed him, gave them a sign, saying, Whomsoever I shall kiss, that same is he; hold him fast. ⁴⁹ And forthwith he came to Jesus, and said, Hail, Master; and kissed him. And Jesus said unto him, Friend, wherefore art thou come? Then came they, and laid hands on Jesus, and took him. And behold, one of them which were with Jesus, stretched	⁴⁴ And he that betrayed him, had given them a token, saying, Whomsoever I shall kiss, that same is he; take him, and lead *him* away safely. ⁴⁵ And as soon as he was come, he goeth straightway to him, and saith, Master, Master; and ⁴⁶ kissed him. And they laid their hands on him, and took him. ⁴⁷ And one of them that stood by, drew a sword, and smote a ser-	And *he* drew near unto Jesus to kiss ⁴⁸ him. But Jesus said unto him, Judas, betrayest thou the Son of man with a kiss? ⁴⁹ When they which were about him saw what would follow, they said unto him, Lord, shall we smite with the sword? ⁵⁰ And one of them smote a servant of the high priest, and cut off his	¹² Then the band, and the captain, and officers of the Jews took Jesus, and bound ¹⁰ him.—Then Simon Peter, having a sword, drew it, and smote the

MATTH. XXVI.	MARK XIV.	LUKE XXII.	JOHN XVIII.
out *his* hand, and drew his sword, and struck a servant of the high [52] priest, and smote off his ear. Then said Jesus unto him, Put up again thy sword into his place ; for all they that take the sword, shall perish with the sword.[a] Thinkest thou that I cannot now pray to my Father, and he shall presently give me more than twelve legions of angels? [54] But how then shall the scriptures be fulfilled, that thus it must be ?	vant of the high priest, and cut off his ear.	[51] right ear. And Jesus answered and said, Suffer ye thus far. And he touched his ear, and healed him.	high priest's servant, and cut off his right ear. The servant's name was Malchus. [11] Then said Jesus unto Peter, Put up thy sword into the sheath : the cup which my Father hath given me, shall I not drink it ?

MATTH. XXVI.	MARK XIV.	LUKE XXII.
[55] In that same hour said Jesus to the multitudes, Are ye come out as against a thief with swords and staves for to take me? I sat daily with you teaching in the temple, and ye laid [56] no hold on me. But all this was done, that the scriptures of the prophets might be fulfilled. Then all the disciples forsook him, and fled.	[48] And Jesus answered and said unto them, Are ye come out as against a thief, with swords and *with* staves [49] to take me? I was daily with you in the temple, teaching, and ye took me not: but the scriptures must be [50] fulfilled. And they all forsook him and fled. [51] And there followed him a certain young man, having a linen	[52] Then Jesus said unto the chief priests, and captains of the temple, and the elders which were come to him, Be ye come out as against a thief, with swords [53] and staves? When I was daily with you in the temple, ye stretched forth no hands against me : but this is your hour, and the power of darkness.

cloth cast about *his* naked *body :* and the young [52] men laid hold on him And ne left the linen cloth, and fled from them naked.

§ 144. *Jesus before Caiaphas. ˉPeter thrice denies him.*—JERUSALEM.

Night introducing the Sixth Day of the Week.

MATTH. XXVI. 57, 58, 69—75.   MARK XIV. 53, 54, 66—72.   LUKE XXII. 54—62.   JOHN XVIII.13—18, 25—27.

¶ And they that [57] had laid hold on Jesus, led *him* away to Caiaphas the high priest, where the scribes and the elders were assembled.	[53] And they led Jesus away to the high priest : and with him were assembled all the chief priests, and the elders and the scribes.	[54] Then took they him, and led *him,* and brought him into the high priest's house.—	[13] And *they* led him away to Annas first ; for he was father-in-law to Caiaphas, which was the [14] high priest that same year. Now Caiaphas was he which gave counsel to the Jews, that it was expedient that one man should die for the people.

---

a **52**. Comp. Gen. 9, 6.

MATTH. XXVI.	MARK XIV.	LUKE XXII.	JOHN XVIII.

MATTH. XXVI.

[58] But Peter follow-ed him afar off, unto the high priest's palace,—

—and went in, and sat with the servants to see the end.—

[69] Now Peter sat without in the palace: and a damsel came un-to him, saying, Thou also wast with Jesus of [70] Galilee. But he denied before *them* all, saying, I know not what thou sayest.
[71] And when he was gone out into the porch, anoth-er *maid* saw him, and said unto them that were there, This *fel-low* was also with Jesus of Naza-[72]reth. And again he denied with an oath, I do not know the man.
[73] And after a while came unto *him* they that stood by, and said to Peter, Surely thou also

MARK XIV.

[54] And Peter fol-lowed him afar off, even into the palace of the high priest:—

—and he sat with the servants, and warmed himself at the fire.—
[66] And as Peter was beneath in the palace, there cometh one of the maids of the high priest:
[67] and when she saw Peter warm-ing himself, she looked upon him, and said, And thou also wast with Jesus of Na-[68]zareth. But he denied, saying, I know not, nei-ther understand I what thou sayest.
And he went out into the porch; and the [68] cock crew. And a maid saw him again, and began to say to them that stood by, This is *one* of [70] them. And he denied it again.
And a little after, they that stood by said again to Peter, Surely thou art *one* of them; for

LUKE XXII.

—And Peter fol-lowed afar off.

[55] And when they had kindled a fire in the midst of the hall, and were set down together, Peter sat down among them.

[56] But a certain maid beheld him as he sat by the fire, and earnest-ly looked upon him, and said, This man was also with him. [57] And he denied him, saying, Wo-man, I know him not.
[58] And after a little while an-other saw him, and said, Thou art also of them. And Peter said, Man, I am not.
[59] And about the space of one hour after, another confidently af-firmed, saying, Of a truth this

JOHN XVIII.

[15] And Simon Pe-ter followed Je-sus, and *so did* another disciple. That disciple was known unto the high priest, and went in with Jesus, into the palace of the high priest. But Peter stood at the door without. Then went out that other disciple which was known unto the high priest, and spake unto her that kept the door, and [16] brought in Peter.—And the servants and officers stood there, who had made a fire of coals; (for it was cold;) and they warmed themselves: and Peter stood with them, and warm-ed himself.—

[17] Then saith the damsel that kept the door unto Peter, Art not thou also *one* of this man's disci-ples? He saith, I am not.—

[25] And Simon Peter stood and warmed him-self. They said therefore unto him, Art not thou also *one* of his disciples? He denied *it*, and said, I am not.

[26] One of the servants of the high priest (be-ing *his* kinsman whose ear Peter cut off) saith

MATTH. XXVI.	MARK XIV.	LUKE XXII.	JOHN XVIII.
art *one* of them; for thy speech bewrayeth thee. **74** Then began he to curse and to swear, *saying*, I know not the man. And immediately the cock crew.	thou art a Galile-an,and thyspeech agreeth *thereto* **71** But he began to curse and to swear, *saying*, I know not this man of whom **72** ye speak. And the second time the cock crew.	*fellow* also was with him; for he is a Galilean. **60** And Peter said, Man, I know not what thou say-est. And imme-diately, while he yet spake, the cock crew.	Did not I see thee in the gar-den with him? **27** Peter then deni-ed again:
76 And Peter re-membered the word of Jesus, which said unto him, Before the cock crow, thou shalt deny me thrice. And he went out, and wept bitterly.	And Peter called to mind the word that Jesus said unto him, Before the cock crow twice, thou shalt deny me thrice. And when he thought thereon, he wept.	and immediately the cock crew. **LUKE XXII.** **61** And the Lord turned, and looked upon Pe-ter. And Peter remem-bered the word of the Lord, how he had said unto him, Before the cock crow, thou shalt **62** deny me thrice. And Peter went out and wept bitterly.	

§ 145. *Jesus before Caiaphas and the Sanhedrim. He declares himself to be the Christ; is condemned and mocked.*—JERUSALEM.

Morning of the Sixth Day of the Week.

JOHN XVIII. 19—24.

19 The high priest then asked Jesus of his disciples, and of his doctrine. **20** And Jesus answered him, I spake openly to the world; I ever taught in the synagogue, and in the temple, whither the Jews always resort; and in **21** secret have I said nothing. Why askest thou me? ask them which heard **22** me, what I have said unto them: behold, they know what I said. And when he had thus spoken, one of the officers which stood by, struck Jesus **23** with the palm of his hand, saying, Answerest thou the high priest so? Je-sus answered him, If I have spoken evil, bear witness of the evil: but if **24** well, why smitest thou me? Now Annas had sent him bound unto Caia phas the high priest.

LUKE XXII. 63—71.

66 And as soon as it was day, the elders of the people, and the chief priests,. and the scribes came together, and led him into their council.

MATTH. XXVI. 59—68.	MARK XIV. 55—65.
59 Now the chief priests, and elders, and all the council, sought false witness against Jesus, to put him **60** to death; ' but found none: yea, though many false witnesses came, *yet* found they none. At the last **61** came two false witnesses, ' and said, This *fellow* said, I am able to de-stroy the temple of God, and to build it in three days.	**55** And the chief priests, and all the council, sought for witness against Jesus to put him to death; and **56** found none. For many bare false witness against him, but their wit-**57** ness agreed not together. And there arose certain, and bare false **58** witness against him, saying, ' We have heard him say, I will destroy this temple that is made with hands, and within three days I will build **59** another made without hands. But nei-ther so did their witness agree together.

MATTH. XXVI.

⁶² And the high priest arose, and said unto him, Answerest thou nothing? what is it which these witness against ⁶³ thee? But Jesus held his peace. And the high priest answered and said unto him, I adjure thee by the living God, that thou tell us whether thou be the Christ ⁶⁴ the Son of God? Jesus saith unto him, Thou hast said: nevertheless, I say unto you, Hereafter shall ye see/ the Son of man sitting on the right hand of power, and coming in the clouds ⁶⁵ of heaven. Then the high priest rent his clothes, saying, He hath spoken blasphemy; what further need have we of witnesses? behold, now ye have heard his blasphemy. ⁶⁶ ' What think ye? They answered and said, He is guilty of death. ⁶⁷ Then did they spit in his face, and buffeted him; and others smote *him* with the palms of their hands, ⁶⁸ ' saying, Prophesy unto us, thou Christ, Who is he that smote thee?

MARK XIV.

⁶⁰ And the high priest stood up in the midst, and asked Jesus, saying, Answerest thou nothing? what is it which these witness against thee? ⁶¹ But he held his peace, and answered nothing. Again the high priest asked him, and said unto him, Art thou ⁶² the Blessed? And Jesus said, I am: and ye shall see the Son of man sitting on the right hand of power, and coming in the ⁶³ clouds of heaven. Then the high priest rent his clothes, and saith, What need we any ⁶⁴ further witnesses? Ye have heard the blasphemy: what think ye? And they all condemned him to be guilty of death.

⁶⁵ And some began to spit on him, and to cover his face, and to buffet him, and to say unto him, Prophesy: and the servants did strike him with the palms of their hands.

LUKE XXII.

⁶⁷ Saying, Art thou the Christ? tell us. And he said unto them, If I tell you, ye will not ⁶⁸ believe. And if I also ask *you*, ye will not answer me, nor let *me* ⁶⁹ go. Hereafter shall the Son of man sit on the right hand of the ⁷⁰ power of God. Then said they all, Art thou then the Son of God? And he said unto them, ⁷¹ Ye say that I am. And they said, What need we any further witnesses? for we ourselves have heard of his own mouth.—

⁶³ And the men that held Jesus, mocked him, and smote *him*. ⁶⁴ And when they had blindfolded him, they struck him on the face, and asked him, saying, Prophesy, who is it ⁶⁵ that smote thee? And many other things blasphemously spake they against him.

§ 146. *The Sanhedrim lead Jesus away to Pilate.*—JERUSALEM.

Sixth Day of the Week.

MATTH. XXVII. 1, 2, 11—14.	MARK XV. 1—5.	LUKE XXIII. 1—5.	JOHN XVIII. 28—38.
¹ When the morning was come, all the chief priests and elders of the people took counsel against Jesus to put him to death.	¹ And straightway in the morning the chief priests held a consultation with the elders and scribes, and the whole council	¹ And the whole multitude of them arose, and led him unto Pilate.	²⁸ Then led they Jesus from Caiaphas unto the hall of judgment, and it was early; and they themselves went not into the judgment-hall, lest they should be defiled; but that they might eat

MATTH. XXVII.	MARK XV.	JOHN XVIII.

And when they had bound him, they led *him* away, and delivered him to Pontius Pilate the governor.—

and bound Jesus, and carried *him* away, and delivered *him* to Pilate.

[29] the passover. Pilate then went out unto them, and said, What accusation bring ye against this [30] man? They answered and said unto him, If he were not a malefactor, we would not have deliver-[31] ed him up unto thee. Then said Pilate unto them, Take ye him, and judge him according to your law. The Jews therefore said unto him, It is not lawful for us to put any man to death:

LUKE XXIII.

[2] And they began to accuse [32] that the saying of Jesus him, saying, We found this might be fulfilled, which *fellow* perverting the na- he spake, signifying what tion, and forbidding to give [33] death he should die. Then tribute to Cesar, saying, Pilate entered into the that he himself is Christ, a judgment-hall a-

[1] And Jesus stood before the governor: and the governor asked him, saying, Art thou the King of the Jews?—

MARK XV.

[2] And Pilate asked him, Art thou the King of the Jews?—

[3] King. And Pilate asked him, saying, Art thou the King of the Jews?—

gain, and called Jesus, and said unto him, Art thou the King of [34] the Jews? Jesus answered

him, Sayest thou this thing of thyself, or did others [35] tell it thee of me? [1] Pilate answered, Am I a Jew? Thine own nation, and the chief priests, have delivered thee unto me. What hast thou done? [36] Jesus answered, My kingdom is not of this world: if my kingdom were of this world, then would my servants fight, that I should not be delivered [37] to the Jews: but now is my kingdom not from hence. Pilate therefore

MATTH. XXVII.	MARK XV.	LUKE XXIII.	said unto him,

[11] —And Jesus said unto him, Thou sayest.

[2] —And he answering, said unto to him, Thou sayest *it*.

[3] —And he answered him and said, Thou sayest *it*.

Art thou a king then? Jesus answered, Thou sayest that I am a king. To this end was I born, and for this cause came I into the world, that I should bear witness unto the truth. Every one that is of the truth, heareth my [38] voice. [1] Pilate saith unto him, What is truth? And when he had said this, he went out again unto the Jews, and saith unto them, I find in him no fault *at all*.

MATTH. XXVII.	MARK XV.

[12] And when he was accused of the chief priests and elders, he answered [13] nothing. Then saith Pilate unto him, Hearest thou not how many things they witness against thee? [14] And he answered him to never a word; insomuch that the governor marvelled greatly.

[3] And the chief priests accused him of many things: but he answered [4] nothing. And Pilate asked him again, saying, Answerest thou nothing? behold how many things [5] they witness against thee. But Jesus yet answered nothing; so that Pilate marvelled.

LUKE XXIII.

[4] Then said Pilate to the chief priests, and *to* the people, I find no fault in [5] this man. And they were the more fierce, saying, He stirreth up the people, teaching throughout all Jewry, beginning from Galilee to this place.

13

§ 147. *Jesus before Herod.*—JERUSALEM.

Sixth Day of the Week.

LUKE XXIII. 6—12.

⁶ When Pilate heard of Galilee, he asked whether the man were a Galilean.
⁷ And as soon as he knew that he belonged unto Herod's jurisdiction, he sent
him to Herod, who himself was also at Jerusalem at that time.
⁸ And when Herod saw Jesus, he was exceeding glad : for he was desirous to see him of a long *season*, because he had heard many things of him ;
⁹ and he hoped to have seen some miracle done by him. Then he question-
¹⁰ ed with him in many words ; but he answered him nothing. And the chief
¹¹ priests and scribes stood and vehemently accused him. And Herod with
his men of war set him at nought, and mocked *him*, and arrayed him in a
gorgeous robe, and sent him again to Pilate.
¹² And the same day Pilate and Herod were made friends together ; for before they were at enmity between themselves.

§ 148. *Pilate seeks to release Jesus. The Jews demand Barabbas.*—
JERUSALEM.

Sixth Day of the Week.

LUKE XXIII. 13—25.

¹³ And Pilate, when he had called together the chief priests, and the rulers,
¹⁴ and the people, ' said unto them, Ye have brought this man unto me,
as one that perverteth the people : and behold, I, having examined
him before you, have found no fault in this man, touching those things
¹⁵ whereof ye accuse him ; ' no, nor yet Herod : for I sent you to him ;
and lo, nothing worthy of death is done unto him:

¹⁶ ' I will there-
fore chastise him,
and release *him*.

MATTH. XXVII. 15—26.	MARK XV. 6—15.	*fore chastise him, and release him.*	JOHN XVIII. 39—40.
¹⁵ Now at *that* feast, the gov- ernor was wont to release unto the people a pri- soner, whom they ¹⁶ would. And they had then a notable prison- er, called Barabbas. ¹⁷ Therefore, when they were gathered toge- ther, Pilate said unto them, Whom will ye that I release unto you? Barabbas, or Jesus, which is called Christ? ¹⁸ For he knew that for envy they had delivered ¹⁹ him. When he was	⁶ Now at *that* feast he released unto them one prisoner, whom- soever they de- ⁷ sired. And there was *one* named Barabbas, *which lay* bound with them that had made insurrection with him, who had committed murder in the ⁸ insurrection. And the multitude crying aloud, began to desire *him to do* as he ⁹ had ever done unto them. But Pilate answered them, saying, Will ye that I release unto you the King of ¹⁰ the Jews? For he knew that the chief priests had delivered him for envy.	¹⁷ For of neces- sity he must re- lease one unto them at the feast.	³⁹ But ye have a custom that I should release unto you one at the passover.— JOHN XVIII. ³⁹ —Will ye therefore, that I release unto you the King of the Jews?

set down on the judgment-seat, his wife sent unto him, saying, Have thou
nothing to do with that just man: for I have suffered many things this
day in a dream, because of him.

MATTH. XXVII.	MARK XV.	LUKE XXIII.	JOHN XVIII.

[9] But the chief priests and elders persuaded the multitude that they should ask Barabbas, and destroy Je- [21] sus. The governor answered and said unto them, Whether of the twain will ye that I release unto you? They said, [22] Barabbas. Pilate saith unto them, What shall I do then with Jesus, which is called Christ? *They* all say unto him, Let him be crucified. [23] And the governor said, Why, what evil hath he done? But they cried out the more, saying, Let him be crucified.

[11] But the chief priests moved the people that he should rather release Barabbas unto them.

MARK XV.

[12] And Pilate answered, and said again unto them, What will ye then that I shall do *unto him* whom ye call the King [13] of the Jews? And they cried out again, Crucify [14] him. Then Pilate said unto them, Why, what evil hath he done? And they cried out the more exceedingly, Crucify him.

MATTH. XXVII.

[18] And they cried out all at once saying, Away with this *man*, and release unto us Barabbas: [19] who, for a certain sedition made in the city, and for murder, was cast into [20] prison. Pilate therefore, willing to release Jesus, spake again to [21] them. But they cried, saying, Crucify *him*, [22] crucify him. And he said unto them the third time, Why, what evil hath he done? I have found no cause of death in him; I will therefore chastise him [23] and let *him* go. And they were instant with loud voices, requiring that he might be crucified: and the voices of them, and of the chief priests prevailed.

[40] Then cried they all again, saying, Not this man, but Barabbas. Now Barabbas was a robber.

[24] When Pilate saw that he could prevail nothing, but *that* rather a tumult was made, he took water, and washed *his* hands before the multitude, saying, I am innocent of the blood of this just person: see [25] ye *to it*. Then answered all the people, and said, His blood *be* on us, and on our children.

MARK XV.

LUKE XXIII.

[26] Then released he Barabbas unto them.—

[15] And *so* Pilate, willing to content the people, released Barabbas unto them.—

[24] And Pilate gave sentence that it should be [25] as they required. And he released unto them him that for sedition and murder was cast into prison, whom they had desired; but he delivered Jesus to their will.

§ 149. *Pilate delivers up Jesus to death. He is scourged and mocked.*— JERUSALEM.

Sixth Day of the Week.

MATTH. XXVII. 26—30.	MARK XV. 15—19.	JOHN XIX. 1—3.

[26] —And when he had scourged Jesus, he de- livered *him* to be cruci- [27] fied. Then the soldiers of the governor took Jesus into the common hall, and gathered unto him the whole

[15] —And *he* delivered Jesus, when he had scourged *him*, to be [16] crucified. And the soldiers led him away into the hall, called Pretorium; and they called together the whole band;

[1] Then Pilate therefore took Jesus, and scourged *him*.

MATTH. XXVII.	MARK XV.	JOHN XIX.
²⁸ band *of soldiers.* And they stripped him, and put on him a scarlet ²⁹ robe. And when they had platted a crown of thorns, they put *it* upon his head, and a reed in his right hand: and they bowed the knee before him, and mocked him, saying, Hail, King ³⁰ of the Jews! And they spit upon him, and took the reed, and smote him on the head.	¹⁷ ' and they clothed him with purple, and platted a crown of thorns, and put it about his *head,* ¹⁸ ' and began to salute him, Hail, ¹⁹ King of the Jews! And they smote him on the head with a reed, and did spit upon him, and bowing *their* knees, worshipped him.	² And the soldiers platted a crown of thorns, and put *it* on his head, and they put on him a purple robe, ⁸ ' and said, . Hail, King of the Jews! and they smote him with their hands.

§ 150. *Pilate again seeks to release Jesus.*—JERUSALEM.

Sixth Day of the Week.

JOHN XIX. 4—16.

⁴ Pilate therefore went forth again, and saith unto them, Behold, I bring ⁵ him forth to you, that ye may know that I find no fault in him. Then came Jesus forth, wearing the crown of thorns, and the purple robe. And ⁶ *Pilate* saith unto them, Behold the man! When the chief priests therefore and officers saw him, they cried out, saying, Crucify *him,* crucify *him.* Pilate saith unto them, Take ye him, and crucify *him:* for I find no fault ⁷ in him. The Jews answered him, We have a law, and by our law he ought to die, because he made himself the Son of God.

⁸ ⁹ When Pilate therefore heard that saying, he was the more afraid; ' and went again into the judgment-hall, and saith unto Jesus, Whence art thou? ¹⁰ But Jesus gave him no answer. ' Then saith Pilate unto him, Speakest thou not unto me? knowest thou not, that I have power to crucify thee, and have ¹¹ power to release thee? Jesus answered, Thou couldest have no power *at all* against me, except it were given thee from above: therefore he that de- ¹² livered me unto thee hath the greater sin. And from thenceforth Pilate sought to release him: but the Jews cried out, saying, If thou let this man go, thou art not Cesar's friend. Whosoever maketh himself a king, speaketh against Cesar.

¹³ When Pilate therefore heard that saying, he brought Jesus forth, and sat down in the judgment-seat, in a place that is called the Pavement, but in ¹⁴ the Hebrew, Gabbatha. And it was the preparation of the passover, and ¹⁵ about the sixth hour: and he saith unto the Jews, Behold your King! But they cried out, Away with *him,* away with *him,* crucify him. Pilate saith unto them, Shall I crucify your king? The chief priests answered, We ⁶ have no king but Cesar. Then delivered he him therefore unto them to be crucified —

§ 151. *Judus repents and hangs himself.*—JERUSALEM.

Sixth Day of the Week.

MATTH. XXVII. 3—10.

[3] Then Judas, which had betrayed him, when he saw that he was condemned, repented himself, and brought again the thirty pieces of silver to [4] the chief priests and elders, ' saying, I have sinned in that I have betrayed the innocent blood. And they said, What *is that* to us ? see thou *to* [5] *that*. And he cast down the pieces of silver in the temple, and departed, and went and hanged himself. [6] And the chief priests took the silver pieces, and said, It is not lawful for to put them into the treasury, be- [7] cause it is the price of blood. And they took counsel, and bought with them the potter's field, to bury [8] strangers in. Wherefore that field was called The field of blood, unto [9] this day. Then was fulfilled that

ACTS I. 18, 19.

[18] Now this man purchased a field with the reward of iniquity ; and falling headlong, he burst asunder in the midst, and all his [19] bowels gushed out. And it was known unto all the dwellers at Jerusalem ; insomuch as that field is called in their proper tongue, Aceldama, that is to say, The field of blood.

which was spoken by Jeremy the prophet, saying,[a] And they took the thirty pieces of silver, the price of him that was valued, whom they of the [10] children of Israel did value ; ' and gave them for the potter's field, as the Lord appointed me.

§ 152. *Jesus is led away to be crucified.*—JERUSALEM.

Sixth Day of the Week.

MATTH. XXVII. 31—34.

[31] And after that they had mocked him, they took the robe off from him, and put his own raiment on him, and led him away to crucify [32] him. And as they came out, they found a man of Cyrene, Simon by name : him they compelled to bear his cross.

MARK XV. 20—23.

[20] And when they had mocked him, they took off the purple from him, and put his own clothes on him, and led him out to crucify him. [21] And they compel one Simon a Cyrenian, who passed by, coming out of the country, the father of Alexander and Rufus, to bear his cross.

JOHN XIX. 16, 17.

[16] —And they took Jesus, and led *him* away. [17] And he bearing his cross,—

LUKE XXIII. 26—33.

[26] And as they led him away, they laid hold upon one Simon a Cyrenian, coming out of the country, and on him they laid the cross, that he might bear *it* after Jesus.

[17] And there followed him a great company of people, and of women, [18] which also bewailed and lamented him. But Jesus turning unto them, said, Daughters of Jerusalem, weep not for me, but weep for [19] yourselves, and for your children. For behold, the days are coming, in the which they shall say, Blessed *are* the barren, and the wombs that never [10] bare, and the paps which never gave suck.[b] Then shall they begin to say

---

[a] 9. Zech. 11, 12 sq Comp. Jer. 32, 6 sq.   [b] 29. Comp. Is. 54, 1.

LUKE XXIII.

[31] to the mountains, Fall on us; and to the hills, Cover us.[a] For if they do these things in a green tree, what shall be done in the dry? [32] And there were also two others, malefactors, led with him to be put to death.

MATTH. XXVII.	MARK XV.		JOHN XIX.

[33] And when they were come unto a place called Golgotha, that is to say, A place [34] of a skull, ' they gave him vinegar to drink, mingled with gall: and when he had tasted *thereof*, he would not drink.

[22] And they bring him unto the place Golgotha, which is, being interpreted, [23] The place of a skull. And they gave him to drink, wine mingled with myrrh: but he received *it* not.

[33] And when they were come to the place which is called Calvary,—

[17]—Went forth into a place called *the place* of a skull, which is called in the Hebrew, Golgotha.

§ 153. *The Crucifixion.*—JERUSALEM.

Sixth Day of the Week.

MATTH. XXVII. 35—38.	MARK XV. 24—28.	LUKE XXIII. 33, 34, 38.	JOHN XIX. 18—24.
	[25] And it was the third hour, and they crucified		
[38] Then were there two thieves crucified with him: one on the right hand, and another on the left.—	[27] him.—And with him they crucify two thieves, the one on his right hand, and the other on his left. [28] And the scripture was fulfilled, which saith,[b] And he was numbered with the transgressors.—	[33]—There they crucified him, and the malefactors; one on the right hand, and the other on the left. [34] Then said Jesus, Father, forgive them: for they know not what they do.	[18] Where they crucified him, and two others with him, on either side one, and Jesus in the midst.—
[35] And they crucified him, and parted his garments,—	[24] And when they had crucified him, they parted his garments,—	And they parted his raiment,—	[23] Then the soldiers, when they had crucified Jesus, took his garments, and made

four parts, to every soldier a part; and also *his* coat: now the coat was without seam, woven from the top [24] throughout. They said therefore among themselves, Let us not rend it,

| casting lots: that it might be fulfilled which was spoken by the prophet,[c] | casting lots upon them, what every man should take. [24] They parted my garments among them, and upon my | [34]—and cast lots. | but cast lots for it whose it shall be: that the scripture might be fulfilled, which saith,[c] They parted my raiment among them, and for my vesture they |
| [36] vesture did they cast lots. And sitting down, they watched him | vesture did they cast lots. And | did cast lots. | did cast lots. These things therefore the soldiers did. |

---

a 30. Hos. 10, 8.   b 28. Is. 53, 12.   c 35 etc. Ps. 22, 18.

MATTH. XXVII.	MARK XV.	LUKE XXIII.	JOHN XIX.
[37] there : ' and set up over his head his accusation written, THIS IS JESUS THE KING OF THE JEWS.	[26] And the super-scription of his accusation was written over, THE KING OF THE JEWS.	[38] And a super-scription also was written over him, in letters of Greek, and La-tin, and Hebrew, THIS IS THE KING OF THE JEWS.	[19] And Pilate wrote a title, and put it on the cross. And the writing was, JESUS OF NAZARETH, THE KING OF THE JEWS.

[20] This title then read many of the Jews: for the place where Jesus was crucified was nigh [21] to the city: and it was written in Hebrew, and Greek, and Latin. Then said the chief priests of the Jews to Pilate, Write not, The King of the [22] Jews ; but that he said, I am King of the Jews. Pilate answered, What I have written, I have written.

§ 154. *The Jews mock at Jesus on the Cross. He commends his Mother to John.*—JERUSALEM.

Sixth Day of the Week.

MATTH. XXVII. 39—44.	MARK XV. 29—32.
[39] And they that passed by, reviled [40] him, wagging their heads, ' and saying, Thou that destroyest the temple, and buildest it in three days, save thyself. If thou be the Son of God, come down from the cross. [41] Likewise also the chief priests mocking *him*, with the scribes and [42] elders, said, ' He saved others ; himself he cannot save. If he be the King of Israel, let him now come down from the cross, and we [43] will believe him. He trusted in God ; let him deliver him now if he will have him : * for he said, I am the Son of [44] God. The thieves also which were crucified with him, cast the same in his teeth.	[29] And they that passed by, railed on him, wagging their heads, and saying, Ah, thou that de-stroyest the temple, and buildest [30] it in three days, ' save thyself, and come down from the cross. [31] Likewise also the chief priests, mocking, said among themselves with the scribes, He saved oth-ers ; himself he can-[32] not save. Let Christ the King of Israel de-scend now from the cross, that we may see and believe.

	LUKE XXIII. 35—37, 39—43.
	[35] And the people stood beholding. And the rulers also with them derided *him*, saying, He saved others ; let him save himself, if he be Christ, the chosen [36] of God. And the soldiers also mocked him, coming to him, and offering him vinegar, [37] ' and saying, If thou be the King of the Jews, save thyself.— [39] And one of the male-factors, which were hanged, railed on him, saying, If thou be

[40] Christ, save thyself and us. But the other answering, rebuked him, saying, [41] Dost not thou fear God, seeing thou art in the same condemnation ? And we indeed justly ; for we receive the due reward of our deeds : but this man hath [42] done nothing amiss. And he said unto Jesus, Lord, remember me when

---

a 43. Comp. Ps. 22, 7. 8.

⁴⁹ thou comest into thy kingdom.   And Jesus said unto him, Verily, I say unto thee, To-day shalt thou be with me in paradise.

JOHN XIX. 25—27.

²⁵ Now there stood by the cross of Jesus, his mother, and his mother's sis-
²⁶ ter, Mary the *wife* of Cleophas, and Mary Magdalene. When Jesus therefore saw his mother, and the disciple standing by whom he loved, he saith
²⁷ unto his mother, Woman, behold thy son! Then saith he to the disciple,
Behold thy mother! And from that hour that disciple took her unto his
own *home.*

· § 155. *Darkness prevails.   Christ expires on the Cross.*—JERUSALEM.

Sixth Day of the Week.

MATTH. XXVII. 45—50.	MARK XV. 33—37.	LUKE XXIII. 44—46.
⁴⁵ Now from the sixth hour there was darkness over all the land unto the ninth hour. ⁴⁶ And about the ninth hour Jesus cried with a loud voice, saying, Eli, Eli, lama sabachthani? that is to say, My God, my God, why hast thou forsaken ⁴⁷ me?ᵃ Some of them that stood there, when they heard *that*, said, This *man* calleth for ⁴⁸ Elias. And straightway one of them ran, and took a sponge, and filled *it* with vinegar, and put *it* on a reed, and gave him a drink. ⁴⁹ The rest said, Let be, let us see whether Elias will come to save him. ⁵⁰ Jesus, when he had cried again with a loud voice, yielded up the ghost.	³³ And when the sixth hour was come, there was darkness over the whole land, until the ninth hour. And at ³⁴ the ninth hour Jesus cried with a loud voice, saying, Eloi, Eloi, lama sabachthani? which is, being interpreted, My God, my God, why hast thou forsaken me?ᵃ And some of them that stood by, when they heard *it*, said, Behold, he call- ³⁶ eth Elias. And one ran and filled a sponge full of vinegar, and put *it* on a reed, and gave him to drink, saying, Let alone; let us see whether Elias will come to take him down. MARK XV. ³⁷ And Jesus cried with a loud voice, and gave up the ghost.	⁴⁴ And it was about the sixth hour, and there was a darkness over all the earth until ⁴⁵ the ninth hour. And the sun was darkened.— JOHN XIX. 28—30. ²⁸ After this, Jesus knowing that all things were now accomplished, that the scripture might be fulfilled,ᵇ saith, I thirst. ²⁹ Now there was set a vessel full of vinegar: and they filled a sponge with vinegar, and put *it* upon hyssop, and put *it* to his mouth. ³⁰ When Jesus therefore had received the vinegar, he said, It is finished: and he bowed his head, and gave up the ghost.-
	LUKE XXIII. ⁴⁶ And when Jesus had cried with a loud voice, he said, Father, into thy hands I commend my spirit: and having said thus, he gave up the ghost.	

ᵃ 46 etc. Ps. 22, 1.   ᵇ 28. Comp. Ps. 69, 21.

§ 156. *The vail of the Temple rent, and graves opened. Judgment of the Centurion. The Women at the Cross.*—JERUSALEM.

Sixth Day of the Week.

MATTH. XXVII. 51—56.	MARK XV. 38—41.	LUKE XXIII. 45, 47—49.
51 And behold, the vail 38 of the temple was rent in twain from the top to the bottom : and the earth did quake, and	And the vail of the temple was rent in twain, from the top to the bottom.	45 —And the vail of the temple was rent in the midst.—

52 the rocks rent ; ¹ and the graves were opened, and many bodies 53 of the saints which slept, arose, ¹ and came out of the graves after his resurrection, and went into the holy city, and appeared unto many.

| 54 Now when the cen- 39 turion, and they that were with him, watching Jesus, saw the earthquake, and those things that were done, they feared greatly, saying, Truly this was 55 the Son of God. And 40 many women were there, beholding afar off, which followed Jesus from Galilee, ministering unto him : 56 ¹ among which was Mary Magdalene, and Mary the mother of James and Joses, and the mother of Zebedee's children. | And when the cen- turion which stood over against him, saw that he so cried out, and gave up the ghost, he said, Truly this man was the Son of God. There were also wo- men looking on afar off, among whom was Mary Magdalene, and Mary the mother of James the less and of Joses, and Salome ; 41 ¹ who also, when he was in Galilee, follow- ed him, and ministered unto him ; and many other women which came up with him unto Jerusalem. | 47 Now when the cen- turion saw what was done, he glorified God, saying, Certainly this was a righteous man. 48 And all the people that came together to that sight, beholding the things which were done, smote their breasts and returned. 49 And all his acquaint- ance, and the women that followed him from Galilee, stood afar off, beholding these things. |

§ 157. *The taking down from the Cross. The burial.*—JERUSALEM.

Sixth Day of the Week.

JOHN XIX. 31—42.

31 The Jews therefore, because it was the preparation, that the bodies should not remain upon the cross on the sabbath-day, (for that sabbath-day was an high day,) besought Pilate that their legs might be broken, and that 32 they might be taken away. Then came the soldiers, and brake the legs of 33 the first, and of the other which was crucified with him. But when they came to Jesus, and saw that he was dead already, they brake not his 34 legs. But one of the soldiers with a spear pierced his side, and forthwith 35 came thereout blood and water. And he that saw it, bare record, and his record is true : and he knoweth that he saith true, that ye might be-

JOHN XIX.

³⁶ lieve. For these things were done, that the scriptures should be fulfil-
³⁷ led,ᵃ A bone of him shall not be broken. And again another scripture saith,ᵇ
They shall look on him whom they pierced.

MATTH. XXVII. 57—61.	MARK XV. 42—47.	LUKE XXIII. 50—56.	
⁵⁷ When the even was come, there came a rich man of Arimathea, named Joseph, who also himself was Jesus' disciple.	⁴² And now, when the even was come, (because it was the preparation, that is, the day before the ⁴³ sabbath,) Joseph of Arimathea, an honourable counsellor, which also waited for the kingdom of God, came, and went in boldly unto Pilate, and craved the body of Jesus. ⁴⁴ And Pilate marvelled if he were already dead: and calling unto him the centurion, he asked him whether he had been ⁴⁵ any while dead. And when he knew it of the centurion, he gave the body to Joseph. ⁴⁶ And he bought fine linen, and took him down, and wrapped him in the linen, and laid him in a sepulchre which was hewn out of a rock, and rolled a stone unto the door of the sepulchre.	⁵⁰ And that day was the preparation, and the sabbath drew on.— ⁵⁰ And behold, there was a man named Joseph, a counsellor: and he was a good man, ⁵¹ and a just: ¹ (the same had not consented to the counsel and deed of them:) he was of Arimathea, a city of the Jews; who also himself waited for the kingdom of God. ⁵² This man went unto Pilate, and begged the body of Jesus. ⁵³ And he took it down, and wrapped it in linen, and laid it in a sepulchre that was hewn in stone, wherein never man before was laid.—	³⁸ And after this, Joseph of Arimathea (being a disciple of Jesus, but secretly for fear of the Jews) besought Pilate that he might take away the body of Jesus: and Pilate gave him leave. He came therefore and took the body of Jesus. ³⁹ And there came also Nicodemus (which at the first came to Jesus by night) and brought a mixture of myrrh and aloes, about an hundred pounds weight. ⁴⁰ Then took they the body of Jesus, and wound it in linen clothes with the spices, as the manner of the Jews is to ⁴¹ bury. Now in the place where he was crucified, there was a garden; and in the
⁵⁸ He went to Pilate, and begged the body of Jesus. Then Pilate commanded the body to be delivered.			
⁵⁹ And when Joseph had taken the body, he wrapped it in a clean linen cloth, ⁶⁰ and laid it in his own new tomb, which he had hewn out in the rock; and he rolled a great stone to the door of the sepulchre, and departed.			

garden a new sepulchre, wherein was never man yet laid.
⁴² There laid they Jesus therefore, because of the Jews'
preparation-day; for the sepulchre was nigh at hand.

MATTH. XXVII.	MARK XV.	LUKE XXIII.
⁶¹ And there was Mary Magdalene, and the other Mary, sitting over against the sepulchre.	⁴⁷ And Mary Magdalene and Mary the mother of Joses beheld where he was laid.	⁵⁵ And the women also, which came with him from Galilee, followed after, and beheld the

---

ᵃ 36. Ex. 12, 46. Ps. 34, 20.　　ᵇ 37. Zech 12, 10

LUKE XXIII.

⁵⁶ sepulchre, and how his body was laid. And they returned, and prepared spices and ointments ; and rested the sabbath-day, according to the commandment. •

§ 158. *The Watch at the Sepulchre.*—JERUSALEM,

Seventh Day of the Week, or Sabbath.

MATTH. XXVII. 62—66.

⁶² Now the next day that followed the day of the preparation, the chief ⁶³ priests and Pharisees came together unto Pilate, ¹ saying, Sir, we remember that that deceiver said, while he was yet alive, After three days I will rise ⁶⁴ again. Command therefore that the sepulchre be made sure until the third day, lest his disciples come by night, and steal him away, and say unto the people, He is risen from the dead : so the last error shall be worse than the ⁶⁵ first. Pilate said unto them, Ye have a watch : go your way, make *it* as ⁶⁶ sure as ye can. So they went and made the sepulchre sure, sealing the stone, and setting a watch.

PART IX.

OUR LORD'S RESURRECTION, HIS SUBSEQUENT APPEARANCES, AND HIS
ASCENSION.

TIME: *Forty days.*

---

§ 159. *Morning of the Resurrection.*—JERUSALEM.

First Day of the Week.

MARK XVI. 1.

[1] . AND when the sabbath was past, Mary Magdalene, and Mary the *mother* of James, and Salome, had bought sweet spices, that they might
come and anoint him.

MATTH. XXVIII. 2—4.

[2] And behold, there was a great earthquake: for the angel of the Lord
descended from heaven, and came and rolled back the stone from the door,
[3] and sat upon it. His countenance was like lightning, and his raiment
[4] white as snow. And for fear of him the keepers did shake, and became as
dead *men.*

§ 160. *Visit of the Women to the Sepulchre. Mary Magdalene returns.*—
JERUSALEM.

First Day of the Week.

MATTH. XXVIII. 1.	MARK XVI. 2–4.	LUKE XXIV. 1–3.	JOHN XX. 1, 2.
[1] In the end of the sabbath, as it began to dawn toward the first *day* of the week, came Mary Magdalene and the other Mary, to see the sepulchre.	[2] And very early in the morning, the first *day* of the week, they came unto the sepulchre at the rising of the [3] sun: [4] and they said among themselves, Who shall roll us away the stone from the door of the sep-	[1] Now upon the first *day* of the week, very early in the morning, they came unto the sepulchre, bringing the spices which they had prepared, and certain *others* with them.	[1] The first *day* of the week cometh Mary Magdalene early, when it was yet dark, unto the sepulchre,

MARK XVI.	LUKE XXIV.	JOHN XX.
⁴ ulchre ? ' (and when they looked, they saw that the stone was rolled away,) for it was very great.	² And they found the stone rolled away from ³ the sepulchre. And they entered in, and found not the body of the Lord Jesus.	and seeth the stone taken away from the ² sepulchre. Then she runneth, and cometh to Simon Peter, and to the other disciple whom Jesus loved, and

saith unto them, They have taken away the Lord out of the sepulchre, and we know not where they have laid him.

§ 161. *Vision of the Angels in the Sepulchre.*—JERUSALEM.

First Day of the Week.

MARK XVI. 5—7.	LUKE XXIV. 4—8.
⁵ And entering into the sepulchre, they saw a young man sitting on the right side, clothed in a long white garment ; and MATTH. XXVIII. 5—7. ⁵ And the angel answered and said unto the women, Fear not ye : for I know that ye seek Jesus, which was ⁶ crucified. He is not here : for he is risen, as he said. Come, see the place where the ⁷ Lord lay. And go quickly, and tell his disciples, that he is risen from the dead, and behold, he goeth before you into Galilee ; there shall ye see	⁴ And it came to pass, as they were much perplexed thereabout, behold, two men stood by them in shining ⁵ garments. And as they were affrighted. ⁶ And he saith unto them, Be not affrighted : ye seek Jesus of Nazareth, which was crucified : he is risen ; he is not here : behold, the place where they ⁷ laid him. But go your way, tell his disciples and Peter, that he goeth before you into Galilee : there shall ye see him, as he said unto you.
	LUKE XXIV. 4—8. continued / JOHN XX. ⁴ And as they were afraid, and bowed down *their* faces to the earth, they said unto them, Why seek ye the living among the dead ? ⁶ He is not here, but is risen. Remember how he spake unto you when he was yet in ⁷ Galilee, ' saying, The Son of man must be delivered into the hands of sinful men, and be crucified, and the third day ⁸ rise again. And they remembered his words.

him : lo, I have told you.

§ 162. *The Women return to the City. Jesus meets them.*—JERUSALEM.

First Day of the Week.

MATTH. XXVIII. 8—10.	MARK XVI. 8.
⁸ And they departed quickly from the sepulchre, with fear and great joy ; and did run to bring his disciples word. ⁹ And as they went to tell his disciples, behold, Jesus met them, saying, All hail.	⁸ And they went out quickly, and fled from the sepulchre ; for they trembled, and were amazed : neither said they any thing to any man ; for they were afraid.

And they came, and held him by the feet, and worshipped ¹⁰ him. Then said Jesus unto them, Be not afraid : go tell my brethren, that they go into Galilee, and there shall they see me.

14

LUKE XXIV. 9—11.

[9] And *they* returned from the sepulchre, and told all these things unto the
[10] eleven, and to all the rest. It was Mary Magdalene, and Joanna, and
Mary *the mother* of James, and other *women that were* with them, which
[11] told these things unto the apostles. And their words seemed to them as
idle tales, and they believed them not.

§ 163. *Peter and John run to the Sepulchre.*—JERUSALEM.

First Day of the Week.

JOHN XX. 3—10.

[3] Peter therefore went forth, and that other disciple, and came to the
[4] sepulchre. So they ran both together: and the other disciple did outrun
[5] Peter, and came first to the sepulchre. And he stooping down, *and looking in*, saw the linen clothes lying;

LUKE XXIV. 12.

[12] Then arose Peter, and ran unto the
sepulchre, and stooping down, he
beheld the linen clothes laid by
themselves,—

[6] yet went he not in. Then cometh
Simon Peter following him, and
went into the sepulchre, and seeth
[7] the linen clothes lie ; ' and' the napkin that was about his head, not
lying with the linen clothes, but
[8] wrapped together in a place by itself. Then went in also that
other disciple which came first to the sepulchre, and he saw,
[9] and believed. For as yet they knew not the scripture, that
he must rise again from the dead.

[12] —and departed, wondering in himself at that which was come to pass.

[10] Then the disciples went away again
unto their own home.

§ 164. *Our Lord is seen by Mary Magdalene at the Sepulchre.*—JERUSALEM.

First Day of the Week.

JOHN XX. 11—18.

[11] But Mary stood without at the sepulchre weeping: and as she wept she
[12] stooped down *and looked* into the sepulchre, ' and seeth two angels in
white, sitting, the one at the head, and the other at the feet, where the body
[13] of Jesus had lain. And they say unto her, Woman, why weepest thou ?
She saith unto them, Because they have taken away my Lord, and I

MARK XVI. 9—11.

[9] Now when *Jesus* was risen early,
the first *day* of the week, he appeared first to Mary Magdalene, out
of whom he had cast seven devils.

know not where they have laid him.
[14] And when she had thus said, she
turned herself back, and saw Jesus
standing, and knew not that it was
[15] Jesus. Jesus saith unto her, Woman,
why weepest thou ? whom seekest

thou ? She, supposing him to be the gardener, saith unto him, Sir, if thou
have borne him hence, tell me where thou hast laid him, and I will take
[16] him away. ' Jesus saith unto her, Mary. She turned herself, and saith
[17] unto him, Rabboni, which is to say, Master. Jesus saith unto her, Touch
me not: for I am not yet ascended to my Father: but go to my brethren, and say unto them, I ascend unto my Father and your Father,

MARK XVI.

[18] *And* she went and told them that

and *to* my God and your God.
[10] Mary Magdalene came and told the

MARK XVI.	JOHN XX.
had been with him, as they mourned ¹¹ and wept. And they, when they had heard that he was alive, and had been seen of her, believed not.	disciples that she had seen the Lord, and *that* he had spoken these things unto her.

§ 165. *Report of the Watch.*—JERUSALEM.

First Day of the Week.

MATTH. XXVIII. 11—15.

¹¹ Now when they were going, behold, some of the watch came into the ¹² city, and shewed unto the chief priests all the things that were done. And when they were assembled with the elders, and had taken counsel, they ¹³ gave large money unto the soldiers, ' saying, Say ye, His disciples came by ¹⁴ night, and stole him *away* while we slept. And if this come to the gover- ¹⁵ nor's ears, we will persuade him, and secure you. So they took the money, and did as they were taught: and this saying is commonly reported among the Jews until this day.

§ 166. *Our Lord is seen of Peter. Then by two Disciples on the way to Emmaus.*—JERUSALEM. EMMAUS.

First Day of the Week.

1 Cor. XV. 5.	LUKE XXIV. 13—35.
⁵ And that he was seen of Cephas.— MARK XVI. 12, 13. ¹² After that, he appeared in another form unto two of them, as they walked, and went into the country.	¹³ And behold, two of them went that same day to a village called Emmaus, which was from Jerusa- ¹⁴ lem *about* threescore furlongs. And they talked together of all these

¹⁵ things which had happened. And it came to pass, that, while they communed *together*, and reasoned, Jesus ¹⁶ himself drew near, and went with them. But their eyes were holden, that ¹⁷ they should not know him. And he said unto them, What manner of communications *are* these that ye have one to another, as ye walk, and are ¹⁸ sad? And the one of them, whose name was Cleopas, answering, said unto him, Art thou only a stranger in Jerusalem, and hast not known the ¹⁹ things which are come to pass here in these days? And he said unto them, What things? And they said unto him, Concerning Jesus of Naza- reth, which was a prophet mighty in deed and word before God, and all ²⁰ the people: ' and how the chief priests and our rulers delivered him to be ²¹ condemned to death, and have crucified him. But we trusted that it had been he which should have redeemed Israel: and besides all this, to-day is the ²² third day since these things were done. Yea, and certain women also of ²³ our company made us astonished, which were early at the sepulchre. And when they found not his body, they came, saying, that they had also seen ²⁴ a vision of angels, which said that he was alive. And certain of them which were with us, went to the sepulchre, and found *it* even so as the ²⁵ women had said: but him they saw not. Then he said unto them, O fools, ²⁶ and slow of heart to believe all that the prophets have spoken! Ought not ²⁷ Christ to have suffered these things, and to enter into his glory? And beginning at Moses, and all the prophets, he expounded unto them in all ²⁸ the scriptures the things concerning himself. And they drew nigh unto the

village whither they went: and he made as though he would have gone
[19] further. But they constrained him, saying, Abide with us: for it is toward
evening, and the day is far spent. And he went in to tarry with them.
[30] And it came to pass, as he sat at meat with them, he took bread, and
[31] blessed *it*, and brake, and gave to them. And their eyes were opened,
[32] and they knew him: and he vanished out of their sight. And they said
one to another, Did not our heart burn within us while he talked with us
[33] by the way, and while he opened to us the scriptures? And they rose up
the same hour, and returned to Jerusalem, and found the eleven gathered
[34] together, and them that were with them, ' saying, The Lord is risen in-

MARK XVI.   deed, and hath appeared to Simon.
[13] And they went and told *it* unto [35] And they told what things *were*
the residue: neither believed they   *done* in the way, and how he was
them.   known of them in breaking of bread.

§ 167. *Jesus appears in the midst of the Apostles, Thomas being absent —*
JERUSALEM.

Evening following the First Day of the Week.

MARK XVI. 14—18.	1 COR. XV. 5.	JOHN XX. 19—23.

[14] Afterward he appeared unto the eleven, as they sat at meat, and upbraided them with their unbelief, and hardness of heart, because they believed not them which had seen him after he was risen.

[5] —Then of the twelve.

LUKE XXIV. 36—49.

[36] And as they thus spake, Jesus himself stood in the midst of them, and saith unto them, Peace *be* unto [37] you. But they were terrified and affrighted,

[19] Then the same day at evening, being the first *day* of the week, when the doors were shut where the disciples were assembled for fear of the Jews, came Jesus and stood in the midst, and saith unto them, Peace *be* unto you.

[38] and supposed that they had seen a spirit. And he said unto them, Why are ye troubled? and [39] why do thoughts arise in your hearts? Behold my hands and my feet, that it is I myself: handle me, and see ; for a spirit hath not flesh and bones, as ye see me have.
[40] And when he had thus spoken, he [20] And when he had so said, he shewed
shewed them *his* hands and *his* feet. unto them *his* hands and his side.
[41] And while they yet believed not Then were the disciples glad when
for joy, and wondered, he said unto they saw the Lord.
[42] them, Have ye here any meat? And
[43] they gave him a piece of a broiled fish, and of an honey-comb. And he
[44] took *it*, and did eat before them. And he said unto them, These *are*
the words which I spake unto you, while I was yet with you, that all
things must be fulfilled which were written in the law of Moses, and *in* the
[45] prophets, and *in* the psalms, concerning me. Then opened he their under-
[46] standing, that they might understand the scriptures, ' and said unto them,
Thus it is written, and thus it behooved Christ to suffer, and to rise from
[47] the dead the third day: ' and that repentance and remission of sins should
[48] be preached in his name among all nations, beginning at Jerusalem.

MARK XVI.   And ye are witnesses   JOHN XX.
[15] And he said unto them, [49] of these things. And [21] Then said Jesus to
Go ye into all the world, behold, I send the pro- them again, Peace *be*

MARK XVI.	LUKE XXIV.	JOHN XX.
and preach the gospel to every creature. He that believeth and is baptized, shall be saved ; but he that believeth not, shall be	mise of my Father upon you : but tarry ye in the city of Jerusalem, until ye be endued with power from on high.	unto you : as *my* Father hath sent me, even so send I you.

¹⁶ to every creature.

¹⁷ damned. And these signs shall follow them that believe : In my name
¹⁸ shall they cast out devils ; they shall speak with new tongues ; ¹ they shall take up serpents ; and if they drink any deadly thing, it shall not hurt them ;
¹² they shall lay hands on the sick, and they shall recover.

JOHN XX.

And when he had said this, he breathed on *them,* and saith unto them,
¹⁸ Receive ye the Holy Ghost. Whose soever sins ye remit, they are remitted unto them ; *and* whose soever *sins* ye retain, they are retained.

§ 168. *Jesus appears in the midst of the Apostles, Thomas being present.*—
JERUSALEM.

Evening following the First Day of the Week next after the Resurrection.

JOHN XX. 24—29.

²⁴   But Thomas, one of the twelve, called Didymus, was not with them when
²⁵ Jesus came. The other disciples therefore said unto him, We have seen the Lord. But he said unto them, Except I shall see in his hands the print of the nails, and put my finger into the print of the nails, and thrust my hand into his side, I will not believe.
²⁶   And after eight days again his disciples were within, and Thomas with them : *then* came Jesus, the doors being shut, and stood in the midst, and
²⁷ said, Peace *be* unto you. Then saith he to Thomas, Reach hither thy finger, and behold my hands ; and reach hither thy hand, and thrust *it* into my
²⁸ side ; and be not faithless, but believing. And Thomas answered and said
³⁰ unto him, My Lord and my God. Jesus saith unto him, Thomas, because thou hast seen me, thou hast believed : blessed *are* they that have not seen, and *yet* have believed.

§ 169. *The Apostles go away into Galilee. Jesus shews himself to seven of them at the Sea of Tiberias.*—GALILEE.

MATTH. XXVIII. 16.	JOHN XXI. 1—24.
¹⁶ Then the eleven disciples went away into Galilee.—	¹ After these things Jesus shewed himself again to the disciples at the sea of Tiberias : and on this wise

² shewed he *himself.* There were together Simon Peter and Thomas called Didymus, and Nathanael of Cana in Galilee, and the *sons* of Zebedee, and
³ two other of his disciples. Simon Peter saith unto them, I go a fishing. They say unto him, We also go with thee. They went forth, and entered
⁴ into a ship immediately ; and that night they caught nothing. But when the morning was now come, Jesus stood on the shore ; but the disci-
⁵ ples knew not that it was Jesus. Then Jesus saith unto them, Children,
⁶ have ye any meat ? They answered, No. ¹ And he said unto them, Cast the net on the right side of the ship, and ye shall find. They cast therefore, and now they were not able to draw it for the multitude of fishes.

14*

JOHN XXI.

7 Therefore that disciple whom Jesus loved saith unto Peter, It is the Lord. Now when Simon Peter heard that it was the Lord, he girt *his* fisher's coat *unto him*, for he was naked, and did cast himself into the sea.
8 And the other disciples came in a little ship (for they were not far from 9 land, but as it were two hundred cubits) dragging the net with fishes. As soon then as they were come to land, they saw a fire of coals there, and fish laid 0 thereon, and bread. Jesus saith unto them, Bring of the fish which ye have 11 now caught. Simon Peter went up, and drew the net to land full of great fishes, an hundred and fifty and three : and for all there were so many, yet 12 was not the net broken. ' Jesus saith unto them, Come *and* dine. And none of the disciples durst ask him, Who art thou? knowing that it was 13 the Lord. Jesus then cometh, and taketh bread, and giveth them, and fish 14 likewise. This is now the third time that Jesus shewed himself to his disciples, after that he was risen from the dead.   .
16 So when they had dined, Jesus saith to Simon Peter, Simon *son* of Jonas, lovest thou me more than these? He saith unto him, Yea, Lord: thou 16 knowest that I love thee. He saith unto him, Feed my lambs. ' He saith to him again the second time, Simon *son* of Jonas, lovest thou me? He saith unto him, Yea, Lord: thou knowest that I love thee. He saith 17 unto him, Feed my sheep. He saith unto him the third time, Simon *son* of Jonas, lovest thou me? Peter was grieved because he said unto him the third time, Lovest thou me? And he said unto him, Lord, thou knowest all things; thou knowest that I love thee. Jesus saith unto him, Feed my 18 sheep. Verily, verily, I say unto thee, When thou wast young, thou girdedst thyself, and walkedst whither thou wouldest: but when thou shalt be old, thou shalt stretch forth thy hands, and another shall gird thee, and carry 19 *thee* whither thou wouldest not. This spake he, signifying by what death he should glorify God. And when he had spoken this, he saith unto him, Follow me.
20 Then Peter, turning about, seeth the disciple whom Jesus loved, follow-ing ; which also leaned on his breast at supper, and said, Lord, which is 21 he that betrayeth thee? Peter seeing him, saith to Jesus, Lord, and what 22 *shall* this man *do?* Jesus saith unto him, If I will that he tarry till I come, 23 what *is that* to thee? Follow thou me. ' Then went this saying abroad among the brethren, that that disciple should not die: yet Jesus said not unto him, He shall not die ; but, If I will that he tarry till I come, what *is that* to thee?
24 This is the disciple which testifieth of these things, and wrote these things: and we know that his testimony is true.

§ 170. *Jesus meets the Apostles and above five hundred Brethren on a Mountain in Galilee.*

MATTH. XXVIII. 16—20.

16 —Into a mountain where Jesus had 17 appointed them. And when they saw him, they worshipped him : but some doubted.
18 And Jesus came, and spake unto them, saying, All power is given 19 unto me in heaven and in earth. Go ye therefore and teach all na-tions, baptizing them in the name of the Father, and of the Son, and of

1 COR. XV. 6.

6 After that, he was seen of above five hundred brethren at once ; of whom the greater part remain unto this present, but some are fallen asleep.

MATTH. XXVIII.

⁵⁰ the Holy Ghost ; ¹ teaching them to observe all things whatsoever I have commanded you : and lo, I am with you always, *even* unto the end of the world. Amen.

§ 171. *Our Lord is seen of James; then of all the Apostles.*—JERUSALEM.

1 COR. XV. 7.

⁷   After that, he was seen of James ; then of all the apostles.

ACTS I. 3—8.

³   To whom also he shewed himself alive after his passion, by many infalli-
⁴ ble proofs, being seen of them forty days, and speaking of the things pertaining to the kingdom of God : ¹ and being assembled together with *them,*
commanded them that they should not depart from Jerusalem, but wait for
⁵ the promise of the Father, which, *saith he,* ye have heard of me. For
John truly baptized with water ; but ye shall be baptized with the Holy
Ghost not many days hence.
⁶   When they therefore were come together, they asked of him, saying,
⁷ Lord, wilt thou at this time restore again the kingdom to Israel ? And he
said unto them, It is not for you to know the times or the seasons which
⁸ the Father hath put in his own power. But ye shall receive power after
that the Holy Ghost is come upon you : and ye shall be witnesses unto me,
both in Jerusalem, and in all Judea, and in Samaria, and unto the uttermost part of the earth.

§ 172. *The Ascension.*—BETHANY.

LUKE XXIV. 50—53

⁵⁰   And he led them out as far as to
Bethany : and he lifted up his hands,

MARK XVI. 19, 20.	and blessed them.	ACTS I. 9—12.
¹⁹ So then, after the Lord had spoken unto them, he was received up into heaven, and sat on the right hand of God.	⁵¹ And it came to pass, while he blessed them, he was parted from them, and carried up into heaven.	⁹ And when he had spoken these things, while they beheld, he was taken up ; and a cloud received him out ¹⁰ of their sight. And

while they looked
steadfastly toward heaven as he went up, behold, two men stood
¹¹ by them in white apparel ; ¹ which also said, Ye men of Galilee,
why stand ye gazing up into heaven ? this same Jesus which
is taken up from you into heaven, shall so come in like manner as
      LUKE XXIV.   ye have seen him go into heaven.
⁵² And they worshipped him, and re- ¹² Then returned they unto Jerusalem,
turned to Jerusalem with great joy :   from the mount called Olivet, which
⁵³ ¹ and were continually in the temple,   is from Jerusalem a sabbath-day's
praising and blessing God. Amen.   journey.

MARK XVI.

²⁰ And they went forth, and preached every where, the Lord working with
them, and confirming the word with signs following. Amen.

§ 173. *Conclusion of John's Gospel.*

John XX. 30, 31. XXI. 25.

[30] And many other signs truly did Jesus in the presence of his disciples, [31] which are not written in this book. But these are written, that ye might believe that Jesus is the Christ, the Son of God ; and that believing ye XXI. [25] might have life through his name.—And there are also many other things which Jesus did, the which, if they should be written every one, I suppose that even the world itself could not contain the books that should be written. Amen.

NOTES

HARMONY OF THE FOUR GOSPELS.

INTRODUCTION.

THE following Notes relate chiefly to the mode and order of *harmonizing* the narratives of the four Evangelists; and touch only incidentally upon other topics. They do not claim, in any sense, to be a Commentary upon the Gospels.

The Gospels of Matthew, Mark, and Luke, along with many diversities, have nevertheless a striking affinity with each other in their general features of time and place. But, when compared with John's Gospel, there is seen to be a diversity no less striking between them and the latter, not only in respect to chronology, but likewise as to the part of the country where our Lord's discourses and mighty works mainly occurred. Matthew, Mark, and Luke speak only of one Passover, that at which Jesus suffered; and from this it would follow, that our Lord's ministry continued at most only about six months. John expressly enumerates three Passovers, and more probably four, during Christ's ministry; which therefore must have had a duration of at least two and a half years, and more probably of three and a half. Again, Matthew, Mark, and Luke place the scene of Jesus' public ministrations chiefly in Galilee; whence he goes up to Jerusalem only just before his death. John, on the other hand, narrates the miracles and discourses of our Lord as occurring principally at Jerusalem, on various former occasions as well as at his last visit.

The apparent difficulty arising from the first difference, is at once set aside by the remark, that although the three Evangelists do expressly mention only one Passover, yet they do not any where, nor in any way, affirm, or even imply, that there were no more; while the testimony of John is express and definite. And further, the incident, narrated by all the three writers, of the disciples' plucking ripe ears of grain as they went through the fields, necessarily presupposes the recent occurrence of a Passover during our Lord's ministry, different from the one at which he suffered; and this is further confirmed by Luke's mention of the "second sabbath after the first" in the same connection. See Matth. 12, 1. Mark 2, 23. Luke 6, 1. See also the Note on § 37.

This difference being thus satisfactorily explained, the existence of the second difference is of course accounted for. If John is right in enumerating several Passovers, he is right in narrating what took place at Jerusalem on those occasions. But, more than this, we find in the other Evangelists several things in which they too seem to allude to earlier visits and labours of Jesus in the Holy City. So the language in which our Lord laments over Jerusalem, as having rejected his efforts, Matth. 23, 37. Luke 13, 34; and, further, his intimate relations with the family of Lazarus, which imply a longer acquaintance than a few weeks, Luke 10, 38. 39; comp. John 11, 1. 2.

For these reasons, I do not hesitate to follow, with most Commentators, the chronology of John's Gospel, and assign to our Lord's ministry four Passovers, or a duration of three and a half years. The second of these Passovers, which is less certain than the rest, and depends upon the interpretation of John 5, 1, will be considered in its place; see Note on § 36.

In view of the same circumstances, it follows also that the Gospel of John was intended to be supplementary to the others, and to narrate only such facts and events as had not been recorded by the other Evangelists. This, too, is manifest on the pages of the Harmony; since up to the last week of our Lord's life, the language of John is in only a single instance parallel to that of the other Gospels, viz. in the feeding of the five thousand, and the accompanying incidents; see §§ 64, 65.

The Gospels, and especially the first three, can in no sense be regarded as methodical annals. It is therefore difficult, and perhaps impossible, so to harmonize them, in respect to time, as in all cases to arrive at results which shall be entirely certain and satisfactory. There is often in them no definite note of time; and then we can proceed only upon conjecture, founded on a careful comparison of all the circumstances. In such cases, the decision must depend very much upon the judgment and taste of the Harmonist; and what to one person may appear probable and appropriate, may seem less so to another.

It is the aim of the present work, not so much to ascertain and exhibit the true chronological order, (although this object is not neglected,) as to place side by side the different narratives of the same events, in an order which may be regarded as at least a probable one. In so doing I may hope to exhibit the legitimate uses of a Harmony, and accomplish a three-fold purpose, viz. to make the Evangelists their own best interpreters; to show how wonderfully they are supplemental to each other in minute as well as important particulars; and in this way to bring out fully and clearly the fundamental characteristic of their testimony, UNITY IN DIVERSITY.

In the arrangement of the Harmony, made in accordance with the probable sequence of the events, and without ascribing any preference to the order of either Evangelist, this unexpected result has been brought out, viz. that the *order of both Mark and John remains every where undisturbed;* with the exception of four short passages in Mark and of three in John; in all which cases the reasons for a change of order are apparent. See Mark 2, 15-22, in § 58. Mark 6, 17-20, in § 24. Mark 14, 22-25, in § 137. Mark 14, 66-72, in § 144. John 12, 2-8, in § 131. John 18, 25-27, in § 144. John 20, 30. 31, in § 173. Besides these there are a few slight transpositions of single verses for the sake of closer parallelism; e. g. in §§ 112, 142, 153, etc.

PART I.

EVENTS CONNECTED WITH THE BIRTH AND CHILDHOOD OF OUR LORD.

§§ 1—13.

§ 2. Zacharias was an ordinary priest of the class of Abia, one of the twenty-four classes instituted by David for the service of the temple, which relieved each other in succession every Sabbath; see 1 Chr. 24, 3-19. 2 Chr. 8, 14. Joseph. Ant. 7. 14. 7. Their service included the daily burning of incense on the altar of incense in the first or outer sanctuary; and this was what Zacharias was now doing; Luke 1, 9. Ex. 30, 6-8. 1 Chr. 23, 13.—It follows, that no inference whatever can hence be drawn as to the year, or season of the year, when the vision took place. Nor is it said how long a time elapsed between the vision and Elizabeth's conception; the expression "after those days" in v. 24 being quite indefinite.

§ 3. The sixth month here refers back, not to the vision, but to the conception of Elizabeth; see v. 36.

§ 4. The conjecture of Reland is probably correct, viz. that *Juda* in v. 39 is a softened form for *Juta*, i. e. *Jutah* or *Juttah* in Hebrew, a city of the priests in the mountains of Judah, south of Hebron; Josh. 15, 55. 21, 16. The place still exists under the same name. See Reland Palæst. p. 870. Bibl. Researches in Palest. II. p. 628.

§ 6. Mary remained with Elizabeth about three months, or nearly until the full time of the latter; and then returned to Nazareth; Luke 1, 56. It was after this and after the birth of John, when Mary was now in her fourth or fifth month, and her pregnancy had become perceptible, that Joseph was minded to put her away.

§ 7. The precise year of our Lord's birth is uncertain. Several data however exist, by which an approximation may be made, sufficiently accurate to show that our present Christian era is not entirely correct.

1. According to Matth. 2, 1-6, Jesus was born during the lifetime of Herod the Great, and not long before his death. Herod died in the year of Rome (A. U.) 750, just before the Passover; see Jos. Antiq. 17. 8. 1. ib. 17. 9. 3. This has been verified by calculating the eclipse of the moon, which happened just before his death; Jos. Ant. 17. 6. 4. Ideler *Handb. of Chronol.* II. p. 391 sq. If now we make an allowance of time for the purification, the visit of the Magi, the flight into Egypt, and the remaining there till Herod was dead,—for all which not less than six months can well be required,—it follows, that the birth of Christ cannot in any case be fixed later than the autumn of A. U. 749.

2. Another note of time occurs in Luke 3, 1. 2, where John the Baptist is said to have entered upon his ministry in the fifteenth year of Tiberius; and again in Luke 3, 23, where Jesus is said to have been "about thirty years of

age" at his baptism. Now if both John and Jesus, as is quite probable, entered upon their ministry at the age of thirty, in accordance with the Levitical custom (Num. 4, 3. 35. 39. 43. 47), then by reckoning back thirty years we may ascertain the year of John's birth, and of course also that of Jesus. Augustus died Aug. 29th, A. U. 767; and was succeeded by Tiberius, who had already been associated with him in the government for at least two years, and probably three. If now we reckon from the death of Augustus, the fifteenth year of Tiberius commenced Aug. 29th, A. U. 781; and going back thirty years, we find that John must have been born not earlier than August, A. U. 751, and our Lord of course not earlier than A. U. 752;—a result disagreeing with that obtained from Matthew by three years. If, on the other hand, we reckon from the time when Tiberius was admitted as co-regent of the empire, which is shown to have been certainly as early as A. U. 765, and probably in A. U. 764; then the fifteenth year of Tiberius began in A. U. 778, and it follows that John may have been born in A. U. 748, and our Lord in A. U. 749. In this way the results obtained from Matthew and Luke are more nearly coincident.

3. A third note of time is derived from John 2, 20, "Forty and six years was this temple in building." Josephus says, in one place, that Herod began to build the temple in the eighteenth year of his reign; while in another he specifies the fifteenth year; Ant. 15. 11. 1. B. J. 1. 21. 1. He also assigns the length of Herod's reign at thirty-seven or thirty-four years; according as he reckons from his appointment by the Romans, or from the death of Antigonus; Ant. 17. 8. 1. B. J. 1. 33. 8. Herod was first declared king of Judea in A. U. 714; Jos. Ant. 14. 14. 4, 5. B. J. 1. 14. 4. comp. Ant. 14. 16. 4. Ideler *Handb. of Chron.* II. p. 390. Hence the eighteenth year of his reign, when Herod began to rebuild the temple, would coincide with A. U. 732; and our Lord's first Passover, in the forty-seventh year following, would fall in A. U. 779. If now our Lord at that time was thirty and a half years of age, as is probable, this would carry back the year of his birth to the autumn of A. U. 748.

4. Further, according to a tradition preserved by the Latin Fathers of the first five centuries, our Lord's death took place during the consulate of the two Gemini, C. Rubellius and C. Fufius, that is, in A. U. 782. So Tertullian, Lactantius, Augustine, etc. See Tertull. adv. Jud. § 8. Augustin. de Civ. Dei XVIII. 54. If now the duration of his ministry was three and a half years, then, as before, the year of his birth would be carried back to the autumn of A. U. 748.

5. Some modern writers, taking into account the abode in Egypt and also the "two years" of Matth. 2, 16, have supposed that Jesus must have been from two to three years old at Herod's death; and hence they assume that he was born in A. U. 747. The same year, A. U. 747, is also fixed upon as the date of Christ's birth, by those who regard the star in the east as having been the conjunction of the planets Jupiter and Saturn, which occurred in that year. So Keppler, Münter, Ideler *Handb. of Chronol.* Berlin 1826.

From all these data it would appear, that while our Lord's birth cannot have taken place later than A. U. 749, it *may* nevertheless have occurred one or two years earlier.

The present Christian era, which was fixed by the abbot Dionysius Exiguus in the sixth century, assumes the year of Christ's birth as coincident with A. U. 754. It follows then from the preceding statements, that this our common era begins in any case *more than four years too late*; that is, from *four to five years*, at the least, after the actual birth of Christ. This era was first used in historical works by the Venerable Bede, early in the eighth century; and was not long after introduced in public transactions by the Frank kings Pepin and Charlemagne.

In respect to the time of the year when Jesus was born, there is still less certainty. John the Baptist would seem to have entered upon his ministry in the spring; perhaps when the multitudes were collected in Jerusalem at the Passover. The crowds which followed him imply that it was not winter. The baptism of Jesus in the Jordan, probably six months later, would then have occurred in autumn. It could not well have been in the winter, for John was still followed by crowds; nor does a winter seem to have intervened. If now we may assume, as is most probable, that John entered on his office when he had completed his thirtieth year; then the time of his birth was also the spring; and that of our Lord, six months later, was the autumn. Archbishop Newcome, referring to Lardner, has the following remark: "Jesus was born, says Lardner, between the middle of August and the middle of November, A. U. 748 or 749. We will take the mean time, October 1." See Lardner's Works, Vol. I. p. 370, 372. Lond. 1835.—There is, on this point, no valid tradition. According to the earliest accounts, the sixth of January, or Epiphany, was celebrated by the eastern churches, in the third and fourth centuries, as the festival of the birth and baptism of Jesus; Cassian. Collat. X. c. 2. In the western churches, after the middle of the fourth century, the twenty-fifth of December (Christmas) began to be kept as the festival of Christ's nativity; this day having been fixed upon, partly at least, as being the then current winter solstice. Thus, as late as the time of pope Leo the Great, (ob. 461,) there were many in Rome, "by whom this day of solemnity was regarded as honourable, not so much on account of the nativity of Christ, as because of the rising of the new sun, as they called it." Leon. Magn. Serm. XXI. c. 6. See the Church Hist. of Neander, Vol. I; also that of Gieseler, Vol. I. The observance of this latter festival (Christmas) spread into the East; while that of the Epiphany, as the baptismal day, was adopted in the West.

§ 10. The visit of the Magi at Bethlehem naturally follows the presentation in the temple; since, after the jealousy of Herod had been once roused, this public presentation could not well have taken place. Joseph and Mary return from Jerusalem to Bethlehem, distant five English miles, where they had now been detained for nearly two months. Luke indeed does not allude to this return (2, 39); but neither does he mention the flight into Egypt.

§ 13. The genealogy in Luke is inverted, for the sake of more convenient comparison. The words "*which was the son*," so often repeated in the English Version, is an addition by the translators merely to fill out the connection.

I. In the genealogy given by Matthew, considered by itself, some difficulties present themselves.

1. There is some diversity among commentators in making out the three divisions, each of fourteen generations, v. 17. It is, however, obvious, that the first division begins with Abraham and ends with David. But does the second begin with David, or with Solomon? Assuredly with the former; because, just as the first begins *from* Abraham, so the second also is said to begin *from*

15

David.   The first extends *to* David, and includes him ; the second extends
until the carrying away into Babylon, i. e. to an epoch and not to a person ;
and therefore the persons who are mentioned as coeval with this epoch (*about
the time* of the carrying away, v. 11), are not reckoned before it.   After the
epoch the enumeration begins again with Jechoniah, and ends with Jesus.   In
this way the three divisions are made out thus :

1. Abraham.	1. David.	1. Jechoniah.
2. Isaac.	2. Solomon.	2. Salathiel.
3. Jacob.	3. Roboam.	3. Zorobabel.
4. Judah.	4. Abiah.	4. Abiud.
5. Phares.	5. Asa.	5. Eliakim.
6. Esrom.	6. Josaphat.	6. Azor.
7. Aram.	7. Joram.	7. Sadoc.
8. Aminadab.	8. Uzziah (Ozias).	8. Achim.
9. Naasson.	9. Jotham.	9. Eliud.
10. Salmon.	10. Ahaz.	10. Eleazar.
11. Boaz.	11. Hezekiah.	11. Matthan.
12. Obed.	12. Manasseh.	12. Jacob.
13. Jesse.	13. Amon.	13. Joseph.
14. David.	14. Josiah.	14. Jesus.

2. Another difficulty arises from the fact, that between Joram and Ozias, in
v. 8, three names of Jewish kings are omitted, viz. *Ahaziah, Joash*, and *Ama-
ziah ;* see 2 K. 8, 25 and 2 Chr. 22, 1.—2 K. 11, 2. 21 and 2 Chr. 22, 11.—2 K. 12,
21. 14, 1 and 2 Chr. 24, 27.   Further, between Josiah and Jechoniah in v. 11,
the name of *Jehoiakim* is also omitted ; 2 K. 23, 34. 2 Chr. 36, 4. comp. 1 Chr.
3, 15. 16.   If these four names are to be reckoned, then the second division,
instead of *fourteen* generations, will contain *eighteen*, in contradiction to v. 17.
To avoid this difficulty, Newcome and some others have regarded v. 17 as a
mere gloss, " a marginal note taken into the text."   This indeed is in itself
possible ; yet all the external testimony of manuscripts and versions is in favour
of the genuineness of that verse.   It is better therefore to regard these names
as having been customarily omitted in the current genealogical tables, from
which Matthew copied.   Such omissions of particular generations did sometimes actually occur, " because they were wicked and impious," according to
the Rabbins; see Lightfoot Hor. Heb. on Matth. 1, 8.   A striking example of
an omission of this kind, apparently without any such reason, is found in Ezra
7, 1-5, compared with 1 Chr. 6, 3-15.   This latter passage contains the lineal
descent of the high priests from Aaron to the captivity ; while Ezra, in the
place cited, in tracing back his own genealogy through the very same line of
descent, omits at least six generations.   The two accounts stand thus :

1 *Chr.* 6, 3-15.	*Ezra* 7, 1-5.	1 *Chr.* 6, 3-15.	*Ezra* 7, 1-5.
1. Aaron.	Aaron.	13. Azariah.	
2. Eleazar.	Eleazar.	14. Johanan.	
3. Phinehas.	Phinehas.	15. Azariah.	Azariah.
4. Abishua.	Abishua.	16. Amariah.	Amariah.
5. Bukki.	Bukki.	17. Ahitub.	Ahitub.
6. Uzzi.	Uzzi.	18. Zadok.	Zadok.
7. Zerahiah.	Zerahiah.	19. Shallum.	Shallum.
8. Meraioth.	Meraioth.	20. Hilkiah.	Hilkiah.
9. Amariah.		21. Azariah.	Azariah.
10. Ahitub.		22. Seraiah.	Seraiah.
11. Zadok.		23. Jehozadak.	
12. Ahimaaz.		24.	Ezra.

A similar omission is necessarily implied in the genealogy of David, as given Ruth 4, 20-22. 1 Chr. 2, 10-12. Matth. 1, 5. 6. Salmon was cotemporary with the capture of Jericho by Joshua, and married Rahab. But from that time until David, an interval of at least four hundred and fifty years (Acts 13, 20), there intervened, according to the list, only four generations, averaging of course more than one hundred years to each. But the highest average in point of fact is *three* generations to a century; and if reckoned by the eldest sons they are usually shorter, or three generations for every seventy-five or eighty years. See Sir I. Newton's Chronol. p. 53. Lond. 1728.

We may therefore rest in the necessary conclusion, that as our Lord's regular descent from David was always asserted, and was never denied even by the Jews; so Matthew, in tracing this admitted descent, appealed to genealogical tables, which were public and acknowledged in the family and tribe from which Christ sprang. He could not indeed do otherwise. How much stress was laid by the Jews upon lineage in general, and how much care and attention were bestowed upon such tables, is well known. See Lightfoot Hor. Heb. on Matth. 1, 1. In the N. T. also, see Phil. 3, 4. 5.

II. Other questions of some difficulty present themselves, when we compare together the two genealogies.

1. Both tables at first view purport to give the lineage of our Lord through Joseph. But Joseph cannot have been the son by natural descent of both Jacob and Heli (Eli), Matth. 1, 16. Luke 3, 23. Only one of the tables therefore can give his true lineage by generation. This is done apparently in that of Matthew; because, beginning at Abraham, it proceeds by natural descent, as we know from history, until after the exile; and then continues on in the same mode of expression until Joseph. Here the phrase is changed; and it is no longer Joseph who "begat" Jesus, but Joseph "the husband of Mary, of whom was born Jesus who is called Christ."

2. To whom then does the genealogy in Luke chiefly relate? If in any way to Joseph, as the language purports, then it must be because he in some way bore the legal relation of son to Heli, either by adoption or by marriage. If the former simply, it is difficult to comprehend, why, along with his true personal lineage as traced by Matthew up through the royal line of Jewish kings to David, there should be given also another subordinate genealogy, not personally his own, and running back through a different and inferior line to the same great ancestor. If, on the other hand, as is most probable, this relation to Heli came by marriage with his daughter, so that Joseph was truly his *son-in-law* (comp. Ruth 1, 8. 11. 12); then it follows, that the genealogy in Luke is in fact that of Mary the mother of Jesus. This being so, we can perceive a sufficient reason, why this genealogy should be thus given, viz. in order to show definitely, that Jesus was *in the most full and perfect sense* a descendant of David; not only by law in the royal line of kings through his reputed father, but also in fact by direct personal descent through his mother.

That Mary, like Joseph, was a descendant of David, is not indeed elsewhere expressly said in the New Testament. Yet a very strong presumption to that effect is to be drawn from the address of the angel in Luke 1, 32; as also from the language of Luke 2, 5, where Joseph, as one of the posterity of David, is said to have gone up to Bethlehem *to enrol himself with Mary his espoused wife* for this is the meaning of the Greek. The ground and circumstances of Mary's enrolment must obviously have been the same as in the case of Joseph himself. Whether all this arose from her having been an only child and heiress, as some suppose, so that she was espoused to Joseph in accordance with Num. 36, 8. 9, it is not necessary here to inquire.

It is indeed objected, that it was not customary among the Jews to trace back descent through the female line, i. e. on the mother's side. There are however examples to show that this was sometimes done; and in the case of Jesus, as we have seen, there was a sufficient reason for it. Thus in 1 Chr. 2, 22, Jair is enumerated among the posterity of Judah by regular descent. But the grandfather of Jair had married the daughter of Machir, one of the heads of Manasseh, 1 Chr. 2, 21. 7, 14; and therefore, in Num. 32, 40. 41, Jair is called the son (descendant) of Manasseh. In like manner, in Ezra 2, 61 and Neh. 7, 63, a certain family is spoken of as "the children of Barzillai;" because their ancestor "took a wife of the daughters of Barzillai the Gileadite, and was called after their name."

3. A question is raised as to the identity, in the two genealogies, of the Salathiel and Zorobabel named as father and son, Matth. 1, 12. Luke 3, 27. The Zorobabel of Matthew is no doubt the chief, who led back the first band of captives from Babylon, and rebuilt the temple, Ezra c. 2-6. He is also called the son of Salathiel in Ezra 3, 2. Neh. 12, 1. Hagg. 1, 1. 2, 2. 23. Were then the Salathiel and Zorobabel of Luke the same persons? Those who assume this, must rest solely on the identity of the names; for there is no other possible evidence to prove, either that they were cotemporary, or that they were not different persons. On the other hand, there are one or two considerations, of some force, which go to show that they were probably not the same persons.

First, if Salathiel and Zorobabel are indeed the same in both genealogies, then Salathiel, who according to Matthew was the son of Jechoniah by natural descent, must have been called the son of Neri in Luke either from adoption or marriage. In that case, his connection with David through Nathan, as given by Luke, was not his own personal genealogy. It is difficult therefore to see, why Luke, after tracing back the descent of Jesus to Salathiel, should abandon the true personal lineage in the royal line of kings, and turn aside again to a merely collateral and humbler line. If the mother of Jesus was in fact descended from the Zorobabel and Salathiel of Matthew, she, like them, was descended also from David through the royal line. Why rob her of this dignity, and ascribe to her only a descent through an inferior lineage?

Again, the mere identity of names under these circumstances, affords no proof; for nothing is more common in Scripture, even among cotemporaries. Thus we have two Ezras; one in Neh. 12, 1. 13. 33; from whom Ezra the scribe is expressly distinguished in v. 36. We have likewise two Nehemiahs; one who went up with Zorobabel, Ezra 2, 2; and the other the governor who went later to Jerusalem, Neh. 2, 9 sq. So too, as cotemporaries, Joram son of Ahab king of Israel, and Joram (Jehoram) son of Jehoshaphat king of Judah; 2 K. 8, 16. comp. v. 23. 24. Also, Joash king of Judah and Joash king of Israel; 2 K. 13, 9. 10. Further we find in succession among the descendants of Cain the following names: Enoch, Irad, Mehujael, Methusael, Lamech, Gen 4, 17. 18; and later among the descendants of Seth these similar ones: Enoch, Methuselah, Lamech, Gen. 5, 21-25.

Various artificial theories of inheritances and intermarriages have at differ ent times been proposed, in order to explain and harmonize the two genealogies. But in the view here taken all these become unnecessary. See Lightfoot Hor. Heb. on Luke 3, 23.

PART II.

ANNOUNCEMENT AND INTRODUCTION OF OUR LORD'S PUBLIC MIN-
ISTRY.

§§ 14—20.

§ 14. For the time when John the Baptist entered upon his public ministry, see Note on § 7. p. 169.—On Matth. 3, 11 and the parallel passages, see the next Note.

§ 15. For the time of our Lord's baptism, see Note on § 7.—We may here, once for all, make a remark upon the difference of the words from heaven, as quoted Matth. 3, 17 and the parallel passages. A like difference is seen in the four copies of the title on the cross, Matth. 27, 37. Mark 15, 26. Luke 23, 38. John 19, 19. And still more, in the solemn words of our Lord at the institution of the cup, Matth. 26, 28. Mark 14, 24. Luke 22, 20. 1 Cor. 11, 25. Similar varieties of expression in the different reports of the same language are found in the following passages, as well as very many others: Matth. 3, 11. Mark 1, 7. Luke 3, 16. John 1, 27.—Matth. 9, 11. Mark 5, 16. Luke 5, 30.—Matth. 15, 27. Mark 7, 28.—Matth. 16, 6-9. Mark 8, 17-19.—Matth. 20, 33. Mark 10, 51. Luke 18, 41.—Matth. 21, 9. Mark 11, 9. Luke 19, 38.—Matth. 26, 39. Mark 14, 36. Luke 22, 42.—Matth 28, 5. 6. Mark 16, 6. Luke 24, 5. 6.—All these examples go only to show, that where the Evangelists profess to record the expressions used by our Lord and others, they usually give them according to the *sense*, and not according to the *letter*; and this must be regarded as a general principle of interpretation in the Gospels and elsewhere.

§ 16. That the temptation of Jesus took place directly after his baptism, appears from the word "immediately" in Mark 1, 12; and also from a comparison of John 1, 29. 35. 44.—According to Mark and Luke, Jesus was subjected to temptation during the forty days. Matthew and Luke specify three instances of temptation, but in a different order. One of these apparently must have occurred at the end of the forty days. The order of Matthew is perhaps the most natural of the two; though, as the accounts were probably derived from the recital of our Lord himself, given at various times, in his intercourse with his disciples, the true order may have been different from either.

§ 18. In v. 21 the Baptist declares that he was not Elias; meaning that he was not Elias risen from the dead. In Matth. 17, 12 Jesus says that "Elias is come already;" meaning that John had come "in the spirit and power of Elias;" Luke 1, 17.

In v. 33, John the Baptist says he knew not Jesus; though in Matth. 3, 14

15*

(§ 15) he appears to have known who he was. That is to say John must have been acquainted with the events of his own childhood and that of Jesus; he had now come preaching and baptizing as his forerunner, v. 31; but he knew not Jesus *personally* before he came to be baptized; at which time God had promised him a sign, by which he might know certainly that Jesus was the Messiah.

§ 20. The *third day* refers back to John 1, 44. The journey in returning to Galilee did not require more than two days; the distance being, in any position of Bethabara, not over about fifty miles. Cana, now *Kâna el-Jelîl*, was situated about seven miles north of Nazareth, and about three miles N. by E. of Sepphoris; see Bibl. Res. in Palest. III. p. 204.

———

PART III.

OUR LORD'S FIRST PASSOVER, AND THE SUBSEQUENT TRANSACTIONS UNTIL THE SECOND.

§§ 21—35.

§ 21. This our Lord's first Passover is mentioned only by John; though the language of the other Evangelists implies, that he had been again in Judea; Matth. 4, 12. Mark 1, 14.

John connects with this first Passover the cleansing of the temple and the casting out of the traders; while the other Evangelists describe a like transaction at his last Passover, Matth. 21, 12 sq. Mark 11, 15 sq. Luke 19, 45 sq. The question is raised, whether these were different transactions; and whether there is not here a neglect of the order of time, either by John or in the other Gospels. As the language and the note of time in all the Evangelists in respect to both the instances, is entirely definite and specific, the answer may be said to depend upon a further question, viz. Whether our Lord would be likely to repeat a highly symbolic and important public act, after an interval of two or three years? That he was accustomed to repeat the substance of his discourses, or at least the more striking parts of them, at different times and before different persons, is sufficiently obvious. Compare Luke 11, 37–54 uttered in Galilee, with Matth. 23, 1–39 delivered at Jerusalem; likewise Matth. 5, 13 in the Sermon on the Mount, with Mark 9, 50 and Luke 14, 34. 35, spoken elsewhere; and also the different examples of the Lord's prayer, Matth. 6, 9–13. Luke 11, 2–4. Further, Matth. 5, 29. 30 compared with Mark 9, 43–47; and Matth. 6. 25–33, with Luke 12, 22–31. Such examples indeed may be multiplied almost indefinitely, as the pages of the Harmony every where show. Now if this is true in respect to the discourses of Christ, why might he not just as well have repeated, after a long interval and before different persons, a public symbolical act, so significant in itself, and so expressive of his character and authority as the Messiah? The Jews, it seems, did not question his right to perform such an act, provided he was a true prophet. They only demanded some **sign** of his authority; John 2, 18. This Jesus gave, and had already given in his mighty works, wrought at the same Passover, v. 13; works which drew from Nicodemus, a Pharisee and a member of the Sanhedrim, the admission, that he was "a teacher come from God;" John 3, 2.

On the "three days" in John 2, 20, see Note on § 49.

§§ 23, 24. The order is here determined by comparing John, 3, 24 with Matth. 4, 12. Mark 1, 14. Jesus goes out with his disciples from Jerusalem into the country of Judea; where he remains until after John was cast into prison. See the next Note.

§ 25. John 4, 35 contains a specification of time which is tolerably definite: "Say not ye, There are yet four months, and *then* cometh harvest?" According to Lev. 23, 5-7. 10. 11. 14. 15, and Jos. Antiq. 3. 10. 5, the first-fruits of the barley-harvest were presented on the second day of the paschal week; while the wheat harvest was two or three weeks later; see Bibl. Res. in Palest. II. p. 99 sq. Hence this journey of our Lord must have been made in the latter part of November or in December, about eight months after the preceding Passover. It follows, that the public ministry of John the Baptist had continued for at least a year and six months, before his imprisonment; that is to say, on the supposition that he commenced his labours about the time of the Passover in the preceding year. See Note on § 7, last paragraph.

§ 28. The visit to Nazareth is inserted here on the testimony of Luke 4, 16 sq. which is supported by Matth. 4, 13. The visit mentioned in Matth. 13, 54 sq. Mark 6, 1 sq. was later, and took place after the raising of Jairus' daughter.

Our Lord's escape from the crowd, Luke 4, 30, does not seem necessarily to imply any thing directly supernatural; see the similar circumstances narrated, John 8, 59. 10, 39.

§ 29. That the call of the four Apostles belongs here, in accordance with Mark's order, is obvious; since they were afterwards present with Jesus at the healing of the demoniac and of Peter's wife's mother, §§ 30, 31.—The three accounts all evidently relate to the same transaction. Luke relates more particularly the former part, including the putting off upon the lake in Simon's boat and also the miraculous draught of fishes; and passes lightly over the latter part. Matthew and Mark, on the other hand, narrate the former part only generally; but the latter part with more detail. In the one part, Luke introduces circumstances which the others omit; in the other part, Matthew and Mark mention facts which Luke has not noted. The remark of Spanheim is here just: "The facts narrated by Luke are not contradicted by Matthew, but only passed over. Nothing is more common than that circumstances omitted by one, should be supplied by another; lest *the sacred writers should seem to have written by compact,* or lest the readers should cleave to one and neglect the others." Dubia Evang. Tom. III. Dub. 72. vii.

PART IV.

OUR LORD'S SECOND PASSOVER, AND THE SUBSEQUENT TRANSACTIONS UNTIL THE THIRD.

§§ 36—66.

§ 36. In John 5, 2, the marginal reading of the English version is adopted, viz. "sheep *gate*" instead of "sheep *market*." We know there was such a gate, Neh. 3, 1. 12, 39 ; but there is no mention of such a market.

On the phrase "a feast [festival] of the Jews," John 5, 1, turns mainly the question as to the duration of our Lord's public ministry. John notes distinctly three Passovers; John 2, 13. 6, 4. 12, 1. If now this festival be another Passover, then our Lord's public labours continued during three and a half years; if not, then the time of his ministry must in all probability be reckoned one year less.

The only reasonable ground of doubt in this case, is the absence (in the Greek) of the definite article before the word signifying *feast*, or rather *festival*. Did the text read "*the* feast of the Jews," (as is actually the case in some Manuscripts and Editions,) then, as most admit, it would with sufficient definiteness denote the Passover; comp. Matth. 26, 5. Luke 2, 42. John 4, 45. 11, 56. etc. At any rate, even as the text now stands, it *may* assuredly in itself just as well denote the great Jewish festival, as any other. The following considerations seem to show, that it does most probably thus stand for a Passover, viz. the *second* in our Lord's public ministry.

1. The same word without the article is put definitely for the Passover, in the phrase "at the feast," where our English version from necessity inserts *the* or *that*, Matth. 27, 15. Mark 15, 6. Luke 23, 17. Comp. John 18, 39.

2. It is not probable, that John means here to imply that the festival was indefinite or uncertain. Such is not his usual manner. The Jewish festivals were to him the measures of time; and in every other instance they are definitely specified. So the Passover, John 2, 23. 12, 1 ; even when Jesus does not visit it, 6, 4 ; and also when it is expressed only by *the feast*, 4, 45. 11, 56. 12, 12. 20. So too the festival of Tabernacles, 7, 2 ; and of the Dedication, 10, 22. This is all natural in him ; for an indefinite festival could afford no note of time.

3. The plucking of the ears of grain by the disciples (§ 37 and Note), shows that a Passover had just been kept ; which tallies accurately with this visit of our Lord to Jerusalem.

4. This feast could not have been the festival either of Pentecost or of Tabernacles next following our Lord's first Passover. He returned from Judea to Galilee not until eight months after that Passover, when both these festivals were already past; see Note on § 25.—That it might by possibility have been the Pentecost after a second Passover not mentioned, and before that in John 6, 4, cannot perhaps be fully disproved ; but such a view has in itself no probability, and is apparently entertained by no one. At any rate

it also would give the same duration of three and a half years to our Lord's ministry.

5. Nor can we well understand here the festival of Purim, which occurred on the fourteenth and fifteenth of the month Adar (March), one month before the Passover; see Esth. 9, 21. 22. 26-28. Against this the following considerations present themselves: (a) The Jews did not go up to Jerusalem to celebrate the festival of Purim. The observance of it among that people throughout the world, consisted solely in reading the Book of Esther in their synagogues on those days, and making them "days of fasting and joy, and of sending portions [dishes] one to another, and gifts to the poor;" Esth. 9, 22. Jos. Ant. 11. 6. 13. But the "multitude," John 5, 13, seems to imply a concourse of strangers at one of the great festivals.—(b) It is very improbable, that Jesus would have gone up to Jerusalem at the Purim, to which the Jews did not go up, rather than at the Passover, which occurred only a month later. His being once present at the festival of Dedication (John 10, 22) is not a parallel case; since he appears not to have gone up for that purpose, but this festival occurred while he remained in or near Jerusalem after the festival of Tabernacles, John 7, 2 sq.—(c) The infirm man was healed on the Sabbath, John 5, 9; which Sabbath belonged to the festival, as the whole context shows, John 5, 1. 2. 10-13. But the Purim was never celebrated on a Sabbath; and, when it happened to fall on that day, was regularly deferred; see Reland Antiq. Heb. IV. 9.

6. The main objection urged against taking this festival as a Passover, is the circumstance, that in such case, as our Lord did not go up to the Passover spoken of in John 6, 4, but only at the subsequent festival of Tabernacles in John 7, 2 sq. he would thus have absented himself from Jerusalem for a year and six months; a neglect, it is alleged, inconsistent with his character and with a due observance of the Jewish law. But a sufficient reason is assigned for this omission, viz. " because the Jews sought to kill him," John 7, 1. comp. 5, 18. It obviously had been our Lord's custom to visit the Holy City every year at the Passover; and because, for the reason assigned, he once let this occasion pass by, he therefore went up six months afterwards at the festival of Tabernacles. All this presents a view perfectly natural; and covers the whole ground. Nor have we any right to assume, as many do, that our Lord regularly went up to Jerusalem on other occasions, besides those specified in the New Testament.

In this instance, the most ancient view is that which interprets the festival as a Passover. So Irenæus in the third century; and the same view was adopted by Eusebius, Theodoret, and others; and in later times has been followed by Luther, Scaliger, Grotius, Lightfoot, Le Clerc, Lampe, Hengstenberg, etc. Cyril and Chrysostom held to a Pentecost; and so, in modern times, Erasmus, Calvin, Beza, Bengel, etc. The festival of Purim was first suggested by Keppler; and at the present day this is the only view, aside from the Passover, that finds advocates. Those who hold it, as Hug, Neander, Olshausen, Tholuck, Meyer, (Lücke and De Wette leave the question undecided,) regard John 6, 4 as having reference to the second Passover during our Lord's ministry; which latter thus becomes limited to two and a half years.

§ 37. The circumstances here narrated show that a Passover had just been celebrated; see Note on § 25. The phrase " second sabbath after the first" in

Luke 6, 1, is more properly translated "the second-first sabbath," and was probably a sort of proper name for *the first Sabbath after the second day of the Passover* or of unleavened bread; that is, the first of the seven Sabbaths reckoned between that day and Pentecost; see the Greek Lexicons, also Scaligei *Emendat. Tempp.* VI. 557.   Our Lord would seem to have hastened away from Jerusalem; for which a reason is found in John 5, 16. 18.

§ 40. The appointment of the Twelve follows here according to Mark and Luke.   Matthew gives their names in c. 10, 24, as having been already appointed. Lebbeus, called also Thaddeus by Matthew and Mark, is the same as Jude the brother of James in Luke.   The epithet *Zelotes*, Zealot, is the Greek translation of the Hebrew word, *Cananite*, Zealot.   Nathaniel, who is mentioned with the Apostles in John 21, 2, was probably the same as Bartholomew, who elsewhere also is coupled with Philip; see John 1, 45 sq.

§ 41. The Sermon on the Mount finds its proper place here, in accordance with the order of Luke.   The correctness of this order, so far as it respects Matthew, depends on the question: Whether the discourse as reported by the two Evangelists is one and the same, and was delivered on the same occasion? The question is answered at the present day by interpreters, with great unanimity, in the affirmative; and mainly for the following reasons.

1. The choice of the Twelve by our Lord, as his ministers and witnesses, furnished an appropriate occasion for this public declaration respecting the spiritual nature of his kingdom, and the life and character required of those who would become his true followers.   Luke expressly assigns this as the occasion; and although Matthew is silent here and elsewhere as to the selection of the Apostles, yet some passages of the discourse as reported by him, seem to presuppose their previous appointment as teachers; see Matth. 5, 13. 14. 7, 6.

2. The beginning and the end of both discourses, and the general course of thought in both, exhibit an entire accordance one with the other.

3. The historical circumstances which follow both discourses are the same, viz. the entrance into Capernaum and the healing of the Centurion's servant.

The main objection which has been felt and urged against the identity of the two discourses, is the fact, that Matthew's report contains much that is not found in Luke; while, on the other hand, Luke adds a few things not found in Matthew, as vv. 24-26. 38–40. 45; and, further, his expressions are often modified and different, as in vv. 20. 29. 35. 36. 43. 44. 46. But this objection vanishes, if we look at the different objects which the two Evangelists had in view. Matthew was writing chiefly for Hebrew Christians; and it was therefore important for him to bring out, in full, the manner in which our Lord enforced the spiritual nature of his dispensation and doctrine, in opposition to the mere letter of the Jewish law and the teaching and corrupt practice of the Scribes and Pharisees.   This he does particularly, and with many examples, in Matth. 5, 18–38. 6, 1-34.   Luke, on the contrary, was writing mainly for Gentile Christians; and hence he omits the long passages of Matthew above referred to, and dwells only upon those topics which are of practical importance to all, whether Jew or Gentile.   In other respects, the discourses, as given by the two writers, do not differ more than is elsewhere often the case in different reports of the same discourse.   Compare Matth. 24, 1-42 with Mark 13, 1-37 and Luke 21,

5-36; also Matth. 28, 5-8 with Mark 16, 6-8 and Luke 24, 5-8. See also Note on § 15.

Some, in order to avoid the like difficulty, have supposed that our Lord first held the longer discourse in Matthew before his disciples on the top of the mountain; and afterwards descended and delivered the same in the briefer form of Luke to the multitudes below. But this is unnecessary; and the order of circumstances would seem rather to have been the following: Our Lord retires to the mountain and chooses the Twelve; and with them descends to the multitudes on the level place or plain, where he heals many. (§ 40.) As they press upon him, he again ascends to a more elevated spot, where he can overlook the crowds and be heard by them; and here, seating himself with the Twelve around him, he addresses himself to his disciples in particular and to the multitudes in general. See Matth. 5, 1. 2. Luke 6, 20; also Matth. 7, 28. Luke 7, 1.

The mountain where these events took place, was doubtless some part of the high ground on the west of the Lake of Tiberias, not far from Capernaum. The Romish church has the tradition, that the singular hill called Tell Hattîn, or Kŭrûn Hattîn, was the spot; and that hill is hence known to travellers as the Mount of Beatitudes. But this eminence is seven or eight miles distant from the probable site of Capernaum; which seems inconsistent with Matth. 8, 5. Luke 7, 1. And further, this tradition is current only among foreign Latin monks, and cannot be traced back, even among them, beyond the twelfth century; while Christians of the Greek church, which has been native upon the soil from the earliest centuries, know nothing of it; and have indeed no tradition whatever connected with the Sermon on the Mount. See Bibl. Researches in Palestine, III. p. 240.

In Matth. 6, 1, p. 34, the marginal reading of the English version is inserted in the text, viz. "righteousness" instead of "alms." This is in accordance with all the critical editions of the Greek Testament, and also with the context; for the word "righteousness" is here general, including the subsequent specifications of alms v. 2, prayer v. 5, and fasting v. 16.

§ 42. In Matthew, the Centurion seems to come in person to Jesus; in Luke, he sends the elders of the Jews. This diversity is satisfactorily explained by the old law-maxim: *Qui facit per alium, facit per se,* "What one does by another, he does himself." Matthew narrates briefly; Luke gives the circumstances more fully. In like manner, in John 4, 1, Jesus is said to baptize, when he did it by his disciples. In John 19, 1, and elsewhere, Pilate is said to have scourged Jesus; certainly not with his own hands. In Mark 10, 35, James and John come to Jesus with a certain request; in Matth. 20, 20, it is their mother who prefers the request. In 2 Sam. 24, 1, God moves David to number Israel; in 1 Chr. 21, 1, it is Satan who provokes him.

§ 44. Matthew places this narrative after the sending out of the Twelve, Matth. 11, 1. 2. This appears to be too late; for, during the absence of the Twelve, John was beheaded; see Mark 6, 30. Matth. 14, 13. The order of Luke is therefore retained. Our Lord was probably at or near Capernaum; comp. § 45.

§ 48. The order of Mark is here resumed, who places these transactions next after the appointment of the Twelve, omitting the Sermon on the Mount and other intervening matters. The narrative of Luke is obviously parallel; although given by him in a different place and order. See in Introd. Note to Part VI. p. 185.

§ 49. The specification in Matth. 12, 40, that Jesus should be "three days and three nights" in the sepulchre, seems at first view not to harmonize with the accounts of his burial and resurrection. From these latter it appears, that he was laid in the tomb before sunset on the sixth day of the week or Friday, and rose quite early on the first day of the week or Sunday; having lain in the grave not far from thirty-six hours. See §§ 159, 160, and Notes. This accords with the usual formula which our Lord employed in speaking of his resurrection, viz. that "he should rise on the *third day;*" Matth. 16, 21. 20, 19. Mark 9, 31. 10, 34. Luke 9, 22. 18, 33. etc. Equivalent to this is also the expression, "after *three days* I will rise again," Math. 27, 63. Mark 8, 31. John 2, 19. etc. This latter idiom is found also in John 20, 26, where *eight days* is put for a week. So too in German, the expression: *nach drey Tagen,* "after three days," is always the same as: *am dritten Tage,* "on the third day," the day after to-morrow; and *acht Tage,* "eight days," is the more common phrase instead of *eine Woche,* "a week."

In the present instance, Matth. 12, 40, the apparent difficulty arises from the form of the expression "three days and three nights," which our Lord uses here, and here alone, because he is quoting from Jonah 1, 17. The phrase "day and night" doubtless in itself implies a day and night of twenty-four hours. But the Hebrew form of expression for *three days and three nights,* was likewise used generally and indefinitely for *three days* simply; as is obvious from 1 Sam. 30, 11. 12 (compared with v. 13), and from the circumstances there narrated. Such also is manifestly the case here.

§ 51. The order here connects back with Luke 11, 36, in § 49. Jesus receives the invitation of the Pharisee *while he was speaking.* See Introd. Note to Part VI. p. 185.

§ 52. Luke c. 12 is directly connected with the preceding by the phrase *in the mean time, meanwhile.*

§ 53. The order is here fixed by v. 1.

§ 54. The order here depends on Matth 13, 1; comp. in § 50. The intervening events in §§ 51–53 are supplied by Luke. The place may be Capernaum; but this is not certain.

§ 56. Mark here fixes the order of time, "the same day at evening." The incident of the Scribe and of another disciple, which Matthew gives definitely here, is related by Luke in a wholly different connection without any note of time. It is transferred hither, because it is of such a nature that it cannot well be supposed to have occurred twice in circumstances so exactly parallel. The conversation takes place, as our Lord was on his way from the house (Matth. 13, 36) to the boat.

§ 57. Origen says that a city *Gergesa* anciently stood on the eastern shore of the lake of Tiberias; Opp. IV. p. 140. Gadara was a larger city, whose district or jurisdiction apparently extended to the lake, and included Gergesa.   In Matth. 8, 28, some critical editions read *Gerasenes*, and others *Gadarenes*.

Mark and Luke speak of only one demoniac; Matthew of two.   Here the maxim of Le Clerc holds true: *Qui plura narrat, pauciora complectitur; qui pauciora memorat, plura non negat;* which may here be thus applied: "He who speaks of two, includes also the one; he who mentions only one, does not deny the two." Something peculiar in the circumstances or character of one of the persons, may have rendered him more prominent, and led the two former Evangelists to speak of him particularly. But their language does not *exclude* another.—A familiar example will illustrate the principle. In the year 1824, Lafayette visited the United States; and was every where welcomed with honours and pageants. Historians will describe these as a noble incident in his life. Others writers will relate the same visit as made, and the same honours as enjoyed, by *two* persons, viz. Lafayette and his son. Will there be any contradiction between these two classes of writers? Will not both record the truth? See Bibliotheca Sacra, 1845. No. I. p. 169.

§§ 58, 59. The *call* of Levi or Matthew is placed by the three Evangelists immediately after the healing of the paralytic in Capernaum; see §§ 34, 35. Very naturally too, they all three connect with his call an account of the *feast* which he afterwards made for Jesus; in order to bring together and present at once all that was personal to Matthew. But from Matth. 9, 18, it appears, that while our Lord was reclining and discoursing at that feast, Jairus comes to beseech him to visit his daughter lying at the point of death; and Jesus goes with him. Now this last transaction, according to Mark and Luke, did not happen until immediately after the return from the eastern shore of the lake. Hence the narrative of the feast is to be transferred to this place; and that too with the more certainty, because the Twelve appear to have been also present at it; Matth. 9, 10. Mark 2, 15.

§§ 63, 64. While the Twelve are absent preaching in the name of Christ, Herod causes John the Baptist to be beheaded in the castle of Machaerus at the southern extremity of Perea, near the Dead Sea; Jos. Ant. 18. 5. 2. In consequence of the preaching of the Apostles, Herod hears the fame of Jesus; is conscience-smitten; and declares him to be John, risen from the dead. The disciples of John come and tell Jesus; and the Twelve also return with the same intelligence; upon which Jesus retires to the northeastern coast of the lake, not far from the northern Bethsaida or Julias; see Bibl. Res. in Palest III. p. 308. All these events seem to have taken place near together.

Matthew and Mark narrate the death of the Baptist in explanation of Herod's declaration. The account of his imprisonment, which is retrospective in these two Evangelists, is transferred to § 24.

According to John 6, 4, the Passover was now at hand, viz. the third during our Lord's ministry. John therefore had lain in prison not far from a year and six months; and was beheaded about three years after entering upon his public ministry. See Note on § 25.

§§ 65, 66. From the region of the northern Bethsaida or Julias, the disciples embark for Bethsaida of Galilee, Mark 6, 45; or for Capernaum according to

John 6, 17. They land on the plain of Gennesareth, Matth. 14, 34. Mark 6, 53. The next day the multitudes follow in boats to Capernaum seeking for Jesus, and find him there; John 6, 24. 25. 59. It follows, as a necessary conclusion, that Capernaum was on or near the plain of Gennesareth; most probably at its northeastern extremity. For the topography of this region, see Bibl. Res. in Palest. III. p. 288 sq. comp. p. 282 sq.

In John.7, 1, a reason is assigned why Jesus did not go up at this time to the Passover mentioned in John 6, 4. This was the third Passover during his ministry.

PART V.

FROM OUR LORD'S THIRD PASSOVER UNTIL HIS FINAL DEPARTURE FROM GALILEE AT THE FESTIVAL OF TABERNACLES.

§§ 67—82.

§ 67 sq. The order of events, as far as to § 79 inclusive, is in accordance with both Matthew and Mark; with whom Luke also coincides, so far as he touches upon the same transactions.

§ 68. Jesus retires from Galilee, first to the region of Tyre and Sidon; then he returns to the Decapolis; and goes afterwards to the district of Cesarea Philippi, now Bâniâs. All these were districts not under the jurisdiction of Herod; whose domain included only Galilee and Perea. Not improbably Jesus may have withdrawn from Galilee at this particular time, because the attention of Herod had been thus turned to him after the death of John the Baptist; and perhaps too on account of Herod's temporary presence in that province, by which his own personal danger would naturally be increased. See Note on §§ 63, 64.

§ 69. The Decapolis was a region comprising *ten cities*, situated chiefly on the S. and S. E. of the Lake of Tiberias. It included Scythopolis (Bethshean), Gadara, Hippo, Pella, Gerasa. The names of the other cities are less certain. Our Lord in returning from Tyre and Sidon had probably passed through Galilee. The feeding of the four thousand obviously took place in the Decapolis; since Jesus immediately afterwards passes over the lake to Magdala on its western shore.

§ 72. The healing of the blind man at the northern Bethsaida, is related only by Mark. It took place on the way from the eastern shore of the lake toward Cesarea Philippi, now Bâniâs.

§ 74. The phrase "after three days" of Mark 8, 31, is equivalent to "the third day" of Matth. 16, 21. Luke 9, 22. See Note on § 49.

§ 75. On Matth. 17, 12, see Note on § 18.

§ 80. The sending out of the Seventy obviously took place at or near Capernaum; see vv. 13. 15. It comes therefore here in its order, before our Lord leaves Galilee to go up to the festival of Tabernacles. The words "after these things" in v. 1, refer to the general series of events narrated in the preceding chapter; not to v. 51 sq. in particular. The incident of the Scribe, which there follows (v. 57 sq.) was in fact much earlier; see in § 56 and Note.

According to Luke 10, 1, the Seventy were to go to every city and place, whither our Lord himself would come. To what part of the country, then, were they sent? Not throughout Galilee; for Jesus apparently never returned to that province; and besides, both himself and the Twelve had already preached in all the towns and villages. Not in Samaria; for he merely passes through that district without making any delay. Possibly into some parts of Judea, whither our Lord himself afterwards came; but more probably along the great valley of the Jordan and throughout the populous region of Perea, which our Lord traversed and where he taught after the festival of Dedication, and as he for the last time went up to Jerusalem; see John 10, 40. Matth. 19, 1. Mark 10, 1. Luke 13, 22.—In accordance with this view, the return of the Seventy took place in Jerusalem or Judea, not long before the festival of Dedication (§ 89); immediately after which festival Jesus withdrew into Perea to follow up their labours, John 10, 40 sq. See Introd. Note to Part VI. p. 185, 186.

Our Lord's instructions to the Seventy have a striking resemblance to those given to the Twelve; see in § 62.

§ 81. Our Lord evades the hypocritical urgency of his relatives, and afterwards goes up to the festival more privately; that is, with less of public notoriety and without being followed as usual by crowds. The journey mentioned in Luke 9, 51 was obviously his last journey from Galilee to Jerusalem; and v. 53 shows that he was passing on rapidly and without delay. In both these circumstances, Luke accords with John; and the two accounts are therefore properly arranged together. See more in Introd. Note to Part VI. p. 184.

§ 82. The healing of the ten lepers evidently connects itself with the same journey through Samaria; and is narrated by Luke out of its proper order. Compare the incident of the Scribe and another, Luke 9, 57 sq. and see Note on § 56.

———

PART VI.

THE FESTIVAL OF TABERNACLES, AND THE SUBSEQUENT TRANSACTIONS UNTIL OUR LORD'S ARRIVAL AT BETHANY SIX DAYS BEFORE THE FOURTH PASSOVER.

§§ 83—111.

INTRODUCTORY NOTE —ORDER OF LUKE AND JOHN.

IN this interval of time, from the festival of Tabernacles to our Lord's last arrival at Bethany, we encounter one of the most difficult portions of the whole Gospel Harmony.

According to John's narrative, Jesus, after leaving Galilee to go up to the festival of Tabernacles in October (John 7, 10), did not return again to Galilee; but spent the time intervening before the festival of Dedication in December, probably in Jerusalem, or, when in danger from the Jews, in the neighbouring villages of Judea; John 8, 59. Luke 10, 38 sq. Had Jesus actually returned to Galilee during this interval, it can hardly be supposed that John, who had hitherto so carefully noted our Lord's return thither after each visit to Jerusalem, would have failed to give some hint of it in this case also, either after c. 8, 59, or after c. 10, 21. But neither John, nor the other Evangelists, afford any such hint.—Immediately after the festival of Dedication, Jesus withdrew from the machinations of the Jews beyond Jordan; whence he was recalled to Bethany by the decease of Lazarus; John 10, 40. 11, 7. He then once more retired to Ephraim; and is found again at Bethany six days before the Passover, John 11, 54. 12, 1.

Matthew and Mark contain no allusion at all to the festival of Tabernacles; nor do we find any express mention of it in Luke. Yet Luke 9, 51 is most naturally referred to our Lord's journey at that time; and it implies also that this was his final departure from Galilee; see Note on § 81. Luke and John are therefore here parallel. The circumstances of danger, which had induced Jesus during the summer to retire from Galilee in various directions (see Note on § 68), as well as the approach of the time when "he should be received up," are reasons of sufficient weight to account for his having transferred, at this time, the scene of his ministry and labours from the north to Jerusalem and Judea, including excursions to the country on and beyond the Jordan.

In regard to the transactions during the whole interval of time comprised in this Part, Matthew and Mark are silent; except where they relate that our Lord, after his departure from Galilee, approached Jerusalem for the last time through Perea and by way of Jericho, where he was followed by multitudes; Matth. 19, 1. 2. 20, 29. Mark 10, 1. 46. With the transactions recorded by these two Evangelists during this last approach, Luke also has some things parallel; Luke 18, 15-43. The arrival at Bethany is common to the three; and in this they all accord with John; Matth. 21, 1. Mark 11, 1. Luke 19, 29. John 12, 1. 12 sq.

There exists consequently no difficulty in harmonizing Matthew and Mark, and so much of Luke as is parallel to them (18, 15 sq.) with John. But in Luke, from c 9, 51, where Jesus leaves Galilee, to c. 18, 14, where the record again becomes parallel with Matthew and Mark, there is a large body of matter peculiar for the most part to Luke, and relating *prima facie* to the time subsequent to our Lord's departure from Galilee. How is this portion of Luke's Gospel to be arranged and distributed, in order to harmonize with the narrative of John? The difficulty of course does not exist in the case of those Harmonists, who, like Calvin, Griesbach, and others, attempt to bring together only the first three Evangelists.

Those Harmonists who have likewise included John's Gospel, have hitherto generally, and perhaps universally, *assumed* a return of our Lord to Galilee after the festival of Tabernacles; and this avowedly in order to provide a place for this portion of Luke's Gospel. But the manner in which it has been arranged, after all, is exceedingly various. Some, as Le Clerc, insert nearly the whole during this supposed journey. Others, as Lightfoot, assign to this journey only what precedes Luke 13, 23; and refer the remainder to our Lord's

sojourn beyond Jordan.   In like manner Schleiermacher, Neander, Olshausen,
and others, assume a return to Galilee before the festival of Dedication; but
differ greatly in their distribution of this part of Luke.

If now we examine more closely the portion of Luke in question (9, 51—
18, 14), we perceive, that although an order of time is discoverable in certain
parts, yet as a whole it is wanting in exact chronological arrangement.   This
indeed is admitted, at the present day, by all Harmonists and Commentators.
It would seem almost, as if, in this portion peculiar to Luke, that Evangelist,
after recording many of the earlier transactions of Jesus in Galilee in accordance with Matthew and Mark, had here, upon our Lord's final departure from
that province, brought together this new and various matter of his own, relating
partly to our Lord's previous ministry in Galilee, partly to this journey, and
still more to his subsequent proceedings, until the narrative (in c. 18, 15) again
becomes parallel to the accounts of Matthew and Mark.   Such, for example, is
the incident of the Scribe and of another in Luke 9, 52 sq.—an occurrence of
such a nature that we cannot well suppose it to have happened twice, and
which Matthew narrates at Capernaum, on the occasion of our Lord's first
excursion across the lake ; see § 56.   The sending forth also the Seventy evidently took place at or near Capernaum, c. 10, 1 sq. see § 80 and Note.   The
transactions narrated in c. 10, 17—11, 13, have marks of chronological connection ; and the scene of them is obviously Jerusalem or its vicinity ; see § 86-
89 and Notes.   The healing of a demoniac and the consequent blasphemy of
the Scribes and Pharisees in Luke 11, 14. 15. 17 sq. is parallel with the same
events in Matthew and Mark, which these two Evangelists describe as having
occurred in Galilee ; see § 48 and Note.   With this passage again Luke 11,
37-54 is immediately connected ; see § 51 and Note.   The transition to the next
chapter (c. 12) is made by a phrase marking proximity of time ; § 52 and Note.
And, further, the words introducing Luke 13, 1, show that the conversation
there given (vv. 1-9) immediately followed.—The remainder of this portion of
Luke, c. 13, 10—18, 14 (with the exception of c. 17, 11-19, which obviously connects itself with the journey in c. 9, 51), contains absolutely no definite notation of time or place ; nor any thing, indeed, to show that the events happened
in the order recorded, or that they did not take place at different times and in
different parts of the country.   The only passage to which this remark does
not perhaps fully apply, is c. 13, 22-35.

For these reasons, like Newcome, I have distributed Luke 9, 51—10, 16, and
11, 14—13, 9, (as also 17, 11-19,) in Parts IV, V, as already specified, among
the transactions of our Lord's ministry in Galilee, between his second Passover
and his journey to the festival of Tabernacles.   The remainder of this whole
portion of Luke, viz. c. 10, 17—11, 13, and 13, 10—17, 10, as also 17, 20 - 18, 14,
remains to be disposed of in the present Part.

With many leading modern Commentators, I prefer here to follow the narrative of John, and infer that our Lord did not again return to Galilee after the
festival of Tabernacles.   So Lücke, Tholuck, Hengstenberg, De Wette, Meyer,
and others.   On this principle, therefore, the present Harmony is constructed.
Hence, Luke 10, 17—11, 13 is inserted between the festival of Tabernacles and
that of Dedication ; see the particulars in the Notes on §§ 86-89.

More difficult is it to assign the proper place for Luke 13, 10—17, 10 ; the
transactions recorded in which all cluster around or follow c. 13, 22, where

16*

Jesus is represented as travelling leisurely through the cities and villages towards Jerusalem. Now this journey cannot have been the same with that in Luke 9, 51 and John 7, 10; because there Jesus went up privately, while here he is accompanied by multitudes, Luke 14, 25. Nor can it have been a later journey *from Galilee;* for that in Luke 9, 51 was the final one. Nor indeed were the Jews accustomed to go up from the country to Jerusalem at the festival of Dedication; see Note on § 91. Lightfoot Hor. Heb. on John 10, 22. Besides, Luke 13, 22 stands in connection with the warning received by our Lord against Herod, vv. 31-33; which under the attendant circumstances cannot well be regarded as having been given in Galilee, and much less in Jerusalem. But Herod was lord also of Perea; and in that province he had imprisoned and put to death John the Baptist; Joseph. Ant. 18. 5. 2. It would therefore be natural, that our Lord, who had been less known in that region, and who now appeared there followed by multitudes, should receive warning of the danger he was thus incurring. Hence, I have ventured to assign this part of Luke (13, 10—17, 10) to that period of our Lord's life and ministry, which was passed in Perea after the festival of Dedication.

Our Lord first withdrew soon after that festival from the plots of the Jews into Perea, the province beyond Jordan : " He went away again beyond Jordan, into the place where John at first baptized; and there he abode. And many resorted unto him and believed ;" John 10, 40-42. How long Jesus remained in that region before he was recalled by the death of Lazarus, can be only matter of conjecture. In that interval Lightfoot places all this part of Luke after c. 13, 22; see Opp. II. p. 39. In this I am unable to accord with that profound scholar; because the language of John does not necessarily imply that our Lord at this time made any journey or circuit in Perea itself. At least, it could not then and there be said of him in any sense, that " he went through their cities and villages, teaching, and journeying towards Jerusalem," Luke 13, 22 ; for he had just departed from Jerusalem, and was recalled to Bethany by a special message from the sisters of Lazarus, John 11, 3. 7. All this would seem to imply rather, that Jesus remained during this excursion, at least mainly, in the district " where John had baptized ;" so that Martha and Mary knew at once where to send for him. It follows also as a natural inference, that this first sojourn beyond Jordan could not well have been a long one, nor probably have occupied more than a few weeks out of the four months intervening between the festival of Dedication and the Passover.

After the raising of Lazarus, Jesus again retired from the machinations of the Jews to "a country near to the wilderness, into a city called Ephraim, and there continued with his disciples ;" John 11, 54. The Evangelist John records nothing more of his movements, until he again appears in Bethany six days before the Passover; John 12, 1. But the expression used by John as to his sojourn at Ephraim, (literally : *there he passed the time,*) does not preclude the idea of excursions from that place, nor of a circuitous route on his return to Bethany and Jerusalem at the Passover. Now Matthew, Mark, and Luke affirm expressly, that on his return Jesus went up to Bethany from Jericho ; and the two former narrate, as expressly, that in thus reaching Jericho he had come "into the coasts of Judea by the farther side of Jordan," where great multitudes followed him, and he healed them and taught them, as he was wont ; Matth. 19, 1. 2. Mark 10, 1. With all this the language of Luke 13, 22 accords perfectly: "And he went through the cities and villages, teaching, and journey-ing towards Jerusalem;" as does also the mention of the multitudes in Luke 14, 25. With this too accords Luke 13, 31–35, including the warning against Herod and our Lord's reply; as also the touching lamentation over Jerusalem, where Jesus was so soon to suffer. With this accords, further, the fact, that the narrative of Luke subsequent to the portion in question, viz. Luke 18, 15 sq. is parallel with that of Matthew and Mark during the same journey; see §§ 105–109.

After long consideration, therefore, I do not hesitate to refer Luke 13, 22, with the transactions and discourses of which it forms the nucleus, mainly to a journey of our Lord through the populous region of Perea, on his return to Bethany after sojourning in Ephraim. There *may* also have been excursions from that city to the neighbouring villages of Judea, or even to the Jordan val-ley. This city Ephraim I hold to be probably identical with Ephron and Ophrah of the Old Testament; and therefore apparently represented by the modern Taiyibeh, situated nearly twenty Roman miles N. N. E. of Jerusalem, and five or six Roman miles N. E. of Bethel, on the borders of the desert which stretches along on the west of the Dead Sea and the Valley of Jordan; see Note on § 93. It occupies a lofty site; and from it one overlooks the adjacent desert, the Jordan with its great valley, and the mountains of Perea beyond, with the Saracenic castle er-Rübüd, near Ajlûn, in the northern part of Perea, bearing about N. E. Even at the present day the hardy and industrious moun-taineers of this place have much intercourse with the valley, and till the rich fields and reap the harvests of Jericho; see Bibl. Res. in Palest. II. p. 121. p. 276. It was therefore quite natural and easy for our Lord, from this point to cross the valley and the Jordan, and then turn his course towards Jericho and Jerusalem; while at the same time he exercised his ministry among the cities and villages along the valley and in the eastern region. Thither, indeed, he not improbably had sent before him the Seventy disciples (see Note on § 80); and some parts of the same district he himself had already visited.

I have therefore inserted the whole of Luke 13, 11—17, 10, after the mention of our Lord's sojourn at Ephraim; as belonging naturally to that period and to this return-journey through Perea. And then it only remained to let Luke 17, 20—18, 14 follow directly afterwards; because there is no mark nor authority for placing it any where else; and because too it immediately precedes, and thus connects with, that portion of Luke which is subsequently parallel to Mat-thew and Mark. Not that I would by any means assert, that all the events and the discourses of our Lord here given, are recorded by Luke in their exact chronological order; for this portion of his Gospel presents very much the ap pearance of a collection of discourses and transactions in themselves discon-nected Yet, as there are no marks nor evidence, internal or external, by which to arrange them differently, it seems hardly advisable, on mere conjecture, to abandon the order in which they have been left to us by Luke himself.

If it be objected, that this arrangement crowds too many incidents and dis-courses into this journey through Perea, the reply is not difficult. Matthew and Mark confine their previous narratives chiefly to Galilee; and give compa-ratively little of what took place later in Perea. Luke, besides recounting the like events in Galilee, has a large amount of matter peculiar to himself, without any definite notation of time and place; and it is therefore not unnatural to suppose, that an important portion of it may relate to this last journey. Again, there is room for allowing to this journey in Perea an interval of time, amply sufficient for all these transactions, and indeed many more. If we assume, that our Lord's first sojourn beyond Jordan, his return to Bethany, and the subsequent departure to Ephraim, occupied even two months (which is a large allowance), there still remained nearly two months before the Passover, in which to make excursions from Ephraim, and also traverse leisurely the distance through Perea to Bethany, requiring in itself, at the utmost, not more than five days of travel. If now we compare the transactions thus spread out over these two months (or not improbably over a longer interval), with those recorded during the following six days next before the Passover (see Part VII), we shall hardly be very strongly impressed with the idea, that too much in proportion is thus allotted to this journey.

§ 83. Jesus had now been absent from Jerusalem a year and six months, since his second Passover.

§§ 86, 87. Our Lord had left the temple, and apparently the city; John 8, 59. The healing of the blind man occurred later; see Note on § 90. While thus absent from the city, and yet in its vicinity, Jesus visits Bethany and is received by Martha and Mary, with whom very probably he may have been earlier acquainted. This visit is placed by Luke in immediate connection with the incident of the lawyer and the parable of the Good Samaritan; which therefore are inserted here. The scene of that parable also implies, that it was spoken in the vicinity of Jerusalem and Bethany.

§ 88. Jesus repeats on this occasion the same model-form of prayer taught in the Sermon on the Mount, § 41. Luke's order is here retained; as there is no evidence by which to assign any other.

§ 89. Luke relates the return of the Seventy in immediate connection with their appointment (Luke 10, 1–16), evidently by anticipation. Their appointment appears to have been one of our Lord's last acts in Galilee; and they went forth, probably into Perea and elsewhere, while he proceeded to Jerusalem; see Note on § 80. Their return to him at or near Jerusalem, is therefore here placed as late as may be, before the festival of Dedication.

§ 90. With the healing of the blind man the discourse in John 10, 1 sq. stands in immediate connection; see c. 9, 40. And in the words of our Lord, John 10, 26, spoken at the festival of Dedication, there is a direct allusion to the figurative representation of the shepherd and his sheep in the same discourse. This implies that the same audience was then present, at least in part; and consequently, that the discourse in question had been delivered not long before. For these reasons the healing of the blind man would seem also to have taken place near the beginning of the festival of Dedication, or at least not long before.

§ 91. The festival of Dedication was instituted by Judas Maccabeus to commemorate the purification of the temple and the *renewal* of the temple-worship, after the three years' profanation by Antiochus Epiphanes. It was held during eight days, commencing on the 25th day of the month Kislev, which began with the new moon of December. See 1 Macc. 4, 52-59. 2 Macc. 10, 5-8. Josephus calls it the festival of lights or lanterns, and speaks of it as a season of rejoicing; Antiq. 12. 7. 6, 7. It was celebrated by the Jews, not at Jerusalem alone, like the great festivals of the law ; but at home, throughout the whole country, by the festive illumination of their dwellings; see Lightfoot Hor. Heb. on Joh. 10, 22.—According to John's narrative, Jesus was now at Jerusalem, not because the Jews were accustomed to go up thither at this festival, but because he had remained in the vicinity since the festival of Tabernacles ; see Introd. Note to Part VI. p. 183, 184.

The place " where John at first baptized" (10, 40) was Bethabara beyond Jordan; or *Bethany* beyond Jordan, according to some manuscripts and editions; see John 1, 28. Nothing more is known as to its situation. On our Lord's sojourn here, and also the probable length of it, see Introd. Note to Part VI. pp. 184, 186.

§ 93. As the Sanhedrim had now determined, in accordance with the counsel of Caiaphas, that Jesus should be put to death, he therefore withdraws from Jerusalem to a city called Ephraim "near to the wilderness;" John 11, 54. This place has only recently been identified with any modern site. There is, however, little reason to doubt, that it was the same with the Ephraim or Ephron of 2 Chr. 13, 19, and also with the Ephron of Eusebius and Jerome, nearly *twenty* Roman miles north of Jerusalem. It lay also near the desert; and corresponds, therefore, in all these particulars with the modern *Taiyibeh*, a most remarkable and commanding site. See Bibl. Res. in Palest. II. p. 121-124.

Indeed, the coincidence of circumstances leaves little room for question, that Ephron and also Ophrah of the Old Testament, and Ephraim of the New, were all identical, and are all represented by the modern Taiyibeh. This then was the place to which our Lord withdrew.

For our Lord's sojourn in Ephraim, and his return thence through Perea to Bethany, see Introd. Note to Part VI. p. 187. For a fuller discussion respecting the identity of Ephraim with Taiyibeh, see Greek Harmony, p. 203, 204.

§ 94. Matthew and Mark, having omitted all mention of our Lord's presence and teaching in Jerusalem at the festivals of Tabernacles and of Dedication, as likewise all notice of the raising of Lazarus and other intervening events, here resume their narrative by relating, that after Jesus had left Galilee he approached Jerusalem, as the Passover drew nigh, by passing through the country beyond Jordan. Both Evangelists speak of the great multitudes that followed Jesus.

Luke 13, 10–21 is inserted here, because it immediately precedes, and is thus connected with, the notice of our Lord's journeying towards Jerusalem in Luke 13, 22 ; see § 95 and Note.

§ 95. For the reasons why Luke 13, 22 is arranged in this connection, see Introd. Note to Part VI. pp. 185, 186. For the appropriateness of this arrangement, so far as it respects vv. 31-35, see the same Note, p. 186, 187.

The lamentation over Jerusalem in v. 34 arises naturally from the mention

of that city in v. 33. In Matth. 23, 37 sq. (§ 123) the same lamentation is repeated in connection with our Lord's denunciation of the Scribes and Pharisees in Jerusalem. Luke's phrase, " Ye shall not see me, etc." is explained by
the like phrase of Matthew, " Ye shall not see me henceforth, etc." implying
that he was now about to withdraw from the world, and that Jerusalem, which
then rejected him, would not again behold him and enjoy the privilege of his
presence, until compelled by his glorious manifestation to acknowledge him as
the true Messiah.

§ 96-103. These sections are placed here for the reasons assigned in the
Introd. Note to Part VI. p. 187.

§ 104. This section properly comes in here before § 105, where Luke is again
parallel with Matthew and Mark.

§ 107. This discourse probably took place in Perea; as Jesus had not yet
arrived at Jericho. The expression *to go up*, is used of any journey to Jerusalem or Judea; see Luke 2, 4. John 7, 8. 12, 20. Acts 18, 22.

§ 108 In Matthew it is the mother of James and John who makes the request;
in Luke it is the two disciples themselves; see Note on § 42.

§ 109. Mark and Luke here speak of *one* blind man; Matthew of *two*. The
case is similar to that of the demoniacs of Gadara; see Note on § 57.
    More difficult is it to harmonize the accounts as to the *place* where the mira-
cle was wrought. Matthew and Mark narrate it as having occurred when
Jesus was *departing* from Jericho; while Luke seems to describe it as happen-
ing during his *approach* to the city. Several ways of solving this difficulty
have been proposed.
    1. The language of Mark is, " They came to Jericho." This, it is said, may
be understood as implying, that Jesus remained some days at least in Jericho,
where he would naturally visit points of interest in the vicinity; as, for example, the fountain of Elisha, a mile or more distant. The miracle, therefore,
may have been wrought, not when he was *finally* leaving Jericho for Jerusalem;
but when he was *occasionally* going out *of*, and returning *to*, Jericho. So Newcome, Harm. Note on § 108.
    2. The Greek verb here rendered *to come nigh*, it is said, may signify not only
to draw nigh, but also *to be nigh* or *near*. Hence, the language of Luke may
include also the idea expressed by Matthew and Mark, i. e. while he was *still
near* the city. So Grotius, Comm. on Matth. 20, 30. Passow in his Lexicon
gives a like definition of the Greek verb, i. e. *to be near, to draw near;* but
neither he nor Grotius brings forward any references to classic authors in support of such a meaning. Indeed, it is very doubtful, whether this definition
can be fully sustained by classic authority. Yet in the New Testament and
Septuagint there are several passages, which go to imply such a usage of the
Greek word. Thus, Luke 19, 29 compared with Matth. 21, 1. So Phil. 2, 3 *he
was nigh unto death.* The usage of the LXX is still more definite; e. g. of
Naboth's vineyard, 1 K. 21, 2 *because it is near unto my house.* Also Deut. 21, 3,
the city next [*nigh*] *unto the slain man.* v. 6. 22, 2; and trop. Jer. 23, 23. Ruth 2, 20.

2 Sam. 19, 42. These instances seem sufficient to bear out the proposed interpretation in Luke; which is also adopted by Le Clerc, Doddridge, Pilkington, and others.—Nor is this method of explanation "made useless for the purpose of reconciling the Evangelists, by Luke 19, 1," as Newcome asserts. In connection with Jericho, Luke first of all relates this striking miracle; then goes back and mentions that Jesus "entered and passed through Jericho;" and lastly records the visit to the house of Zaccheus, apparently within the city. Luke 19, 1 therefore is not more at variance with this view respecting the miracle, than it is with the visit to Zaccheus. It is a passing announcement of a general fact, in connection with which other more important circumstances are related, not indeed in the order of time, but partly by anticipation.

3. Less probable than either of the above is the solution of Lightfoot and others, who assume that Jesus healed one blind man before entering the city, and another on departing from it. See Lightfoot Opp. II. p. 42.

§ 111. The phrase " out of the country," John 11, 55, does not refer to the region of Ephraim; for those coming from that vicinity would hardly have made such inquiries. The phrase therefore signifies *from the country* generally, as distinguished from Jerusalem; compare in Luke 21, 21.

"Six days before the Passover" is equivalent to "the sixth day" before that festival; see Note on § 49. As our Lord ate the paschal supper on the evening following Thursday, (which evening was reckoned in the Jewish manner to Friday,) the sixth day before the Passover was the first day of the week or Sunday, reckoning back from Friday itself as one day, as is done in all like cases. Jesus then came to Bethany on the first day of the week, from Jericho.

John 12, 2-8, where the supper at Bethany is described, is postponed in accordance with the order of Matthew and Mark; see Note on § 131.

PART VII.

OUR LORD'S PUBLIC ENTRY INTO JERUSALEM, AND THE SUBSEQUENT
TRANSACTIONS BEFORE THE FOURTH PASSOVER.

§§ 112—132.

INTRODUCTORY NOTE.—SCHEDULE OF DAYS.

THE Jewish day of twenty-four hours was reckoned from sunset to sunset, as is still the case in oriental countries. The paschal lamb was killed on the fourteenth day of Nisan towards sunset; and was eaten the same evening, after the fifteenth day of Nisan had begun; Ex. 12, 6. 8. Our Lord was crucified on the day before the Jewish Sabbath, that is, on Friday, Mark 15, 42; and as he had eaten the Passover on the preceding evening, it follows that the fourteenth of Nisan fell that year on Thursday, reckoned from the preceding sunset. Hence, the sixth day before the Passover, when Jesus came to Bethany, was the first day of the week or Sunday (see Note on § 111); and the transactions of the week, comprised in Parts VII and VIII, may be distributed according to the following Schedule; which differs somewhat from the *Schema* of Lightfoot; see his Hor. Heb. on Joh. 12, 2.

SCHEDULE OF DAYS.

Day of Nisan.	Day of Week.		
9.	7. SAT.	*reckoned from sunset.* The Jewish Sabbath. Jesus remains at Jericho.
10.	1. SUND.	*from sunset.* Jesus arrives at Bethany from Jericho, John 12, 1.
11.	2. MOND.	*from sunset.* Jesus makes his public entry into Jerusalem, § 112; and returns at night to Bethany, Mark, 11, 11.
12.	3. TUESD.	*from sunset.* Jesus goes to Jerusalem; on his way the incident of the barren fig-tree. He cleanses the temple, § 113; and again returns to Bethany, Mark 11, 19.
13.	4. WEDN.	*from sunset.* Jesus returns to the city; on the way the disciples see the fig-tree withered, Mark 11, 20. Our Lord discourses in the temple, § 115–126; takes leave of it; and, when on the Mount of Olives, on his way to Bethany, foretells his coming to destroy the city, and proceeds to speak also of his final coming to judgment, §§ 127–130.
14.	5. THURS.	*from sunset.* The rulers conspire against Christ. On the eve of this day, (i. e. the evening following Wednesday,) our Lord had partaken of the supper at Bethany; where Mary anointed him, and where Judas laid his plan of treachery, which he made known to the chief priests in the course of this day.
		Jesus sends two disciples to the city to make ready the Passover. He himself repairs thither in the afternoon, in order to eat the paschal supper at evening.
15.	6. FRID.	*from sunset.* At evening, in the very beginning of the fifteenth of Nisan, Jesus partakes of the paschal supper; institutes the Lord's Supper; is betrayed and apprehended; §§ 133–143. He is brought first before Caiaphas, and then in the morning before Pilate; is condemned, crucified, and before sunset laid in the sepulchre; §§ 144–158.
16.	7. SAT.	The Jewish Sabbath. Our Lord rests in the sepulchre.
17.	1. SUND.	Jesus rises from the dead at early dawn; see § 159 and Note.

§ 112. The time is specified in John 12, 12. The other Evangelists do not notice the fact, that Jesus had remained at Bethany the preceding night.

§ 113. Mark 11, 11. 12 specifies the time very exactly. On the cleansing of the temple, see Note on § 21.

Luke 21, 37. 38 is inserted here, because in Luke's order it is only retrospective; being placed after our Lord's discourses on the Mount of Olives, when he had already taken leave of the temple, to which he returned no more.

§§ 114–130. These sections include the numerous discourses and transactions of the fourth day of this week.

§ 114. The account of the withering away of the fig-tree might in itself well be connected with the preceding Section. But according to Mark 11, 20 this occurrence took place on the subsequent day.

§ 123. In Matthew, verses 13 and 14 are transposed, as in the best critical editions.

125. This incident of the Greeks is inserted here on the fourth day of the week, rather than on the second, because of John 12, 36; which implies that Jesus afterwards appeared no more in public as a teacher. He immediately takes leaves of the temple.

§ 126. The Evangelist John here gives his own reflections upon the unbelief of the Jews. From v. 44 we are not to understand, that Jesus, after having .eft the temple, returned and uttered this additional discourse. It is rather the vivid manner of the Evangelist himself; who thus introduces Jesus as speaking, in order to recapitulate the sum and substance of his teaching, which the Jews had rejected.

§§ 127-130. The topics of these Sections are more fully discussed in an article by the author of this work, in the *Bibliotheca Sacra*, 1843, No. III. pp. 531 sq.

§ 127. Our Lord takes leave of the temple, to which he returns no more; at the same time foretelling its impending destruction. On his way to Bethany, he seats himself for a time upon the Mount of Olives, over against the temple, where the city was spread out before him as on a map; and here four of his disciples put to him the question, "When shall these things be?" According to Matthew they add: "And what the sign of thy coming, and of the end of the world?" They were still in darkness; and believed, like the other Jews, that the Messiah was yet to go forth as an exalted temporal prince, to subvert the then present order of things, to overthrow their enemies and subdue all nations, and thus restore pre-eminency and glory to the Jewish people, and reign in peace and splendour over the world; see Luke 24, 21. Acts 1, 6. This was the expected coming and the end of the world, or present state of things, referred to in Matth. 24, 3; as also in Luke 17, 20 sq. 19, 11. See *Biblioth. Sacra*, ib. pp. 531-535.

Jesus does not directly answer the question of the four Apostles; but speaks of deceivers and calamities and persecutions, that should arise. His language here is strictly introductory to the next Section.

§ 128. That the "abomination of desolation" Matth. 24, 15 etc. refers to the Roman armies by which Jerusalem was besieged and destroyed, is shown conclusively by Luke 21, 20.

The subsequent desolation and calamity spoken of in Matth. 24, 29-31 and the parallel passages, may be most appropriately referred to the overthrow and complete extirpation of the Jewish people fifty years later under Adrian; when they were sold as slaves and utterly driven out from the land of their fathers. See Münter's *Jewish War*, translated by W. W. Turner in the *Biblioth. Sacra*,

1843. No. III. p. 393 sq. Compare ibid. p. 550 sq. This was the final war and catastrophe of the Jewish nation under the celebrated and mysterious Bar-Cochba, "Son of a Star." It was a catastrophe far more terrible than that of the destruction of Jerusalem; though the latter, in consequence of the vivid description of it by Josephus, has come to be usually considered as the last act in this great tragedy. Such, however, it was not.

The figurative language of these verses (Matth. 24, 29-31, etc.) is similar to that of many passages in the Old Testament, which refer to civil commotions and historical events, of far less importance than the destruction of Jerusalem and the overthrow of the Jewish state; see Is. 13, 9 sq. 19, 1. 5 sq. 34, 2. 4 sq. Ezek. 32, 2. 7. Ps. 18, 7-14. 68, 1 sq. etc. See also *Biblioth. Sac.* 1843, No. III. p. 545 sq. Further, Luke 21, 28 shows decisively, that these verses cannot have reference to the general judgment of the great and final day; the language of Luke directly expresses temporal deliverance, and that only. That some near catastrophe is meant, appears also from the limitation to " this generation," in Matth. 24, 34 and the parallel passages.

Matth. 24, 36–42 connects itself directly with what precedes, see v. 36; and refers likewise to the overthrow of the Jewish people and dispensation; comp. Luke 17, 20 37. But with v. 42 of Matthew, all direct reference to the Jewish catastrophe terminates. This appears from the nature of the language; and also further from the fact, that thus far both Mark and Luke give parallel reports; while at this very point their reports cease, and all that follows belongs to Matthew alone. This goes to show, that the discourse of our Lord up to this point is to be regarded as a whole, which is here completed; having reference to his coming for the overthrow of Judaism. At this point a new topic is introduced.

§§ 129, 130. Our Lord here makes a transition, and proceeds to speak of his final coming at the day of judgment. This appears from the fact, that the matter of these Sections is added by Matthew, after Mark and Luke have ended their parallel reports relative to the Jewish catastrophe; and Matthew here commences with v. 43, the same discourse which Luke has given on another occasion, in Galilee; Luke 12, 39 sq § 52. (See Note on § 21.) This discourse in Luke has reference obviously to our Lord's final coming; and that it has here the same reference, is apparent from the appropriateness of the subsequent warnings, and their intimate connection with Matth. 25, 31-46; which latter all interpreters of note agree in referring to the general judgment. See *Biblioth. Sac.* 1. ib. 553 sq.

§ 131. On the fifth day of the week the chief priests and others, after deliberation, came to the formal conclusion to seize Jesus and put him to death; Matth. 26, 3. 4. etc. As the means by which this purpose was aided and accomplished, the first three Evangelists narrate the treacherous intent of Judas; which again Matthew and Mark introduce by describing the circumstances under which it arose during the supper at Bethany. According to Matthew and Mark this supper would most naturally seem to have taken place on the preceding evening; that is, the evening which ushered in, and was reckoned to, the fifth day of the week. John's order would apparently assign it to the evening after the day on which Jesus came to Bethany.

As in the accounts of this supper itself, neither of the Evangelists has specified any note of time, we are left to infer from other circumstances, whether
it more probably took place on the evening after the arrival of Jesus at
Bethany, as John seems to imply; or, on the evening following the fourth day of
the week, in accordance with Matthew and Mark, after our Lord had taken his
final leave of the temple. The following are some of these circumstances.

1. The formal determination of the chief priests to put Jesus to death, was
made early on the fifth day of the week, Matth. 26, 1-5. Mark 14, 1. etc. It
was not until *afterwards* that Judas came to them with his proposal of treachery,
which they received with joy, Matth. 26, 14. Mark 14, 10. 11. etc.

2 Matthew and Mark relate the supper as the occasion which led to the
treachery of Judas. Stung by his Master's rebuke, he is represented as going
away to the chief priests and offering to betray him. This act would then
seem to have been done under the impulse of sudden resentment; and this view
of the matter receives also some support from his subsequent remorse and
suicide. All this accords well with the order of Matthew and ·Mark. But if
the supper took place on the evening after Jesus came to Bethany, then Judas
had already cherished this purpose of treachery in his heart for several days
without executing it; and that too while our Lord was daily teaching in the
temple, and there was abundant opportunity to betray him. Such a supposition, under the circumstances, is against probability.

3. The language of Matthew, "then Judas went," v. 14, seems necessarily
to connect the visit of Judas to the chief priests *immediately* with the supper,
which therefore must have taken place on the. preceding evening. On the
other hand, it would be very natural for John to anticipate the time of the supper and narrate it where he does, in order there to bring together and complete
all that he had to say further of Bethany; which indeed he mentions no more.

There is no sufficient reason for supposing, with Lightfoot and others, that
the supper in John is a different one from that in Matthew and Mark. The
identity of circumstances is too great, and the alleged differences too few, to
leave a doubt on this point. Matthew and Mark narrate it as in the house of
Simon the leper; John does not say where it took place, but he speaks of Lazarus as one of those who reclined at the table, implying that the supper was not
in his own house. It was not, and is not now, customary in the East, for females
to eat with the males; and therefore Lazarus, in his own house, would have
been the master and giver of the entertainment. In the two former Evangelists,
the woman anoints the head of Jesus; in the latter his feet; yet neither ex-
cludes the other., Matthew and Mark do not here name Mary; nor have they
any where else mentioned her or Martha or Lazarus. Nor do they in this connection name Judas; whom we know as the fault-finder only from John.

§ 132. "The first day of unleavened bread" is here the fourteenth of Nisan;
on which day, at or before noon, the Jews were accustomed to cease from
labour and put away all leaven out of their houses; Ex. 12, 15-17. Lightfoot
Hor. Heb. on Mark 14, 12 On that day towards sunset the paschal lamb was
killed; and was eaten the same evening, after the fifteenth of Nisan had begun;
at which time, strictly, the festival of unleavened bread commenced and continued seven days. In popular usage, however, the fourteenth day, being thus
a day of preparation, was spoken of as belonging to the festival; and there-

fore is here called the "first" day. That such a usage was common, appears also from Josephus; who, having in one place expressly fixed the commencement of the festival of unleavened bread on the fifteenth of Nisan (Antiq. 3. 10. 5), speaks nevertheless in another passage of the fourteenth as the day of that festival, B. J. 5. 3. 1. comp. Ant. 11. 4. 8. In this way, further, the same historian could say, that the festival was celebrated for *eight* days; Jos. Ant. 2. 15. 1.

On this fifth day of the week, as the circumstances show, our Lord, after sending Peter and John to the city to prepare the Passover, himself followed them thither with the other disciples, probably towards evening.

. On the Passover in general, see Introd. Note to Part VIII.

PART VIII.

THE FOURTH PASSOVER; OUR LORD'S PASSION; AND THE ACCOMPANYING EVENTS UNTIL THE END OF THE JEWISH SABBATH.

§§ 133—158.

INTRODUCTORY NOTE.—THE PASSOVER.

As the events of our Lord's Passion were intimately connected with the celebration of the Passover, it seems proper here to bring together, in one view, those circumstances relating to that festival, which may serve to illustrate the sacred history. A more complete article upon this whole subject, was published by the author of these Notes in the *Bibliotheca Sacra* for August 1845, pp. 405-436; to which the reader is referred. See also Greek Harmony, p. 211 sq.

I. *Time of killing the Paschal Lamb.* The paschal lamb (or kid Ex. 12, 5) was to be selected on the tenth day of the first month, Ex. 12, 3. On the fourteenth day of the same month, (called Abib in the Pentateuch, and later Nisan, Deut. 16, 1. Esth. 3, 7,) the lamb thus selected was to be killed, at a point of time designated by the expression *between the two evenings*, as in the marginal reading of our version, Ex. 12, 6. Lev. 23, 5. Num. 9, 3. 5; or, as is elsewhere said, *at evening about the going down of the sun*, Deut. 16, 6. The same phrase, *between the two evenings*, is put for the time of the daily evening sacrifice, Ex. 29, 39. 41. Num. 28, 4. The time thus marked was regarded by the Samaritans and Karaites, as being the interval between sunset and deep twilight; while the Pharisees and Rabbinists held the first evening to commence with the declining sun, and the second evening with the setting sun. Hence, according to the latter, the paschal lamb was to be killed in the interval between the ninth and eleventh hour, equivalent to our three and five o'clock, p. m. That this was in fact the practice among the Jews in the time of our Lord, appears from the testimony of Josephus; B. J. 6. 9. 3. The daily evening sacrifice also was offered at the ninth hour or three o'clock, p. m. Jos. Antiq. 14. 4. 3. See Acts 3. 1.

The true time, then, of killing the Passover in our Lord's day, was between the ninth and eleventh hour, or towards sunset, near the close of the fourteenth day of Nisan.

II. *Time of eating the Passover.* This was to be done the same evening. "And they shall eat the flesh in that night, roast with fire, and unleavened bread, and with bitter herbs shall they eat it," Ex. 12, 8. The Hebrews in Egypt ate the first Passover, and struck the blood of the victims on their door-posts, on the evening before the last great plague; at midnight the Lord smote all the first-born; and in the morning the people broke up from Rameses on their march towards the Red Sea, viz. "on the fifteenth day of the first month, on the morrow after the Passover," Num. 33, 3.

It hence appears, very definitely, that the paschal lamb was to be slain in the afternoon of the fourteenth day of the month; and was eaten the same evening; that is, on the evening which was reckoned to and began the fifteenth day.

III. *Festival of unleavened Bread.* From Ex. 12, 17. 18, comp. Deut. 16, 3. 4; and from Lev. 23, 6, comp. Num. 28, 17; it appears, that the festival of un-leavened bread began strictly with the passover-meal, at or after sunset follow-ing the fourteenth day, and continued until sunset at the end of the twenty-first day. Comp. Jos. Ant. 3. 10. 5.

We have already seen that it was customary for the Jews, on the fourteenth day of Nisan, to cease from labour at or before mid-day; to put away all leaven out of their houses before noon; and to slay the paschal lamb towards the close of the day; see above and Note on § 132. Hence, in popular usage, the four-teenth day very naturally came to be reckoned as the beginning or first day of the festival, Matth. 26, 17. Mark 14. 12; and Josephus also could say, that the festival was celebrated for eight days; see Note on § 132.

It is hardly necessary to remark, that in consequence of the close mutual relation between the Passover and the festival of unleavened bread, these terms are often used interchangeably, especially in Greek, for the whole festival, in-cluding both the paschal supper and the seven days of unleavened bread; see Luke 22, 1. John 6, 4. Acts 12, 3. 4. Jos. Ant. 2. 1. 3. comp. B. J. 5. 3. 1.

IV. *Other Paschal Sacrifices.* 1. In Num. 28, 18–25, it is prescribed, that on the first and last days of the festival, the fifteenth and twenty-first of Nisan, there should be a holy convocation, in which, "no manner of servile work" should be done. And on each of the seven days, besides the ordinary daily sacrifices of the Sanctuary, there was to be "a burnt offering unto the Lord; two young bullocks, and one ram, and seven lambs of the first year;" also a meat-offering, and "one goat for a sin-offering." The first and last days of the festival, therefore, were each a day of convocation and of *rest*, and hence were strictly *sabbaths;* distinct from the weekly Sabbath, except when one of them happened to fall upon this latter.

2. On the morrow after this first day of rest or sabbath, that is, on the six-teenth day of Nisan, the first fruits of the harvest were offered, together with a lamb as a burnt-offering; Lev. 23, 10–12. This rite is expressly assigned by Josephus, in like manner, to the second day of the festival, the sixteenth of Nisan; Antiq. 3. 10. 5. The grain offered was barley; this being the earliest ripe, and its harvest occurring a week or two earlier than that of wheat; Jos. ib. Bibl. Res. in Palest. II. p. 99. Until this offering was made, no husbandman could begin his harvest; nor might any one eat of the new grain; Lev. 23, 14. It was therefore a rite of great importance; and in the time of our Lord and later was performed with many ceremonies. See *Biblioth. Sacra,* ib. p. 408.

17*

Comp. Lev. 2, 14–16. Jos. Ant. 3. 10. 5. Lightfoot Hor. Heb. on John 19, 31. Reland Antiqq. Sac. 4. 3 8.

3. There was also another sacrifice connected with the Passover, known among the later Hebrews as the *Khagigah*, or *festival;* of which there are traces likewise in the Old Testament. It was a festive thank-offering, (Engl. Vers. peace-offering,) made by private individuals or families, in connection with the Passover, but distinct from the appointed public offerings of the temple. Such voluntary sacrifices or free-will offerings were provided for and regulated by the Mosaic law. The fat only was burned on the altar (Lev. 3, 3. 9. 14); the priest had for his portion the breast and right shoulder (Lev. 7, 29–34. 10, 14); and the remainder was eaten by the bringer with his family and friends in a festive manner, on the same or the next day; Lev. 7, 16–18. 22, 29. 30. Deut. 12, 17. 18. 27. 27, 7. These private sacrifices were often connected with the public festivals, both in honour of the same, and as a matter of convenience; Num. 10, 10. Deut. 14, 26. 16, 11. 14. comp. 1 Sam. 1, 3–5. 24. 25, 2, 12–16. 19. They might be eaten in any clean place within the city (Lev. 10, 14. Deut. 16, 11. 14); but those only might partake of them, as likewise of the Passover, who were themselves ceremonially clean; Num. 18, 11. 13. John 11, 55. comp. Num. 9, 10–13. 2 Chr. 30, 18. Jos. B. J. 6. 9. 3.

Such voluntary private sacrifices in connection with the Passover seem to be implied in the Old Testament, in Deut. 16, 2. 2 Chr. 30, 22. 24. 35, 7–9; see more in *Biblioth. Sacra*, ib. p. 409 sq. Hence, as being a sacrifice, thus connected with a festival, these private free-will offerings were themselves called, at least among the later Hebrews, by the name *Khagigah*, i. e. *festival*. The earlier Rabbins connect the Khagigah directly with Deut. 16, 2, as above ; Lightfoot Hor. Heb. on John 18, 28. There was, however, some difference of opinion among them, as to the particular day of the paschal festival, on which the Khagigah ought to be offered, whether on the fourteenth or fifteenth of Nisan; but the weight of authority was greatly in favour of the fifteenth day. Yet the later accounts of the mode of celebrating the paschal supper seem to imply, that a Khagigah was ordinarily connected with that meal. Indeed, mention is made of a "Khagigah of the fourteenth day," so called in distinction from the more important and formal ceremonial Khagigah of the passover-festival ; which latter was not regularly offered until the fifteenth day, when the paschal supper had already been eaten. The former was then a mere voluntary oblation of thanksgiving, made for the purpose of enlarging and diversifying the passover-meal. See Lightfoot Ministerium Templi 13. 4. ib. c. 14. Reland Antiqq. Sac. 4. 2. 2.

V. *The Paschal Supper.* For a full account of this meal, both in its original institution and as it was probably celebrated in the time of our Lord, see *Biblioth. Sacra*, ib. p. 411 sq. That the Jews in the course of ages had neglected some of the original precepts, and also introduced various additional ceremonies, is evident from the manner in which our Lord celebrated the supper, as narrated by the Evangelists. What all these additions were, we have no specific historical account from cotemporary writers; yet the precepts preserved in the Mishnah and Talmud of Jerusalem, (compiled in the third century from earlier traditions,) probably refer to the most important of them, and serve to throw light upon some of the circumstances connected with the institution of the Lord's Supper. See Lightfoot Minist. Templi c. 13. Hor. Heb. on Matth. 26,

26, 27. Werner *de poculo Benedict.* in Ugolini Thesaur. T. XXX. See too *Biblioth. Suc.* ib. p. 411 sq.

According to these authorities, four cups of red wine, usually mingled with one fourth part of water, were drunk during the meal, and served to mark its progress. The *first* was merely preliminary, in connection with a blessing invoked upon the day and upon the wine; and this corresponds to the cup mentioned in Luke 22, 17. Then followed ablutions, and the bringing in of bitter herbs, the unleavened bread, the roasted lamb, and also the Khagigah of the fourteenth day, and a broth or sauce made with spices. After this followed the instructions to the son, etc. respecting the Passover; and the first part of the *Hallel* or song of praise (Pss. 113. 114) was repeated. The *second* cup was now drunk. Next came the blessing upon each kind of food, and the guests partook of the meal reclining; the paschal lamb being eaten last. Thanks were then returned, and the *third* cup drunk, called *the cup of blessing*; comp. 1 Cor. 10, 16. The remainder of the *Hallel* (Pss. 115-118) was now repeated and the *fourth* cup drunk; which was ordinarily the end of the celebration. Sometimes a *fifth* cup might be added, after repeating the *great Hallel*, Pss. 120-137.

The institution of the Lord's Supper probably took place at the close of the proper meal, immediately before the third cup, or cup of blessing, which would seem to have made part of it; comp. 1 Cor. 10, 16.

VI. *Did our Lord, the night in which he was betrayed, eat the Passover with his Disciples?* Had we only the testimony of the first three Evangelists, not a doubt upon this question could ever arise. Their language (see § 132) is full, explicit, and decisive, to the effect, that our Lord's last meal with his disciples was the regular and ordinary paschal supper of the Jews, introducing the festival of unleavened bread, on the evening after the fourteenth day of Nisan. Mark says expressly, 14, 12 : *when* THEY *killed the passover;* which, whether the subject *they* refer to the Jews or be indefinite, implies at least the regular and ordinary time of killing the paschal lamb. Luke's language is, if possible, still stronger, 22, 7 : "Then came the day of unleavened bread, *when the passover* MUST *be killed*," i. e. according to law and custom. This marks of course the fourteenth day of Nisan; and on that same evening our Lord and his disciples sat down to that same passover-meal, which had thus by his own appointment been prepared for them, and of which Jesus speaks expressly as the Passover, v. 15. Philologically considered, there cannot be a shadow of doubt, but that Matthew, Mark, and Luke, intended to express, and do express, in the plainest terms, their testimony to the fact, that Jesus regularly partook of the ordinary and legal passover-meal on the evening after the fourteenth of Nisan, at the same time with all the Jews.

When, however, we turn to the Gospel of John, we seek in vain in this Evangelist for any trace of the paschal supper, as such, in connection with our Lord at that time. John narrates indeed (c. 13) our Lord's last meal with his disciples; which the attendant and subsequent circumstances show to have been the same with that, which the other Evangelists describe as the Passover. Upon just that point, however, John is silent; but from this silence the inference can never be rightfully drawn, that this last meal was *not* the Passover; any more than John's similar silence in respect to the Lord's Supper warrants the conclusion that no such rite was ever instituted. John, as all admit, wrote his Gospel as a supplement to the others; and hence, in speaking of this last meal, he narrates only such circumstances as had not been fully set forth by the other Evangelists. He does not describe this meal as being the Passover, nor make any mention of the Eucharist, because this had been done, in both cases, in the most explicit manner, by Matthew, Mark, and Luke. In this way the' difference in the two reports of the same occasion, is satisfactorily accounted for.

But there are a few expressions in John's Gospel, in connection with this meal, and especially with our Lord's Passion, which taken together might, at first view, and if we had only John, seem to imply, that on Friday, the day of our Lord's crucifixion, the regular and legal Passover had not yet been eaten, but was still to be eaten on the evening after that day.

The point of the whole inquiry relates simply to the time of the Passover. According to all the four Evangelists, our Lord was crucified on Friday, the day before the Jewish Sabbath; and his last meal with his disciples took place on the preceding evening, the same night in which he was betrayed. The simple question, therefore, at issue is, Did this Friday fall upon the fifteenth day of Nisan, or upon the fourteenth?' Or, in other words, did our Lord on the evening before his crucifixion eat the Passover, as is testified by the first three Evangelists; or was the Passover still to be eaten on the evening after that day, as John might seem to imply?

This question has been more or less a subject of discussion in the church ever since the earliest centuries; chiefly with a view to harmonize the difficulties. It is only in recent years, that the alleged difference between John and the other Evangelists, has been urged to the extreme of attempting to make it irreconcilable.

John obviously wrote his Gospel as supplementary to the other three. He had them then before him, and was acquainted with their contents. He was aware that the other three Evangelists had testified to the fact, that Jesus partook of the Passover with his disciples. Did John believe that their testimony on this point was wrong; and did he mean to correct it? If so, we should naturally expect to find some notice of the correction along with the mention of the meal itself, which John describes, as well as they. Indeed, that would have been the appropriate and only fitting place for such a correction. But John has nothing of the kind; and we are therefore authorized to maintain, that it was not John's purpose thus and there to correct or contradict the testimony of the other Evangelists; and if not there, then much less by mere implication in other places and connections.

Let us examine the passages referred to in John's Gospel; and see whether they require to be so understood or interpreted, as to present any appearance of discrepancy. They are the following:

a) John 13, 1: "before the feast of the passover." This form of expression, it is said, shows that our Lord's last meal with his disciples took place *before* the Passover; and could not, therefore, itself have been the paschal supper.

But we must here take into account the meaning of the Greek word thus rendered *feast*, the true and only proper signification of which is *festival*; that is, it implies every where a yearly day or days of festive commemoration; never a single meal or entertainment. So in Num 28, 16. 17, where the paschal *supper*, prepared on the fourteenth of Nisan and eaten at evening, is distinguished from the *festival*, (Engl. Ver. *feast*,) which began on the fifteenth and continued for seven days. See farther Luke 2, 41. 22, 1. In this view, the phrase in question does not mean "before the paschal supper," but "before the festival of the Passover," i. e. of unleavened bread (Luke 22, 1). It is equivalent therefore to the Engl. *festival-eve;* and here marks the evening before the *festival* proper of seven days' continuance; on which evening, during the (paschal) supper, our Lord 'manifested his love for his disciples unto the end,' by the touching symbolical act of washing their feet. It is therefore evident, that this passage does not sustain the inference attempted to be drawn from it.

b) John 18, 28 : "and they themselves [the Jews] went not into the judgment-hall, lest they should be defiled ; *but that they might eat the passover.*" From this last phrase, it has been inferred, that the Jews were expecting to partake of the paschal supper the ensuing evening; and of course had not eaten it already.

But to bring out this inference, the phrase "to eat the passover" must be taken in the most limited sense, "to eat the paschal supper." This certainly cannot be necessary, unless the context requires such a limitation ; which is not the case here.

The word *passover* in the New Testament is found in no less than three main significations : *a) The paschal lamb ;* Mark 14, 12. Luke 22, 7. 1 Cor. 5, 7. *b) The paschal meal ;* Matth. 26, 18. 19. Luke 22, 8. 13. Heb. 11, 28. *c) The paschal festival,* comprising the seven days of unleavened bread ; Luke 22, 1. 2, 41 comp. 43. Matth. 26, 2. John 2, 13. 6, 4. etc.—As now there is nothing in the circumstances or context of John 18, 28, to limit the meaning of the word *passover* in itself either to the paschal lamb or paschal meal, we certainly are not bound by any intrinsic necessity so to understand it here in the phrase "to eat the passover." If, on the other hand, we adopt for it in this place the wider sense of *paschal festival,* two modes of interpretation are admissible, either of which leaves no room for the above inference.

1. By modifying the force of the verb *to eat,* so as to make the phrase "to eat the passover" equivalent to the more common expression, "*to keep* or *celebrate* the passover." Precisely this form of expression occurs in the Hebrew in 2 Chron. 30, 22, literally : "*and they did eat the festival seven days ;*" where the English Version has it : "*throughout* seven days." The Septuagint translates correctly according to the sense, though not according to the letter : "*and they fulfilled* (*kept*) *the festival of unleavened bread seven days.*"   -

2. Or we may assign to the word *passover* (paschal festival), by metonymy, the sense of *paschal sacrifices,* that is, the voluntary peace-offerings and thank-offerings made in the temple during the paschal festival, and more especially on the fifteenth of Nisan ; called in later times the *Khagigah ;* see p. 198 above. A like metonymy is found in Ps. 118, 27 : "bind the sacrifice (festive offering, lit. *festival*) with cords." See too Ex. 23, 18. Mal. 2, 3. The same metonymy is assumed by some in the passage above quoted, 2 Chr. 30, 22 ; which they then render thus : "and they did eat the festival *offerings* seven days."

It is manifest, that both the above methods of interpretation are founded on fair analogies ; and that either of them relieves us from the necessity of referring the phrase in question to the paschal supper, and thus removes the alleged difficulty. The chief priests and other members of the Sanhedrim, on the morning of the first day of the festival, were unwilling to defile themselves by entering beneath the roof of the Gentile procurator ; since in that way they

would have been debarred from partaking of the sacrificial offerings and ban-
quets, which were customary on that day in the temple and elsewhere; and in
which they, from their station, were entitled and expected to participate.

This view receives some further confirmation from the circumstance, that
the defilement which the Jews would thus have contracted by entering the
dwelling of a heathen, could only have belonged to that class of impurities.
from which a person might be cleansed the same day by ablution; the *ablu
tions of a day*, so called by the Talmudists. See Lev. 15, 5 sq. 17, 15. 22, 6. 7.
Num. 19, 7 sq. Lightfoot Hor. Heb. on Joh. 18, 28. If now the *passover* in
John 18, 28 was truly the mere paschal supper, and was not to take place until
the evening after the day of the crucifixion, then this defilement of a day could
have been no bar to their partaking of it; for at evening they were or might be
clean. Their scruple, therefore, in order to be well-founded, could have had reference only to the *Khagigah* or paschal sacrifices offered during the same day
before evening.

c) John 19, 14 : " and it was the preparation of the passover, about the sixth
hour." Does this "preparation" refer, as usual, to the Jewish Sabbath, which
actually occurred the next day? or does it here refer to the festival of the Passover as such, and as distinct from the Sabbath? It is only on the latter supposition, that the passage can be made, in any way, to conflict with the testi
mony of the other Evangelists.

This "preparation" is defined by Mark (15, 42) to be "the day before the
Sabbath," i. e. the *fore-sabbath*, the day or hours immediately preceding the
weekly Sabbath, and devoted to preparation for that sacred day. No trace of
any such observance is found in the Old Testament; though the strictness of
the Mosaic law respecting the Sabbath, which forbade the kindling of fire and of
course the preparation of food on that day (Ex. 35, 2 3. comp. 16, 22-27), would
very naturally lead to the subsequent introduction of such a custom; as we find
it in the times of the New Testament. In the still later Hebrew of the Talmudists, it bore the specific appellation *ere*, as being the *eve of the Sabbath*; Buxtorf Lex. col. 1659. The Greek word "preparation," is also every where translated by the like Syriac form for *eve*, in the Syriac Version of the New Testament.

Primarily and strictly, this "preparation" or "eve" would seem to have
commenced not earlier than the ninth hour of the preceding day; as is implied,
perhaps, in the decree of Augustus in favour of the Jews, where it is directed
that they shall not be held to give pledges on the Sabbath, nor during the preparation before the same *after the ninth hour;* see Jos. Ant. 16. 6. 2. But in
process of time the same Hebrew word for "eve" or "preparation" came in
popular usage to be the distinctive name for the *whole day* before the Jewish
Sabbath, i. e. for the sixth day of the week or Friday; Buxtorf Lex. col. 1659.
Scaliger Emend. Temp. VI. p. 569. The same was the case in Syriac; and we
know, too, that the corresponding word in Arabic for *eve* was likewise an ancient name for Friday; see Golius' Arabic Lexicon, p. 1551. Freytag III. p.
130. It appears then, that among the Jews, Syrians, and Arabs, the common
word for *eve*, to which corresponded the Greek word "preparation," meaning
the preparation of the weekly Sabbath, became at an early date a current appellation for the sixth day of the week. That is, Friday was known as the *Preparation* or *Fore-sabbath;* just as in German the usual name for Saturday is
now *Sonnabend*, i. e. "eve of Sunday."

In the later Talmudists a *passover-eve* is likewise spoken of; Buxtorf Lex, col. 1765. But what this could well have been, so long as the passover (paschal supper) continued to be regularly celebrated at Jerusalem, it is difficult to perceive. The *eve* before the passover-*festival* could have included, at most, only the evening and the few hours before sunset at the close of the fourteenth of Nisan; as in the primary usage in respect to the *fore-sabbath*, as we have just seen. But according to all usage of language, both in the Old and New Testament, those hours and that evening were part and parcel of the *passover-festival* itself, and not its preparation; unless indeed the paschal meal and its accompaniments be called the preparation of the subsequent festival of seven days; which again is contrary to all usage. It would seem most probable, therefore, that this mode of expression did not arise until after the destruction of the temple and the consequent cessation of the regular and legal passover-meal; when of course the seven days of unleavened bread became the main festival.

But even admitting that a passover-eve did exist in the time of our Lord; still, the expression could in no legitimate way be so far extended as to include more than a few hours before sunset. It could not have commenced apparently before the ninth hour, when they began to kill the paschal lamb; see p. 196 above. On the other hand, the Hebrew term for *eve*, for which the Greek "preparation" stands in the New Testament, was employed, as we have seen, as a specific name in popular usage for the whole sixth day of the week or Friday, not only by the Jews, but also by the Syrians and Arabs. Hence, when John here says: "and it was the preparation of the passover, about the sixth hour," there is a twofold difficulty in referring his language to a preparation or *eve* of the regular Passover; *first*, because apparently no such eve or preparation did or could well then exist; and *secondly*, because, it being then the sixth hour or mid-day, the eve or time of preparation (supposing it to exist) had not yet come, and the language was therefore inapplicable. But if John be understood as speaking of the weekly preparation or fore-sabbath, which was a common name for the whole of Friday, then the mention of the sixth hour was natural and appropriate.

We come then to the conclusion, that if John, like Mark in c. 15, 42, had here defined the phrase in question, he would probably have written on this wise: "and it was the preparation of the passover, that is, the *fore-sabbath* of the passover," implying that it was the paschal Friday, the day of preparation or *fore-sabbath* which occurred during the paschal festival. In a similar manner Ignatius writes: "Sabbath of the Passover," Ep. ad Phil. c. 13; and Socrates also: "Sabbath of the festival," Hist. Ecc. V. 22. And further, in the only other two instances where John uses the word "preparation" in this way, he applies it to this very same day of our Lord's crucifixion, and in this very same sense of the weekly preparation preceding the weekly Sabbath; John 19, 31. 42.

d) John 19, 31: "for that sabbath-day was an high day." Here, as is alleged, it is the coincidence of the first festival day with the Sabbath, that made the latter a "high" or more properly a "great" day. This would certainly be the effect of such a coincidence; but the Sabbath of the Passover would also be still a "great" day, even when it fell upon the second day of the festival. The last day of the festival of Tabernacles is called "that great day," though in itself not more sacred than the first day; John 7, 37. comp. Lev. 23.

33–36. So *the calling of assemblies*, Is. 1, 13, is translated "a great day" by the Seventy, implying that in their estimation any day of solemn convocation was a great day. The Sabbath, then, upon which the sixteenth of Nisan or second day of the festival fell, might be called "great" or "high" for various reasons. *First*, as the Sabbath of the great national festival, when all Israel was gathered before the Lord. *Secondly*, as the day when the first fruits were presented with solemn rites in the temple; a ceremony paramount in its obligations even to the Sabbath; see above p. 197. Lightfoot Hor. Heb. on John 19, 31. Reland. Antiqq. Sac. 4. 2. 4. p. 227. *Thirdly*, because on that day they began to reckon the fifty days until the festival of Pentecost, Lev. 23, 15 sq. In all these circumstances there is certainly enough to warrant the epithet "great," as applied to the Sabbath on which the sixteenth of Nisan might fall, as compared with other Sabbaths. There exists, therefore, no necessity, and indeed no reason, for supposing, that John by this language meant to describe the Sabbath in question as coincident with the first paschal day or fifteenth of Nisan.

The preceding four passages are those mainly urged against the consistency of John with the other Evangelists. One or two other considerations are also sometimes brought forward.

e) John 13, 27–30. Here the words: "Buy that we have need of *against the feast* [festival]," having been spoken apparently near the close of the meal, imply, as some suppose, that the *passover*-meal was yet to come. But this again is to mistake the *festival* for the *paschal supper*, a signification which is quite foreign to the word; see p. 200 above. The disciples thought Judas was to buy the things necessary for the *festival* on the fifteenth and following days. If now our Lord's words were spoken on the evening preceding and introducing the fifteenth of Nisan, they were appropriate; for some haste was necessary, since it was already quite late to make purchases for the next day. But if they were uttered on the evening preceding and introducing the fourteenth of Nisan, they were not thus appropriate; for then a whole day was yet to intervene before the festival. This passage therefore confirms, rather than contradicts, the testimony of the other Evangelists.

f) There remains the objection sometimes brought forward, that a public judicial act, like that by which Jesus was condemned and executed, was unlawful upon the Sabbath and on all great festival days; see Lightfoot Hor. Heb. on Matth. 27, 1. This consideration has, at first view, some weight, and has been often and strenuously urged; yet it is counterbalanced by several circumstances which very greatly weaken its force.

The execution itself took place under Roman authority; and therefore does not here come into account.   And as to the proceedings of the Sanhedrim, even admitting that the prohibitory precepts already existed at this early time, (which is very doubtful,) yet there are in the Talmud other precepts of equal antiquity and authority, which actually direct and regulate the meeting and action of that body on the Sabbath and on festival days; see Tholuck's Comm. on John, p. 304 sq. Edit. 6. But besides all this, the chief priests and Pharisees and scribes, who composed the Sanhedrim, are every where denounced by our Lord as hypocrites, 'who say, and do not; who bind heavy burdens upon others, but themselves touch them not with one of their fingers;' Matth. 23, 1 sq. Such men, in their rage against Jesus, would hardly have been restrained even by their own precepts. They professed likewise, and perhaps some of them believed, that they were doing God service; and regarded the condemnation of Jesus as a work of religious duty, paramount to the obligations of any festival. Nor are other examples of such a procedure by any means wanting. We learn from John 10, 22. 31, that on the festival of Dedication, as Jesus was teaching in the temple, "the Jews took up stones to stone him." On the day after the crucifixion, which, as all agree, was a Sabbath and a "great day," the Sanhedrim applied to Pilate for a watch; and themselves caused the sepulchre to be sealed, and the watch to be set; Matth. 27, 62 sq. A stronger instance still is recorded in John 7, 22. 37. 44. 45; where it appears, that on the last *great* day of the festival of Tabernacles, the Sanhedrim having sent out officers to seize Jesus, "some of them would have taken him, but no man laid hands on him;" so that the officers returned without him to the Sanhedrim, and were in consequence censured by that body. The circumstances show conclusively, that on this last great day of that festival, the Sanhedrim were in session and waiting for Jesus to be brought before them as a prisoner. Nor was it merely a casual or packed meeting, but one regularly convened; for Nicodemus was with them, v. 50. And finally, according to Matth. 26, 3-5, the Sanhedrim, when afterwards consulting to take Jesus and put him to death, decided not to do it on the festival. Why? because it would be unlawful? Not at all; but simply "lest there should be an uproar among the people." But when, through the treachery of Judas, this danger was avoided, the occasion was too opportune not to be gladly seized upon even on a great festival day.

All these considerations seem to me to sweep away the whole force of this objection; on which Scaliger and Casaubon, as also Beza and Calov, laid much stress; and which Lücke has again brought forward and urged with no little parade.

Such then is a general review of the passages and arguments, on the strength of which the alleged discrepancy between John and the other Evangelists in respect to this Passover has usually been maintained. Nothing has here been assumed, and nothing brought forward, except as founded on just inference and safe analogy. After repeated and calm consideration, there rests upon my own mind a clear conviction, that there is nothing in the language of John, or in the attendant circumstances, which upon fair interpretation requires or permits us to believe, that the beloved disciple either intended to correct, or has in fact corrected or contradicted, the explicit and unquestionable testimony of Matthew, Mark, and Luke.

For a fuller discussion of the subject, see the Greek Harmony, p. 211–224. For a review of other proposed methods of conciliation, and for the literature of the subject, the student is referred to the author's article above mentioned, in the *Biblioth. Sacra*, for Aug. 1845, p. 405–436.

§ 133 For the cup mentioned by Luke in v. 17, see the preceding Introductory Note, p. 199.

The contention among the disciples had apparently occurred quite recently, perhaps even in the guest-chamber while taking their places at the table. That they were prone to yield to such a spirit, is evident from the instances recorded in § 79 and also § 108. Our Lord on this solemn occasion reproves them; especially by the touching act of washing their feet; see § 134.

18

§ 134. The washing of the disciples' feet by their Lord and Master was an impressive lesson, that they should live in harmony and love and humility one with another. The occasion of this act was their previous.contention, as related by Luke in § 133. Compare Luke 24, 26 sq. with John 13, 16 sq. John's narrative is supplementary to that of Luke; and therefore he does not speak of the contention itself, because the latter had already described it.

On the phrase "before the feast of the passover," v. 1, see above in Introd. Note, p. 200.—The phrase "supper being come," v. 2, is here equivalent to "during supper;" see v. 4 and v. 12. The time of the action was probably after they had taken their places at table, and before they had partaken of the proper meal; perhaps between the first and second cups of wine; see p. 199 above.

§ 135. The sequence of the transactions during the supper appears to have been the following: The taking of their places at table; the contention; the first cup of wine; the washing of the disciples' feet and reproof (§§ 133, 134); the pointing out of the traitor and his departure (§ 135); the foretelling of Peter's denial (§ 136); institution of the Lord's Supper (§ 137), etc. Luke's order differs from that of Matthew and Mark, in placing by anticipation the institution of the Eucharist before the pointing out of the traitor, etc. He was apparently led to this by the mention of the first cup of wine, vv. 17. 18. Afterwards he returns and narrates the previous circumstances.

In the present section, Jesus first declares that one of the twelve shall betray him; they in amazement inquire, "Lord, is it I? is it I?" and Peter makes a sign to John, leaning on Jesus' bosom, that he should ask, who it was. John does so; and Jesus gives him privately a sign by which he may know the traitor, viz. the sop. The amazement and inquiry still continuing, Jesus gives the sop to Judas; who then conscience-smitten, but desiring to conceal his confusion, asks as the others had done, "Lord, is it I?" Jesus answers him, and he immediately goes out, before the institution of the Eucharist; comp. John 13, 26 sq.—For John 13, 28. 29, see Introd. Note, p. 204.

§ 136. Mark says, "Before the cock crow *twice*," v. 30; the other Evangelists have simply, "Before the cock crow;" see Note on § 144.

§ 137. The institution of the Lord's Supper took place obviously at the close of the passover-meal, and in connection with the "cup of blessing," or third cup, which terminated the meal proper; comp. 1 Cor. 10, 16, and see p. 199 above. With this view accords the expression "after supper," in Luke 22, 20; and so 1 Cor. 11, 25. Matthew and Mark speak of Jesus as breaking the bread "as they were eating;" which implies nothing more than "during the meal," while they were *yet* eating; and does not require the institution of the bread to be separated from that of the cup.

§ 142. Matthew relates that our Lord went away *thrice* and prayed. Mark speaks of his going away twice only, but mentions his coming again the *third* time, v. 41; and therefore accords with Matthew. According to Luke, Jesus goes away and prays, and an angel strengthens him; after which he prays the "more earnestly," v. 44. The three Evangelists, therefore, agree in their narratives.

§ 143. Jesus advances to meet the crowd, and declares himself to be the person whom they sought. At the same time Judas, in order to fulfil his bargain, comes up and salutes him with a kiss.

§ 144. An oriental house is usually built around a quadrangular interior court; into which there is a passage (sometimes arched) through the front part of the house, closed next the street by a heavy folding gate, with a smaller wicket for single persons, kept by a porter. In the text, the interior court, often paved or flagged, and open to the sky, is the place where the attendants made a fire; and the passage beneath the front of the house, from the street to this court, is the *porch* in Matth. 26, 71. Mark 14, 68. The place where Jesus stood before the high priest, may have been an open room or place of audience on the ground-floor, in the rear or on one side of the court; such rooms, open in front, being customary. It was close upon the court; for Jesus heard all that was going on around the fire, and turned and looked upon Peter; Luke 22, 61.

Peter's *first* denial took place at the fire in the middle of the court, on his being questioned by the female porter.—Peter then, according to Matthew and Mark, retreats into the porch or passage leading to the street, where he is again questioned, and makes his *second* denial. Luke and John do not specify the place. The Evangelists differ in their statements here, as to the person who now questioned him. Mark says the same maid saw him *again*, and began to question him, v. 69; Matthew has "another maid," v. 71; Luke writes "another," i. e. another man, v. 58; while John uses the indefinite form, *they said*. As, according to Matthew (v. 71) and Mark (v. 69), there were several persons present, Peter may have been interrogated by several.—The *third* denial took place an hour after, probably near the fire, or at least within the court, where our Lord and Peter could see each other; Luke 22, 61. Here Matthew and Mark speak of several interrogators, Luke has still "another," and John specifies the servant of the high priest.

The three denials are here placed together for convenience, although during the intervals between them the examination of Jesus was going on before the high priest; the progress of which is given in § 145.

Mark relates that the cock crowed *twice*, vv. 68. 72; the others speak only of his crowing *once*. This accords also with their respective accounts of our Lord's prophecy; see § 136. The cock often crows irregularly about midnight or not long after; and again always and regularly about the third hour or day-break. When therefore "the cock-crowing" is spoken of alone, this last is always meant. Hence the name *cock-crowing*, for the third watch of the night, which ended at the third hour after midnight; Mark 13, 35. Mark therefore here relates more definitely; the others more generally.

§ 145. This examination by Caiaphas, John 18, 19-23, took place soon after Peter's first denial; see § 144. Not improbably the high-priest again withdrew, after having sent off messengers to convoke the Sanhedrim, which met at early dawn, Luke 22, 66.—Luke 22, 63–65 is transposed, in accordance with Matthew and Mark.

§ 146. On John 18, 28, see Introd. Note, p. 201.

§ 149. The *scarlet* robe of Matth. 27, 28, and the *purple* robe of John 19, 2, are put for the *paludamentum* or red military cloak worn by officers ; see Adam's Rom. Antiqq. p. 371. The Greek word in Matthew signifies properly *coccus-dyed, crimson*, and seems to be nearly synonymous with *purple ;* just as *purple-red* and *crimson* are often interchanged in English.

§ 150. On the phrase "preparation of the passover," v. 14, see the Introd. Note, p. 202. In the same verse, the expression "about the sixth hour," does not accord with the " third hour" of Mark 15, 25 ; see in § 153. But the "third hour" of Mark, as the hour of the crucifixion, is sustained by the whole course of the transactions and circumstances ; as also by the fact stated by Matthew, Mark, and Luke, that the darkness commenced at the *sixth* hour, after Jesus had already for some time hung upon the cross ; see § 155. The reading *sixth* in John is therefore probably an early error of transcription for *third,* arising out of the similarity of the Greek numeral letters. Indeed, this last reading is found in two of the best manuscripts, as well as several other authorities ; so that its external weight is marked by Griesbach as nearly or quite equal to that of the common reading ; while the internal evidence in its favour is certainly far greater.—The suggestion of some commentators, that John here computes the hours from midnight, seems to be without any historical foundation. The time also which would thus result, viz. sunrise, would be much too early for the course of events.

§ 151. Judas repented, it would seem, as soon as he saw that Jesus was delivered over to be crucified. Till then he had hoped, perhaps, to enjoy the reward of his treachery, without involving himself in the guilt of his Master's blood.

According to Matthew (v. 5), Judas "strangled," i. e. hanged himself. Luke says in Acts 1, 18, "falling headlong he burst asunder in the midst." These two accounts are not inconsistent with each other ; the rope breaking, the fall might easily be such as to cause the bursting of the abdomen.

In Acts 1, 18 the word "purchased" is to be taken as expressing the idea : *he gave occasion to purchase,* was the occasion of purchasing. For such an usage, see Matth. 27, 60. Rom. 14, 15. 1 Cor. 7, 16. 1 Tim. 4, 16. etc.

The quotation in Matth. 27, 9. 10, is found, not in Jeremiah, but in Zech. 11, 12 sq. The reading *Jeremiah* is therefore most probably an early error of a transcriber, misled by a reminiscence of Jer. 18, 1 sq. The Syriac version, the earliest of all, as also several other versions and manuscripts, have simply "by the prophet ;" which is apparently the true reading. Other later authorities read *Zechariah.*

§ 152. Jesus bore his cross at first ; but he being probably faint from exhaustion, Simon was compelled to bear it after him.

The "vinegar mingled with gall" of Matthew 27, 34, is the same with the "wine mingeld with myrrh" of Mark 15, 23, viz. cheap acid wine mingled with bitter myrrh. Such a drink was given to persons about to be executed, in order to stupify them. See Lightfoot Hor. Heb. on Matth. 27, 34.

§ 153. Various slight transpositions in the verses are made in this Section, in order to present their parallelism to the eye.—On the four different forms of the title on the cross, see Note on § 15.

§ 154. According to Matthew and Mark, both the malefactors reviled Jesus; while according to Luke, one was penitent. In the former Evangelists, there is here an enallage of number; the plural being put for the singular. This is often done, where the predicate relates strictly to one subject, while yet the writer expresses the idea generally. So Matth. 26, 8 comp. John 12, 4. Matth. 2, 20. 9, 8. Mark 7, 17 comp. Matth. 15, 15. Mark 5, 31 comp. Luke 8, 45. Matth. 24, 1 comp. Mark 13, 1. John 19, 29 comp. Matth. 27, 48. etc.

For the "vinegar" in Luke 23, 36, see note on § 155.

In John 19, 25, the marginal reading of the English version is the proper one, viz. *Clopas* instead of *Cleophas*. It is strictly a Greek form of a Hebrew name, which is elsewhere represented by *Alpheus.*—The *Cleopas* of Luke 24, 18, is a different name of regular Greek derivation, and belongs to another person.

§ 155. In Matth. 27, 46 *Eli* is the Hebrew word for *my God;* and in Mark 15, 34 *Eloi* is the corresponding Aramæan word for the same.

The "vinegar" in Matth. 22, 48 and the parallel verses, is here the *poscu* or common drink of the Roman soldiers, viz. cheap acid wine mingled with water. In Matthew and Mark the sponge is said to be put upon a reed; in John, upon hyssop. Here probably a *stalk* or *stem* of hyssop is to be understood; the cross not being of any great height. The particular plant designated by the *hyssop* of the Hebrews, has not yet been fully ascertained by botanists. It probably included not only the modern hyssop of the shops, but also other aromatic plants, as mint, wild marjoram, etc.

§ 156. Matth. 27, 55. 56, etc. refers to a later point of time than John 19, 25 sq. Mary and the other women had now retired to a distance from the scene of suffering.

§ 157. On the phrase: "that sabbath-day was an high day," John 19, 31, see Introd. Note, p. 203.

It was according to custom among the Jews, that the bodies of persons publicly executed should be taken down and buried before sunset. Thus Josephus, B. J. 4. 5. 2: "So great care did the Jews take respecting sepulture, that even the bodies of those condemned to be crucified they took down and buried before sunset."

18*

PART IX.

OUR LORD'S RESURRECTION, HIS SUBSEQUENT APPEARANCES, AND HIS ASCENSION.

§§ 159—173.

INTRODUCTORY NOTE.

A FULL discussion upon this part of the Gospel History, embracing a review of the main difficulties in the way of harmonizing the accounts of the four Evangelists, was published by the author of these Notes, in the *Bibliotheca Sacra* for Feb. 1845, p. 162 sq. To this the student is referred for a more complete examination of the subject.

It is no doubt true, that more of these apparent difficulties are found in this short portion of the Gospels, than in almost all the rest. This has its cause in the circumstance, that each of the sacred writers here follows an *eclectic* method, and records only what appertained to his own particular purpose or experience. Thus many of the minor and connecting facts have not been preserved; and the data are therefore wanting to make out a full and complete harmony of all the accounts, without an occasional resort to something of hypothesis. Had we all the facts, we may well rest assured, that this part of the sacred history would at once prove to be as exact, as consistent, and as complete, as any and every other portion of the Word of God.

The general results of the investigations upon which we are now entering, may be presented in the following summary view of the events and circumstances connected with our Lord's resurrection and ascension, in the order of their occurrence.

The resurrection took place at or before early dawn on the first day of the week; when there was an earthquake, and an angel descended and rolled away the stone from the sepulchre and sat upon it; so that the keepers became as dead men from terror. At early dawn, the same morning, the women who had attended on Jesus, viz. Mary Magdalene, Mary the mother of James, Joanna, Salome, and others, went out with spices to the sepulchre in order further to embalm the Lord's body. They inquire among themselves, who should remove for them the stone which closed the sepulchre. On their arrival they find the stone already rolled away. The Lord had risen. The women knowing nothing of all that had taken place, were amazed; they enter the tomb, and find not the body of the Lord, and are greatly perplexed. At this time Mary Magdalene, impressed with the idea that the body had been stolen away, leaves the sepulchre and the other women, and runs to the city to tell Peter and John.

The other women remain still in the tomb; and immediately two angels appear, who announce unto them that Jesus is risen from the dead, and give them a charge in his name for the Apostles. They go out quickly from the sepulchre, and proceed in haste to the city to make this known to the disciples. On the way Jesus meets them, permits them to embrace his feet, and renews the same charge to the Apostles. The women relate these things to the disciples; but their words seem to them as idle tales, and they believe them not.

Meantime Peter and John had run to the sepulchre, and entering in had found it empty. But the orderly arrangement of the grave-clothes and of the napkin, convinced John that the body had not been removed either by violence or by friends; and the germ of a belief sprung up in his mind, that the Lord had risen. The two returned to the city. Mary Magdalene, who had again followed them to the sepulchre, remained standing and weeping before it; and looking in she saw two angels sitting Turning around she sees Jesus; who gives to her also a solemn charge for his disciples.

The further sequence of events, consisting chiefly of our Lord's appearances, presents comparatively few difficulties. The various manifestations which the Saviour made of himself to his disciples and others, as recorded by the Evangelists and Paul, may accordingly be arranged and enumerated as follows:

1. To the women returning from the sepulchre. Reported only by Matthew. See § 162.
2. To Mary Magdalene, at the sepulchre. By John and Mark. § 164.
3. To Peter, perhaps early in the afternoon. By Luke and Paul. § 166.
4. To the two disciples going to Emmaus, towards evening. By Luke and Mark. § 166.
5. To the Apostles (except Thomas) assembled at evening. By Mark, Luke, John, and Paul. § 167.
   N. B. These five appearances all took place at or near Jerusalem, upon the first day of the week, the same day on which the Lord arose.
6. To the Apostles, Thomas being present, eight days afterwards at Jerusalem. Only by John. § 168.
7. To seven of the Apostles on the shore of the Lake of Tiberias. Only by John. § 169.
8. To the eleven Apostles and to five hundred other Brethren, on a mountain in Galilee. By Matthew and Paul. § 170.
9. To James, probably at Jerusalem. Only by Paul. § 171.
10. To the eleven at Jerusalem, immediately before the ascension. By Luke in Acts, and by Paul. § 171.

Then follows the ascension. § 172.

§ 159. The women had rested on the seventh day, according to Luke 23, 56; and the Sabbath being past, Mark relates (v. 1) that they brought spices to anoint the body. This purchase would seem to have been made before the Sabbath; see Luke 23, 56.

The angel had descended and the earthquake had taken place, before the arrival of the women. Our Lord therefore had arisen from the tomb at or before early dawn. See the next Note.—Verses 2–4 of Matthew are here transposed into their natural order. As they stand in Matthew, they should be read as in the pluperfect: "*had* been" and "*had* rolled away."

. The body of our Lord was laid in the sepulchre before sunset on Friday; and he rose early on the morning of Sunday. He therefore rose on the third day; having lain in the tomb during one whole day and a part of two others; in all not far from thirty six hours. On the expressions: *the third day* and *after three days*, see Note on § 49

§ 160. The point of time when the women visited the sepulchre is very definitely marked by all four of the Evangelists, by expressions which all go to fix
the time at what we call *early dawn*, or *early twilight*; after the break of day,
but while the light is yet struggling with darkness.

But Mark, in v. 2, has added the phrase: "*at the rising of the sun.*" These
words seem, at first, to be directly at variance with the language of the other
three Evangelists, and with the "very early" of Mark himself. Yet as Mark,
by the expression "very early," has definitely fixed the time in accordance
with all the other Evangelists, we cannot suppose that by the subsequent phrase
"at the rising of the sun," he meant to contradict himself and them. He must
therefore have employed this latter expression in a broader and less definite
sense, not inconsistent with the other. As the sun is the source of light and
day, and his earliest rays produce the contrast between night and dawn, so the
term *sun-rising* might easily come in popular usage, by a metonymy of cause
for effect, to be put for all that earlier interval, when his rays still struggling
with darkness do yet usher in the day.

Accordingly, we find such a popular usage existing among the Hebrews and
in the Old Testament. Thus in Judg. 9, 33, Zebul, after directing Abimelech
to lie in wait with his people in the field during the night, goes on to say:
"And it shall be, in the morning, as soon as the sun is up, thou shalt rise early
and set upon the city." Here we have the very same reference to the *sun-rising*;
and yet we cannot for a moment suppose that Abimelech was to wait till the
sun actually appeared above the horizon, before he made his onset. So the
Psalmist, Ps. 104, 22, speaking of the young lions that by night roar after their
prey, proceeds thus: "The sun ariseth, they gather themselves together, and
lay them down in their dens." But beasts of prey do not wait for the actual
appearance of the sun above the horizon ere they shrink away to their lairs; the
break of day, the dawning light, is the signal for their retreat. See also Sept.
2 K. 3, 22. 2 Sam. 23, 4 In all these passages the language is entirely parallel
to that of Mark 16, 2; and they fully illustrate and confirm the principle, that
the *sun-rising* is here used by Mark in a popular sense, as equivalent to the
rising of the day, or early dawn.

There was probably something in respect to Mary Magdalene, which gave
her a peculiar prominence in these transactions. This may be inferred from
the fact, that John mentions Mary Magdalene, and her alone; while the other
Evangelists likewise name her first, as if holding the most conspicuous place.
—On the different names and number of the women, as narrated by the different Evangelists, see Note on § 57.

Mary Magdalene, amazed at not finding the body of Jesus, and supposing
it to have been stolen, leaves the other women, probably in the sepulchre, and
returns to the city to tell Peter and John. To them she uses the phrase "*we
know not*," v. 2, meaning herself and the other women; but afterwards, when
she speaks to the angels, it is "*I know not*," v. 13.

§ 161. Luke speaks of two angels; Matthew and Mark of only one; see the
Note on § 57.—Mark says he was sitting; Luke speaks of them apparently as
standing, v. 4. But the Greek word, in its appropriate and acknowledged
usage, is *to appear suddenly, to be suddenly present*, without reference to its etv-
mology; comp. Luke 2, 9. Acts 12, 7.

In Matthew, the angel addresses the women apparently while still sitting on the stone outside of the sepulchre; in Mark and Luke, on the contrary, the conversation takes place in the sepulchre. But although Matthew does not speak of the women as entering the tomb, yet in v. 8 he describes them as *coming out* of it; so that of course his account too implies, that the interview took place within the tomb, as narrated by Mark and Luke.

In recording the charge sent by the angels to the Apostles, Matthew and Mark dwell more upon Galilee; and Luke more upon the Lord's previous announcement of his resurrection.

§ 162. It is evident that Mary Magdalene was not with the other women, when Jesus thus met them on their return. Her language to Peter and John forbids the supposition, that she had already seen the Lord; see John 20, 2. See too *Biblioth. Sacra*, Feb. 1845, p. 171.

§ 163. Mary Magdalene had gone to Peter and John only; who would seem to have lodged by themselves in a different part of the city. The other women went apparently to the rest of the disciples. When therefore it is here said of John, on his entering the sepulchre (v. 8), that "he saw and believed," this is not at variance with v. 9, nor yet with Luke 24, 11. What was it that John thus believed? Not the mere report of Mary Magdalene, that the body had been taken away; for so much he must have known and believed, when he stooped down and looked into the sepulchre. His belief must have been of something more and greater. The grave-clothes lying orderly in their place, and the napkin folded together by itself, made it evident that the tomb had not been rifled, nor the body stolen by violent hands; for these garments and the spices would have been of more value to thieves, than merely a naked corpse; at least, thieves would not have taken the pains thus to fold the garments together. The same circumstances showed also that the body had not been removed by friends; for they would not thus have left the grave-clothes behind. All these considerations excited in the mind of John the germ of a belief, that Jesus was risen from the dead. He believed *because* he saw; "*for* as yet they knew not the Scripture," v. 9. He now began to recall and understand our Lord's repeated declaration, that he was to rise again on the third day; a declaration on which the Jews had already acted in setting a watch. See Matth. 16, 21. 17, 23. Luke 9, 22. 24, 6, 7. etc. Matth 27, 63 sq. In this way, the apparent want of connection (sometimes urged) between verses 8 and 9, disappears.

§ 164. Mary Magdalene now manifestly sees the angels for the first time; and this circumstance also goes to show, that she had previously left the other women at the sepulchre before the angels appeared to them.

A main difficulty occurs here in fixing the order of time, between our Lord's appearance to Mary Magdalene and that to the other women in § 162. This arises from the use of the word *first* in Mark 16, 9, which seems to imply that this appearance to Mary Magdalene was the first of all: "he appeared first to Mary Magdalene." Yet the whole course of events and circumstances shows conclusively, that Jesus had previously appeared to the other women. We are therefore compelled, and that in accordance with good and ordinary usage, to regard "first" as put here not absolutely, but *relatively*. That is to say, Mark narrates three and only three appearances of our Lord; of *these three* that to Mary Magdalene takes place *first*, and that to the assembled disciples the same evening occurs *last*, Mark 16, 14, where our translators have used the word *afterward*, which is less correct. Now as the word for *last* is here put relatively, and does not exclude the subsequent appearances of our Lord to Thomas and in Galilee; so too *first* stands here relatively, and does not exclude the previous appearance to the other women.

In this way the whole difficulty in the case before us vanishes; and the complex and cumbrous machinery of earlier commentators becomes superfluous. See more in the Greek Harmony, p. 232.

§ 166. This appearance of our Lord to Peter, is mentioned only by Paul and by Luke, v. 34. It had not taken place when the two disciples left Jerusalem for Emmaus; or at least they had not heard of it. It had occurred when they returned; and that long enough before to have been fully reported to all the disciples and believed by them. It may perhaps have happened about the time the two disciples set off, or shortly afterwards.

On the name *Cleopas*, see Note on § 154   This is a different person from the Cleophas (Clopas) of John 19, 26.

§ 167. Paul speaks of the Apostles by their usual appellation, as *the twelve*, 1 Cor. 15, 5; Matthew, Mark, and Luke here speak of them as *the eleven;* Matth. 28, 16. Mark 16, 14. Luke 24, 33. Yet on this particular occasion, only *ten* were actually present; see John 20, 24.

When the disciples beheld their risen Lord, they thought they saw a spirit. Jesus reassures them; and presents to them indubitable evidence, that the same body of flesh and bones which had been crucified and laid in the sepulchre, was now risen and alive before them. On the general subject of the nature of our Lord's resurrection body, see a full discussion by the author of these Notes in the *Bibliotheca Sacra* for May, 1845, p. 292 sq.

Then follows our Lord's charge and commission to the eleven Apostles, delivered to them here in private by themselves; and distinct from the public and more general commission recorded in Matth. 28, 19. 20.—As a symbol of this commission to them in particular, and of the power which they should shortly receive through the Spirit imparted from on high, " he breathed on them, and said, Receive ye the Holy Ghost;" John 20, 22. There was in this emblem a recognition and reiteration of the gracious promise of the Spirit before made; which was to be abundantly fulfilled on the day of Pentecost. See John 14, 26. 16, 7 sq. Acts 2, 1 sq.

§ 169. This appearance of our Lord to the seven disciples at the Lake of Galilee, is shown to have preceded that upon the mountain, by John 21, 14. It was his third appearance to the *Apostles;* see §§ 167, 168. They were now waiting the appointed time, to meet Jesus upon a certain mountain; Matth. 28, 16.

§ 170. The set time had now come; and the eleven disciples went away into the mountain, "where Jesus had appointed them." It would seem probable, that this time and place had been appointed by our Lord for a solemn and more public interview, not only with the eleven whom he had already met more than once, but with all his disciples in Galilee; and that therefore it was on this same occasion, when, according to Paul, "he was seen of above five hundred brethren at once." That the interview in Matthew was not confined to the eleven alone, seems evident from the fact that "some doubted;" for this could hardly be supposed true of any of the eleven, after what had already happened to them in Jerusalem and Galilee, and after having been appointed to meet their risen Lord at this very time and place. The appearance to the five hundred must at any rate be referred to Galilee; for even after our Lord's ascension, the number of the names in Jerusalem were together only about an hundred and twenty; Acts 1, 15. And further, Paul in enumerating the appearances of Jesus, in 1 Cor. 15, 5-8, specifies only those to *Apostles*, with this one single exception; which therefore seems of itself to imply, that the eleven also were here included. I therefore, with many leading commentators, do not hesitate to regard the interviews thus described by Matthew and Paul, as identical. It was a great and solemn occasion. Our Lord had directed, that the eleven and all his disciples in Galilee should thus be convened upon the mountain. It was the closing scene of his ministry in Galilee. Here his life had been spent. Here most of his mighty works had been done and his discourses held. Here his followers were as yet most numerous. He therefore here takes leave on earth of those among whom he had lived and laboured longest; and repeats to all his disciples in public the solemn charge, which he had already given in private to the Apostles: "Go ye therefore and teach all nations;—and lo, I am with you always, even unto the end of the world." It was doubtless the Lord's last interview with his disciples in that region; his last great act in Galilee.

§ 171. Luke relates, in Acts 1, 3, that Jesus showed himself alive to the Apostles "after his passion, by many infallible proofs, being seen of them forty days, and speaking of the things pertaining to the kingdom of God." This would seem to imply interviews and communications, as to which we have little more than this very general notice. One of these may have been the appearance to James, mentioned only by Paul (1 Cor. 15, 7), and subsequent to that to the five hundred brethren. It may be referred with most probability to Jerusalem, after the return of the Apostles from Galilee.

Afterwards, our Lord again, according to Paul, "was seen of all the Apostles." This was apparently an appointed meeting; the same which Luke speaks of in Jerusalem, immediately before the ascension. It was of course the Lord's last interview with his Apostles.

§ 172. During the preceding discourse, Acts 1, 7. 8 (§ 171), or in immediate connection with it, our Lord leads the Apostles out *as far as to Bethany;* and lifting up his hands he blessed them; Luke 24, 50. This act of blessing must be understood, by all the laws of language, as having taken place at or near Bethany. "And it came to pass, while he blessed them, he was parted from them, and carried up into heaven." Our Lord's ascension, then, took place at or near Bethany. Indeed, the sacred writer could hardly have found words to express the fact more definitely and fully; and a doubt on this point could never have suggested itself to the mind of any reader, but for the language of the same sacred writer in Acts 1, 12, where he relates that after the ascension the disciples "returned unto Jerusalem from the mount called Olivet." Luke obvi-

ously did not mean to contradict himself; and the most that this expression
can be made to imply, is, that from Bethany, where their Lord had ascended,
which lies on the eastern slope of the Mount of Olives, a mile or more below
the summit of the ridge, the disciples returned to Jerusalem by a path across
the mount. Indeed, Bethany is described in the New Testament as connected
with, or as part of, the Mount of Olives; as "*at* the Mount of Olives," Mark
11, 1. Luke 19, 29. And further, where Matthew and Mark speak of Jesus,
during the week of his passion, as going out at evening from Jerusalem to
lodge at *Bethany*, Luke says expressly that he went out at night and abode in
the *Mount of Olives;* see Matth. 21, 17. Mark 11, 11. 19. 20. Luke 21, 37.
This serves to show, that Luke, in c. 24, 50 and Acts 1, 12, uses the terms
Bethany and Mount of Olives interchangeably, and almost as synonymous.

   Yet from this remark in Acts there arose, probably early in the fourth century, the legend which fixed the place of the ascension on the reputed summit
of the Mount of Olives. If that was indeed the true spot, then our Lord
ascended from it in full view of all the inhabitants of Jerusalem; a circumstance not hinted at by the sacred writers, nor at all in accordance with the life
and character of the Saviour.